W9-ARF-265

DATE DUE			
APR 04 2000			

Kierkegaard's
Fear and Trembling:
Critical Appraisals

Kierkegaard's
Fear and Trembling:
Critical Appraisals

EDITED BY

Robert L. Perkins

The University of Alabama Press
University, Alabama

Copyright © 1981 by
The University of Alabama Press
All rights reserved
Manufactured in the United States of America

Library of Congress Cataloging in Publication Data

Main entry under title:

Kierkegaard's Fear and trembling

Includes bibliographical references and index.
1. Kierkegaard, Søren Aabye, 1813–1855.
Frygt og bæven—Addresses, essays, lectures.
2. Christianity—Philosophy—Addresses, essays,
lectures. 3. Ethics—Addresses, essays, lectures.
I. Perkins, Robert L., 1930–
BR100.K5216K53   230   79–16984
ISBN 0-8173-0028-7

Contents

Acknowledgments

Thanks are due the following publishers for granting permission to quote from the publications listed here.

Princeton University Press: Søren Kierkegaard's *Fear and Trembling* [and *The Sickness Unto Death*], translated with an introduction and notes by Walter Lowrie, copyright 1941, 1954; Princeton Paperback, 1968. Reprinted by permission of Princeton University Press.

Fordham University Press: John Donnelly's *Logical Analysis and Contemporary Theism,* copyright 1972. Used by permission.

University of Pennsylvania Press: Louis Mackey's *Kierkegaard: A Kind of Poet,* copyright 1971. Used by permission.

The Review of Metaphysics: Henry Allison's "Christianity and Nonsense," copyright 1967. Used by permission.

Harcourt Brace Jovanovich: Milton Steinberg's *Anatomy of Faith,* copyright 1962. Used by permission.

Harcourt Brace Jovanovich (New York): lines from T.S. Eliot's "Four Quartets" from *Complete Poems and Plays, 1909–1950* (1962); and Faber & Faber, Ltd. (London): Idem from *Collected Poems 1900–1962* (1963). Used by permission.

Preface

This volume of previously unpublished essays on Søren Kierkegaard's *Fear and Trembling* is an outgrowth of many minds and reflects a number of very different philosophic perspectives and methods. This is entirely appropriate, for Kierkegaard has influenced many disciplines and methodologies.

The contributors to the volume are all either theologians or philosophers, but it is doubtful whether a blind reading could identify most of them as one and not the other. According to one's perspective, this bespeaks something either good or ill of the two disciplines at the present time. The methodologies represented are historical, comparative, systematic, analytic, existential, and phenomenological. What we hope is accomplished here is the continuing discipline, scrutiny, and criticism of the subject matter under consideration and the consequent illumination of human existence itself by any and all methodologies. The work of Kierkegaard is a potent catalyst in this critical and illuminating activity, and it is only proper that he, too, should be so examined. Given his dim view of professors, the scholarly criticism of Kierkegaard has always made professors aware of the self-ironizing effect of their professional efforts for or against him.

These essays tend to affirm Kierkegaard's insights. Perhaps some reviewer will grant us the grace of time and patience in order to become our teacher.

Quite a number of acknowledgments are called for, particularly when there are so many authors. However, in order to permit the reader to proceed to the real matters at hand, we shall acknowledge only the need for acknowledgments and let those who might have been identified be bemused by their being unnamed.

Robert L. Perkins

Introduction

Fear and Trembling has four beginnings: a Preface, a Prelude, a Panegyric, and a "Preliminary Expectoration"—all before Kierkegaard ostensibly gets down to the problems of the book. Of course, these beginnings are very deceptive because the thesis (or theses), analysis, ethics, aesthetics, theology, irony, philosophy, and whatever else there is, all start with the title. With this bad example before us, it would be utterly un-Kierkegaardian simply to begin. The reader will not find four false starts here. In fact, there may not be a start here at all, false or otherwise. Still, it seems that something of a scholarly introduction is called for in a book of "critical appraisals," and if we cannot have four beginnings, we must settle for less.

I. HISTORICAL AND LITERARY CONTEXT

Fear and Trembling was published on the same day, 16 October 1843, as *Repetition* and *Three Edifying Discourses*. The first two have subtitles, "A Dialectical Lyric" and "An Effort in Experimental Psychology," respectively, and pseudonomous authors, Johannes de Silentio and Constantine Constantius, respectively. Only the *Three Edifying Discourses* came forth unadorned by subtitle and pseudonym.

Sometime in November 1842 Kierkegaard finished the manuscript of *Either/Or* and while he did the proofreading and other chores for this he embarked on a small book, *Johannes Climacus or De Omnibus Dubitandum Est*, in which he made his break with modern philosophy final and clear to himself. About Easter 1843 he stopped work on *Johannes Climacus*; he would never complete it, although some ideas developed in it appeared in later works. On May 8 he made a second journey to Berlin, where he remained for almost two months. Toward the end of May he wrote his closest friend, Emil Bosen, that he would soon be home, and that he had finished a work that was very important to him and had begun another. The manuscripts of the pseudonomous works were finished by July and he dated the foreword to the *Three Edifying Discourses* on 9 August 1843, the fifth anniversary of his father's death. Most commentators think *Repetition* was written first.

The two pseudonomous works, though hastily written, are perhaps Kierkegaard's most perfect. They were born out of the struggle to explain himself to his former fiancée, Regina Olsen, and to raise the possibility within the ethical of repetition, i.e., the restoration of the broken engagement or, in terms of *Fear and Trembling,* receiving back in faith his beloved. Both books were antiquated before they were published: Regina was again engaged to her first intended. The ending of *Repetition* had to be rewritten, but *Fear and Trembling* had been developed in such a way that no changes were necessary.

The consumate art of *Fear and Trembling* was as evident to Kierkegaard as it has been to his latter-day readers: "Oh, when once I am dead—then *Fear and Trembling* alone will be enough to give me the name of an immortal author. Then it will be read, then too it will be translated into foreign tongues."

There are very few entries in the *Papers* about *Fear and Trembling*. They appear in *Søren Kierkegaards Papirer* (Udgivet af P.A. Heiberg og V. Kuhr; Glydendalske Boghandel Nordisk Forlag, 1912 [volume 4, pp. 229–47]). There were four reviews of the book. The signed ones were by J.F. Hagan and J.P. Mynster (literary pen name, Kts). Explicit reference to the reviews are in Jens Himmelstrup's, *Søren Kierkegaard International Bibliografi* (Nyt Nordisk Forlag, 1962); see numbers 49–52.

II. INTRODUCTION TO THESE *CRITICAL APPRAISALS*

The present volume is in itself an expression of unity in diversity. Some of the essays are scholarly and heavily documented, while others rely more on analytic methods of argument to develop their point. Problems of theology, ethics, and philosophical method jostle the reader of this book as they do the reader of *Fear and Trembling*. The essays touch on many of the major points, but they have neither individually nor collectively exhausted the riches of *Fear and Trembling*. Still, the twelve essays do illuminate much of the text and demonstrate the breadth of interest provoked by the biblical story.

Professor Jacobs' article indicates the varieties of the Jewish interpretation of Genesis 22:1–18. This is the first such overview of Jewish tradition as it bears on Kierkegaard's effort.

Professor Pailin sets the problem of the offering of Isaac in the context of Enlightenment theology. Special difficulties were encountered in that period because of the unstable condition of the concept of authority. Pailin updates the problem in his final section by relating his previous discussion to some contemporary issues in hermeneutics.

Professor Perkins attempts to find some points held in common by both Kant and Kierkegaard by reexamining the conventional wisdom regarding their differences. The result is as much a Kierkegaardian exposition of the salient points of Kant's ethics as it is a Kantian interpretation of *Fear and Trembling*.

Professor Westphal first sets out the logical status of faith in both Kierkegaard and Hegel and then proceeds to show the practical consequences of both views. Westphal argues persuasively that the differences about the concept of faith lie at the root of Kierkegaard's criticism of the Hegelian notion of the social order.

Professor Holmer re-creates something of the feeling that Abraham must have experienced when he realized what it was necessary for him to do in order to remain faithful to God. Holmer first stresses the moral character of Abraham and elicits a sympathy for him, and then he re-creates the emptiness and confusion occasioned by God's command. Yet the whole essay is essentially about the nature of selfhood vis-à-vis ethics and the religious.

The articles mentioned so far are more introductory and historical in nature than those in the next sequence, which concentrate on specific parts of *Fear and Trembling*.

Professor Mooney focuses on the "Preliminary Expectoration" and argues that *Fear and Trembling* is, among other things, a polemic against the rise of the capitalistic spirit of acquisitiveness. If this is so, then Kierkegaard's attack on bourgeois society in the last years of his life was continuous with some of his earliest impulses.

Professor Donnelly attempts an entirely novel interpretation of "Problem I" and "Problem II." Kierkegaard asked, "Is there such a thing as a teleological suspension of the ethical?" and "Is there such a thing as an absolute duty to God." Kierkegaard is usually understood to have answered both questions in the affirmative. Donnelly argues that it is possible to mount a plausible defense of Abraham qua knight of faith, "a distinctively moral, rational, and philosophical justification." Donnelly argues that the first question must be answered in the negative, but that there is still an affirmative answer to the second question.

Professor Evans argues that it is possible to universalize the concept of the teleological suspension of the ethical. The question of universalizing the case of Abraham gives us logical cramps only because we are mistaken in thinking that every ethical obligation requires a universal rule. Professor Donnelly's and Professor Evans' articles complement each other.

Professor Wren explores the question of silence raised by Kierkegaard in "Problem III" and relates Abraham's silence to the notion of absurdity as it is discussed in the *Concluding Unscientific Postscript*. The prolematics of silence are here related to aesthetics, ethics, subjectivity, and the absurd.

Professor Taylor examines the notion of silence in the wider contexts of Kierkegaard's illustrative hermeneutic principle of the stages. From this discussion Taylor implies some interesting suggestions about social and political philosophy and the notion of community.

Professor Crumbine compares Albert Camus' *The Stranger* and Kierkegaard's *Fear and Trembling* and attempts to show the character of Abraham through the characterlessness of Mersault. The operative term is "inwardness" referring to a quality that protects the person from being so socialized that he is merely a reflection of the social environment.

Finally, Professor Gill claims that in *Fear and Trembling* it is Johannes de Silentio, not necessarily Kierkegaard himself, who is attempting an irrational justification of Abraham. According to Silentio, justification on rationalist grounds is not possible. According to Gill, justification on irrationalist grounds is also not possible. If Silentio is right and if Gill is right, the ground is cut, to a very considerable extent, out from under the several critical appraisals in this volume!

A fitting and proper irony.

1. The Problem of the *Akedah* in Jewish Thought

LOUIS JACOBS

THE NARRATIVE IN THE TWENTY-SECOND CHAPTER OF THE BOOK OF GENESIS, IN which Abraham is instructed by God to offer up his son Isaac as a burnt offering, is known in the Jewish tradition as the *Akedah*,[1] "the binding" (of Isaac on the altar). The *Akedah* features prominently in the Jewish liturgy. It is, for instance, the Pentateuchal reading in the synagogue on the second day of the New Year festival, and it is recited daily by some pietists. It became the prototype for Jewish martyrdom. And it has exercised a powerful fascination over the minds of Jewish biblical exegetes and Jewish thinkers generally throughout the ages, each of whom has tried to bring his own understanding to the narrative.

This essay is concerned with Jewish attitudes toward the most difficult problem connected with the *Akedah:* How could God have ordered a man to murder his son? The problem is aggravated by the fact that in no less than sixteen other passages in the Bible (Leviticus 18:21;20:1–8; Deuteronomy 12:31;18:10; 2 Kings 13:27;16:3;17:17,31;21:6;23:10; Jeremiah 7:31;19:5; Ezekiel 20:31; Micah 6:7; 2 Chronicles 28:3; 33:6) child sacrifice is condemned as an abomination before God. Arising out of the initial problem are the further questions regarding Abraham's intention to carry out the terrible deed. How could Abraham have been so sure that God had, indeed, commanded him to kill his innocent child? Even if he was convinced that God had so commanded him, was it his duty to obey? Is obedience to God's will so supreme an obligation that it can override man's moral sense, demanding of him that he commit a criminal act of the very worst kind for the greater glory of God? Can or should one worship a being who wishes to be served by an act of murder? Moreover, the very God who demanded the sacrifice of Isaac had himself performed the miracle of giving Isaac to Abraham and Sarah when they were of advanced age and had promised Abraham that, through Isaac, Sarah would be a mother of nations (Genesis 17:15–19;18:10–15; and 21:1–12).

Three different attitudes to the problem have been adopted by Jewish thinkers. The first stresses the story's "happy ending." Abraham is, in fact, eventually commanded not to slay his son. The whole episode was only a "test," a divine vindication of Abraham's absolute trust in God. There was never any divine intention for Abraham to kill Isaac. God, being God, could never so deny his own nature as to wish a man to commit a murder in obedience to him. The second attitude stresses, on the contrary, the original command. This view, very close to Kierkegaard's attitude, can imagine God commanding Abraham to slay his son. True the order is revoked at the last moment but the point has been made, nonetheless, that, in Kierkegaard's terminology, there can be, so far as "the knight of faith" is concerned, a "teleological suspension of the ethical." As "ethical man" as well as "knight of faith," Abraham goes in "fear and trembling" but the ultimate for him is not the ethical norm but his individual relationship to his God. A third attitude seeks to dwell on both aspects of the narrative. On this view, it is impossible that God could ever, in reality, be false to his own nature and command a murder, and yet *if* he could, then Abraham would indeed be obliged to cross the fearful abyss. These three attitudes, it must be said, are rarely given sharply defined expression in the Jewish sources. They tend to shade off into one another, and among some of the Jewish thinkers, all three are combined without any awareness that a contradiction is involved. It is thus far more a matter of where the emphasis is placed than one of precise categorization.

The first attitude seems to have been the earliest among the Jewish thinkers. It is not without significance that the *Akedah* hardly appears at all as a distinct theme in the early rabbinic literature. The only reference to it before the third century is in the Mishnah (Taanit 2:4). Here there is a vivid description of the procedure adopted on a public fast-day when the rains had failed to come. The people congregated, we are told, in the town square where they were led in prayer by a venerable man free of sin and experienced in offering supplication to his maker. One of the prayers he was to offer is given as: "May He who answered our father Abraham on Mount Moriah answer you and hearken to the voice of your crying this day." But this is said to be only one of the special "May He who answered . . ." prayers. Others recited on that day contained references to other biblical characters, such as Joshua and Jonah, whose prayers in a time of crisis and danger were answered. Abraham's crisis, it is implied, was basically no different from that of the other heroes. When God answered Abraham's prayer it was to spare Isaac. Implied, too, is the idea that God's "answer," his true will, was revealed not in the original command but in the second command for Abraham to stay his hand and save Isaac. In a later talmudic passage (Taanit 4a) it is stated explicitly that God never intended Abraham to kill his son any more than God wishes Baal worshippers to carry out human sacrifices. In a comment to Jeremiah's fierce castigation of the people for burning their sons in fire as burnt offerings for Baal "which I commanded not, nor spoke it, neither came it into My mind" (Jeremiah 19:5), this passage elaborates: " 'which I commanded not' refers to the sacrifice of the son of Mesha, the king of Moab (2 Kings 3:27); 'nor spoke it' refers to the daughter of Jephtah (Judges 11:31); 'neither came it into My mind' refers to the sacrifice of Isaac, son of Abraham." Similarly, a rabbinic midrash (Genesis Rabbah 56:8) describes Abraham, after the angel had told him in the name of God to spare Isaac, puzzled by the contradictory statements: "Recently Thou didst tell me

(Genesis 21:12): 'In Isaac shall seed be called to thee,' and later Thou didst say (Genesis 22:5): 'Take now thy son.' And now Thou tellest me to stay my hand!" God is made to reply in the words of Psalm 79 verse 35: "My covenant will I not profane, nor alter that which is gone out of My lips." "When I told thee: 'Take thy son,' I was not altering that which went out from My lips [i.e., the promise that Abraham would have descendants through Isaac]. I did not tell thee: 'Slay him' but bring him up [i.e., take him to the mountain and make him ready to be sacrificed]. Thou didst bring him up. Now take him down again."

In addition to this idea emerging from specific comments to the *Akedah*, it seems to be implied in the typical rabbinic view that God himself keeps his laws. In the Jerusalem Talmud (*Rosh Ha-Shanah* 1:3), for example, the Greek maxim is quoted that the law is not written for the king (i.e., the law is for the king's subjects whereas the king himself is beyond the law). God, it is said, is not like a human king who decrees laws for others but need not keep them himself. God orders man to rise in respect before the aged and God did this himself, as it were, out of respect for Abraham.

All this lends powerful support to an anti-Kierkegaardian understanding of the *Akedah*. Drawing on passages such as those we have quoted it is easy (far too easy, as we shall see) to generalize and to argue that there is no room in Judaism for a doctrine that accepts any teleological suspension of the ethical.

This is, in fact, the attitude adopted by the late Milton Steinberg in an essay entitled: "Kierkegaard and Judaism."[2] In a lethal attack on the Danish thinker's interpretation of the *Akedah*, Steinberg roundly declares that there is nothing in Judaism to correspond to Kierkegaard's teleological suspension of the ethical and continues:

> From the Jewish viewpoint—and this is one of its highest dignities—the ethical is never suspended, not under any circumstances and not for anyone, not even for God. *Especially not for God* [*italics* Steinberg's]. Are not supreme Reality and supreme Goodness one and co-essential to the Divine nature? If so, every act wherein the Good is put aside is more than a breach of His will; it is in effect a denial of His existence. Wherein the rabbis define sin as constituting not merely rebellion but atheism as well.
>
> What Kierkegaard asserts to be the glory of God is Jewishly regarded as unmitigated sacrilege. Which indeed is the true point of the *Akedah*, missed so perversely by Kierkegaard. While it was a merit in Abraham to be willing to sacrifice his only son to his God, it was God's nature and merit that He would not accept an immoral tribute. And it was His purpose, among other things, to establish that truth.[3]

The opposite view, the "pro-Kierkegaardian" interpretation of the *Akedah,* is, however, also found in Jewish thought, and certainly not as infrequently as Steinberg implies. Philo (*De Abrahamo,* 177–199) replies to hostile critics of Abraham who point out that many others in the history of mankind have offered themselves and their children for a cause in which they believed. Among examples these critics cite are the barbarians whose Moloch worship was explicitly forbidden by Moses, and Indian women who gladly practise suttee. Philo retorts that Abraham's sacrifice was unique in that he was not governed by motives of custom, honor, or fear but solely by the love of God. It is, then, for Philo a token of Abraham's great love that he was ready to suspend the ethical norm; his love for God overriding all else.

The Talmud (*Sanhedrin* 89b), in a legal context, asks why Isaac (who, in one tradition, was not a docile infant but a mature man) allowed himself to be led to the slaughter. True Abraham was a prophet but is even a prophet to be heeded when he orders another in the name of God to commit an illegal act, in this instance, what amounts to suicide? The reply given is that, indeed, an established prophet can be relied upon, not to cancel any of God's laws entirely but to demand, in God's name, a temporary suspension of them. The commentators[4] rightly remark that no question is even raised about Abraham's readiness to kill his son since the prophet himself is obviously obliged to heed God's command even if it involves an illegal act. In the "Remembrance" prayer, dating, according to the majority of historians, from the third century and still recited in synagogues on the New Year festival, there occurs the phrase: "Remember, unto us, O Lord our God, the covenant and the loving kindness and the oath which Thou swore unto Abraham our father on Mount Moriah: and consider the binding with which Abraham our father bound his son Isaac on the altar, how he suppressed his compassion in order to perform Thy will with a perfect heart. So may Thy compassion overbear Thine anger against us; in Thy great goodness, may Thy wrath turn aside from Thy people, Thy city and Thine inheritance."

Indeed, there was current in the Middle Ages a curious legend that Abraham actually killed Isaac at the command of God and that later Isaac was resurrected from the dead, the call of the angel to Abraham, commanding him to stay his hand, coming too late. The medieval Spanish commentator, Abraham Ibn Ezra (to Genesis 22:19) quotes this opinion (which, he says, seeks to explain why there is no reference in the narrative to Isaac returning home with his father) but rejects it as completely contrary to the biblical text. Yet in a splendid monograph Shalom Spiegel[5] has demonstrated how widespread such views were in the Middle Ages, possibly, Spiegel suggests, in order to deny that Isaac's sacrifice was in any way less than that of Jesus; or as a reflection of actual conditions when the real martyrdom of Jewish communities demanded a more tragic model than that of a mere intended sacrifice. It was not unknown for parents to kill their children and then themselves when threatened by the Crusaders.[6]

It is highly improbable that Kierkegaard knew of it, but the Talmud (*Sanhedrin* 89b), in the passage following the legal one we have quoted, has a Midrashic exposition of the drama of the *Akedah* in which there is expressed all the "fear and trembling" of which Kierkegaard speaks, as Abraham, both "ethical man" and "knight of faith," is torn in his anguish. The passage deserves to be quoted in full:

> "And it came to pass after these words that God did tempt Abraham" (Genesis 22:1). What is the meaning of *after*? Rabbi Johanan said in the name of Rabbi Jose ben Zimra: *After* the words of Satan. It is written: "And the child grew up and was weaned: and Abraham made a great feast the same day that Isaac was weaned" (Genesis 21:8). Satan said to the Holy One, blessed be He: "Sovereign of the Universe! Thou didst give a son to this old man at the age of a hundred, yet of all the banquet he prepared he did not sacrifice to Thee a single turtle-dove or pigeon!" God replied: "Did he not do all this in honor of his son! Yet were I to tell him to sacrifice that son to Me he would do so at once." . . . On the way (as Abraham was leading Isaac to be sacrificed) Satan confronted him and said to him: "*If we assay to commune with thee, wilt thou be grieved? . . . Behold, thou hast instructed many, and thou hast strengthened the weak hands. Thy words have upholden him that was falling, and thou hast strengthened the feeble knees. But now it is come upon thee, and thou faintest*" (Job 4: 2–5) (i.e., Abraham is being asked to commit a wrong against which his whole teaching has hitherto been directed"). Abraham replied: "*I will walk in my integrity*" (Psalm 26:2). Satan said to him: "*Should not thy fear be thy confidence?*" (Job 4:6). He replied: "*Remember, I pray thee, whoever perished being innocent?*" (Job 4:6). Seeing that Abraham would not listen to him, Satan said to him: "*Now a thing was secretly brought to me*" (Job 4:12). I have heard from behind the Veil "*the lamb, for a burnt offering*" (Genesis 22:7) "but not Isaac for a burnt offering." Abraham replied: "It is the punishment of a liar that he is not believed even when he tells the truth." In the parallel passage in the Midrash (Genesis Rabbah 56:4) Satan says to Abraham: "Tomorrow He will condemn thee as a murderer"[8] but Abraham replies: "Nevertheless!"

The analysis of the *Akedah* given by Moses Maimonides (1135–1204),[9] the greatest of the medieval Jewish thinkers, similarly comes very close to the Kierkegaardian understanding. Maimonides observes that the *Akedah* teaches two fundamental ideas (neither of these, it should be noted, has anything to do with the "happy ending" of the narrative). The first of these is that man, out of the love and fear of God, is obliged to go even to the limits to which Abraham was prepared to go. According to Maimonides' reading of the *Akedah,* the "test" was not in order to provide God with information about Abraham's steadfastness that God did not possess, but rather it was to provide a "test case" of the limits to which a man can and should go in his love for God. Maimonides stresses not alone the natural love that Abraham had for the child of his extreme old age but the fact that in this child was centered all Abraham's hope of establishing a religious community to carry on his teachings. Maimonides adds: "Know that this notion is corroborated and explained in the *Torah,* in which it is mentioned that the final end of the whole of the Torah, including its commandments, prohibitions, promises and narratives, is one thing only—namely, fear of Him, may He be exalted. This is referred to in its dictum: *If thou wilt take care to observe all the words of this Law that are written in this book, that thou mayest fear this glorious and awful Name, and so on* (Deuteronomy 28:58)."

The second idea contained in the *Akedah,* according to Maimonides, is that the prophets consider as true what comes to them from God in a prophetic revelation. If the prophetic vision ever allows the prophet to remain in some doubt, Abraham would not have hastened to commit an act so repugnant to nature. The man, Abraham, who taught that God does reveal himself to man, was the most suitable instrument for conveying the further truth that there is complete conviction in the mind of the prophet that he is really the recipient of a divine communication so that he is ready to act on it no matter how severe the moral as well as physical demands it makes on him. Maimonides' statement, that the final end of the whole Torah (as he says, including its commandments, which means, the ethical as well as the purely religious commandments) is one thing only, the fear of God, is as close to the idea of, at least, a possibility that the ethical can be suspended for this particular telos as makes no difference. The thirteenth-century exegete Bahya Ibn Asher[10] develops the same line as Maimonides, that the *Akedah* teaches the great love of Abraham and adds that the reason that Abraham took only two lads with him (and ordered even these to remain at the foot of the mountain) was because Abraham knew that if others were present they would, in their horror of the deed he intended to perform, seek to prevent him from carrying it out.[11]

The renowned contemporary Orthodox teacher Professor J.B. Soloveitchick is the most determined exponent of a Kierkegaardian interpretation of the *Akedah.* In a famous essay, entitled *Ish Ha-Halakhah* (The Man of Halakah),[12] Soloveitchick observes that the midrash (to which reference has previously been made) in which Abraham's dialogue with Satan conveys all the anguish and uncertainty of the man of faith, is much closer to Kierkegaard than any idea of religion as offering "peace of mind." The ultimate aim of "the man of Halakah," the man who follows the *Halakah,* the legal side of Judaism, is to obey God's revealed will which transcends man's merely rational aspirations for the good life. The psalmist who speaks of the Lord as his shepherd who leads him beside the still waters (Psalm 23), affirms this only as the ultimate aim of the religious life. He does not mean to imply, according to Soloveitchick, that the religious way itself has anything to do with "still waters." On the contrary, as Kierke-gaard affirms, the deeper aspects of religious faith are only to be found in the man tormented by the demands God seems to be making both on his intelligence and his conscience. Soloveitchick only refers to Kierkegaard's interpretation in connection with Abraham's anguish and doubt, not with regard to the teleological suspension of the ethical, but J.B. Agus[13] may be right in reading Soloveitchick's essay as a statement that the full Kierkegaardian view is compatible with Judaism.

Although some Jewish thinkers have stressed the "happy ending" as the chief point of the *Akedah* narrative and others have stressed the original command to sacrifice as the chief point of the story, a compromise position in which both aspects are avowed is not as contradictory as might appear at first glance. It can be argued that, after all, the story does consist of these two parts, the original command and the "happy ending"; that this is the only occasion on which God is said to have commanded a man to commit murder as a test of obedience; that, on the other hand, to read the story simply as a homily on the sacredness of human life tends to reduce it to banality; and, at the same time, to overlook the finale is to ignore an element that the narrator never intended should be overlooked. For this reason some modern thinkers, especially, have tried to preserve both insights as essential parts of the *Akedah*.

W. Gunther Plaut,[14] in an essay entitled "Notes on the Akedah," implying, perhaps, an avoidance of too tidy a schematic presentation of the complicated narrative, states the problem but offers more than one solution. Plaut first quotes Franz Rosenzweig's understanding[15] of the whole idea of God tempting man. God must, at times, conceal his true purpose. He must mislead man (as he misled Abraham into thinking that he was the kind of God who demanded that a murder be committed for his glorification) because if everything were clear men would become automatons. In Rosenzweig's words, "the most unfree, the timid and the fearful would be the most pious. But evidently God wants only the free to be His: He must make it difficult, yea, impossible, to understand His actions, so as to give man the opportunity to believe, that is, to ground his faith in trust and freedom." Plaut continues: "What kind of God is He? How can the compassionate God of the Bible be presented as asking the sacrifice of a child?" Plaut replies by referring to two different solutions that have been offered. The first is that the test came out of a time when human sacrifice was still an acceptable possibility; in terms of its own age, therefore, it was merely the extreme test and, after all, God did not exact the final price. The real test of faith and obedience consists in being ready to do the totally unexpected, the impossible, for the sake of God. Another solution is that God never intended the sacrifice to be made. According to this way of reading the narrative, concludes Plaut, Abraham's test both succeeded and failed. It succeeded in that it proved Abraham to be a man of faith and obedience. And it failed in that Abraham's understanding of God's nature remained deficient. This latter observation does not seem to tally, however, with the narrative. It is nowhere suggested that Abraham failed in any way in his test, as Plaut would have it. Even if the *Akedah* be interpreted as a lesson on the sacredness of human life and the true nature

of God it is nowhere implied that Abraham was mistaken in his understanding of the demand made on him.

The religious thinker and educationist Ernst Simon,[16] in a discussion of
how the *Akedah* narrative should be taught in religion classes, refers to the
two different interpretations of the *Akedah* in the Jewish tradition. He calls
them the "rationalist" and the "existentialist" and believes that between
these two extremes some intermediate possibilities exist, "not necessarily
of a compromising nature, but authentic in themselves." Simon refers to
Kierkegaard's analysis in his *Fear and Trembling* and remarks that though
Kierkegaard was not aware of the Jewish traditions his attitude toward
Abraham as the "knight of faith" is, in some ways, kindred to them.

Simon formulates the basic problem of the *Akedah* as: "How could
Abraham believe that God asked from him the sacrifice of his son? Is that a
moral demand? And if not, how can it be a religious one?" The "rationalist" view is that God never intended the sacrifice to be made. This line of
interpretation can be followed all the way to Maimonides' view[17] that God
does not really want even animal sacrifices and that these are commanded
only as a concession to the psychology of the ancient Israelites who, under
the influence of their milieu, could not conceive of divine worship without
sacrificial offerings. The "existentialist" school of thought, on the other
hand, sees man's highest perfection in the absolute submission of his will to
God's command, even when this seems most absurd. "According to this
view," writes Simon, "the real victim was not the innocent Isaac, but the
knowing Abraham who brought a sacrifice of his intellect and his will, of
his emotions and even of his morals, that is, of his whole human personality, *ad maiorem gloriam Dei.*"[18]

Yet Simon believes that it is possible to read the narrative in a way in
which both extremes are avoided but in which justice is done to the insights
provided by both. The command to sacrifice can be read as a warning
against too facile an identification of religion with naturalistic ethics.
Ultimately, it is in the command of God that ethical conduct is grounded.
The "happy ending," on the other hand, precludes any religious approach
that encourages ideas repugnant to our moral feelings. An antiethical
religion such as that described in Gustave Flaubert's historical novel
Salambo, about Moloch worship in Semitic Carthage, is a real possibility.
Thus the *Akedah* teaches that Judaism is neither a secular system of morals
nor a blind devotion to a supernatural power. Furthermore, the *Akedah* is
the great exception, not the rule. The rule in Judaism is that religious and
moral commands are very close to each other.

To sum up, there is more than one Jewish interpretation of the *Akedah.*
In this and similar matters of biblical interpretation there is no such thing
as an "official" Jewish viewpoint and it is extremely doubtful whether the
whole concept of "normative Judaism" is more than a myth. Both Stein-

berg and Soloveitchick are, therefore, correct in claiming that their understanding of the *Akedah* is authentically Jewish. They are both wrong in appearing to claim that theirs is the only possible authentically Jewish interpretation. It is not as if there is any question of the Jew ever being obliged to emulate Abraham's example. Judaism supplies a categorical answer to the question whether a murder is ever permitted when it is believed that God has so commanded and the answer in all the Jewish sources is in the negative. The command to Abraham was, on any showing, a once-and-for-all matter, never to be repeated and not carried out in practice even in the instance of Abraham himself. Yet this does not allow a Jewish thinker to dimiss the Kierkegaardian "midrash" as utter nonsense. There is point in the reminder, and sufficient support from the classical Jewish writings, that a true religious outlook demands of "ethical man" that he acquire a vertical direction to his life and that when the brave "knight of faith" goes out to do battle he does not tilt at windmills.

2. Abraham and Isaac: A Hermeneutical Problem Before Kierkegaard

DAVID A. PAILIN

KIERKEGAARD'S *FEAR AND TREMBLING* IS A PROVOCATIVE STUDY OF THE STORY of Abraham's attempt to sacrifice Isaac. It highlights the question whether it is correct that faith may involve the "teleological suspension of the ethical" since "faith is precisely this paradox, that the individual as the particular is higher than the universal."[1] Consequently, what ethics would condemn as murder, religion may praise as sacrifice.[2] This "contradiction" produces "the dread which can well make a man sleepless." It makes Johannes de Silentio confess that "Abraham I cannot understand, in a certain sense there is nothing I can learn from him but astonishment."[3] Most of this symposium is concerned with the ethical, religious, and philosophical issues raised by Kierkegaard's treatment of the story of the sacrifice of Isaac.

Kierkegaard's treatment of the story, however, while probably the longest, is by no means the first discussion of the issues it raises for religious understanding. For example, Augustine, Abélard and Aquinas discuss issues raised by the story.[4] Two centuries before *Fear and Trembling* was written, Joseph Hall anticipated both Johannes de Silentio's puzzlement (in terms of a savage heathen observing the incident from the secrecy of some bushes) and Kierkegaard's use of the story to exemplify the character of faith. He writes of Abraham that

> Faith hath wrought the same in him, which cruelty would in others, Not to be moved. He contemns all feares, and overlookes all impossibilities.[5]

In this essay, I want to consider various ways in which the story of Abraham and Isaac was treated by some, mainly English, works in the seventeenth and eighteenth centuries.

It is not surprising that during this period a number of theologians and preachers dealt with this story, since it apparently challenges the compatibility of two of their basic religious convictions. On the one hand, it was very widely accepted as self-evident that faith and belief must be essentially reasonable. From the Cambridge Platonists to Paley this principle was regarded by most people, both believers and nonbelievers, as practically unquestionable. A faith that ran counter to reason was, to them, untenable. There were some interesting exceptions to this position, but this essay is not the place to discuss them. On the other hand, it was probably as widely accepted that Christian faith and belief involved treating the Bible as an accurate record of God's dealings with men. Since, therefore, the story of Abraham and Isaac is part of the biblical record, it was necessary for Christian believers to show how God's demand and Abraham's response could be seen to be reasonable. Some of the ways in which they attempted to do this remind us of those "men of nice and acute perceptions, excellent metaphysicians, and by no means pedants" who, according to Voltaire, try to justify Abraham's conduct toward his wife![6]

In this paper, then, I want to do three things:

first, to outline some of the treatments of the Abraham and Isaac story produced during the seventeenth and eighteenth centuries. Since most of these treatments are not easily accessible today, I will spend a large portion of this paper in describing them. I do not pretend that the list of works consulted is exhaustive—there is a limit to the volumes of theology and, even more, of sermons that I can cope with—but it does, I believe, provide a fair indication of the different kinds of interpretation that were advanced;

second, to consider why the different interpretations of the story were advanced;

third, to indicate, briefly, what this study suggests about hermeneutics, especially in relation to what is regarded as an intrinsically authoritative text.

This program means that the first two parts of this paper belong to the history of thought and the third to contemporary understanding of hermeneutics. The legitimacy of this combination is defensible on the grounds that a study of past hermeneutical activity may show what happens in practice more clearly than a study of present modes of interpretation. This is because the different cultural context and exegetical presuppositions of a past age make it easier to see how such factors prejudice the understanding of a text than is the case when, as contemporaries of the interpreters we are studying, we share their basic approach and so find it hard to become completely aware of the prejudices at work.

Nevertheless, the views expressed in the first two parts must be placed under the judgment of the conclusions we draw from them in the third part. It is important not to forget this, since one of the conclusions reached by studying what is revealed by the first two parts of this paper is that the attempt to understand past expressions of thought is, to a significant degree, methodologically unsure. Somewhat paradoxically, then, the conclusions reached in part three, while derived from an analysis of evidence provided by parts one and two, include the claim that the kind of understanding found in those parts is in principle suspect! This may well be regarded as a self-defeating result. Such a judgment, however, would fall into the trap of absolutizing a relative: the fact that no understanding of past thought can ever wholly escape (or, at least, can ever be able to show that it has wholly escaped) from being affected by current problems and prejudices does not show that any such understanding must be wholly or even largely a reading of those problems and prejudices into the expressions of that past thought. There is an important difference between holding that all attempts to understand texts of another culture must be tentative to some extent and maintaining that no claim to such understanding is at all justifiable. As I see it, then, this study does not reach a pointlessly self-defeating conclusion but illustrates the difficulty of understanding past thought. It is always illegitimate for us to claim finality and incorrigibility for our understanding of the expressions of such thought.

Having thus indicated the justifiability of this project, it is time to stop worrying about the nature of the conclusions to be reached and to show how to reach them! How, then, was the story of Abraham and Isaac understood in the seventeenth and eighteenth centuries?

I. HOW WAS THE STORY INTERPRETED?

The material available to the interpreters of the story of Abraham and Isaac was, of course, the record in Genesis 22:1–18 and the comments on it in Hebrews 11:17–19 and James 2:21–23. The remarks about Abraham in Romans 4:2f and Galatians 3:6–9 (both presumably echoing Genesis 15:6) could also have been in mind. Most of the treatments of this source material are in terms of the Authorized Version translation, although some of the Hebrew and Greek terms in the originals are occasionally referred to. The various interpreters of the story thus receive it as the record of a historical event in which Abraham was "tempted" by God (Genesis 22:1) or "tried" and responded in an act of "faith" (Hebrews 11:17). Hebrews 11:19 attaches both belief in resurrection and a notion of "figurative" significance to the story.

The various interpreters seem to confine their use of the available source material to the passages in Genesis and Hebrews. The comment on it in James 2:21–23 is generally ignored, as are the comments on Abraham in Romans and Galatians. Fuller is an exception: he attempts to reconcile James's understanding with that of Paul.[7] The interpreters find little to explain in the words of their sources. There are some discussions of the meaning of the terms "tempt" (Genesis 22:1), "try" (Hebrews 11:17) and "accounting that" (Hebrews 11:19) but generally the interpreters seem to have no difficulties with the terms used either in the translation or in the original text. Charnock, though, suggests that Genesis 22:14 should be translated "*In the Mount the Lord Jehovah shall be seen;* the Particle (*of*) not being in the *Hebrew* Text."[8] The vast majority of the interpretations which we shall consider do not, furthermore, doubt that the Genesis story—as any such report in the Bible—is an accurate report of a series of events that actually occurred.[9] They do not cast doubt on the historicity of the story and, apart from the author of the note on Abraham added to the enlarged English edition of Bayle's dictionary and Kant, there is no suggestion that Abraham might only have "thought" that God was so ordering him. Indeed, with these rare exceptions, there seems to be little doubt about the reliability of the knowledge of God's intentions contained in the biblical materials.

The problem for the interpreters, then, was not in deciding the *meaning* of the biblical material about Abraham and Isaac. The texts as such raised no great problems and their meaning was clear. They provide a record of a past event from which, at the human level at least, we can accurately reconstruct what occurred. Their problem was to determine the *significance* of that story or, rather, of the event it described. They sought to do this in three respects, in terms of God, of Abraham, and of themselves and their readers. The composite question they were trying to answer was: What do we learn from this story about God, about Abraham, and about ourselves in relation to God? Some of them felt, as we shall see, that their interpretations must include a moral justification of the actions of God and Abraham; others felt under no such constraint because the report concerned God and was biblical. What, then, did the various interpreters make of the story? Although they run together their different answers to the three underlying questions, I will deal with their views in terms of those questions and not according to the individual interpreters.

The works of the individuals that I have used can be found in the appended notes. Some of them offer only very brief comments on the story, while others give it extended discussion. From my own notes I seem to have found these references through looking at some 230 authors in the period! They are a mixed bag—including an Archbishop of Canterbury, a radically minded glover, and a Master of Trinity College, Cambridge.

What, first, was understood to be the significance of the story so far as it concerned God? In this respect the interpretations can be treated as answers to one or more of three questions: Why did God command Abraham to sacrifice Isaac? If God did it to test Abraham, why was such a test necessary? Was God's command to Abraham morally justifiable? It was generally assumed that these questions must be answerable since God did not do things without a good reason. Consciously or not the canon of reason was applied to God in this period, so that most commentators were not prepared to entertain the notion that God's motives might be unfathomable to them or his actions gratuitous. Here at any rate Chubb speaks for the vast majority when he maintains that "God will not *prostitute* his authority by using it to answer no good purpose."[10]

As for the primary question, 'Why did God do it?', the obvious answer was that it was to test Abraham and, in particular, to prove the quality of his faith. This answer follows the "tempt" of Genesis 22:1 and the "try" of Hebrews 11:17. Collyer describes it as "the sorest affliction, and most severe trial" of Abraham's faith in and obedience to God.[11] According to Fuller, God sees fit "to *try* the righteous" since he sets great value "upon the genuine exercises of grace" which are produced in such situations.[12]

Stackhouse's comments, though, suggest that God inflicts the test not for his own benefit but in order that others might perceive "the Excellency of the Patriarch's Conduct" and, especially, "the Firmness and Steadfastness of his Faith."[13]

Another and frequent answer to the question—and one that takes up the notion of figurative action suggested in Hebrews 11:19—was that God commanded the event in order to provide a typological indication of the future redemptive death and/or resurrection of Jesus Christ. Fuller, for instance, puts it that "in this transaction there seems to be a still higher design; namely, to predict in a figure the great substitute which God in due time should 'see and provide.' " He nicely goes on to suggest that God's "high approbation" of Abraham might be due to the fact that it offered "some faint likeness" of what God himself would "shortly" do.[14] Some interpreters treat the incident as a prophetic foreshadowing of Christ without mentioning any divine design in the matter, but most clearly regard the figurative significance as deliberately intended by God. The typology is developed in various ways. Abraham offers his only son (at least, the only son by his wife) as God is to offer his; Isaac carrying the wood preenacts Christ carrying his cross; the provision of a ram anticipates God's provision of a substitute—and, according to Charnock, "intimates that there would be some interval of time before the blessed Seed should be offer'd" although Abraham himself might not at the time have understood the "Prophetick" significance of his remark in Genesis 22:8.[15] The "three days" between the command to sacrifice Isaac and its withdrawal reflects the fact of Christ's resurrection on the third day.[16] Pearson, who holds that "a clearer type can scarce be conceived of the Saviour of the world . . . than Isaac was," denies that the differences between the two incidents (e.g., that Isaac was not in fact killed) are significant: "the saving of Isaac alive doth not deny the death of the Antitype, but rather suppose and assert it, as presignifying his resurrection from the dead."[17]

A third view was that God staged the incident in order to make clear his disapproval of human sacrifices. Jenkin, indeed, argues that Abraham "too well understood the Divine Attributes, to believe God could delight in human Blood" but, having "a full Knowledge of the whole Dispensation of the Gospel," acted "not out of a Principle of Dread and Horror, but of Love" in order to "prefigure" the death and resurrection of Christ. He does, though, also see the story as a declaration by God of "how much he disapproved of such Sacrifices."[18] Waterland puts it that God's design was "to discourage and discountenance *human* sacrifices" while simultaneously showing that "he requires all men to be strictly obedient to his commands, and to prefer him above any the nearest and dearest relations."[19] Chubb, while offering it, describes this interpretation as only "a bare conjecture."[20] This interpretation possibly received added stress because of Tindal's argument that the incident indicated that the Jews did not regard killing a child as "absolutely unlawful" since "Abraham was highly extoll'd for being ready to sacrifice his only Son, and that too without the least Expostulation."[21] Voltaire similarly suggests that the story "seems to show that, at the time when this history was written, the sacrifice of human victims was customary amongst the Jews."[22] Leland replies to Tindal that the incident

> proves the quite contrary to what he produces it for. For tho' God requir'd *Abraham*, as the most signal Proof to all Generations of his Self-denial and absolute Obedience and Resignation to the divine Will, to be ready to give up his own Son . . . yet his not suffering him to execute his Purpose, but providing a Ram in his Son's stead, plainly shew'd that human Sacrifices were not what God approv'd, not even in this extraordinary Instance; and probably it was so order'd with this View, that no body might make use of this as a Precedent.[23]

Hall suggests a further understanding of God's attitude to the sacrifice. He considers that the Ram is provided because "God cannot abide that good purposes should be frustrate" and so acts to enable Abraham to offer a sacrifice of some kind. Apparently his God practices the principle, "Waste not, want not!"[24]

A further attempt to explain the reasons for God's command was that it emphasized the status of Isaac as one who was totally "*dedicated* to the Lord" and so a fit means for the fulfillment of God's promise to Abraham. I have, though, only found this view hinted at by a secular historian, although he may have had theological promptings.[25]

Although the view that God's purpose was to test Abraham was the most frequent response to the question, "Why did God do it?" and, in view of the biblical material, the most obvious response, it was an answer that raised a further question, "Why was such a test necessary?" In particular it was felt by a number of commentators who saw the incident as a test of Abraham's faith that they must explain why it was necessary for God so to test Abraham since, as God, he must already know everything, including the precise quality of Abraham's faith. If, then, God must have infallibly known the result of the test before it was set, what was the point of setting it? Tillotson puts it that it seems "contrary to Reason; because God who knows what every Man will do, needed not to make Tryal of any Man's Faith or Obedience."[26] The problem posed by God's omniscience is aggravated by the fact that Genesis 22:12 suggests that God did learn something from the event when it states, "Now I know that thou fearest God." The start of the verse indicates that it is "an angel of the Lord" who is speaking but the "me" at the end of the comment suggests that it is God who is speaking. Tillotson attempts to solve this issue by holding that when God says "*Now I know that thou lovest me* . . . we are to understand this as spoken after the manner of Men."[27] Charnock, on the other hand, suggests that since "*Knowledge* is sometimes taken for Approbation; then the sense will be, now I approve this Fact as a Testimony of thy fear of me."[28]

One response to the major problem of why an omniscient God needed to test Abraham was that the test was not for God's own sake but in order that Abraham and those who later were to hear about him might be made vividly aware of Abraham's character. Thus Tillotson remarks that "God does not try Men for his own information; but to give an illustrious Proof and Example to others of Faith and Obedience."[29] Leland describes it as "the most signal Proof to all Generations . . . a noble Proof . . . of his intire Submission to God and steady Faith in him."[30] As "Bayle" points out, following Le Clerc, this solution is not supported by the biblical evidence.[31] Another response was that the test was set in order to allow God to reward Abraham on a successful pass. Chillingworth, for instance, says that God tempted Abraham "not to satisfie his curiosity, but meerly out of a good inclination to the party; both hereby to confirm his graces in him, and to reward them with a greater measure of Glory."[32] It is not shown, though, why the omniscient God needed to set the test before awarding a prize! In the end, as with other attempts to understand God's actions, the introduction of the notion of his omniscience plays havoc with the meaningfulness of the understanding offered. Perhaps those commentators are wisest who leave this issue alone and so do not raise questions they cannot satisfyingly answer! Thus Hall apparently sees the incident as the tenth and severest "trial" by which God made sure of the purity of Abraham's faith. He writes that "it was fit that . . . the Father and pattern of the faithfull, should be thoroughly tryed: for in a set copy every fault is important, and may prove a rule of error."[33]

The moral justifiability of God's action in commanding Abraham to sacrifice his son was, however, a much more disturbing problem for many commentators—but not for all.[34] Believers held—perhaps it would be more accurate to say presupposed—that God was morally perfect. How then could this cruel order be seen to be morally good? "Bayle" puts the problem thus:

> That a merciful Being who does not delight in the misery of his creatures, should require human sacrifices, and order a father to butcher his own son, is what can never be reconciled with right reason. And that the father of mankind should delight in cruelty, is absolutely inconsistent with his moral character. . . . Mr. Chub thinks, that in the case of Abraham the thing commanded was morally unfit; and so we presume every sensible man will think. How then could such command be given by a good and benevolent Being?[35]

"Bayle" himself suggests that one way to evade this problem is to hold that in fact God did not command Abraham to sacrifice his son. He mentions Le Clerc's view "that it was only an Angel" who decided to discover "how deeply Abraham's virtue was rooted in his heart" by testing him in this way. He seems uncertain about this solution, though, and leaves it to the reader to judge how far it agrees with the biblical evidence about Abraham. His own conjecture, about which he seems equally tentative, is that we should understand the story according to the "well known" view that "the Scripture often ascribes to God some actions, as tho' he were the immediate author of them, though he only permits them providentially." He accordingly suggests that the idea of sacrificing Isaac was originally Abraham's. He sought, that is, to follow the practices of his contemporaries in order "to give to the true God" a "testimony of love and faith." God, then, did not initiate the action. While, though, he was pleased with its motive, "he abhorred the sacrifice itself" and therefore stopped Abraham from carrying it out.[36] This solution, though, was open to the serious criticism that its "interpretation" ran counter to the plain text of the evidence: "God did tempt Abraham." (Genesis 22:1) On the other hand, the widespread conviction about the reasonableness of belief and God's moral perfection made any solution that hid behind the mystery or unfathomableness of God's actions equally unacceptable for most interpreters in this period. Wilson does suggest that questions about the morality of God's actions are likely to bring trouble upon the questioner:

> God cannot escape the licentious tongues of His own creatures, who will not be satisfied unless He will give them an account of all His proceedings; and when they have such an account, they make a jest of it. But God will not be mocked without a just resentment.[37]

Most interpreters, though, were not afraid to attempt to justify the ways of God to man, at least in the case of Abraham and Isaac. Wilson, indeed, holds that in this case God's actions are understandable. Chubb pointed out that God did not object when Abraham elsewhere queried his behavior.[38] How, then, did the interpreters try to find a moral justification for Abraham's behavior?

It was generally agreed by them that it would be wrong for God to induce a man to evil. This view was backed by the biblical assurance that God does not so "tempt" men (James 1:13). As Abernethy put it, "all religion resteth upon this principle, utterly inconsistent with his tempting any man or any creature, that God is only pleased with rational agents doing that which is right."[39] Accepting this principle and aware of James 1:13, many interpreters begin to justify God's action by arguing that when the word "tempt" is used in Genesis 22:1, it does not mean that God sought to attract Abraham to do evil but that God "tested" or "proved" Abraham. Thus Tillotson suggests that "God tempts no Man, with a design to draw him into Sin; but this doth not hinder, but he may try their Faith and Obedience with great difficulties, to make them the more illustrious. Thus God tempted *Abraham*. . . ."[40] Such "testing" was held not to be morally objectionable. Hartley describes it as one of the methods that "Reason and Experience dictate as the proper ones, for advancing and perfecting true Religion in the Soul."[41]

The case for the moral justifiability of God's test of Abraham could not, however, rest here. It was widely felt to be necessary to show that the command to Abraham was morally good even though its execution would apparently have been morally evil. Chillingworth attempts to get round this problem by holding that it was "only a temptation." Since God did not intend it to be executed, there was nothing morally wrong in his action.[42] Chubb, though, hints that such a defense of the morality of God's action may not be an unqualified success. If God is to escape moral censure on the grounds that he never intended his command to Abraham to be fulfilled, he is then left open to the moral censure that he deliberately deceived Abraham about his will.[43] Nevertheless, in spite of recognizing the possibility of such an objection to God's conduct, Chubb himself holds elsewhere that while the death of Isaac could never have been morally justified, the command to kill him was just. This is because it "was not given in order to execution, and with an intent that it should be obeyed, but only to *try* the understanding, the faith and the obedience of Abraham."[44]

Others preferred a more radical defense of the morality of God's action. They argued in various ways that since God's will is sovereign, it is always good and to be obeyed.[45] Joseph Butler, however, is in difficulties when he puts forward this defense because he apparently follows the Lockean view that reason must judge what is authentic revelation and morality. Thus he seems to want to hold both that reason judges the morality of what is supposedly revealed and that it is subordinate to revelation.[46] The defense itself, though, could be (and was) put in terms of a thorough-going voluntarist view of the relation of moral goodness to God's will: whatever God commands must be good simply because it is commanded by God. William Law, for instance, denies that "any actions have any *absolute* fitness, of and in *themselves*." Accordingly, when "God by his will makes anything fit to be done, he does not make the thing fit in *itself* . . . but it becomes fit for the person to do it, because he can only be happy, or do that which is fit for him to do, by doing the will of God." Thus in Abraham's case, the command of God so fixes the circumstances of the act of killing Isaac that it makes it "lawful for *Abraham* to kill his son."[47] In practice, though, most interpreters, probably because they are deeply influenced by the canon of reason, do not advance such a full-blooded voluntarism. They are content to hold that in the kind of case at issue, God's will is competent to determine what is good. Samuel Clarke, for instance, holds that while not even God can vary "*That part of* the Law of Nature, which is founded . . . on the very *Existence of God* and on the *essentially and eternally immutable Nature and Relation of Things*," he can change those moral rules that are established by his mere command or by a

Law of Nature founded originally on his will. Since the prohibition on killing an innocent person does not derive from the "*essential* Nature of Things" but is merely what is established by "the *Will* and *Free Gift* of God," there is nothing to prevent God ordering Abraham to kill Isaac. What would have been morally impossible, though, according to Clarke, would have been for God to command Abraham to hate Isaac or to delight in cruelty since, in his view, these states are contrary to the essential and unalterable character of things.[48]

One way in which this view was developed was by holding that the moral character of an action is determined by its circumstances. The express will of God is, then, regarded as a deciding circumstance. William Law, in the passage quoted earlier, holds that the command of God "adds *new circumstances* to an action, that is neither fit, nor unfit, moral, nor immoral, in *itself,* but *because* of its circumstances."[49] Waterland similarly asserts that "the Divine command is a circumstance which changes the very nature and quality of the act, which makes *killing* no *murder,* no iniquity, but duty, and strict justice."[50] This view was persistently attacked by Chubb:

> if it was fit to take away *Isaac's* life, that fitness *did not* arise from, nor was it founded upon the *divine command,* but upon such *other circumstances* as attended the case . . . antecedent to any divine determination concerning it.[51]

He maintained that morality could not be simply a matter of God's "sovereign pleasure" since that would make nonsense of morality. It was, rather, a matter of the intrinsic fitness of an act viewed in its natural situation.[52]

Most interpreters followed a different way of developing the justification of God's command. At heart their commitment to reasonableness probably made them feel, as Kant was to put it in his *Lectures on Ethics,* that "we ought, therefore, to do a thing not because God wills it, but because it is righteous and good in itself—and it is because it is good in itself that God wills it and demands it of us."[53] None of the interpreters, though, seemed to feel that there was any way of arguing that the killing of Isaac could be regarded as a positive good. They were content, therefore, with trying to show that God's command to Abraham could at least be regarded as morally justified, bearing in mind who gave the command. The way in which many tried to do this was by reference to God's supposed rights over the lives of his creatures. Since it was implicitly denied that the creature had any intrinsic right to his life over against the Creator who gave it to him, and since it was held that death was inflicted by God, it was argued that there could be no difference in principle between God taking a life through disease or accident and taking it through an executioner at his order. Tillotson, for example, sees no reason why Abraham should have moral scruples about killing Isaac

> at the Command of God, who being the Author of Life, hath power over it, and may resume what he hath given, and take away the Life of any of his Creatures when he will, and make whom he pleaseth Instruments in the Execution of his Command.[54]

Similarly Waterland asks

> For why should not God have as much right to demand the life of any, even the most innocent man, by a *knife,* or a *sword,* as by a *fever* or *pestilence,* by a *lion* or *bear,* or other instrument whatever? And if a man be employed in it by God's express order, he is God's executioner in doing it, and only pays a debt which God has at any time a sovereign power and right to demand of him . . . .[55]

God's command was thus seen as morally justified on the basis that as an owner has unrestricted rights over his property, so God has unrestricted rights over his creatures.[56]

Chubb, on the other hand, rejects any such attempted defense of God's action. He is quite clear that Abraham's filicide could never be morally justified, even at God's command.[57] There were no circumstances whatsoever "which rendered it fit that he should die."[58] Chubb systematically rejects eight theories, some extremely speculative, which had been put forward by Stone to suggest how Isaac's death could have been justifiable—that Isaac was wicked, that he would be wicked, to translate him elsewhere in the universe, to sanctify him in heaven, to recompense him for earthly loss, to show Abraham's and Isaac's obedience, to give evidence of the resurrection. Even if any of these theories could be substantiated by evidence, Chubb points out that none of them would justify Abraham's killing Isaac in the prescribed manner. As for the theory that the command might be "merely to shew God's absolute sovereignty over his creatures," Chubb remarks that such behavior would "*dishonour*" God, revealing him as "acting *below himself,* and *unsuitable* to his character."[59] The debate between Chubb and Stone illustrates the phrenetic character of the extreme attempts to justify the command of God to Abraham. Chubb's confidence that the execution of the command could never have been justified, even if ordered by God, was positively backed by two considerations. First, since God brought mankind "into being without their consent . . . reason requires that he should take care of their *well-being.*"[60] God's parental sovereignty was thus regarded as imposing a duty to foster his creatures' good, not as bestowing a right to do what he liked with his own.[61] Here Chubb shows the more radical kind of commitment to the canon of reason that was found in this period. Chubb stands up to God on the basis of what Chubb's reason tells him is right, no matter what the biblical evidence and orthodox faith might suggest. He sees his position, though, as justified secondly by the fact that God himself withdrew the command to kill Isaac when Abraham was about to do it. If the command had been morally good, God would have insisted that it be carried out. It was only justifiable as a deceptive "try-on" that God never intended to be carried through.[62] God's command thus did not impugn his moral goodness.[63]

Having considered how the interpreters treated the story in relation to God, we must now review their understanding of Abraham's part. In this respect they were basically concerned with two questions: Why did Abraham obey God's command? and Was Abraham's obedience reasonable—and therefore correct for him and an example to us? Though the answers to the first question might also suggest why it was reasonable for him to obey, the reason found for his action need not justify it. Thus while their answers to the two questions may overlap, they need to be considered separately. Furthermore, although their answers were to some extent affected by how they interpreted God's role in the story, their studies of Abraham also reveal other problems that they had to overcome if they were to reconcile the conviction of the reasonableness of belief with the biblical records. The ways in which their problems were overcome illustrates at times how interpreters may increasingly have to produce ideas not explicitly supported by their text in order to sustain their exegeses.

Before suggesting why Abraham obeyed, many of the interpreters stress how very hard it must have been for Abraham to obey. Here some preachers allow themselves to go far beyond the text as they describe what they imagine to have been Abraham's agony as he prepared to carry out the command and traveled to Moriah. Tillotson tells his hearers that Abraham "was to offer up his Son but once; but he sacrificed himself and his own Will every Moment for three Days together."[64] Fuller highlights the magnitude of Abraham's trial by pointing out that God was ordering him to kill his son, for whom he had waited many years and in whom his hopes resided, by unusually cruel means, for no apparent reason, and seemingly in contradiction of God's promises.[65] The innocence of Isaac and the interval between the command and its appointed execution were also seen as aggravating the harrowing nature of the incident. Hall imagines Abraham as possibly being aware of the indefensibility of his intended action to his contemporaries and his anguish on the journey. He has Abraham say to Isaac, "I need not tell thee, that I sacrifice all my worldly joyes, yea and my selfe in thee; but God must be obeyed. . . ."[66] Others, however, were so convinced of the reasonableness of Abraham's obedience (which we shall investigate shortly) that they did not consider that it would have been so very difficult for him! It was even suggested that human sacrifice, including filicide, would not have been so dreadful for Abraham since it was commonly practiced then.[67]

Whatever his feelings might have been, Abraham did as God commanded. Three reasons were suggested for this response. First, it was argued that Abraham obeyed because he trusted God and so believed that all would come right in the end if he did what God wanted. Secondly, it was suggested that Abraham obeyed because he knew without doubt that God had commanded this action. Various interpreters seek to explain how it could be that Abraham could know without a peradventure that the command came from God. Thirdly, and above all, Abraham's response in this case was seen as a consequence of his regular and thorough obedience to God. It was held that since Abraham would in general never think of questioning, let alone of disobeying, God's orders, so neither would he think of not obeying in this particular case. Thus Abraham "contemns all feares, and overlookes all impossibilities. . . . In a holy wilfulnesse he either forgets Nature, or despises her, he is sure that what God commands, is good"; faith has "taught him not to argue, but [to] obey."[68] Delaney, incidentally, is one of those who do not forget to give due praise to Isaac, who "equalled, if not exceeded, the faith and piety of his father Abraham, in suffering himself to be bound, and calmly submitting himself to be sacrificed."[69]

Granted, though, that these were the reasons why Abraham was prepared to obey, the question remained whether, in the circumstances, his obedience was reasonable. Only if it were could his behavior be regarded as an example for men who presupposed the canon of reason and the essential reasonableness of true faith. Interpreters thus examined closely the supposed reasons for his conduct and other relevant factors in order to establish whether Abraham could be held to be rationally and morally justified in doing what he did. As Ogden points out, the fact that Abraham was prevented from actually killing Isaac makes no real difference to the justification of his conduct since the intention was there and "the will before God is the deed."[70] Chubb, as we have already noted, suggests that whereas God's command could be justified on the grounds that God never intended it to be executed, Abraham's action in obeying could never be so justified since he intended to do what could never be morally right.

There were several grounds for casting doubt on the reasonableness of Abraham's conduct. They all presupposed what was widely accepted, namely, that a man's conduct and, in particular, his entertainment of something as a revelation from God, must be guided by his reason, including his moral sense. Locke expressed this dominant conviction when he held that a man must believe or disbelieve "according as reason directs him" for

> he that takes away reason, to make way for revelation, puts out the light of both, and does much what the same, as if he would persuade a man to put out

his eyes, the better to receive the remote light of an invisible star by a telescope.[71]

On this basis it was uncertain whether Abraham should have accepted the command as being from God and have been prepared to obey it. How could he have legitimately persuaded himself that the command did come from God and that there were good reasons for doing what he did, at least in God's understanding of the total issue?[72] Was it not more likely that he was faced with "the Suggestion and Illusion of an evil Spirit, than any Command of God?"[73]

In the first place, what Abraham planned to do is unnatural. It is contrary to natural inclinations and affections for a father to kill his son. Since, however, it was assumed that man's natural inclinations and affections were planted in him by God, it was also held to be unreasonable and immoral for him to act contrarily to them. As Tillotson puts it, "The horrid Nature of the thing commanded" makes it appear "very barbarous and unnatural, and look liker a Sacrifice to an Idol, than to the true God." Why should it be believed that God orders something so opposed to man's strongest affections when the very naturalness of such affections shows them to have been implanted by God and so to be good?[74] Chubb, in a more secular approach, points out that it is contrary to the public good for parents to harm their children—unless, that is, those children are themselves a threat to that good, which was not the case with Isaac.[75] Stackhouse attempts to defend Abraham by suggesting that his grief over losing Isaac may have "satisfied the Laws of Nature" but this hardly justifies the morality of the action itself.[76] From the human side, the cruelty of what Abraham was prepared to do is aggravated by the fact that Isaac was to be killed by his father's hand and that Isaac was innocent of any crime.[77] From the divine side the enormity of the act is accentuated by the fact that it would destroy God's greatest blessing to Abraham in his old age,[78] seemingly prevent the fulfillment of God's promise to Abraham that through his seed should all nations be blessed,[79] oppose God's usual commands,[80] be contrary to other revelations from God,[81] and suggest that God is tormentingly sadistic.[82] Finally there was the scandalous character of the act. Stackhouse might describe these objections to the reasonableness of Abraham's action as "the Reasoning of a *carnal* Mind"[83] but, as Hall suggests, most men would have difficulty in justifying conduct like Abraham's to themselves, let alone to others. Hall writes,

Who but *Abraham* would not have expostulated with God? What? Doth the God of mercies now begin to delight in bloud? Is it possible that Murder should become Piety? . . . Can I not be faithfull unlesse I be unnaturall? . . . What will the Heathen say, when they shall heare of this infamous massacre? How can thy Name, and my profession escape a perpetuall blasphemy? . . . Or who will beleeve, that I did this from thee?[84]

Whoever would believe Abraham when he claimed that what he did was in obedience to God's revelation? Would they not hold that if a "confident pretence to Revelation be admitted, the worst Actions may plead this in their excuse?" Would not such a defense thus only seem to aggravate Abraham's fault "by adding the boldest Impiety to the most barbarous Inhumanity?"[85]

The reasonableness of Abraham's faith and conduct had thus to be established in the face of formidable objections. Chubb, indeed, considered that it could never be established since not only was the action intrinsically unreasonable but also the evidence about "Abraham's opinion concerning this matter" is not available.[86] Others, though, were happy to let their imaginations conjecture where concrete evidence was lacking. Tillotson consequently felt able, in spite of recognizing the objections, to represent Abraham's faith as "the result of the wisest Reasoning, and soberest Consideration"[87] while Conybeare holds that his faith was the exemplary product of "duly attending" to "common Sense and Reason."[88] On what grounds were Abraham's faith and conduct held to be reasonable?

They were primarily held to be reasonable because they were in accordance with a revelation of God's will that Abraham knew to be authentic. Since he was sure that "the order was from God, . . . he readily submitted," having "never learned to dispute with unerring Wisdom."[89] Those who offered this justification realized, however, that the problem with it was to show how Abraham could have been rationally convinced that the revelation was from God and not a devilish deception.[90] Hartley tried to avoid the issue by suggesting that in that "early Age there had as yet been few or no false Pretences, or Illusions."[91] Others ducked the issue by simply asserting that Abraham could not have so acted and God would not have so commanded unless the revelation had been authenticated beyond reasonable doubt. Thus Conybeare holds that it "cannot be doubted" that God always provides sufficient supporting evidence for any revelation.[92] More speculative commentators tried to answer the question by suggesting that Abraham was so familiar with the characteristics of a genuine revelation from God (without specifying what those characteristics might be) that he could not have been duped concerning the authenticity of the revelation in this case. In the first place, for instance, Tillotson maintains that God has the power to produce in a man "a firm Perswasion" of what he reveals and that he never requires of a man a belief that "plainly contradicts the Natural and Essential Notions of his Mind," including his grasp of "the Essential Perfections of the Divine Nature." Secondly, he argues that

this was not the first of many Revelations that had been made to him, so that he knew the manner of them, and had found by manifold experience, that he was not deceived. . . . And it is very probable the first time God appeared to *Abraham,* because it was a new thing, that to make way for the Credit of future Revelations, God did shew himself to him in so glorious a manner, as was abundantly to his Conviction.[93]

Consequently when God's command was revealed to Abraham "by an audible Voice, . . . he was fully satisfied by the Evidence which it carried along with it, that it was from God."[94] Clarke adds that Abraham had the "peculiar security" of knowing that God would not allow him to be deceived when "he was sure his own Heart was perfectly right."[95] Kant, though, as we shall see later, did not accept his argument. He considered that the possibility of mistaken identity could not be put beyond reasonable doubt in such a case as this.[96]

Having established that Abraham could know that the command genu-, inely came from God, the reasonableness of his action was defended, secondly, on the grounds that it was God whom he was obeying. His obedience, that is, was justified in the view of many commentators in the same way as the morality of God's command, namely, by reference to the ultimate and absolute nature of God's authority. Clarke, for instance, says that Abraham's action "seems contrary at first sight to the eternal Law of Nature; But he is justified by the *immediate* Command of God, who has undeniably a supreme Right over all: A *Right,* not to make Virtue to be Vice, and Vice Virtue; but a *Right* over the *Life* of every man whom he has created."[97] William Law puts it that "it had been as unlawful for *Abraham* to have disobeyed God in this extraordinary command, as to have cursed God at any *ordinary calamity* of providence."[98] Chubb argues that Abraham's intercession for Sodom and Gomorrah shows that he did not accept that God had a right to destroy the innocent with the guilty and hence that he ought to have appreciated the unfitness of his intention to kill Isaac.[99] The prevalent view, however, was that Abraham could not be faulted for obeying God. Some commentators, furthermore, consider that Abraham's awareness of God's wisdom, power and benevolence make his obedience all the more reasonable. He acts on the basis of his assurance that God would not command anything inconsistent with his perfection and Abraham's ultimate good. His conduct thus reflects his trust in God's goodness to him.[100] It was also suggested that Abraham would recognize that God had a peculiar right to Isaac on account of the miracle of his birth: "he was sensible that the offering up his son to God was no more than paying a debt, resigning up a trust, or returning a loan."[101]

A few commentators suggested that the reasonableness of Abraham's action became clearer when it was viewed in the light of what they supposed to be current practices. Tillotson, for example, states that in those times "the Paternal Power was more absolute and unaccountable" than it was after the Law of Moses had limited it amongst the Jews. This is held to reduce "the horror and scandal" of Abraham's intention to kill his son.[102] Apart from Hurd's view that the event reflects the sacerdotal power in the heads of families at that time,[103] the claim that the action was sanctioned by current practices of human sacrifice seems to have been restricted to rationalist critics of orthodox belief.[104]

Another widespread defense of the reasonableness of Abraham's conduct took the line that Abraham was justified in what he did because he believed in the power of God—and, in particular, in the power of God to raise Isaac from the dead. This widespread view was clearly influenced by the comment in Hebrews 11:19. Abraham, according to this view, could act reasonably and without too much anxiety in preparing to kill Isaac because he believed God could bring him back to life. Some interpreters argue that Abraham was justified in having this belief because of past favors to him[105] and, especially, because of the miraculous nature of Isaac's birth.[106] Tillotson and Collyer both recognize, though, the remarkable character of Abraham's belief in that there were no previous instances of resurrection on which he could base his faith.[107] In contrast Toland, as not infrequently in other matters, was unqualified in his remarks about Abraham's reasonableness. He held that Abraham's belief in God's resurrecting power was not only a means by which he could reconcile God's command with his earlier promises. It was also a product of "very strict Reasoning from Experience [i.e., of the miracle of Isaac's birth], from the Possibility of the thing, and from the Power, Justice and Immutability of him that promis'd it."[108] Nevertheless, whatever the grounds for his belief—whether it was based on reasoning or on revelation—many commentators found a justification for Abraham's action in a belief in the resurrecting power of God. Arguing that *"True Faith* is always founded upon *Reason,"* Samuel Clarke states that Abraham could offer Isaac "because *Reason* told him, that, whatever Improbabilities appeared at present; yet God, who has Power over the *Future* as well as the *Present* State, was able to fulfil his Promises even by a *Resurrection from the Dead.*"[109] Robert Jenkin went further. He argues that Abraham knew God too well to believe he would desire such a sacrifice and that he also had "a full knowledge of the whole Dispensation of the Gospel" revealed to him. Consequently he reasonably "concluded" from the events that were to be typified that Isaac "was to . . . prefigure the Son of God, both in his Death, and in his Resurrection." Here, then, a revealed knowledge of the far future gave Abraham reasonable grounds for predicting the near future![110] Some commentators, though, were not convinced by these types of argument. Delaney felt that it could not explain why Abraham acted as he did—only the origin of the command in God could do that.[111] Chubb ingeniously argued that Abraham's belief that God would raise Isaac was "a *groundless presumption*" since God could never have had such an intention as he never intended that Isaac should actually die![112] "Bayle" offers a different kind of objection. He quotes Saurin's suggestion that if Abraham knew Isaac would be resurrected, his action cannot be counted as all that meritorious: "What great self-denial was it to cut off the head of his son, if he knew, that he would immediately come to life again?"[113]

Tindal hints that Abraham may deserve censure on the grounds that whereas "he was importunate with God to save an inhospitable, idolatrous, and incestuous City," he never offered "the least Expostulation" to save his "innocent child."[114] Waterland gives a threefold reply to this criticism of Abraham. First, it would have been selfish of Abraham to plead for his own son's life: "he could plead for *others;* . . . for *himself* he could not plead; such was his modesty, ingenuity, and disinterested piety." Secondly, the Sodomites were evil and needed an intercessor if they were to escape God's wrath. Isaac, in comparison, was innocent, "an object of *Divine love,* and certain to be a gainer by it." Thirdly, the Sodomites were to be punished but Isaac was to be "an occasion of further manifestation of Divine goodness."[115] By means that were sometimes more ingenious than ingenuous commentators thus sought to assert the reasonableness of Abraham's conduct. For most of them it was this reasonableness that allowed Abraham's faith and action to be presented as an example to their contemporaries. In this way the dominant acceptance of the canon of reason controlled both their understanding of the story and of its current religious significance.

What, then, were the "lessons" that commentators drew from the story for their contemporaries? Some of them were more obvious than others.

Waterland describes Abraham as "a man of the fairest and brightest character to be met with in all history."[116] By far the most popular "moral" to be drawn from the story is that Abraham provides us with an eminent example of religious faith, trust, and obedience. The story of Abraham and Isaac gives us "a remarkable Instance of *Faith.*"[117] Abraham continues to trust God even though what he is to do apparently destroys the means of fulfilling God's promises.[118] Abraham was "justified by faith" because he did not let the appearances of improbability destroy his steadfast belief.[119] Thereby he provides a "standard" of what is "acceptable to God."[120] The story reminds us that faith involves action as well as intellectual belief.[121] The activity of faith is found in unquestioning obedience to God's commands. Consequently Abraham is presented as showing exemplary obedience—"upon the first summons of the Divine Command without scruple or hesitancy, readily and cheerfully yielding up his only Son."[122] For Tillotson, Abraham displays "one of the most miraculous" and virtuous "acts of Obedience" since he performed it "deliberately, and upon full consideration" of all the difficulties. If we believed "as firmly as *Abraham* believed God in this case; what should we not be ready to do, or suffer, in obedience to him?"[123] Indeed, whereas Clarke suggests Abraham's obedience was "founded upon the *Expectation* of a *Future State*"[124] and Voltaire speaks of "the resignation" that a man owes to God,[125] some commentators so present his example as one of unquestioning readiness to obey in spite of all problems that they are liable to undermine the arguments to show the reasonableness of his conduct![126] Isaac's acceptance of his role is similarly held to be a pattern of faith and obedience.[127]

This understanding of Abraham's conduct was further developed as an illustration of the way that faithful obedience may demand the surrender of everything to God. The story, that is, does not just illustrate and prefigure God's gift of his son and the passion of Jesus.[128] It also reminds us, in Hall's words, that "the only way to finde comfort in any earthly thing, is to surrender it (in a faithfull carelessnesse) into the hands of God" since "those shall never rest with *Abraham,* that cannot sacrifice with *Abraham*" their dearest possessions.[129] Wilson puts it that Christians "ought" similarly "to resign their dearest children, when God calls for them, . . . a sacrifice of their obedience to His good pleasure."[130] Lest, however, some parents might be tempted to anticipate God's clear command in such matters, Hurd apparently felt it necessary to remind his readers that "the case of Isaac was of a peculiar nature, and no way applicable to the common state of affairs in the world, which would put an end to the existence of civil society."[131] There is no precedent here of a way to solve the problem of what to do with the children on holiday!

The story of Abraham's obedience was also held, by Stackhouse for instance, to make the point that such obedience would be backed by "extraordinary Comfort and Support" and would receive "a glorious Reward."[132] It was claimed that Abraham's example indicates that obedience to God ultimately leads to the fulfillment of his promises and the good of his faithful,[133] even though it would probably be mistaken to hold that the provision of the ram shows that God will always come to the aid of his faithful in times of extremity.[134] Clarke uses the story of Abraham's faith to argue that "*True Faith* in *God* never leads men to the Practice of any thing, that is essentially and in its own nature *Immoral*."[135] The only possible suspension of the ethical by God is, as we have already seen, in matters under the immediate command of God or established by his will.

In view of the way in which the canon of reason controls most of the interpretations of the story, making it incumbent upon the commentator to establish the reasonableness of God's command and of Abraham's response, it is amusing to note that the story is held to illustrate the need for reason in matters of faith. Reason, for instance, is said to be needed to reconcile the apparent contradiction between God's character and his command or between his promise and his command. It is maintained that only reason can assure a believer of what he ought to do when faced with such apparent contradictions. Thus Tillotson sees illustrated by the story

the great and necessary use of Reason, in matters of Faith. For we see here that *Abraham's* Reason was a mighty strengthning and help to his Faith.

> Here were two Revelations . . . which seemed to clash with one another; and if *Abraham's* Reason could not have reconciled the Repugnancy of them, he could not possibly have believed them both to be from God; because this natural Notion, or Principle, that *God cannot contradict himself,* every Man does first, and more firmly believe, than any Revelation whatsoever.[136]

This moral was certainly in accord with the temper of the times. It contains, though, a potential source of conflict with the supposed Protestant principle that what Scripture reveals, our mind "is not to search and speculate about . . . but with a pious Credulity to embrace."[137] A large part of the story of religious faith in the seventeenth and eighteenth centuries is the story of the increasingly unhappy attempts to establish its reasonableness. The treatment of the Abraham and Isaac story is a small illustration of this larger debate.

The attempt to show the reasonableness of Abraham's action led to a further lesson being drawn from the story, namely, that God ensures that those to whom he reveals himself are properly certain that the revelation has come from God. Even though we may not be able to determine what were the authenticating marks in the case of Abraham with any precision, the story of Abraham and Isaac is held to show that when God does command something, the person receiving the command will be left in no doubt about its source and authority. The various commentators who urged this view do not seem to have been worried by the need to produce evidence to justify its validity. It was apparently enough that the presupposition of its truth and its applicability in the case of Abraham made it possible for them to judge Abraham's conduct as reasonable. They did little more, that is, than offer a hypothesis to meet a specific problem and then propose to treat it as a general rule on the grounds that it seemed reasonable! It was, nevertheless, a practice followed by respectable preachers—and probably is the kind of rational howler that preachers are prone to make! Tillotson, for instance, on the basis that Abraham would only have acted as he did because he was sure the command came from God, affirms that

> Humane Nature is capable of clear and full satisfaction, concerning a Divine Revelation . . . And nothing is more reasonable, than to believe that those, to whom God is pleased to make immediate Revelations of his Will, are some way or other assured that they are Divine; otherwise they would be in vain, and to no purpose. But how Men are assured concerning Divine Revelations made to them, is not so easie to make out to others . . .[138]

Conybeare says this principle "cannot be doubted"[139] and Stackhouse agrees, though he admits that "the Scripture has no where informed us" how the assurance is given to men.[140] Such, then, was the intrinsic authority given to reason in matters of faith that a "reasonable" hypothesis which offered a "reasonable" explanation was unlikely to be challenged, even though there was no evidence for it beyond its apparent ability to provide a "reasonable" understanding of why things had happened as they had.

Another lesson drawn from the story was that believers must not permit the appearance of problems and unpleasantness to hinder their faithful obedience to God's commands. Unless they know the matter to be impossible even to God, believers are urged to trust and obey without question. Thus Conybeare exhorts his hearers that

> in Matters of Religion, we should not give way to the first Appearances of Difficulty, . . . nor attend too much to the Solicitations of Passion: Had *Abraham* done so, we should have wanted this excellent Pattern of Faith and Obedience. . . . How different is the Behaviour of our modern Objectors against Religion! They are carried away with the first Shew of Difficulty; and, being impatient of Examination, reject the Truth of every Article they cannot immediately master. . . . But *Truth* is still *Truth* . . . and in the Search after it, Men should rather consult their own cool and impartial Reason, than their vain and extravagant Humours.

Accordingly he argues that, following Abraham, believers should in "common Modesty" prefer "the Divine Testimony" to apparent difficulties unless "the Thing objected against" can be shown to be "absolutely impossible." Thus God is to be trusted to fulfil his promises in some way at some time.[141] Since, however, the obedience displayed by Abraham is far from easy, Fuller also sees the story as illustrating how God enables men to obey him: "we have here, then, a surprising instance of the efficacy of Divine grace, in rendering every power, passion, and thought of the mind subordinate to the will of God."[142]

Not everyone saw the story of Abraham and Isaac as providing a good example of faith and conduct. As we have already noted, Tindal and Chubb suggest that Abraham may be open to criticism for not trying to save Isaac. It is at least surprising that he did not protest when he had previously been "importunate with God to save" Sodom.[143] Tindal, furthermore, saw the story as evidence that "the *Jews* cou'd not think it absolutely unlawful for a Father to sacrifice an innocent Child" since they "highly extoll'd" Abraham for what he did.[144] Voltaire suggested that the story indicates such acts were "customary among the Jews."[145] Hurd adopts a more neutral approach when he sees the story as evidence of their being "at that time, a sacerdotal, as well as civil power, lodged in the master of every family."[146] The vast majority of those who dealt with the story, though, so accepted, implicitly or explicitly, the authority of the Bible as a not-to-be-questioned guide in faith and morals that they considered their task to be that of finding the good morals in the story!

The sacrificial element in the story, however, did raise a question about who copied whom! One of the apologetic arguments for the truth—or finality—of the Christian religion (with its Jewish ancestry) maintained, contrary to what might seem to be historically probable from the origin of the Jewish people,[147] that the non-Jewish nations of the ancient world first learnt (and subsequently often corrupted) many things from the Jews, including writing and philosophy. Theophilus Gale's *Court of the Gentiles*, for example, was an extensive attempt, following hints in Grotius and others, to confirm "*the* Authoritie of the Scriptures; *and so by consequence the* Christian Religion" through showing "*the* Traduction *of* Human Arts *and* Sciences *from the* Scriptures, *and* Jewish Church."[148] The question that arose concerning the Abraham and Isaac story was whether it provided the original for non-Jewish religious practices and stories. Did, for example, non-Jews copy a possibly distorted report of Abraham's conduct when they told of human sacrifices or the substitution of an animal for a man? John Edwards writes that

> *Sacrificing of Men*, especially of their Sons, which some Pagan Stories relate, might have its original from *Abraham*. It is recorded by *Porphyrius*, saith *Eusebius*, that *Saturnus* an antient King of *Phoenicia*, that he might appease the Gods, and save his Kingdom . . . offer'd his *Only Son* on an Altar. This *Saturn* is the Antient Patriarch *Abraham* . . . *Pelopidas* (saith *Plutarch* in his Life) was bid in a Vision to sacrifice a Virgin; but it so happen'd that a Mare-Colt came running through the Camp, whilst they were disputing whether the Vision should be obey'd, and by the advice of the Augur was taken and sacrificed instead of a Virgin. . . May we not conceive that this was done in imitation of what they had heard by Tradition [about Isaac]?[149]

Stackhouse comments that "the Heathen World was not altogether ignorant of this Sacrifice of *Abraham*." In support he cites the stories of Iphigenia and the fawn, Helena and the heifer, and "many more Stories of the like Nature." He further maintains that Abraham was giving a "new and unusual Example." He could not have been following current custom since such practices were not then to be found in Babylon, Mesopotamia, Chaldea and Beersheba.[150] Waterland, in contrast, denies that the story of Abraham and Isaac was the first case of human sacrifice and later copied by others. He argues that it is more likely that God used the incident to discourage an existing custom of human sacrifice than that he unwittingly brought about the "occasion of introducing that barbarous practice."[151]

The final interpretation of the story which I want to mention is that given by Kant in his *Der Streit der Facultäten*, which appeared in 1798. In his *Religion Within the Limits of Reason Alone*, published five years before, Kant argued that an inquisitor who proposes to execute a man on the basis of a revealed command of God should refrain because he cannot be certain of the justification of his action. The revelation has only reached him through man and as interpreted by man. Consequently, "even did it appear to have come to him from God himself (like the command delivered to Abraham to slaughter his own son like a sheep) it is at least possible that in this instance a mistake has prevailed."[152] In *The Conflict of the Faculties* he explicitly rejects Abraham's example as one to be followed. Since he does not accept the voluntarist view of ethics, he holds that God can declare but not determine by his fiat what is right and wrong. God's moral uniqueness is that his holy will is "incapable of any maxim conflicting with the moral law,"[153] not that he chooses what the law shall be. Consequently in his understanding faith cannot involve a teleological suspension of the ethical.[154] As for the story of Abraham and Isaac itself, Kant comments thus:

> For if God really were to speak to man, the latter could after all never know that it is God who is speaking to him. It is utterly impossible for man to apprehend the Infinite through his senses, to distinguish him from sensible objects and thereby to know him. He can, though, no doubt convince himself in some cases that it cannot be God whose voice he believes he hears; for if what it commands him to do is contrary to the moral law, he must regard the manifestation as an illusion, however majestic and transcending the whole of Nature it may seem to him to be.
>
> For example, consider the story of the sacrifice which Abraham was willing to make at the divine command by slaughtering and burning his only son—what is more, the poor child unwittingly carried the wood for the sacrifice. Even though the voice rang out from the (visible) heavens, Abraham ought to have replied thus to this supposedly divine voice, "It is quite certain that I ought not to kill my innocent son, but I am not certain and I cannot ever become certain that you, the 'you' who is appearing to me, are God."[155]

Here, then, the moral of the story is that Abraham ought not to have done it: he should have preferred his moral reasoning to any supposed revelatory order from God.

II. WHY WERE THE DIFFERENT INTERPRETATIONS ADVANCED?

Having outlined some of the ways in which the story of Abraham and Isaac was treated in the seventeenth and eighteenth centuries, we must consider briefly what led to the different interpretations. In doing this it is important to recognize that some commentators present more than one view of the story's significance. Frequently the different views can be regarded as complementary. Barrow, for example, presents mutually compatible aspects of the story when he sees it both as typological and as an illustration of faith's readiness to believe the incredible.[156] On occasions, though, an interpreter offers views of the story which are not easy to harmonize—as when Stackhouse both emphasises the great virtue of Abraham's obedience to God in view of what God commanded and holds that Abraham's action shows that he believed in the miraculous power of God to restore Isaac to life.[157] Similar tensions arise between other attempts to show the reasonableness of Abraham's conduct and claims about the exemplary character of his unquestioning obedience to God's commands. The more his act was obviously reasonable, the less was the virtue of his unquestioningness. The more he believed in the eventual restoration of Isaac, the less magnificent was his offering of Isaac! We have already mentioned "Bayle's" reference to Saurin's recognition of this point. In such cases the interpreters seem to be trying to have both their penny and the bun as well! Where such tensions arise, they are frequently to be understood as instances of preacher's license! The commentator is more concerned to draw out what he regards as the valuable lessons to be learnt from the story than to ensure that they are consistent with each other in relation to the story from which they are drawn. The existence of such tensions, however, indicates why the interpreters approach the story: they approach it in order to draw out lessons from it. For the great majority of the commentators, the presence of the story in the Bible implies that it must teach some religious "moral," be it ethical or theological or both. Their problem, as they understand it, is to decide what the "moral" is and to expound it for their contemporaries' benefit. Their view of the nature of the Bible as well as their customary use of it means that they probably could never seriously entertain the possibility that the story may not have any such point. It means, rather, that they not only seek a moral from the story but also consider that some moral is intrinsic to it. God does not utter without purpose and the Bible, for them, is his word. If, then, the intrinsic moral can be identified, it enjoys for them the support of divine authority. This last consideration shows why the treatment of the story is considerably controlled by the interpretative comments contained within the story, in Hebrews 11:17–19 and, to a lesser extent, in James 2:21–23. On the whole it just does not occur to most of the persons we are concerned with to regard such comments as simply indications of how the human authors of Genesis, Hebrews, and James understood the story. They regard these comments, rather, as divinely guided remarks about the story's proper significance. For similar reasons, the interpreters could not avoid the problem of reaching a "reasonable" understanding of what happened by suggesting that this part of the biblical narrative could be ignored. Chubb, the independently minded glover from Salisbury, does mention doubts about the credibility of the story but he makes it clear that he himself is not denying its truth.[158] Such a protestation was probably necessary since, whatever Chubb himself might privately think, his comments on the story would only have had a chance of overcoming suspicions about his radicalism if they appeared to readers to begin from the prevalent presupposition of its basic truthfulness qua biblical. Since all of the Bible was generally regarded as divinely given and inspired, it was inferred that no part of it could be doubted without casting doubts on it as a whole. God could not be envisaged as authorizing a document that contained inaccurate or false reports. Consequently what the story of Abraham and Isaac says about God and what it implies about the nature of faith had to be regarded as part of the essential content of faith.

Another influence on the interpretations is the lack of what may be called "historical sensibility" at the time they were produced. Even today we tend to understand the past in terms of the present—and it may be queried if any other way is possible—even though the growth of historical consciousness in the past two centuries makes us pay at least lip service to the need to observe the distinctions between different ages. In the seventeenth and eighteenth centuries this need was far less appreciated. The modern sense of history was only beginning to appear. As a result some interpreters fail to distinguish between understanding Abraham's conduct in terms of his own time and in terms of their own. They apparently assume, probably without conscious consideration, that a satisfactory explanation of the propriety of Abraham's conduct must hold good both for his day and for their own. There is, consequently, some confusion in their interpretations of the story. Even where they recognize differences between Abraham's day and their own, it is not always made clear whether Abraham's actions are being recommended as a good example bearing in mind their day or simply as good in themselves and for any day.

Behind most of the interpretations which we have mentioned stands the view that a proper act of faith must be justified by sound reasons and restricted to what can be so justified. Barrow might preach about Abraham's conduct as an "illustrous Precedent" of a faith that is ready "to believe things incredible, and to rely upon events impossible,"[159] but most interpreters took as axiomatic the Lockean canon of reason, namely, that

> he governs his assent aright, and places it as he should who, in any case or matter whatsoever, believes or disbelieves, according as reason directs him.[160]

This principle unites Locke, Hume, and Kant. It fashions the thought of the Enlightenment. It is to be found in Chillingworth[161] and dominates English theology, with some interesting and some eccentric exceptions, from the Cambridge Platonists to Paley.

Locke himself seems never to have discussed the story of Abraham and Isaac, although he does discuss the general problem of whether God's command can suspend the validity of the natural law with reference to the Israelites spoiling the Egyptians.[162] His contemporary Tillotson, though, exemplifies the Lockean approach to understanding the story's moral when he seeks to display for the edification of his hearers "the Reasonableness of his [Abraham's] Faith" as "the result of the wisest Reasoning, and soberest Consideration."[163] The acceptance of the canon of reason, that is, means that the story's commentators presuppose that any genuine revelation from God and belief about God must be rationally, including morally, justifiable. If it is not so justifiable, it cannot have come from God and be an example of authentic faith. Since it is in the Bible, though, it must have such a source and be such an example. As a result of accepting these two presuppositions, the commentators struggle, at times desperately to our minds, to display the fundamental reasonableness of God's command and Abraham's response, including his awareness that the command was genuinely from God. Because most of them implicitly consider the canon of reason as beyond dispute even in matters of religious faith, they cannot treat the story as exemplifying the mystery of God and the transcendence of faith. The story can only be part of the record of authentic faith and significant for their faith if the actions involved in it can be shown to be such that a reasonable man (in their view of what is reasonable) will approve of them. We have seen the extent to which they go in order to meet these criteria. The "significance" they find in the story is thus determined to a large extent by the interpreters' presuppositions.

The majority of interpreters were faced with a critical problem when they dealt with the story of Abraham and Isaac. On the one hand, with most of their contemporaries, they accepted the canon of reason. Either, therefore, the story reported what, in spite of appearances, was eminently reasonable or it could not be regarded as belonging to the record of authentic faith. On the other hand, as Christians, they accepted the Bible as a whole as a divinely authorized document whose authority was fundamental to their faith. If, therefore, the biblical story of Abraham and Isaac could not be shown to belong to the record of authentic faith, the authority of the Bible and so of the Christian faith supposedly based upon it would be threatened. Hence the "proper" meaning of the story of the sacrifice of Isaac (as well as of other stories, such as Jephtha's vow) was a matter of considerable concern to the interpreters. It raised the question of whether two basic authorities of their religious understanding were reconcilable.

The attempts to show in different ways the "reasonableness" of God's demand and of Abraham's response thus reflect the current acceptance of the canons of reason and of sacred Scripture. In a different culture, among people who do not accept those canons, the story would not pose such problems. The exegeses that we have studied would be less likely to occur. A modern interpreter, for instance, might avoid the problems faced by his seventeenth- and eighteenth-century forebears by holding from the start that the story is mythical (whatever that might then be held to mean!) and not historical. Alternatively, he might simply interpret it as a report of Abraham's response to what he "thought" was being asked of him.[164] Another way of interpreting the story, as Kierkegaard was to indicate, would be through severely restricting the scope of the canon of reason in religious matters. If, on the other hand, we are to appreciate the understandings of the story offered in the seventeenth and eighteenth centuries, we need to approach them in the light of the presuppositions of its interpreters, presuppositions that are largely determined by their cultural context. It was these presuppositions, not the story itself, which largely decided how the story was understood.

The study of the different interpretations also indicates that an understanding of the story does not merely reflect the cultural context that the interpreter shares with his contemporaries in the society to which they belong. It also depends upon the faith and understanding of any subgroup to which he may also belong and upon the individual himself as a distinct, self-determining person. In this latter respect, there is always a danger in studies of the history of thought that the attempt to understand a thinker in terms of his context may lead to a systematic failure to appreciate his individuality. The nature of understanding may make such appreciation difficult, but it ought not to be allowed to obscure the personal contribution of the individual. As Locke appreciated, though, the effect of such individual freedom as well as of cultural and group conditioning upon exegesis can be that

> the scripture serves but, like a nose of wax, to be turned and bent, just as may fit the contrary orthodoxies of different societies. For it is these several systems, that to each party are the just standards of truth, and the meaning of the scripture is to be measured only by them.[165]

Locke's solution was to urge men never to demand, for the Christian faith, more than what "was at first required by our Saviour and his apostles" in their own preaching as recorded in the Bible.[166] Such a solution fails once questions are raised about what the biblical text means and, as in the case of Abraham and Isaac, about how one of its reports can be reconciled with other elements. Such questions cannot be answered by parroting the sacred text since it is that text which gives rise to the questions. No interpretation of the Bible, furthermore, seems able to escape the criticism that in practice it is significantly controlled by the interpreter's existing faith and cultural background. Some of those we have mentioned, for example, seem to find no problem with the morality of God's behavior, apparently because their faith never permits them even to think of questioning the propriety of God's actions and the accuracy of the biblical record of them.

Others find a problem here and have to deal with it. In the latter case their concern about moral justification is apparently stronger in practice than their respect for biblical reports about God. Similarly their understandings of the story and the lessons they derive from it seem largely to reflect their own existing faiths.

So far, then, as the text is regarded by the interpreter as authoritative, it seems that he is compelled to allow his existing faith to dominate his appreciation of it. However, the relationship may be more reciprocal than the evidence suggests. By the time an author comes to write or a preacher to preach about Abraham and Isaac, it is likely that he will have found a way to reconcile his faith and his understanding of this story. The result may consequently appear to be that the faith has determined the interpretation whereas in fact wrestling with the significance of the story may have been one (perhaps small) factor in determining the character of his faith. In the cases I have examined, unfortunately, I have not been able to find signs of such a process. This is not surprising. Such evidence would be more likely to appear in private notes than in published opinions. It is even more likely not to appear at all but to belong to the individual's secret musings. Such is the systematic elusiveness of the basic materials of any attempt to grasp the history of thought as it actually occurred!

These comments on why the interpreters interpreted as they did clearly call for comparison with contemporary views about biblical and other forms of exegesis. How far, for instance, do the practices agree with current theories? In many ways the hermeneutical views of the seventeenth and eighteenth centuries were somewhat commonsensical (though not to be looked down upon for all that by modern pundits, who seem at times to prefer anything to common sense!). They frequently reflect problems that arise with translating and understanding classical texts. There was, however, some awareness of the problems of understanding in one culture the materials of another.[167] Unfortunately the literature is far too large and diverse to be considered here. It demands an article or more to itself! The awareness of hermeneutical problems, though, did not begin with Schleiermacher, Bultmann, or Gadamer! The authors that we have discussed came from a period when many of these problems were beginning to be discussed, even if only in a preliminary fashion.

III. WHAT DOES THIS STUDY SUGGEST ABOUT HERMENEUTICS?

The length of this essay so far precludes any extended discussion about the lessons to be learnt from seventeenth- and eighteenth-century interpretations of the story of Abraham and Isaac. Nevertheless, a few closing remarks about the hermeneutical insights suggested by this study may be permissible.

What to my mind clearly emerges from this study (and so controls my interpretation and presentation of the materials—a nice hermeneutical circle!) is that the problems posed for an interpreter and the answers that he will offer largely depend upon the faith and ways of understanding that he brings to the project. The qualifier "largely" is important, though, because the interpreter's faith will to some extent be affected by the material he seeks to understand. The extent of any such influence in the case of a particular text will depend upon the significance given to it in relation to all the other factors forming his faith. In the case of Abraham and Isaac, the interpreters discussed seem to have faced a story that is peripheral to the formation of their faith, although troublesome to its cogency. Coming to the story with a faith that is based upon their understanding of other matters, they seek to make it conform to that faith. Consequently its potential for influencing the faith by which it is interpreted seems rather slight. This is probably the case with most texts taken individually, since the forces that mold faith initially are likely to be much more determined by cultural background, social upbringing, and personal reflection than by the appreciation of any particular text, "sacred" or not. Nevertheless, whether or not wrestling with the text alters the interpreter's faith, it is his faith and the cultural context in which it is actualized that determine how he understands the text. There is, therefore, just no way for the interpreter to be able to show that his interpretation coincides with the "original meaning" of the text, whatever that phrase might be held to refer to. It may coincide, but that it does must remain forever unknowable since the interpreter can never have a standpoint for judging his interpretation that is independent of the principles of understanding that determine his interpretation. Thus while we may be tempted to adopt a superior attitude to seventeenth- and eighteenth-century interpreters because they seem to us to have been clearly influenced in their works by their faiths and cultural context, it is a temptation to be resisted. Although we can probably be only partially aware of it, our interpretations (including our interpretations of what they did as interpreters) are presumably as influenced by our faith and cultural context as theirs were by their faith and cultural context. There is no way to escape this hermeneutical relativity and to justify claims to be able to understand correctly the original meaning of a text from another culture. The understanding of the meaning, let alone of the significance, of texts of a past cultural era is methodologically unsure to a degree that must always be taken into account in any attempt to understand and to interpret.

The interpretation of a passage, then, depends upon the faith and principles of understanding accepted by the interpreter. It is these that determine what presents problems to him and what he regards as making "sense." Similarly the cogency of his interpretation will likely be judged to a large extent according to the faith and principles of understanding accepted by his readers. In the case we have considered, the legitimacy (or illegitimacy) of Abraham's conduct depends upon whether the interpreter is prepared to accept it because it is biblical (cf., John Edwards), or because he can find grounds to justify it (cf., Tillotson), or because he doubts the possibility of any such grounds (cf., Kant). This suggests that it is misleading to talk about the "correct" understanding of a passage, as if the text intrinsically has a particular significance and the goal of the interpreter is to identify it in some contextually independent manner. Even as a regulative ideal, there seems to be nothing that such "correctness" could refer to absolutely. This is particularly the case if we accept the thesis of the intentional fallacy and so rule out reference to the author's expressed purpose in determining the "true" significance of a passage. The author's interpretation of his work may be given a privileged status. It may tell us why he thinks that he wrote the material in the first place (though even here his answers can vary according to the question in his mind: for instance, why am I writing this article?—to respond to a request from the editor or to sort out some material that has been interesting me or to display my knowledge or to support my skepticism about biblical authority or what?) or what he later makes of it—and the two may not be the same. But how far ought it to determine our view of his work? There is at least a danger of later rationalizations affecting even the author's judgments on his own products. The question is controversial and we can happily evade it in the case of stories like that of Abraham and Isaac because there is no way of determining the author's (or authors') purpose in relating the story except by inference from the story itself—and this is where the problem lies! In any case, there is also the need to understand what the author says about his intentions. If the text comes from a past cultural age, its author's comments on his intentions in writing it will raise problems of interpretation in terms of current understanding similar to those found in dealing with his text itself.

On the other hand, judgments need to be made on the tenability of the interpretations of a text, even if we may doubt whether it is legitimate to speak of a "correct" understanding in any absolute manner. Thus it does seem possible and useful, in the first place, to suggest that a certain interpretation seems to harmonize better than another with a particular way of understanding. In this case the acceptability of an interpretation is a matter of its reconcilability with a specific faith-stance rather than simply a matter of the consideration of the text itself. (This, incidentally, is how the first two parts of this essay may be judged: do the comments in the second part agree with the interpretations in the first?) A more interesting and debatable question, secondly, concerns the degree to which texts can limit the range of viable interpretations that can be made of them. How, for example, can fidelity to the narrative legitimately be held to outlaw certain uses of it that are acceptable to faith? I am not sure what criteria would be involved in any such judgment, but I am sure that some such judgments can be made and apparently rightly made. To claim, for example, Jesus' support for total abstinence by claiming that the "wine" he is recorded in the Gospels as drinking was "nonalcoholic grape juice" seems highly implausible to me, however attractive it might be to certain groups. Similarly I am most doubtful whether the biblical narrative of the Exodus can be used to show the desacralisation of politics. What this study of the story of Abraham and Isaac does suggest, however, is that while common sense can declare certain interpretations to be implausible because of the text (and I leave the criteria for such a judgment for further investigation), and while the standpoint of the interpreter may outlaw others, in the end there is no final way of showing in a certain cultural context that a text properly has just one significance.

Hermeneutical studies have often been concerned with the problem of understanding religious statements, moral precepts, and philosophical principles. In the case of Genesis 22:1–18, however, we are faced with a story of something that is supposed to have happened. Admittedly the story is problematic for historians, since it includes references to God but, nevertheless, it is a story and does not (like a fable of Aesop or La Fontaine) carry an appended moral. It is, furthermore, probably mainly because the story is contained in the Bible that most interpreters try to find a moral in it. The primary hermeneutical questions in relation to such a story, then, are whether it is legitimate to attempt to draw moral or religious insights from it and, if so, how such insights are to be validated. When we step from the meaning of the story as reporting what Abraham (and perhaps also what God) did to drawing conclusions about its significance for our faith and morals, we seem to be in danger of making the logical type-jump that Lessing showed in his "On the Proof of the Spirit and of Power" to be a basic stumbling block in the use of history for religious purposes. Although the seventeenth- and eighteenth-century interpreters seem not to have recognized this problem, apparently assuming that the story must have a moral because it is biblical, the justifiability of such a use of the story needs to be established. How do we get from a story of a historical event to a justifiable claim that some universally true moral is thereby indicated? This important question has been overlooked in most hermeneutical studies. The views of interpretation in Schleiermacher, Dilthey, and Bultmann (in terms of a postulated universal humanity making it possible for one age to understand another), and its recent criticisms by Gadamer (raising doubts about the notion of a common humanity and advancing the method of fusing the intellectual horizons of different ages) and by Pannenberg (in favor of a final perspective given provisionally in Jesus) have primarily been concerned with understanding the moral and religious teaching contained in the Bible. The Abraham and Isaac story, however, reminds us that a preliminary issue has first to be settled before we can claim to find religious or moral significance in the great amount of historical and quasi-historical material contained in the Bible. The question is: How do we bridge the gulf between a historical event or its record and the religious-moral teaching that it is held to convey? The solution of this question is crucially important for a faith that professes, like traditional and orthodox interpretations of the Jewish and Christian faiths, to be based on the story of certain events rather than on certain authoritative moral and religious instructions.

I have not space to develop a possible answer to this question here but in brief I suggest that the significance of stories such as that of Abraham and Isaac or, supremely for the Christian faith, that of Jesus is what is found by the intending interpreter as he wrestles with them and with the whole train of events to which they belong, including the histories of their different interpretations. Pannenberg suggests that the significance of an event can be held to include all its effects throughout history, including how it has been understood its *Geschehenszusammenhang!* Similarly the signifi- cance of a story such as that of Abraham and Isaac does not lie in its text alone but in the insights into moral and religious understanding that it has evoked over the centuries in its interpreters. The significance of such texts, then, is as "pretexts" for insight. They have value to the extent to which they are found to be provocative sources of it, including insight that goes far beyond what can be regarded as directly stimulated by the text itself. In this respect the importance of historical investigations of the historical backgrounds and contexts of a story and of its interpretations is that they provide more material for evoking insights in the current interpreter. The upshot of these hermeneutical hints is, therefore, that the religious and moral significance of stories does not lie in the stories themselves but in the understanding they evoke. The justification of the understanding, how- ever, is not found by examining the hermeneutical processes that have produced it but by finding independent (probably metaphysical) grounds for holding that it is true.

Can we accept that this is the value of supposedly authoritative and even sacred texts like the biblical stories—that their significance does not lie in what they relate but in the truthful insights (to be independently justified) they provoke in those who reflect on them? This, at any rate, is the conclusion that I would see suggested by this study of seventeenth- and eighteenth-century interpretations of one story. It highlights both the freedom and the responsibility of the interpreter. The text is there, a given, for him to interpret within the limits of commonsense plausibility. This is his freedom—a freedom that is inescapably culturally relative and limited by his principles of understanding. The truth of the significance he finds in it is for him to establish. He cannot hide for justification behind the text he interprets. This is his responsibility. Perhaps, then, this study of the story of Abraham and Isaac comes to a conclusion that Kierkegaard himself would not have found utterly uncongenial!

3. For Sanity's Sake: Kant, Kierkegaard, and Father Abraham

ROBERT L. PERKINS

USUALLY IT IS ASSUMED THAT THE CONTRASTS BETWEEN KANT AND KIERKE- gaard are entire, that a fundamental philosophic abyss separates them from each other, that one is rational and the other is irrational, that one argues for a universalist ethic and the other maintains a subjectivistic and individ- ualist ethic, that one talks simply about duty and the other talks about duty to God, that one is secular and the other is theological, that one insisted that the language of morals was public and the other insisted upon the incommunicability of our deepest moral convictions. These contrasts con- stitute the conventional wisdom, and this conventional wisdom has been offered as the result of philosophic analysis to graduates and undergradu- ates for a number of years. However, one of the functions of philosophy, at least, is not to repeat the conventional wisdom but rather to subject it to examination now and again.

Let us look at certain salient features of Kant's philosophic program, his ethics, and his philosophy of religion particularly as they bear on the case of Abraham, for that is a paradigm he has in common with Kierkegaard. This examination may not only enforce some of the contrasts indicated by the conventional wisdom, but also suggest some surprising likenesses and unsuspected similarities.

Perhaps we can also thereby delimit some of Kant's and Kierkegaard's ambiguous relations to the enlightenment.

By way of introduction, let us note a fundamental similarity between Kant's and Kierkegaard's concepts of faith. Both made a fundamental distinction between faith and knowledge. Knowledge of God as a result of theoretical or practical reasons was for Kant impossible. For Kant to consider a knowledge-claim to be true it would have to be based on empirical evidence or inference from empirical evidence. The knowledge- claim that God exists is justifiable for Kant only on the basis of empirical evidence or reasoning from empirical evidence. Such would-be knowledge is impossible as his whole epistemology shows. Faith, on the other hand, is by definition different from "theoretical knowledge," simply because there is no evidence to support it.

> No one, indeed, will be able to boast that he *knows* that there is a God, and a future life: if he knows this, he is the very man for whom I have long and vainly sought. All knowledge, if it concerns an object of mere reason, can be communicated; and I might therefore hope that under his instruction my own knowledge would be extended in this wonderful fashion. No, my conviction is not *logical,* but *moral* certainty, and since it rests on subjective grounds (of

the moral sentiment), I must not even say, "*It is* morally certain that there is a God," etc., but "*I am* morally certain, etc."[1]

This skepticism regarding the possibility of knowledge of God is apparent in Kierkegaard. In the *Philosophical Fragments* Kierkegaard subjects the traditional proofs for God's existence to a radical examination and comes to the same skeptical conclusion as Kant (and Hume). The proofs for God's existence contain insuperable logical difficulties, and since the existence of God is such a momentous notion, it should not be supported by any argument exhibiting bad logic no matter how well intended. I have explored elsewhere in considerable detail Kierkegaard's epistemological preferences.[2] Kierkegaard agrees with the epistemological skepticism of Kant as well as the existential conviction ironically expressed in the above quotation. Very much in the same mood Kierkegaard wrote:

> If I am capable of grasping God objectively, I do not believe, but precisely because I cannot do this, I must believe. If I wish to preserve myself in faith I must constantly be intent upon holding fast to the objective uncertainty, so as to remain out upon the deep, over seventy thousand fathoms of water, still preserving my faith.[3]

Setting these two statements, one by Kant and the other by Kierkegaard, over against each other suggests at least that the conventional wisdom stands in need of qualification. In order to reassess the relations between these two Titans of recent thought, let us examine their philosophical programs.

The program of the critical philosophy has a pragmatic and phenomenological basis that is rarely overlooked in papers of this sort. Kant was confronted with two phenomena that appeared to be in contradiction. The first phenomenon was the philosophy of David Hume, which challenged and denied the possibility of science as Kant understood it. Hume, faced with this result of his philosophy, could and did leave the study and went to shoot a game of billiards. He did so because the limitations of his philosophy had been reached and the implications of its salient points had been drawn. He could proceed no further with the terms of his philosophy, and so it was as much desperation over his conclusions as it was wisdom that prompted him to go shoot billiards and turn his subsequent intellectual efforts to the writing of the history of England. Kant faced the phenomenon of Hume's philosophy squarely and determined neither to shoot billiards nor to write history but rather to re-create philosophy. The second phenomenon suggests why he took up the challenge of Hume and doggedly stayed in the study in pursuit of philosophy. He was determined to ascertain, "How is science possible?" The growth, development, and achievements of science were precisely the factors of modern life that most mystified Kant after he read Hume and was awakened from his dogmatic slumber. The conflict between a sophisticated philosophy that denied the possibility of science (as he, Kant, understood it) and the obvious historical fact of the success of science drove Kant to his deepest and most profound philosophic endeavor. Let us briefly examine the way he approached the task of finding a new fundamental ground of understanding that would allow the truth of Hume's position to remain and yet also account for the fact of science as Kant understood it.

Kant framed the problem of knowledge with the question, "How is science and/or knowledge possible?" In the answer he attempted to set forth the conditions of knowledge.

Given the analysis of the *Critique of Pure Reason,* Kant felt that he had explained both the truth of Hume's philosophy and the fact of the existence of a priori necessary scientific propositions. Of course, this has been the battleground about the critical philosophy in the twentieth century, but that Kant thought he had solved the problem is no less indisputable.

As Kant sought the grounds of knowledge, he examined the human capacity and faculty of knowledge by means of itself. *The Critique of Pure Reason* is a reflective analysis of knowledge and science. This *Critique* is, in Aristotle's expression, thought thinking itself. Kant, in the first fundamental move of his philosophy, goes behind the lived-world of knowledge and assertion to find the conditions of knowledge. Though this analysis appears to be a Hegelian reading expressed in the jargon of recent phenomenology, it is nevertheless intended as a cautious, highly generalized explanation of the program of Kant.

His procedure could be called a regressive argument, and I will use that expression in this paper. Kant, accepting the facts of his intellectual landscape—the philosophy of Hume, on the one hand, and the evident successes of Newtonian science, on the other—searches for the foundations. The archaeological digs take place not in further examination of the external world or in science itself, but in the knowing capacity of the human mind. His task is properly archaeological, phenomenological, and hermeneutical. Our effort at this point is not to write an essay on Kant's theory of knowledge, but simply to show how he approached his program.

Kant used the same approach in his moral theory. Men in the lived-world assess blame and give credit for behavior. Again Kant begins with a phenomenological base, something that is noticed and noticeable in all climes and places: that men approve of some and disapprove of other behaviors. Kant then attempts to set forth the conditions on which we do this. The basic substructure or *arche* of our moral philosophy is set forth in Kant's marvelous *Foundations of a Metaphysics of Morals.* In this book, which is so richly philosophic and important for the understanding of recent moral philosophy, Kant begins with the ordinary, common-sense, everyday, lived-world experience of moral blame and approbation and seeks to set forth as economically as possible the minimal conditions necessary for an explanation of morality. This is another example of his regressive mode of arguing.[4]

Turning to Kierkegaard, we note that he had a well-conceived conception of a philosophic-theological program. Kierkegaard wrote in his *Point of View Regarding My Work as an Author* that his purposes were clear from the very beginning.[5] This may have been an overstatement on Kierkegaard's part, but that he was able to look back over his authorship and feel that there had been a plan working through it is certainly undeniable. What precisely was that plan? According to Kierkegaard's own estimate, the purpose of his authorship was not to raise the question of the truth of Christianity, but rather to cause men to inquire how they could become Christians. According to modern prejudices, this was not an ordinary philosophical program, to be sure, but nonetheless, it was the stated purpose of his authorship. In pursuit of this program Kierkegaard did not make many long excursions into a number of areas that we today take for granted in philosophy, and the lack of which now perhaps reflects badly on him according to the Emily Posts of current philosophic good taste. On the other hand, Kierkegaard analyzed some notions and ideas with such a singleness of mind that his pursuit of them has to some extent become identified with his own position. Kierkegaard's program, though it had a strange purpose (considered strictly as philosophy), led him into an examination of a number of philosophical perspectives. In other words, his unusual program made him a philosopher.

The fundamental approach to becoming a Christian according to Kierkegaard begins in a philosophical anthropology. Kierkegaard has a fairly well worked-out philosophical anthropology expressed in terms derived from Aristotle and Hegel was well as from Christian theology. This philosophical anthropology is to a great extent a reflection upon man's place in life (*Sitz-in-Leben*). It is a pursuit of human understanding, that is, an understanding of man that is fundamentally ethical rather than scientific, sociological, or behavioral.

Very much like Kant's, Kierkegaard's philosophical program had its origins in the intellectual commonplaces of his time and place. Unlike Kant, Kierkegaard, though quite well versed in physics and mathematics (as the university records show), was not at all overwhelmed by Hume or the Newtonian science. The things that appear to have been most important within Kierkegaard's horizon were the ethical implications of German romanticism and the philosophy of German idealism (Kant's perhaps less than Hegel's form thereof, at least if we judge by the number of references he makes to each).

Kierkegaard strove to present his philosophy so that "he who runs may read it," but the very literary form of his philosophical expositions has served to make his position more difficult for professional philosophers to understand. He should not be blamed for this any more than the news media should be blamed for the crimes they report. Neither should one blame the victim—and certainly Kierkegaard has been victimized by a horrendous philosophical misunderstanding.

Kierkegaard's literary methodology has been truly offensive to many professional philosophers who apparently have little sense of literature and who did not learn the educational philosophy of Plato's *Meno*. The program as presented by Kierkegaard is at least as startling philosophically as the purpose stated above, because the program is carried out through the writing of novellas, literary criticisms, essays in defense of marriage, and psychological analyses, as well as philosophical arguments. All the early and more philosophic literature of Kierkegaard was written under a series of pseudonyms. No wonder that the professional philosopher who insists that words should mean one thing and one thing only and who has cultivated a professional intolerance of literature and literary beauty in philosophy should object to Kierkegaard, who does not so much analyze words (though he does a great deal of that) as he shows his meaning through works in various literary genres.

The fact is, Kierkegaard attempts a conceptual analysis, and his analysis has one decisive advantage over much recent analysis: it is presented through a literary production that has been judged many times by competent critics as being of a very high quality indeed. Unfortunately, philosophers of little literary talent or taste or both have failed to perceive the subtlety and irony of Kierkegaard's philosophic descriptions and analysis. Philosophic analysis and existential showing are not opposed in Kierkegaard's work, for he renders the idea clear and distinct by using the advantages of each to meet the disadvantages of the other.[6]

Kierkegaard's philosophical anthropology is sketched around three topics that he called "spheres" or "stages" on life's way—in today's jargon, "life-styles." These three life-styles are the aesthetic, the ethical, and the religious, with the last divided into religion A and religion B.

In his discussion of the aesthetic life-style Kierkegaard achieves conceptual clarification through critical, literary analyses. If one reads the works of the German romantics (particularly those published in the journal called the *Athenaeum*) with Kierkegaard's characterization of German romanticism in mind, one realizes that Kierkegaard has not been unfair to German romanticism, but rather has offered an analysis and critique that is penetrating and conceptually clarifying, for he has shown us the ethical and theological implications with the utmost of clarity.[7]

If one compares the sketch of bourgeois ethics and the discussion of the family in Hegel's *Philosophy of Right* with the picture offered by Kierkegaard one realizes that, once again, he has performed the task of conceptual clarification by means of literary presentation.[8] There is not a false line in the whole effort. Hegel, in his characterization of bourgeois life, has written *about* the family as the immediate stage of concrete ethical life:

Kierkegaard has *shown* us this life-style, and it is not at all certain that Kierkegaard's depiction is any less revealing conceptually than Hegel's philosophical analysis is.

When one turns to Kierkegaard's *Fear and Trembling,* which contains the paradigm of the religious in contrast to the ethical, one realizes that Kierkegaard is again attempting conceptual clarification by means of description and picturing. Kierkegaard confronts a phenomenon, the fact that people make religious professions: they go to church, they sing hymns, they recite creeds, they perform all sorts of acts in the name of God, saying that such and such is a divine command or God's will. Kierkegaard, like Kant, always attempts to save the appearances. In fact, Kierkegaard is even more radical than Kant in attempting to save the appearances, for Kierkegaard takes the religious phenomenon simply as he finds it and addresses himself to the problems of the conceptual clarification of the phenomenon itself. Kant, unfortunately, confuses many issues owing to his uncritical acceptance of the dubious distinction between natural and revealed religion.[9]

This effort on Kierkegaard's part is not unique in the history of philosophy. Plato himself, in the *Euthyphro,* attempted to show what an unexamined religion can lead to. In the dialogue, Socrates catches his antagonist, Euthyphro, in numerous conceptual dilemmas because Euthyphro has not thought through what is intended by religious belief. Finally, of course, Euthyphro gets fed up with Socrates' needling and simply stomps out. I fear that Kierkegaard has suffered the same sad experience of Socrates, for all too many people have simply tuned Kierkegaard out or stomped off in self-righteous indignation. Kierkegaard is not attempting to impose a fictitious view of what the religious means. He is not attempting (and failing) to present a rational faith. He is not attempting to praise human sacrifice or to do any of a number of other things that have been suggested. What he is attempting to do is to present the phenomenon of the religious in conceptual clarity; to unearth the essence of the religious itself, and to make it stand there independent and autonomous—for that is the only way that any phenomenon can be understood. To revert to more familiar jargon, he attempts to render the religious clear and distinct. Kierkegaard accepted the phenomenon of religious profession and experience and attempted to save the appearances in his analysis of the case of Abraham.

In summary of this first part, it should be clear now that however different the philosophic programs of Kant and Kierkegaard appear to be, they hold certain assumptions in common. First and foremost, they are both concerned with the phenomenon, its independence and autonomy. Kant attempts to save the appearances, as does Kierkegaard. Both describe the phenomenon and set forth the conditions necessary to explain it. Both are skeptical regarding the possibility of rational knowledge of God.

Let us now turn to their analyses of the religious. We must briefly examine Kant's moral theology first, and then turn to the analysis of the

Abraham story, for, as mentioned above, Abraham is a paradigm they have in common.

As is well known, Kant postulates three notions to support and complete his ethical theory. These three tenets of rational religion—the existence of God, freedom, and immortality—were criticized in the first *Critique*. We can never prove or disprove them theoretically, according to Kant. These postulates of morality are necessary for understanding and giving final justification to the moral life. They have the same pragmatic basis as the regulative ideas; they enable us to order and to understand the phenomena of our moral life. These postulates comprise Kant's theology, and it is notable that the concept of God is derived from man's effort to ground, justify, and understand the ethical. At no point in his thought does Kant show himself to be more the child of his age than in this moral theology, which uses God as a crutch to support a universalist ethic.[10]

For Kant, the form of ethical decision is universality. This is evident in the first and most important formulation of his famous categorical imperative. "Act only according to that maxim which you can at the same time will that it should become a universal law."[11] This form of universality is the connection between the individual's freedom and will and the social context within which he does freely will. The implications of the concept of universality in Kant are far reaching and cannot be examined here. However, it is precisely this form of approach to universality that begins with the individual's act of will. For Hegel, universality is not created by the test of logical consistency but is rather found in the structures of society. Universality, though arrived at in entirely different fashion by Kant and Hegel, is nevertheless affirmed by them both.

A second factor that we notice in Kant's ethical theory serves as a unifying factor in the second *Critique,* and that is the ethical telos of the good. In the very beginning of the *Foundations* Kant writes, "Nothing in the world—indeed nothing even beyond the world—can possibly be conceived which can be called good without qualification except a *good will.*"[12] This fundamental concept of the good is undefined in Kant, and its lack of definition has caused scholars to say that the term is vacuous. The good for Kant is rather the sum total of all the willing according to the categorical imperatives that are based on freedom. Thus the good is not something in addition to the individual acts of free and responsible willing, but the good is the telos, the totalizing concept of all the individual acts of will. As with Plato, so with Kant: the good is a transcendental category that requires no further explanation, but it indeed explains. It does not require justification; rather, it justifies.

A third factor in Kant's ethics that must be characterized here is the principle of autonomy. Kant characterized it as the "supreme principle of morality." Negatively Kant opposed autonomy to heteronomy.[13] This latter principle seems to serve at least four functions in Kant's ethics. First he suggests that the principle of heteronomy is identified with the desire for pleasure and with our inclinations. These are not moral principles. The second usage of heteronomy refers generally to authoritarianism. Kant's sarcasm regarding this use of heteronomy is evident in this passage from "What is Enlightenment?":

> If I have a book which understands for me, a pastor who has a conscience for me, a physician who decides my diet, and so forth, I need not trouble myself. I need not think, if I can only pay—others will readily undertake the irksome work for me.[14]

For a third instance, any revealed morality is by definition heteronomous. As an exemplary passage one can quote:

> [If the will is moral] it is not merely subject to law, but subject in such a way that it must also be regarded as imposing the law on itself, and subject to it for that reason only. . . . All past efforts to identify the principle of morality have failed without exception. For while it was seen that man is bound by his duty to laws, it was not seen that he is subject only to his own, albeit at the same time universal legislation, and obligated to act according to his own albeit universally legislating will. So long as one thought of man merely as subject to a law, whatever its content, without this law originating in his own will, one had to think of him as impelled to action by something other than himself. The law had to carry with it some interest which induced or impelled him to action. But in this way all labour to discover the supreme ground of duty was lost beyond recovery. For one could never thus arrive at duty, but merely at the necessity of acting for some interest.[15]

As a fourth instance of heteronomy, having an "interest" is at best only an impure morality, for it is subject to the present evaluation of the interest rather than to the reverence for law as such. Kant means by all this that universality, though it is an important moment of the ethical, cannot be its fundamental principle. His fundamental point is that no law, even though it is universal, can morally obligate us if it is mixed with an interest. A law may be prudent, wise, beneficial, universal, but if it is mixed with an interest, i.e., if it is in any of these four senses heteronomous, it is not moral. Moral obligation is entirely autonomous and Kant rejects heteronomy in every way.

On the basis of his ethic, which has been so briefly characterized here, Kant made three postulates: freedom, immortality of the soul, and God.

Freedom is no doubt the most revealing of the three, at least so far as revealing something about persons is concerned. By requiring us to do something that we may not do, the moral law reveals to us that we are agents. The person is an initiatory cause of effects in the world. Furthermore, if there were no rational free choices, we could not possibly impute responsibility to persons for their acts. Here we see another of Kant's regressive arguments, and the fact that it is a commonplace in popular moral thinking should not prohibit philosophers from comprehending its philosophic importance.

Before proceeding to discussion of the second and third postulates we must consider briefly Kant's conception of the summum bonum.[16] This term is quite important in the further development of Kant's philosophy. First, in seeking each individual moral telos in this act and that act, in this situation and that situation, as we unconditionally obey the moral law and the dictates of the categorical imperative, we are also seeking a totality, which Kant calls the highest good. This highest good is itself unconditioned, for it is a perfect (i.e., complete) good in the sense that it is a logical totality of all the goods that we pursue through individual acts of will. The second meaning of this term in Kant's philosophy is that men desire it as well as morally seek it. Men by nature do seek happiness, and, therefore, the summum bonum for Kant is a conjunction of virtue and happiness. Kant has argued throughout his moral philosophy that virtue is a condition of happiness. Insofar as we are virtuous, we have a right to happiness. He has also argued that as we submit our wills to the moral law, we are in rational pursuit of happiness. That is, moral action is a condition of happiness. However, this conjunction of virtue and happiness is not very apparent in the world. The virtuous sometimes are miserable and the wicked sometimes prosper. So we have arrived at what must be an antinomy in Kant's moral philosophy, for these two concepts, virtue and happiness, on the one hand, necessarily go together as the condition and consequent, while on the other hand, in practical experience they simply do not.

Kant's solution to this difficulty is to suggest that the conjunction does not occur in this world, but that there may be another type of existence, another level of existence where the conjunction would be not merely fortuitous and contingent but necessary. The view that virtue produces happiness is not absolutely false. It is only conditionally false. If we can think of ourselves as existing as noumena in an intelligible and supersensible world, we can thereby conceive of ourselves in a position where virtue and happiness would be necessarily combined.

This is the first approach and suggestion of the postulate of immortality in Kant's philosophy. But we must insist that the moral law does not command us to pursue virtue because it will make us happy. The moral law commands us, according to practical reason, to pursue virtue, and this in turn is the condition of happiness. The moral law is concerned with virtue, not with happiness. We can conceive of the condition of a complete concordance of rational will commanded by the moral law and our feelings. This complete concordance is holiness, a perfection that apparently is not possible in the sensible world. Yet this ideal of rational moral perfection and its conjunction with happiness is necessary if we are to explain and justify man's moral striving in this world. This is Kant's most important argument for the immortality of the soul as a postulate of pure, practical reason. Immortality is a necessary condition for making sense of man's search for virtue and happiness in this world.

The moral law that causes us to postulate immortality causes us also to postulate the existence of God as the condition that is necessary for this conjunction between virtue and happiness. Immortality grants us time to pursue this conjunction of virtue and happiness but does not guarantee the locus or the conditions in which this connection may be attained. That is possible only if we postulate the existence of a God who is distinct from nature and who is also the cause of nature. If we are to attain this connection between virtue and happiness, it will have to be finally guaranteed by one who is the creator of not only the world in which this conjunction has been obviously denied, but also of another world in which it will be guaranteed. This God must be conceived as being not only capable of guaranteeing a world in which virtue and happiness will be properly proportioned but also wise enough to know all our inner states and to proportion happiness to virtue accordingly.

Kant is *not* affirming here, in the second *Critique,* what he denied in the first! The existence of God is not provable by theoretical reason; it is a postulate, an act of faith of pure practical reason. We can postulate the existence of God as a possibility, but we cannot demonstrate that such a God exists according to the necessary canons of theoretical reason. However, Kant argues that we are able to postulate these concepts "from a practical point of view." These concepts—that man is free, that the soul is immortal, and that God exists—are not given to us as objects of intuition and therefore "knowledge" of them is not, properly speaking, knowledge of supersensible objects. These three objects are not objects of any intellectual intuition. However, we cannot conceive of our moral life as meaningful unless these three postulates are made. Without these postulates man's moral striving is insane, meaningless, a gratuitous gesture, and man is reduced to the position that would later be so admirably put by Albert Camus in his *Myth of Sisyphus.* Moral sanity requires these postulates.

This summary treatment of Kant's moral theology is a testimony to the tenacity of Kant's dedication to "natural religion." Perhaps no eighteenth-century thinker drew the conclusions of this ad hoc academic philosophical theology with the logical rigor of Kant. The *Critique of Practical Reason* and Kant's other books on religion are classical statements. Yet there are some differences that we cannot pursue here. The main point that emerges form the above analysis is that, for Kant, revelation is in principle unnecessary. Revelation is not proven to be impossible, but it is certainly superfluous. Without the concept of revelation, religion, in the sense it is commonly understood in the West, is threatened; its foundation is removed. Christianity, certainly, is a religion of revelation. The secularist implications of German idealism were appreciated by no one better than Søren Kierkegaard, to whom we now turn.

Reading the thought of Søren Kierkegaard, one is struck first and foremost by the contrasts between it and the philosophy of Kant. These contrasts tend to confirm the conventional wisdom. The first of them is Kierkegaard's insistence that there is a teleological suspension of the ethical. Kierkegaard accepts the Kantian and Hegelian definition of the ethical as the "universal" in the sense that it applies to everyone. However, he also emphasizes its temporality by suggesting that it also applies every moment. The ethical is, for Kierkegaard as for Kant, immanent within itself; it has no purpose or goal beyond itself but is rather the telos of everything outside it. This means that all intersubjective relations are incorporated into the ethical and that there is no appeal beyond it to any other telos.

If one accepts this characterization of the ethical, then the particular individual relates to the ethical by willing it. "Willing" is a particularly Kantian expression, but the same distinction between universal and individual also appears in Hegel. The emphasis in Hegel is not so much upon willing as it is upon the removal of one's individuality and particularity so that one's life is in conformity with the social institutions of one's place and time. Whether you follow the moral philosophy of Kant or Hegel, whenever the individual has an impulse to assert himself as individual, i.e., as an exception to the moral law or as operating and living outside social institutions, he is in temptation. If there is no other telos than the ethical, then man's existence and his values are conterminous with the ethical, and the ethical becomes a religious object and a substitute for man's eternal happiness. We have seen how this is certainly the case in Kant. However, it is not Kant who is named in Kierkegaard's discussion but rather Hegel. Explicit reference is made to a section in Hegel's *Philosophy of Right* entitled "The Good and the Conscience." Nevertheless, the point applies just as well to Kant.[17]

At this point Kierkegaard has agreed with the definition of the ethical according to Kant and Hegel, but he then suggests that faith is the paradox that the particular is higher than the universal. This assertion brings him into direct conflict with both Kant and Hegel. The concept of faith as a result transforms the universal into a temptation. Yet if this is the case, then an either/or emerges for which all mediation is impossible, including Kant's attempt to develop a rational faith and Hegel's attempt to transmute religion into philosophical truth. It is in this way that Kierkegaard asserts the autonomy of the religious, in contrast to its identification with the ethical in Kant's ethics and in contrast to its functional role in Hegel's social philosophy.[18]

Kierkegaard argues that the case of Abraham does contain such a teleological suspension of the ethical and that Abraham's situation is utterly different from that of a tragic hero. Kierkegaard suggests three examples of tragic heroes who were caught in the same position as Abraham, at least to some extent. They are Agamemnon, Jephthah, and Brutus. All three had to sacrifice their children. Agamemnon has to sacrifice Iphigenia in obedience to a command of the Greek gods. Jephthah must sacrifice his daughter in order to fulfill a reckless and foolish vow he has made to God. (Jephthah is quite difficult for us to understand because the whole business of keeping promises is so fuzzy in contemporary philosophy and in modern life.) Brutus is forced to sentence his son to death for crimes against the Roman Empire. All three are comprehensible because of the contexts in which their personal tragedies occurred. In each case some rational explanation is possible. However, Abraham is not in such a happy situation.[19]

Abraham's situation is entirely different, for by his act he is outside of the ethical and is possessed by some telos that is nonethical. To be sure, the tragic hero is great by reason of the personal strength of character that enables him to do what is required by his situation. Abraham's greatness lies in the fact that he is able to step beyond the ethical into the religious or temptation or madness. So, in the case of Abraham the ethical is itself a temptation. If we are to understand Abraham at all, we must have some new category other than the universal or the ethical. The only possible category available, according to Kierkegaard, is that of faith.

In Kant's view this new category, faith, is heteronomous, unnatural, irrational, and ununiversalizable; it reduces persons to means and violates the realm of ends. It appears that the conventional wisdom is entirely correct. Yet there is one more issue to be considered. In both Kierkegaard and Kant the self is an agent. Though Abraham is commanded, he *can* say no. He is no automaton; it is entirely possible that he will refuse to obey God's command. Faith is characterized by Kierkegaard as obedience, the act of an agent. The conflict between God's command and our instincts and inclinations (all of which, in this instance, are on the side of Kant) raises the intensity of the drama to an almost unbearable pitch. Yet the conflict, presented by Kierkegaard in terms derived from the dramatic concept of conflict, is such only because Abraham is seen as an agent. Only on the basis of a shared concept of agency does Kierkegaard's effort confront Kantian ethics with a serious challenge.

In fact, Kierkegaard seems determined to show that Kant's ethics is the truth of man's moral situation. He argues that Abraham is singular, full of dread, perhaps seduced by the demonic, and caught in an insuperable paradox. Whether Abraham obeys or refuses to obey God's command, God's promise to make of him a great nation is negated. The fact is, for Kierkegaard, Kant's ethics is the truth about man's moral situation *unless* the case of Abraham shows otherwise. Kant spent many of his most important arguments in refutation of the suggestion that inclination is a sufficient basis for morality or should even be of concern in matters of morality. He argued that reason must discipline our inclinations and make them rational. Kierkegaard shares Kant's suspicion of the inclinations. In the case of God's command to Abraham, the natural inclination of a father toward his son, indeed the duty of a father toward his son, should incline Abraham to disobey the command. Thus the religious, as Kierkegaard attempts to conceptualize it here, is very much like Kant's view of inclination in his moral philosophy. That is, religion is not supported by inclination and conceptually is not dependent upon inclination.[20]

If it is suggested that we could or should judge Abraham according to the result, by the fact that, in the end, Isaac was not sacrificed, one misses the whole point, because the issue at stake is not whether Isaac was or was not sacrificed. In fact, the faith of Abraham did not save Isaac's life: God provided the sacrifice. The greatness of Abraham and his personal virtue and strength of character lay in the fact that, ambiguous though the command was, he was willing to obey it because he thought it was from God. The paradox of Abraham's life is that a loving father is in an absolute relation to something that violates his deepest love. Abraham's faith, through which he goes beyond the ethical, is neither sentimental romanticism nor Hegel's immediacy nor Kant's moral faith. Abraham's faith is fraught with dread, distress, and paradox. Kierkegaard has brought us face-to-face with an either/or. Either the story of Abraham contains a teleological suspension of the ethical or Abraham should be indicted for murder rather than glorified as a father of faith in the Jewish and Christian religions. By the either or the or Kierkegaard has shown the religious to be autonymous from ethics. Given the facts of the case, that Abraham is honored as the father of faith, moral sanity requires us to accept the theological explanation or to write off the history of man's religious experiences in Judaism and Christianity as founded upon madness.

The second question that Kierkegaard addresses relative to distinguishing the ethical and the religious is the question: "Is there such a thing as an absolute duty toward God?" Kierkegaard begins by referring back to the concept of the ethical as the universal and interprets this concept to show that it means that all duties are duties to one's fellow man. A duty is such that it brings us into an ethical relation with our fellow man, not into relation with God. This is apparent in the ethical philosophies of both Kant and Hegel, though neither is referred to by name. If we say that it is a divine command that we love our neighbor, then we are really using the word *divine* in a vacuous way, unless we are willing to assert the notion of revelation in a full sense. "In this way all of human existence is rounded off like a sphere and the ethical is at once its limit and its content." If this is a correct analysis of the universal as the ethical, then the expression *God* is a vacuous expression and God does become a phantom. The case will be entirely different if there is an Abraham, but the case of Abraham brings the ethical into question. Abraham introduces the concept of the incommensurable. There is at least one behavior in the universe that is not commensurable, explainable, and understandable in ethical terms, and that is the behavior of Abraham. Faith is this paradox, that the ethical is bracketed and made relative by a religious command.

To be sure, this is not the concept of faith as Kant understood it in his view of moral theology. Neither is it the concept of faith that Hegel understood as the immediate from which one should divest oneself and beyond which one should move in the direction of philosophy. And, to be sure, this is not a romantic conception of faith as a new kind of inwardness full of warm feelings and passion. Neither is it a Schleiermacherian feeling of dependence. Rather the faith of Abraham is isolating, singular, individual; it is highly internalized and cannot possibly be equated with either idealist or romantic interpretations of faith.

The paradox of faith is simply this: the individual is higher than the universal. Faith is the quality that determines the relation of the individual to the ethical—contrary to Kant, for whom the ethical determined the quality and content of faith itself. The ethical is reduced to a position of relativity in Kierkegaard's thought. On the other hand, if the story of Abraham does not present us with a case that is utterly incommensurable then, as Kierkegaard argues, we should settle for the concept of the universal and stop uttering silly, empty, and vain talk about God.

On the other hand, if there is a theological dimension to man's moral situation, then it must partake of many of the same characteristics of the Kantian ethic. If there is a religious command, it is personal as in the case of Abraham, but paradoxically *all* so commanded have a duty to God, the duty of obedience. Again Kierkegaard seems convinced that Kant's terms are adequate; "duty" is appropriate in a theological ethic. Also, the criterion of universality is restored. There are natural duties suggested in the order of creation and graceful duties implied by redemption; but Kierkegaard does not catalog what any of these duties are. Kant, in the *Foundations* and in the second *Critique,* did not suggest any specific duties, and Kierkegaard, like Kant, is concerned with the logic of duty—in this case, theological or theonomous duty. Hence *Fear and Trembling* supplies no content for the concept of theonomous duty; it is an effort to map the boundaries.

The third issue confronting Kierkegaard's discussion has to do with the problem of language. The question that Kierkegaard raises is: Was it ethically defensible for Abraham to keep silent about his purpose before Sarah, before Eleazar, and before Isaac? Beginning again with the concept of the ethical as the universal, one questions whether one could explain the case of Abraham. Whether conceived in the Kantian fashion or the Hegelian fashion, the ethical is not a bare or abstract notion. For Kant it has universality and other forms of the categorical imperative; for Hegel it has social custom to give it content.

The religious as a category, taking Abraham as its paradigm, has neither the language of universality nor the language of society through which it can explain itself. In matters of ethics we should be able to explain ourselves fully, presenting cogent reasons for and against what is proposed or what has been done, should we not? Books on ethics are full of such arguments. Again Kierkegaard refers explicitly to Hegel, but the application of his analysis to Kant is not unwarranted. The problem is simple: how *could* Abraham have justified his intentions to Sarah, to Eleazar, and to Isaac? Even in aesthetic situations it is possible that we can speak and that we can talk and explain ourselves. In ethical situations, to be sure, we can do this too, though it is seldom possible to get universal agreement. In the religious situation, however, silence is all that is possible. There is simply no way for Abraham to make himself explicit through the universal to anyone. If he started to explain himself to anyone his argument would seem to be based on egotism, madness, pride, hatred, or some other determinant and would not pass as a moral explanation.

These categories are sufficient to show that there are marked and remarkable differences between Kant and Kierkegaard, and these are usually claimed to be the conventional wisdom concerning the two thinkers. We have already suggested some important likenesses. However, there are several other issues between Kant and Kierkegaard that also deserve mention, just to set the record straight. To begin with, Kant's moral philosophy is strikingly like Kierkegaard's analysis of faith in the sense that both involve striving. The ethical man, according to Kant, must strive to attain his ethical integrity. He must do this because of the heteronomy of his inclinations, interests, peers, and various authority figures against whom he must struggle in order to be self-directed and autonomous. This moral and ethical striving is not done once and for all but must continue for as long as inclinations, authorities, peers, and interests attempt to deprive him of his moral autonomy. The ethical life for Kant, then, is one of considerable moral striving much like that depicted in the dramas of Schiller.

Regarding the inclinations, what is remarkable is that in the present comparison, the inclinations support the ethics of Kant. Kant, it will be recalled, had difficulty with the inclinations because they were heteronomous, particular, and private. He was quite embarrassed by occasions when the inclinations supported the moral law, and he declared that such instances had no moral value. Kierkegaard has very similar and serious reservations about the inclinations and, if we may add, the passions. Still, his position would differ from Kant's if and when the person's inclinations and the higher goal—in this case faith rather than the moral law—agreed.

Kierkegaard would *not* say that such an instance was without religious significance. Kierkegaard could only rejoice that the person was happy. What Abraham through his whole life was in process achieving through much agony, the grocer or the tax collector may achieve with joy. However, be the man of faith tested as Abraham was or confident in life like the grocer and the tax collector are, faith is always in process of being appropriated and is never a possession.

For Kierkegaard, faith is a task for a lifetime. Kierkegaard rejects the Kantian definition of faith as implied, suggested, and postulated by morality. Neither did Kierkegaard understand faith in a Hegelian sense as the immediate. For Kierkegaard, faith is very much like the ethical striving of the Kantian moral hero. Indeed, Kierkegaard uses the expression "the hero of faith" precisely because the hero of faith must continue endlessly and forever to attain his faith again and again by obedience. It is not "his" once and for all; he must come to it now and again, ever and ever. Faith, like Kant's ethics, is a task for a lifetime."[21]

That Kierkegaard had in mind the concept of an ethical hero is obvious from his use of the examples of Agamemnon, Jephthah, and Brutus, all tragic heroes, in contrast to Abraham, the hero of faith. Kant, of course, did not indulge in the language of heroes, and it was left to his sometime literary disciple, Schiller, to dramatize the Kantian moral philosophy. But that it is capable of dramatization is important and even noteworthy, for not every moral philosophy is capable of such presentation.

There is also a very important likeness between Kierkegaard and Kant if one interprets Kant as giving primacy to practical reason. The order of Kant's *Critiques* is considered philosophically proper by modern taste, but existentially the second one is primary. The primacy of practical reason is an important mark of the Kantian philosophy, because it is existentially required for our life together, a fundamental condition of the science he sought to justify. Kierkegaard, likewise and much more emphatically than Kant, argues for the primacy of practice and action as against speculation and theory. Indeed, this characteristic is one of the hallmarks of Kierkegaard's philosophical critique of philosophy. That this is a shared mark with Kant is generally neglected in the conventional wisdom.

It is important to note that Kant and Kierkegaard have radically different views of the afterlife. This touches upon their relation to the Enlightenment. Kant accepted the major tenets of the Enlightenment views of religion as vouchsafed and guaranteed to him through the writings of Rousseau and Lessing, among others. The distinction between the natural religion and revealed religion was one of the characteristic hallmarks of the Enlightenment view in both France and Germany. Lessing was so dogmatic on this point that he argued that the Old Testament was not written to reveal religion because it did not contain an argument for an afterlife. On the factual ground, Lessing was quite right; there is no view and no possibility for an afterlife for Old Testament religion until after the Jews are taken into captivity in Babylon in 586 B.C. and exposed there to the teachings of Zoroastrianism. Lessing's implication may not be as certain. Kierkegaard agrees that there is no faith in the afterlife for Abraham. There is no hope that Abraham can barter away this life for an afterlife, and so the religious as Kierkegaard presents it here in his categorical description is not anything other than obedience to God and implies no promise of an afterlife. Kierkegaard at this point reverts to the genuine primitive faith of the Old Testament. Kant, though usually so much more stringent in his thinking and much more aware of the limitations of the Enlightenment, has on this point hewed to the Enlightenment line. Kant is determined to have a guarantee for his ethics and he does indeed guarantee the conjunction of happiness and virtue through his promise of freedom and immortality and God. But no such happiness is in the offing for Father Abraham; his hope is for this life only, and he obeys God simply because of the divine command itself. The final conjunction of virtue and happiness in Kant jeopardizes Kant's view of the ethical as an end in itself and suggests that he is finally infected by what Nietzsche called the "reward disease." For Kierkegaard, Abraham serves God for no other reason than that God is God. Kierkegaard's argument is uncompromising in its assertion of religion's autonomy from ethics and even from the common human expectations for happiness.

Kierkegaard and Kant, as has been observed above, agree that faith is not an object of knowledge. Kierkegaard draws from that an epistemological consequence for religion when he suggests that the command to Abraham may not indeed be a divine command, and that it might be a demonic command. This is a conclusion that Kant also drew, and it is interesting that Kierkegaard's concept of the religious category is broad enough and strong enough to contain this suggestion. For Kant, the religious is narrowly constricted by the limitations of his moral philosophy; his view of the religious has no place for the demonic and consequently no place for the idolatrous. Phenomenologically, Kierkegaard is in the stronger position, for the religious, as he understands it, does contain possibilities of the demonic and the idolatrous. Kierkegaard faces the facts, the ambiguities, the murkiness of the historical phenomenon of religion; whereas Kant legislates from an ad hoc position what can count as religious.

There are two places where Kant directly addresses the problem posed by Abraham. In the *Streit der Facultäten,* Kant claims that the voice of God could be known negatively in the sense that God could never require that which violated the moral law. Kant even lectures Abraham's tempter: "It is certain that I ought not to kill my son. I am not convinced and never will be even if your voice resounds from the visible heavens." The sanctity of the moral law is upheld; Kant cannot conceive of God so tempting

Abraham. In *Religion Within the Limits of Reason Alone,* Kant argues that in every visionary and historical faith the possibility of error remains. Thus this reference to Abraham is only a passing one in the protracted discussion of clericalism in general and inquisition in particular, the whole critique of revealed religion is raised epistemologically: it might have been a mistake.[22] Kierkegaard agrees with both points: it *is* inconceivable that God could so tempt Abraham and it *is* possible that Abraham was deceived by a demon or at least was mistaken. But that is the way it must be if the religious is to be autonomous from the ethical.

For Kant, the quality of the ethical is determined by the universalizability of the maxim, not by the result of the action. In no place is the likeness of Kierkegaard and Kant so explicit, for Kierkegaard agrees with Kant that the religious dimension has no concern for the result, end, or effect. The obedience to the universalizable maxim is very like Kierkegaard's obedience of faith. The tension between the subjective maxim and the universal moral law is solved by Kant by his concept of willing "as if." Kierkegaard uses the language of obedience as if the command were of God. Results are not the issue in either.

The paradox between God's promise to bless all nations through this son Isaac and his command that Isaac be sacrificed was puzzling to Kant, as he remarked in the book, *Streit der Facultäten.* However, we would want'to suggest that if anyone thinks that Abraham compromises or is a danger to the public morality he should be disabused. Most people are implicitly Kantians in their views of morality at least to the extent that they will not endure the possibility of paradoxes and contradictions. Most people require at least formal consistency of conduct. And so, though Kierkegaard argues that the case of Abraham establishes the autonomy of the religious, it does not do so in such a way as possibly to endanger the ethical or public order. Most of us would rather remain in the relatively still waters of the Kantian moral philosophy, which Kant himself thought mirrored the commonsense view of the ordinary man.

For Kant and for Kierkegaard, faith and knowledge are two entirely separate but related things. Perhaps here at the end we should suggest one other likeness between them with respect to the concept of faith. Kierkegaard argues many times in *Fear and Trembling* that faith is not an aesthetic emotion as faith has been described by the romantics and by Hegel. Rather faith occurs only through obedience, an obedience that at times can be costly or even horrendous. Faith is in precisely the same position with reference to ethical striving in the philosophy of Kant because philosophical faith is lately arrived at after the categorical imperative has exercised its constraint upon inclinations and all the forms of heteronomy. Philosophical faith is postulated only toward the conclusion of Kant's philosophical analysis, and existentially could be arrived at only by those who had submitted to the discipline of ethics. Thus there is a strong similarity in Kant's and Kierkegaard's views of faith as appearing as a result of and after a strong discipline and testing.

Kant suggested that the summum bonum was a totalizing concept of all of our ethical acts. This is quite similar to Kierkegaard's view of faith in God, which for him was the highest good. Faith is the obedient response to revelation that enables us to gain coherence and consistency in our lives.

I have not disagreed with the conventional wisdom about the relations of Kant and Kierkegaard; in fact, I have assumed it and attempted to show its logic. However, the obvious was not the whole truth, as the above analysis shows. Kant and Kierkegaard, for all their differences, have at least as much in common as separates them. Owing to Kant's having been led by the prejudices of the Enlightenment, one wonders whether Kierkegaard did not work out the logic of what they held in common better than Kant did. In other words, Kierkegaard seems to have perceived the conceptual relation of ethics and religion more clearly than Kant did.

Religion is autonomous with respect to ethics, is not derived from it, and is not supported by it. The autonomy of religion respects the phenomenon of religion, permits a natural ethic, but the logic requires only that men not reverence ethics as an idolatrous object. This autonomy suggests the risk involved in going beyond moral experience as Kant defined it, and suggests also that the risk must be taken under command.

4. Abraham and Hegel

MEROLD WESTPHAL

It has been rumored that Abraham will shortly receive an Oscar nomination for his supporting role in the greatest love story since Abélard and Héloïse, that of Søren and Regina. If confirmed, these reports will come as no surprise, since the setting of *Fear and Trembling* in its author's life is known to every reader of this dazzling but untimely meditation.

Reading this version of the Abraham story as a piece of spiritual autobiography may serve to increase its lyrical intensity but not to illuminate its dialectical intrigue. For that illumination we must turn to another setting of the story, its place in the history of the Enlightenment. In its English, French, and German versions, deist and materialist, this movement erected an either/or between the Christian faith and reason, of which Lessing's "ugly, broad ditch" is perhaps the most vivid symbol.[1] The metaphysical and historical claims that lie at the heart of the Christian faith were set aside as superstitions unacceptable to "modern man come of age."[2] Christian ethics were more or less spared; it is not uncommon for the leaders of a victorious coup d'etat to set up their headquarters in the palace of the deposed monarch.

The Enlightenment's triumph was ambiguous, however, for romanticism emerged to testify to a hunger for the Infinite and Eternal that enlightened reason could not satisfy. Kant had been right in arguing that reason could only demand the Unconditioned, not achieve it.

But yearning (*Sehnsucht*) is not salvation either, and romanticism sank under the weight of its own sentimentality and irrationalism. The Enlightenment shrugged off the adolescent doubts of the romantic interlude and reconquered much of the modern world, though not always with the faith in scientific reason that had swaddled the movement in its childhood. The heroes of this conquest do not all look alike, as a few names will suggest: Marx, Nietzsche, and Freud—Sartre and Camus—Russell and Carnap. But beyond their important differences they share a thorough confidence in the original either/or between religious faith and modern man and an equally uncompromising attitude toward any romantic mitigation of a world without grace.

This hurried history is neither original nor, I suspect, very controversial. But it is incomplete—not just as any short schematic account is bound to be, but essentially, for it leaves out the numerous attempts to negotiate a nonromantic compromise between the Enlightenment and Christian faith, among which Hegel's attempt to preserve the content of the latter in the form of the former is by far the most impressive. One of the most noteworthy features of the Hegelian synthesis is the quality of the opposition it attracted, most notably Marx and Kierkegaard. In the case of Kierkegaard, the battle begins with brief skirmishes in *The Concept of*

Irony, but it is in *Fear and Trembling* that the first full-scale battle is waged. It is to this conflict that we must turn if we would fully appreciate the dialectical dexterity of Kierkegaard's story telling.

Like David choosing five stones from the brook with which to face Goliath, Kierkegaard chooses a most unlikely weapon, Abraham. But it is not an arbitrary choice. If Christian faith is to show itself immune to the Hegelian synthesis, why not focus on the one whom St. Paul presents in Romans 4 and Galatians 3 as the paradigm of faith and to whom Hebrews 11 gives more attention than anyone else in its catalogue of the heroes of faith? Why not stage a confrontation between Abraham and Hegel?

With the help of Abraham, so to speak, Kierkegaard plans a double assault on the central thesis of Hegel's mature speculation, to which, for example, the opening five paragraphs of the *Encyclopedia* are devoted. That would be the claim that his philosophy contains the same content as the Christian religion but in the superior form of the philosophical concept, *Begriff,* rather than the religious form he labels *Vorstellung.* (*Begriff* is an ordinary German word for concept, but in Hegel's usage it becomes a technical term for the specifically philosophical concepts generated by his system, especially the Logic. *Vorstellung,* which etymologically means to place before or to re-present, similarly has no satisfactory English equivalent in its Hegelian usage; it refers to prephilosophical concepts, especially in their metaphorical or analogical senses, and in the dependence of their meaning on sensory contents.) The first challenge will be to the supremacy of the concept, the second to the identity of content.[3]

●   ●   ●

It is supposed to be difficult to understand Hegel, but to understand Abraham is a trifle. To go beyond Hegel is a miracle, but to get beyond Abraham is the easiest thing of all.[4]

The first issue is joined in the Preface and Epilogue, which form a satirical frame for retelling the Abraham story. In both the idea of going beyond faith is scathingly pilloried.[5] The Preface suggests that by this means Christianity has been reduced to such a bargain price that there will no longer be any customers; while the Epilogue remembers the Holland spice merchants who dumped several cargoes into the sea to peg up prices and considers this a model for what might be needed in the realm of the spirit. In other words, Kierkegaard (via Johannes de Silentio, his pseudonym) will try to present faith as a more costly commodity than those who have gone further would take it to be. After all, doesn't Jesus teach in the Gospels that the Kingdom is like a pearl of great price for which one would sell everything else? Such a pearl is surely not to be found in the bargain basement or at the local discount center.[6]

In the midst of his satirical forays Johannes remains serious enough to present us with his own idea of what faith really is, the task of a lifetime and the highest passion in a man. Of the first he writes: "In our time nobody is content to stop with faith but wants to go further. It would perhaps be rash to ask where these people are going, but it is surely a sign of breeding and culture for me to assume that everybody has faith, for otherwise it would be queer for them to be . . . going further. In those old days it was different, then faith was a task for a whole lifetime, because it was assumed that dexterity in faith is not acquired in a few days or weeks."[7]

It is the Abraham picture itself that must show concretely how faith could be a lifetime task, but the frame does present us with two analogies, doubting and loving. Modern philosophy begins with doubt, but of course quickly goes further.[8] This is surely a bargain-basement doubt compared to that of the "ancient Greeks (who also had some understanding of philosophy)" and who viewed doubt as "a task of a whole lifetime, seeing that dexterity in doubting is not acquired in a few days or weeks . . . "[9] Today we might have chosen the Vedantist or the Buddhist as an example, for Kierkegaard is here following Hegel's notion that the truly philosophical skepticism is not a Humean or positivist skepticism but one that comes to see "the given" itself as most highly problematical.[10] Such doubt is no casual or temporary project but an endless task so long as one has not yet left the human condition and, to use the Eastern examples, passed over into undifferentiated union with Brahman or into Nirvana.[11]

The other analogy is from the Epilogue. There love is the task of a lifetime. The one who has reached faith "does not remain standing at faith, yea, he would be offended if anyone were to say this of him, just as the lover would be indignant if one said that he remained standing at love, for he would reply, 'I do not remain standing by any means, my whole life is in this.' Nevertheless he does not get further. . . ." Why not? Because the seriousness of the task of loving lies in its "authentically human factor," passion. "Thus no generation has learned from another to love. . . ."[12]

In that significant *thus* we are reminded of the way the Preface contrasts passion with learning. The point is not to suggest that reflection is necessarily dispassionate, but to protest the way in which the age has made it so by its commitment to objectivity.[13] At the same time we are reminded that what is essential to love (and faith) is an element of passion that is neither reducible to nor deducible from any form of learning, the theoretical learning of the learned or the practical learning of the socialized. Love is not education or culture (*Bildung*). Nor is faith, and God has no grandchildren. Satire aside for the moment, Johannes turns hortatory. "But the highest passion in a man is faith, and here no generation begins at any other point than did the preceding generation, every generation begins all over again, the subsequent generation gets no further than the foregoing. . . . If the generation would only concern itself about its task, which is the highest thing it can do, it cannot grow weary, for the task is always sufficient for a human life. . . . Faith is the highest passion in a man. There are perhaps many in every generation who do not even reach it, but no one gets further."[14]

Since Hegel clearly viewed his thought as the culmination of a development spanning many generations, it looks as if there is a fundamental difference between faith as understood by Kierkegaard and philosophy as understood by Hegel. Doubt is prerequisite to both, but in strikingly different ways, and philosophy benefits from the achievements of preceding generations, while faith does not. But Hegel, too, affirms that religious faith and philosophical wisdom are significantly different—in form though not in content. It needs to be shown that and how the polemic against going beyond faith is a critique not just of the *Phenomenology's* relation to the system,[15] but also of the more important Hegelian theory of the relation between religious *Vorstellungen* and philosophical *Begriffe*. That it is intended to be such a critique is overt. Johannes writes in the Preface: "Even though one were capable of converting the whole content of faith into the form of a concept, it does not follow that one has adequately conceived faith and understands how one got into it or how it got into one."[16]

Two misunderstandings must be avoided if the issue is to be sharply focused. The first thing to notice is that in the passage before us Kierkegaard does not present us with the truism that faith is not understanding. Nor does he challenge the idea that faith should seek understanding. The question is whether in reflecting on its content or object faith also comes to an understanding of itself, or rather loses sight of itself. Kierkegaard prefers Socratic to Hegelian dialectic because the former never neglects the Delphic command, "Know thyself," while the latter commits precisely this sin, in what the *Postscript* will call a world-historical fit of absent mindedness. Such, at any rate, is the allegation.

We might say that Hegelian reflection is faith seeking to understand God while Kierkegaardian reflection is faith seeking to understand itself. After all, it is of Abraham and not God that Johannes writes: "No one is so great as [he]! Who is capable of understanding him?"[17] But that would be to misrepresent Kierkegaard's point, which is not to direct our attention away from God but toward him so as to realize that a proper knowledge of this "object" must involve the knower's "infinite, personal, passionate interest" in his own relation to what is known. Because it is essentially related to the knower's own personal existence, this knowing can be called essential knowledge. It belongs to a context in which the properly conceived *what* is ever so useless if the *how* is inappropriate. For what shall it profit a man if he comprehend God comprehensively but fail to trust and obey him?[18]

The other misunderstanding would be to confuse the issue here with that between Hegel and the philosophies of immediacy (Jacobi, Schleier- macher, etc.). The possibility of such a misunderstanding lies in two facts. Kierkegaard speaks of faith as an immediacy and Hegel speaks of knowl- edge as mediation. In doing the latter Hegel uses the very language of "going beyond" that the frame satire employs. Objects can be given to consciousness in many ways, but to reflect upon them is to go beyond their givenness. Thus every form of thought involves "the negation of what we have immediately before us." It is this negative movement that is called mediation. "For to mediate is to take something as a beginning and to go onward to something else."[19]

From his critique of Jacobi in *Glauben und Wissen* (*Faith and Knowl- edge,* 1802) to the end of his life Hegel felt the need to defend philosophy as mediating thought against an appeal to immediacy that he took to be a virulent disease of the spirit. The time and energy he devoted to opposing it suggest that he saw it as having assumed epidemic proportions. It is, briefly put, the romantic solution to the Kantian dilemma. We demand the Unconditioned, but reason, understood here as mediating thought in all its forms, is unable to provide us with it. Rather than draw a positivist conclusion from the first *Critique,* the alternative is to claim a direct, noninferential, even nonconceptual prehension of the Infinite and Eternal. We could again avail ourselves of Vedantist or Buddhist analogies were it not for the fact that instead of portraying this immediate awareness of the Absolute as the result of a long and arduous discipline, it is presented as given with the same primordial obviousness as that with which we experi- ence, for example, our own bodies.

There is no need to elaborate the details of Hegel's polemic against this view.[20] The important point is that although Hegel regularly speaks of faith as an immediacy and the movement from *Vorstellung* to *Begriff* as media- tion, he consistently portrays religious faith as thoroughly mediated and only relatively immediate. The thrust of his argument, then, is that one mode of mediation requires another, relative to which the first has a kind of immediacy. This is quite different from refuting an appeal to pure immediacy as the only legitimate "knowledge" of God.

There are for Hegel two senses in which even prespeculative knowledge of God is mediated. God is not, like the objects of other sciences, among the "natural admissions of consciousness."[21] To have faith in God is to rise above and beyond the sensible world that empiricism allows as given to consciousness. This elevation (*Erhebung*) is at once the essence of faith and a paradigm of mediation.[22]

Corresponding to this logical mediation is the psychological process that Hegel calls culture (*Bildung*). The ideas we have of God are not innate but the result of a long and gradual process of training and socialization. The cultured person has a mind whose contents have not been left in their natural state but have been humanized through the educational process.[23]

In the same logical and psychological senses religious faith is relatively immediate. When it is not meant as a polemic against further reflection, Hegel will even accept the idea that the consciousness of God is immediately given with consciousness of the self, i.e., that its status is the same as that of the *cogito*. While in neither case, that of the self nor of God, does Hegel permit this to preclude further discussion as to their nature, it seems that there is at least a formal sense in which he wants to make awareness of the Infinite transcendental in the Cartesian and Kantian sense. Even the concrete contents of religious consciousness come to have the kind of self-evidence that gives them the logical priority of presuppositions or assumptions. In this capacity as functionally a priori Hegel speaks of them as an "unconscious immediacy."[24]

To call this logical priority functional is to say that it derives from a sociopsychological familiarity. Acculturation (*Bildung*) is not only a process; it is also a result, which Hegel refers to as our ordinary, popular modes of thought (*gewöhnliches* or *gemeines Bewusstsein*).[25] Our ideas of God are thus at first in the form of *Vorstellung,* finally in that of *Begriff.*[26] Philosophy is often discredited through a "hankering after an image with which we are already familiar."[27] It is just this familiarity that transforms the results of complicated mediations into the immediacy of self-evidence. So in religious consciousness we are dealing with "a result that at once does away with itself as result." It "is in a state of constant unrest between immediate sensuous perception on the one hand and thought proper on the other." While I can believe in God I cannot in that sense either believe that there is a sky above me or that the Pythagorean theorem is true. Faith falls between the immediacy of sensible presentness and the mediation that yields rational necessity.[28]

The immediacy of religious consciousness for Hegel is thus quite distinct from the immediacy to which Jacobi appeals. Correspondingly, Hegel's case for the need to move from *Vorstellung* to *Begriff* is quite distinct from his polemic against romantic philosophies of feeling and intuition. Nor is there any misunderstanding on Kierkegaard's part. In *The Concept of Irony* and in *Either/Or* he presents a thoroughly Hegelian critique of the romantic subjectivism that Hegel finds implicit in the appeal to immediacy. More important, when Kierkegaard speaks of faith as a second immediacy, distinct from any "aesthetic emotion" or "immediate instinct of the heart" and subsequent to the movement of infinite resignation, he too affirms that whatever immediacy faith involves is relative and permeated with mediation.[29]

What we have to consider, then, is not Hegel's general thesis that every mode of life and thought involves mediation,[30] but the special thesis that the richly mediated position of religious faith, which comes to have a functional immediacy, requires a further mediation in which *Vorstellung* is replaced by *Begriff*; and we have to consider this thesis in the light of Kierkegaard's concern that knowledge of God should involve the knower's existence.

The further mediation that speculation provides is necessary because while religion provides us with our earliest acquaintance with what is also the subject matter of philosophy, namely God as Truth, that acquaintance is "inadequate." It is only when this content has been transformed from *Vorstellung* to *Begriff*, or pure thought (*Gedanke*), that it is "for the first time put in its proper light."[31] Contaminated by the accretion of elements that do not really belong to it, it stands in need of the "purification" that only this new mediation can provide.[32] Philosophy thus takes up a polemical stance toward the form of religious consciousness as such.[33] In the course of following this polemic the differences between *Vorstellung* and *Begriff* as Hegel understands them will come to light.

Though he usually names the religious form of consciousness simply as *Vorstellung,* Hegel feels free to subdivide its modes for the sake of more detailed analysis. When he does this he most frequently distinguishes three moments of faith: feeling, intuition or perception, and *Vorstellung.* Feeling is an important element in religion in that in feeling the divine is given to man with certainty and the unity with what is other is directly experienced. What is other to me, I make my own (*Was mir ein Anderes ist, vermeinige ich*). Put by itself, feeling will not do. At this level God loses both the content and the independent reality that religion itself affirms, for since feeling is prior to the subject-object distinction, it is a unity without difference.[34]

Perception is treated only very briefly. Hegel turns immediately to art, particularly to the mythological religion of ancient Greece, which he so loves to discuss. The critique is simple. In this mode, the divine becomes an object of consciousness and gains the determinateness and objectivity that pure feeling could not provide, but it does so in an unqualifiedly sensible way that is inappropriate to the sacred. As in the previous case, Hegel intends this critique to be one that Christian faith would join him in making.[35]

It is only in the discussion of *Vorstellung* proper that the debate between Hegel and Kierkegaard comes into focus. To each of Hegel's major points Kierkegaard's reply will be the same. It will be the invitation to put Abraham through the "purification" that Hegel proposes in order to see whether what gets washed away is something unessential or Abraham himself. Kierkegaard will speak through Johannes de Silentio, the satirist turned lawyer for the defense.

1. To distinguish *Vorstellung* proper from *Anschauung* Hegel begins by stressing that it is not the mode of pure image (*Bild*). As thought, it has a

universality and an objectivity that surpass imagination. But although it is
negative toward the sensible it is not fully freed from it. Abstracting from
the sensible, *Vorstellung* becomes abstract and thereby dependent on sense
images for determination. This involves religion in the analogical use of
such terms as *son, begetting, wrath, repentance, vengeance,* etc. in which
the palpably human is attributed to God, though not literally. This is an
unstable position between sense perception and the authentic thought that
frees itself from this dependence on sense.[36]

  And Johannes:

> But what is left of my Abraham? His faith presupposes that God is the giver
> and keeper of promises, one who can be trusted and who must be obeyed.
> The absolute trust of Abraham is the highest passion in a man, and to learn
> his sort of obedience is the task of a lifetime. But now I am told that talk of
> God as giver and keeper of promises is too sense bound and that we must go
> beyond this to a more purely categoreal vocabulary. What then happens to
> the passion and the task? What is left of my Abraham?

  2. For Hegel the historical as such belongs to *Vorstellung* as well.
Though we take the history of Jesus Christ to be history and not myth, the
same task of finding "the inward, the true, the substantial element" of the
narrative, i.e., of distinguishing the meaning from the external form,
applies to historical as well as to mythical texts. The trouble with *Vorstellung* is that it portrays the divine action, "divine, timeless events," as if
they were historical events.[37]

  And Johannes:

> But what is left of my Abraham? The divine acts on which his trust is
> grounded are no "timeless events," but the very particular and temporal
> experiences of coming to Canaan and having a son in his old age. Nor is the
> demand that he offer up his son a timeless truth. Its entirely sudden eruption
> into his life evokes tremendous passion, and learning to live with such a God
> is surely the task of a lifetime. But if God's activity is to be understood as
> timeless events, what happens to the passion and the task? What is left of my
> Abraham?

  3. By contrast with feeling, which expresses unity without difference,
Vorstellung expresses difference with insufficient unity. For example, when
creation is spoken of at this level of thought, the relation of God to the
world has a contingency and externality quite distinct from the necessity
required by speculative thought.[38]

  And Johannes:

> But you simply haven't been listening. If God's relation to the world is
> transformed into rational necessity the situation is changed beyond recogni-
> tion. Given a rational necessity to God's requirement we would still have a
> passionate Abraham. But his would be the passion of a tragic hero, not of the
> knight of faith. Not everyone can be a tragic hero, for it is no simple task to

learn infinite resignation in the face of impersonal fate. But then it is not the task of a lifetime either. What is left of my Abraham?

4. At the level of the philosophical concept "the givenness, the authority, and externality of the content over against me vanish." What was dark and impenetrable becomes transparent. In both these respects the Platonic theory of recollection becomes the appropriate model for our knowledge of God. Because the truth is within man, thought can be entirely free and self-sufficient.[39]

And Johannes:

> It seems I can't get through. It is just because the authority of God's command remains so dark and impenetrable that Abraham's passion is raised to a peak. And to describe how Abraham might have gotten himself into this predicament via Platonic recollection—*that* would be the task of a lifetime if it were not so patently foolish. When nothing is commanded and everything is clear, what is left of my Abraham?

5. While the fourth point grows out of the third, since rational necessity is the best candidate for the kind of truth that is within man, the fifth point is a kind of corollary of the fourth. As authority is replaced by rational necessity, the paraenetic character of discourse about God is lost. "It is not the purpose of philosophy to edify. . . ." It can presuppose the existence of faith and therefore need not concern itself with evoking it. Of course, it knows that in the realm of human freedom what is and what ought to be do not always coincide and that there are individuals who, through self-will, perversity, indolence, and obstinacy, stand outside the truth, but "the fact is no man is so utterly ruined, so lost, and so bad, nor can we regard any one as being so wretched that he has no religion whatever in him, even if it were only that he has the fear of it, or some yearning after it, or a feeling of hatred towards it." For this reason we can say that though men are ungodly "it is not, however, the aim of knowledge to lead to piety, nor is it meant to do so." It is the task of the concept to comprehend whatever religion does exist.[40]

And Johannes:

> You say that philosophy must beware of the wish to be edifying. I say the Jutland pastor was right when he preached that "only the truth which edifies is truth for you." I have always said that "the thing is to find a truth which is true *for me,* to find *the idea for which I can live and die.* . . . What good would it do me if truth stood before me, cold and naked, not caring whether I recognized her or not. . . . What is truth but to live for an idea?"[41] I am no philosopher. I surely don't understand the System and I probably don't even understand Kant. But ever since I read him at the university I have been moved by the heart of his great Critique, the Transcendental Deduction. The

transcendental unity of apperception is justified as a first principle of knowledge because without it the content of my knowledge and experience would not be mine. This seemed to me the truly revolutionary theme in Kant, that philosophical reflection primarily concerns itself with the conditions under which the various contents of experience can be mine.[42] It seemed to me that Kant went about this in a highly abstract and formal way, and when I first heard how philosophy had gone beyond Kant I was thrilled, especially since it was clear that knowledge of the Infinite and Eternal was no longer to be excluded. But then I read that philosophy must beware of the wish to be edifying, and I realized that reflection was trying to divest itself of its natural passion, and that philosophy had gone beyond Kant by leaving out his most important insight. I was reminded of the disciple of Heraclitus who went beyond his master by reverting to the Eleatic thesis which denies movement.[43]

When you said that philosophy presupposes the existence of faith I at first began to smile. For when Abraham is taken as the paradigm of faith it is comically preposterous for any philosophy, especially a presuppositionless philosophy, to presuppose the existence of faith in its hearers. But you went right on to indicate that the faith you presuppose is somewhat less rigorous and that even a feeling of hatred toward religion will count as faith so far as the concept is concerned (or should I say unconcerned). Then I began to wonder. Suppose Abraham had come by faith to Canaan and by faith had received a son in his old age, but then, seeing that he had but little time left, had gone beyond faith to the concept. He would have learned that when the truth is purified of its inadequacies and seen for the first time in its proper light it is less concerned than he had thought about his trusting and obeying. He would have learned that the Truth was quite distinct from the God with whom he had been in covenant. No doubt Abraham would have enjoyed a relaxation from the strenuousness of faith, but what would be left of my Abraham?

6. It is time to consider a feature of Hegel's position that has not come to light in the discussion so far. There are passages that indicate that he is no more enthusiastic for philosophy without a heart than he is for a faith without understanding. "Philosophic thought and religious faith are part of a living whole, *each fragmentary by itself.*"[44] The *Vorstellungen* of faith are "metaphors" of philosophical concepts. One can have the metaphor without understanding its meaning for thought; but the converse is also true. "It is one thing to have thoughts and *Begriffe,* and another to know what *Vorstellungen,* perception, and feelings correspond to them."[45] On the other hand it is possible for the two modes of consciousness to accompany one another, and in fact it is necessary that they do so.[46] The reason for this necessity is that the content must become "identical with me" until I am "so penetrated through and through with it that it constitutes my qualitative, determinate character. . . . It thus becomes my feeling." This does not guarantee its truth, but it does mean that the

72   Merold Westphal

content "makes itself actively felt in the life of the individual and governs his entire conduct, active and passive."[47]

In other words, "we must have God in our heart." This is not a matter of momentary feelings but of that "continuous, permanent manner of my existence" (*Existenz*) that we call character. For when we speak of God it is clear that "I, as actual, as this definite individual, am to be determined through and through by this content." The cultured person is one whose heart and feelings have been humanized by the influence of reason and thought and, conversely, whose mind is not dissociated from his character.[48]

Perhaps Johannes has been a bit hasty in his complaint that "it is dishonest of philosophy to give something else instead of [faith] and to make light of faith. . . . Least of all should [philosophy] fool people out of something as if it were nothing."[49] Particularly in his various lectures on religion, Hegel seems to hold that faith is by no means nothing and that, while it is something distinct from philosophy, it is no less important an element of *Bildung* than philosophy. Whether this will satisfy Johannes we will have to hear from his own lips.

And Johannes:

> So you think we need to have God in our hearts after all. While I do not profess myself to be a man of Abraham's faith, I am glad to hear you say this, but am at a loss to reconcile it with your polemic against the religious form of consciousness. If the link between my life and my ideas of God is so all important as you say should it not be to the inadequacy of the concept which reflection calls attention? Can there really be any sense to the idea that only at the level of *Begriffe,* where this link has been systematically cut, as we seem to agree, do our ideas of God appear in their "proper light"? From what point of view is the abstraction from this "existential" dimension, to coin a phrase, a "purification" from the unessential. It seems to me that your reflection is governed by the ideal of Aristotle's knight of intellectual virtue, while mine is trying to come to grips with Abraham as the knight of faith. I know that Aristotle portrays pure contemplation, theoria, as the most divine activity, but that hardly fits the God who called and tested Abraham and who sent his Son into the world to save it; and in any case, I've always assumed that the task was to be human. But now we're touching on another subject. To ask what conception of God is presupposed by your exaltation of *Begriff* above *Vorstellung* is to go beyond the question of form to the question of content. I am about to express my suspicion that the content of your philosophical speculation is not the same as that of the Christian religion, in spite of your claim that it is.[50]

•   •   •

How often have I shown that fundamentally Hegel makes men into heathens, *into a race of animals gifted with reason.* For in the animal world "the individual" is always less important than the race. But it is the peculiarity of the human race that just because the individual is created in the image of God "the individual" is above the race.

This can be wrongly understood and terribly misused: *concedo*. But that is Christianity. And *that* is where the battle must be fought.[51]

We have been considering the frame. It is time to turn to the picture itself, the retelling of the Abraham story, where Johannes' doubts about the identity of content come to the fore. He proceeds by posing three questions about the story, whose discussion makes up the body of his little book. Hegel is mentioned by name at the beginning of each of these discussions and the confrontation between Abraham and Hegel is intensified. Each time the structure is the same. The ethical is understood as the universal. If this is the ultimate framework for human existence, then the Hegelian philosophy is correct on this or that central theme, but in such a way that consistency would require Hegel to turn on Abraham as a murderer rather than honoring him as the father of the faithful. On the other hand, the kind of faith that Abraham exhibits requires that the individual, in his God relation, be higher than the universal. If this be not the case, then Abraham is lost.[52]

The point is clear. No one claims that Abraham is a philosopher. But if Hegelian philosophy requires that he no longer even be honored as the father of faith this can only be because that philosophy, in content as well as in form, differs from the Christian faith of the New Testament, which holds up Abraham as a prototype of man's true relation to God.

It is important to take seriously the fact that it is Hegel and not Kant who is under scrutiny. To call the ethical the universal in the Kantian context means that moral principles have a priori status, i.e., the universal validity that derives from rational necessity, and that as such they are unexceptionable. This is not the issue between Kierkegaard and Hegel, for whatever type of rational necessity moral principles have for Hegel, it does not mean that they are unexceptionable. The tragic heroes whom Kierkegaard presents (Agamemnon, Jephthah, and Brutus) remain comfortably within the framework of the universal, although they teleologically suspend their duty to their children and slay them. Since this is not the teleological suspension of the ethical that Kierkegaard describes, it is clear that Kant's essay "On the Supposed Right to Lie from Altruistic Motives" is not Kierkegaard's target.

It is quite another universality that defines the ethical in the Hegelian scheme, the concrete universality of the social order. Kierkegaard is explicit in indentifying the universal he has in mind as being the nation, the state, the laws, society, a people.[53] Agamemnon, Jephthah, and Brutus remain within the ethical because they teleologically suspend the lesser universality of family responsibilities for the greater universality of the nation. In Hegelian terms, then, the universality of the ethical designates not *Moralität,* with its inner conviction of personal conscience, but *Sittlichkeit,* the public life of a people, institutionalized in family, civil society, and the state.[54]

What, then, is the issue that Kierkegaard seeks to pose? In the following formulation one must fill in "society" for "universal" and "God" for "absolute" to get the proper meaning.

> The paradox of faith is this, that the individual is higher than the universal, that *the individual . . . determines his relation to the universal by his relation to the absolute, not his relation to the absolute by his relation to the universal.* The paradox can also be expressed by saying that there is an absolute duty toward God; for in his relationship of duty *the individual as an individual stands related absolutely to the absolute. . . .* If this duty is absolute, the ethical is reduced to a position of relativity. From this it does not follow that the ethical is to be abolished, but it acquires an entirely different expression.[55]

Implicit in these formulae is the charge that Hegel absolutizes the ethical. This would mean that man's relation to God is so thoroughly mediated via the social order that faith becomes indistinguishable from socialization and the individual's relation to God is no longer a personal one. The knight of faith "becomes God's intimate acquaintance . . . and . . . says 'Thou' to God in heaven, whereas even the tragic hero only addresses Him in the third person." Why so? To Kierkegaard the answer is plain. "The tragic hero does not enter into any private relationship with the deity, but for him the ethical is the divine."[56] But if the social order itself is the divine then it no longer stands under the judgment of God. This is as alien to Kierkegaard's understanding of the Christian view as the depersonalizing of the individual's God relation. "Every individual ought to live in fear and trembling, and so too there is no established order which can do without fear and trembling. . . . And fear and trembling signifies that a God exists—a fact which no man and no established order dare for an instant forget."[57] It is these two themes that Kierkegaard wishes to develop with his claim that for faith the individual is higher than the universal.

It would be a misunderstanding, however, to think that he means the natural individual, "conceived immediately as physical and psychical."[58] This individual has his telos in the universal. The aesthetic must sublimate itself in the ethical and the id learn to subordinate itself to the super-ego.[59] On this point there is no quarrel between Hegel and Kierkegaard, except for the fact that Hegel's analysis seems merely two dimensional to Kierkegaard in tending to remain at the level of interplay between the preethical individual and society.[60] So persistently and energetically does Hegel hammer away at the superiority of the universal to the preethical individual that the finitude of the ethical itself is forgotten.

But while Kierkegaard is eager to relativize the universal as something finite, it would be another misunderstanding to view this as abolishing it or depriving it of all spiritual significance. In its teleological suspension it is "not forfeited but . . . preserved."[61] Kierkegaard always rejects the view that the finite is worthless, and his knight of faith is strictly to be distinguished from the knight of infinite resignation, whether of the stoic or monastic type, just because he continues to love the finite. "Abraham, though gray-haired, was young enough to wish to be a father." He is persuaded that "God is concerned about the least things." For him "finiteness tastes . . . just as good as to one who never knew anything higher." He enjoys its blessings "as though the finite life were the surest thing of all," for he is "the heir apparent to the finite."[62]

What distinguishes the knight of faith from the tragic hero, then, is not that one denies while the other affirms spiritual significance for the family and the nation. The issue is the nature of that significance, and Kierkegaard's complaint is that for Hegel the ethical is divine, meaning that "the whole existence of the human race is rounded off completely like a sphere, and the ethical is at once its limit and its content. God becomes an invisible vanishing point, a powerless thought, His power being only in the ethical which is the content of existence."[63] In such a case, Abraham would be lost. But so would Hegel, for it would be shown that the content of his speculation is substantially different from the content of biblical faith, and it is a central claim of his philosophy that just the opposite is true. We must ask whether Kierkegaard's is a fair and accurate reading of Hegel.

Hegel's central affirmation about the state, taken in the broad sense equivalent to value-structured social life rather than in the narrowly political sense, is that it is the actuality (*Wirklichkeit, Realisierung*) of reason and freedom. It is as an Aristotelian, not as a Platonist, that he says this, for far from scorning the real in relation to the ideal, he stands in awe of what he calls "the prodigious transfer of the inner into the outer, the building of reason into the real world." It is as the state that inwardness becomes actuality, that the universal Idea comes to appearance. But in this instance at least, appearance (*Erscheinung*) is itself the essential (*das Wesentliche*).[64]

By itself, this would not evoke Kierkegaard's complaint. But Hegel consistently interprets the original affirmation to mean that the state, as the actuality of reason and freedom, is the actuality of the truth, the knowledge of which, in one of its modes, constitutes religion.[65] This enables him to speak of religion as an abstract essence whose concrete existence is the state.[66]

Hegel's motives are not far to seek. He feels obliged to enter the lists against the "atheism of the ethical world," which finds reason only in nature but not in the world of spirit and consequently lapses into various forms of antisocial subjectivism.[67] This makes of religion an antisocial principle, for it is "the highest and unholiest contradiction to seek to bind and subject the religious conscience to a secular legislation which for it is something unholy." Hegel finds such a dualism intolerable. "There cannot be two kinds of conscience, one religious and another ethical."[68] This is the sense in which religion is the foundation of the state. For it is in religion that man's conscience "first feels that it lies under an absolute obligation," and consequently "it is in religion [that] we first have any absolute certainty and security as regards the dispositions of men, and duties they owe to the state."[69]

While Hegel is concerned about the dissolution of law and order, Kierkegaard is fearful of their deification. His sensitive ear pricks up immediately at the suggestion that the laws of the state are something holy toward which, with the help of religion, man owes an absolute obligation. Things are not looking up for Abraham. Is the boundary between God and the social order being threatened? Kierkegaard's anxieties are not lessened when he reads that "everything which man is he owes to the state, in which alone he has his essence. All worth which man has, all spiritual actuality, he has only through the state." Furthermore, the culture of a nation that animates the actual state and is the spirit of a people is the holy.[70] This is no mere metaphor. Since "the secular is capable of being an embodiment of the true . . . it is now perceived that morality and justice in the state are also divine and commanded by God, and that in point of substance *there is nothing higher or more sacred*." Again, "secular life is the spiritual kingdom in reality [*im Dasein*]," and "*nothing must be considered higher and more sacred than good will towards the state*."[71]

It is possible to sacralize the ethical in this way because we are dealing with the Idea in its actuality. "The Idea in its truth is rationality actualized; and this it is which exists as the state." In other words, "what is divine about the state is the Idea, as it is present on earth."[72] This introduces us to a new aspect of the problem. It is no longer only a question of whether the state stands in fear and trembling before God. The Idea is what Hegel understands by perfection. To call the state its presence on earth is to substitute the state for the Incarnation. Instead of answering the question "Where on earth is God to be found?" by pointing to Jesus of Nazareth, Hegel points to the state.[73] The detailed arguments of *Philosophical Fragments* are designed to show how strenuous an act faith is when it understands Jesus to be the unique and decisive presence of God in human history. For such a faith Abraham is a splendid model, for in his case as well God breaks into human experience in such a way as to call for an intensely personal response for which even the highest culture is no substitute, and hardly even a preparation.

The statements in which Hegel finds the state to be God's incarnation are most striking. He sometimes speaks in a Spinozistic vein, as when he writes in the preface to the *Philosophy of Right* that "the great thing is to apprehend in the show of the temporal and transient the substance which is immanent and the eternal which is present." This could be taken simply as an affirmation of Providence, against which Kierkegaard would have no quarrel except for the implied identification of Providence with the state. But when Hegel goes beyond Spinozistic categories to speak of God as will and as love the overtones of incarnation become stronger. "The state is the divine will, in the sense that it is spirit present on earth, unfolding itself to be the actual shape and organization of a world"; and "the love which God is, is in the sphere of actuality conjugal love."[74]

Finally, there are passages where the ethical is identified as the actuality simply of God himself, without qualification. "It is in the organization of the state that the divine has passed into the sphere of actuality . . . and the secular realm is now justified in and for itself. . . . The true reconciliation whereby the divine realizes itself in the region of actuality is found in the ethical and legal life of the state. This is the true disciplining of secular life."[75] "Man must therefore venerate the state as an earthly deity [*Irdisch-Göttliches*]."[76] "The ethical life [*Sittlichkeit*] is the divine spirit as indwelling in self-consciousness, in its actual presence *as* a nation [*Volk*] and the individuals of the nation."[77]

This last statement belongs to a context that deserves closer scrutiny. At the beginning of the supplement to paragraph 552 of the *Encyclopedia* Hegel expresses his agreement with Kant's view that belief in God proceeds from practical reason. This is because the ethical involves a purification of consciousness from subjective opinion and selfish desire. "True religion and true religiosity only issue from the ethical life. Religion is the ethical life as thinking [*die denkende Sittlichkeit*], i.e., becoming aware of the free universality of its concrete essence. Only from the ethical life and by the ethical life is the Idea of God seen to be free spirit. Outside the ethical spirit it is vain to seek for true religion and true religiosity."

At first it seems that Kierkegaard would agree. On his view of the stages of existence, the religious presupposes the ethical, for until the subjectivism of the aesthetical attitude has succumbed to the subjectivity that can be called seriousness, the self is in no position for talk about God to make any sense at all. But Hegel's second and fourth sentences diverge completely from Kierkegaard's way of agreeing with Kant. Religion, as he understands it with the help of Abraham, is not the self-consciousness of the established order, but the individual's personal relation to God, a relation which relativizes his participation in the life of his people. In that sense, it is only beyond or outside the ethical spirit that true religion and true religiosity are to be found, for in religion the individual finds an allegiance that transcends political, economic, and family bonds.[78]

It is to these three institutions that Hegel directs our attention in the passage before us. He is very fond of contrasting the Reformation's affirmation of these institutions with the Roman Catholic monastic vows of chastity, poverty, and obedience.[79] This time that contrast is followed by a reaffirmation of *Sittlichkeit* as the immanence of the divine spirit.

> The divine spirit must interpenetrate the entire secular life. . . . But that concrete indwelling is only the aforesaid ethical organizations. It is the morality of marriage as against the sanctity of the celibate order, the morality of economic and industrial action against the sanctity of poverty and its indolence, and the morality of an obedience dedicated to the law of the state as against the sanctity of an obedience from which law and duty are absent and where conscience is enslaved.

This is to say that true religion affirms the family, the economy, and the state as the decisive presence of God on earth and that true religiosity consists in thoroughgoing socialization. Nothing could be further from the faith of which Abraham is the father! And yet it is in the very passage before us that two important qualifications of Hegel's position come to light. First, it is not just any state that Hegel has in mind; it is the modern, secular, Protestant state. This is consistent with his mature philosophy of history, according to which there are three crucial ingredients in the modern world. To begin with, it was Christianity that introduced into the world the idea that all are free. Then the Reformation reintroduced this idea with an intensity of inwardness that gave it new depth. And when, in addition, the Reformation affirmed marriage, labor, and the state it established the principle that this freedom was not to be something merely inward but was to inform the whole of man's life on earth. Finally, it was the French Revolution that took this principle at face value and sought to introduce into worldly life the principle that man as man is free. If the real is the rational and vice versa it is because the real *has become* rational and vice versa.[80] It is most frequently in the setting of these themes from the philosophy of history, as in the passage before us, that Hegel speaks of the state as the divine spirit's earthly manifestation.

A second and even more important qualification of Hegel's view is expressed in the statement that "the divine spirit *must* interpenetrate the entire secular life."[81] It is regularly with the grammar of imperatives, subjunctives, and optatives that Hegel speaks. The state or ethical substance *must* or *should* be the earthly manifestation of God, for this is its *task*. It is only ideally (*in sich*) rational or infinite, based on a principle that it does not fully realize. Though the principle of the modern world was articulated by the Reformation, "we have as yet no reconstruction of the state, of the system of jurisprudence. . . . Spirit does not assume this complete form immediately after the Reformation."[82] Nor has this defect been finally remedied. During the epoch of the French Revolution the world was filled with a jubilation and spiritual enthusiasm "*as if* the reconciliation between the divine and the secular was now first accomplished." But after forty years Hegel sees "the powerlessness of victory" and concludes both his lectures on the philosophy of history and those on the philosophy of religion with a gloomy report on the present scene.[83] We need to take seriously the fact that even in the preface to the *Philosophy of Right* Hegel describes reason as "the rose in the *cross of the present.*"

Will Kierkegaard's anxieties be assuaged by these restrictions on the Hegelian thesis? It is important to keep in mind that his problems are primarily theological and not narrowly political. The question is not whether Haym, Carritt, Popper, Hook, et al. are right in finding an obsequious Prussianism, crypto-Nazism, and various other offenses against modern liberal sensibility in Hegel's view of the state. (Unfortunately, Kierkegaard would not have been as upset about these allegations as we might like.) The question is whether that view, whatever we may think of its specifically political character, is compatible with the kind of faith that knows what fear and trembling before God is all about and that has Abraham as its father.

And Johannes:

You surely cannot expect me to be impressed by the suggestion that it is only to the modern state that Hegel's comments fully apply. That would be to tell me that Abraham and the faith he represents have become obsolete with the passing of time. I, for one, am not able to see the greatness of Abraham as so ephemeral a thing. But even if I could I would never claim that my view was the same in content as the Christian faith. I think it would be more honest to say that I found that faith to be outmoded. (All honor to Lessing.) As it is I can only say that while I admire Abraham's faith more than my limited literary skill can express, I cannot honestly claim to have such a faith, much less to have gone further.

The second point is more delicate. I have no wish to dispute the view that while men profess allegiance to higher principles than they used to, the world is still far from what it ought to be and the task which those principles set before us remains undone. But from this fact I conclude that the state, like the individuals who make it up, is both finite and sinful and not even in principle the incarnation of the sacred. While you concede the facts which lead me to this conclusion, you deny their import. For you "philosophy concerns itself only with the glory of the Idea mirroring itself in the history of the world. Philosophy escapes from the weary strife of passions that agitate the surface of society [*Wirklichkeit*] into the calm region of contemplation.[84] But if the Idea mirrors itself in a "weary strife of passions" from which philosophy must make its escape, that social reality, even if not wholly God-forsaken, can scarcely be described as "the image of the invisible God," or as "the effulgence of God's splendor and the stamp of God's very being. . . ."[85] And it remains puzzling to me how philosophy can afford the luxury of a contemplation divorced from repentance and exhortation. But that is an issue we have already discussed. I cannot help but wonder, though—if Abraham had found his social order, imperfect as it was, to be the highest earthly manifestation of the divine, would he ever have been my Abraham?

5. About Being a Person: Kierkegaard's *Fear and Trembling*

PAUL HOLMER

I

KIERKEGAARD WAS SO TALENTED AND SO WITTY THAT EVEN AS A YOUNG MAN, when barely thirty and his authorship just beginning (1843), his personal reputation already assured the sale of much that he wrote. So an acquaintance came to him one day complaining that in good faith he had purchased *Two Edifying Discourses,* assuming their author's cleverness and diverting propensities. Kierkegaard could only promise him his money back if he so wished, for that book was surely not the expected idle elegance.

In a strange but commanding way, however, Kierkegaard's life and authorship never suffered comparison. It was not as if Kierkegaard wrote so much better than he lived or that he indulged designs of human life that he was reluctant to perform. Kierkegaard of all people knew very well that his wit and his talent, even though they were the means to his writing better than others, were not an indulgence granting him the right to act worse than others. His powers were so easy and his endowments so profligate that flights of fancy, sallies of wit, and spates of pleasantries could frame his rigors of argument and lighten his severe dialectical distinctions. As a reader, therefore, one can never willfully choose Kierkegaard's poetic delights and omit his intellectual thrust and still say that one had understood his books. Likewise, to thrill with Kierkegaard's argument and to neglect his passional appeal is surely to miss his point, whatever the book.

This is to remark, then, upon two features of Kierkegaard's relationship to his own books. First, his life does not tell us much of what his writings portend. And this is not because his life is so much less than his writings or vice versa. His writings are not a personal expression, and he practices a craft that is not subjective, not self-disclosing, and surely never emotive or directly passional. He does not illustrate, clearly enough, the popular conception of what an existentialist writer should be like. Second, though he wrote a great deal about his books (in the *Postscript,* in *The Point of View For My Work as an Author,* and at length in his *Papirer*), he never quite gratified that easy deceit that an author is "in a purely legal sense the best interpreter of his own words." Neither did he assume that because he, the author, had intended this or that, that the reader would be helped by a confession to that effect. Nor does he allow one to assume that because something is promised in a preface that it is, therefore, realized in the text.[1]

Both of these points are negative, and they could be used to suggest that Kierkegaard was a rank subjectivist, illustrating the notion that there are no objectivities and no criteria for the arch existentialist that he is supposed to be. But this, too, would be wrong, for Kierkegaard was neither a subjectivist nor an existentialist in any of the popular senses. He is not even "schoolish" or an advocate of a philosophic position or cause. Even if the historical objectivities of his life and the clarity of his intentions were available—as I think they can be with little effort—Kierkegaard scoffs at the notion that these give the meaning of his books. So, the broken engagement with Regina, serious as it is in being a moral breach, is not a clue to the meaning of *Fear and Trembling*. Some critics have insisted that the earnestness in showing that there is a teleological suspension of a moral duty must reflect a deep psychological need to justify breaking a promise and restoring a little continuity to his life. But surely even this must be a mistaken interpretative notion.

But these denials do not require that a book's meaning is whatever the reader declares it to be. There are not as many meanings as there are resourceful readers. Kierkegaard suggests over and over again a large number of limitations upon such wanton interpretation. Also, the things he says about his entire literature, when he considers it as a totality, and what he says about particular books seem to provide a "confinium," a limited arena, in which restraints are not only being asserted but in which a certain range of logical considerations are brought to bear by the author. There are logical curbs upon the person who suggests that meaning is private or social, or that there are multiple meanings, or that meaning, in any case, is only subjective.

This is an exceedingly important consideration for an author like Kierkegaard. For there is a way in which he, too, writes an entire literature whose spirit is outside the main strands of western theological and philosophical thought. Something like Wittgenstein who said this kind of thing about his pages on mathematical and logical problems, Kierkegaard did not write in easy congruence with the pedogogical style of his day nor with the popular theology and philosophy. Wittgenstein said very tellingly about an early work that it did not build "ever larger and more complicated structures," that it did not add "one construction to another, moving on and up, as it were, from one stage to the next." On the contrary, it stayed where it was, seeking clarity and perspicuity right there, and "what it tries to grasp is always the same."[2] Kierkegaard wrote no new metaphysics, contrived no new doctrines, and spun no theories about fundamental matters. In this respect, he was not an originating thinker; for he was not carrying further the thought of the age and he was not suggesting an unheard of mutation. Therefore, his works spoke to the age and yet were not what the age required. Kierkegaard himself said both of these things.

If one had thought there was nothing different in either Kierkegaard or Wittgenstein because they did not realize an expectation one might entertain from the thought of their day, then it looks again as if another standard way to assess their meaning is being disparaged. And so it is. But this again does not imply that there is no right or wrong understanding or that the literature means what one chooses it to mean. The bugaboo for so many academic people is always subjectivity; for subjectivity suggests that carefully acquired learning, deep acquaintanceship with a period of culture, and scrupulous detail about the problems of reflection to which an author addresses himself are irrelevant to ascertaining what that author is about. But often what is forgotten in this context, bracketed by the cryptic notion that either one must be objective or otherwise subjectivity runs riot, is that such dichotomous reasoning is misleading on a whole range of issues. Just what issues and why—that will be part of the point of subsequent remarks.

For in what follows, I want to allude to another set of conditions that bear upon understanding the sort of religious and even deep matters of the human spirit (we could call them ethico-philosophical) that Kierkegaard writes about. Our considerations will bear upon the meanings that constitute his books, not least *Fear and Trembling*. It might be tempting to say, as a very singular critic of our time has done, "the meaning of a book is the series or system of emotions, reflections, and attitudes produced by reading it. . . . The ideally true or right 'meaning' would be that shared (in some measure) by the largest number of the best readers after repeated and careful readings over several generations, different periods, nationalities, moods, degrees of alertness, private preoccupations, states of health. . . ."[3] But here the question of "meaning" and the related issue of "understanding" are described as though the reader's capacities required either an anterior consensus or the assistance of the literary critic. Kierkegaard thinks that there are times when the critics can help; but he is more concerned about a kind of understanding that does not come because of an intermediary and, in fact, cannot come about in that way. Instead, there is an understanding and meaning that only the reader can endanger but one that is not, for that cause, subjective, private, or idiosyncratic. Other conditions can be transmitted, but not the meaning. It is the logic of such meaning and such understanding that obtains between the story of Abraham and its reader, between the New Testament and its authors, between oneself and a page of moral advice. There is a logic not only between propositions but also between spoken sentences and their speakers or readers. This is then to anticipate our remarks.

II

Johannes de Silentio asks about Abraham: "Who is capable of understanding him?"[4] And right away we sense a great difference between Kierkegaard and most religious authors, including learned commentators. For one thing, he always shows us that religious matters are discontinuous and heterogeneous with our ordinary "patois" about the world and our common life. The fact is that if we think we have understood Jesus' crucifixion, his dying for our sins, and Abraham's tough and ready faith, then Kierkegaard is certain that all our descriptions and talk about them are much like language on a holiday, that is, not meshing at all with our lives. But the issue is starker than that. Who is in the position ("*istand til*"), who has the capacity ("*duelighed*," "*egenskab*") to understand? Understanding requires more than knowledge and especially knowledge given you by a third party, say a learned critic. And "capacity" here does suggest that one must have some room in his life (perhaps like the expression "*rummelighed*" suggests), but that can be deceptive too.

No, the capacity is not merely a matter of capaciousness, nor is it simply a skill. So, most students in a modern university can be taught to read Hebrew and some will read a great deal. Some will read so widely in ancient lore that they will have access to the history hidden from the rest of us. But if Kierkegaard is right, these skills and all the attendent advantages they bring will not add up to the capacity to understand Abraham. The difficulty here is not to be met with more information or even with an historical empathy.

The difficulty to which Kierkegaard alludes here is a breach of consciousness itself, something far deeper than a different culture, a nomadic people, another ethos, etc., could suggest. And it is not a breach like that between the cultivated and the bumpkins, the drooling idiot and the person of taste and discrimination, or the scientists versus the persons of letters. Neither is it like that between the good and the evil, drastic and thorough though this breach might be.

The breach of consciousness of which Kierkegaard speaks has to be differently conceived. But first we must sketch a bit what we mean by a person being conscious. The familiar feature that stands out in being conscious is simply that people typically learn to see, hear, think in an "about" mood. That is, their attention becomes focused and their psychological activities become transitive. They see the world, hear sounds, and some go on to talk about the world around them. The most familiar way we have of summarizing all this is to say that people begin to learn "about" something. They acquire knowledge. Of course, this supposes a variety of strengths and capacities, skills and crafts. The result is that knowing the world is done in social ways, in language that must be public and for purposes that are recognizable and by and large stateable. But the principal feature is, again, the transitivity, the intentional and referential thrust that is given everything psychological, so that it becomes a medium for "aboutness."

There is nothing in Kierkegaard's pages to suggest that knowing the world does not have all kinds of advantages. Kierkegaard is not an antiintellectualist if by that one means that he suggests any other way to understand current events, or the past, or even the physical world around him. He never says (like Bergson) that a concept must deceive because the concept is static while reality is in flux and that, therefore, knowledge is only like the movie, an illusion of motion created cinematographically. Neither does he say (like John Locke) that we know only our ideas and not the world itself. There is no pervasive skepticism putting knowledge or the reflective consciousness into jeopardy. On the contrary, Kierkegaard trusts ideas and concepts because general skepticism is only a bit of nonsense. So, we can say that becoming a reflective person, acquiring a reflective consciousness, is like moving from a *terminus a quo,* which in this case is ignorance, to the *terminus ad quem,* which is knowledgeability.

The point is that human beings are host to a certain kind of consciousness. We become conscious "of," become attentive "to," more and more in extent, if we so choose, or contrariwise, we become competent in respect to ever greater detail, if we so choose. Either way, humans begin to distinguish themselves from animals by acquiring all that allows them to intend the world in its very rich and ever-changing manifold. In brief, we could say that man shows spiritual potential by this kind of development. And, of course, we can extend ourselves to new instances, to things heretofore unknown and even to those deemed unknowable. I believe Kierkegaard thought that this kind of cognitive personality growth was *uno tenore,* almost without a breach and in a single breath, and mostly without serious crisis and confounding personal disarray. Here there need be no paradoxes, except local ones to be resolved by better conceptual tools and a refinement of judgement.[5] The limits of thought keep getting moved by better observations and better hypotheses.

So, there need be no paradox in technical scholarship about Abraham. Instead, a refined knower finds more generous rubrics and a host of ways of subsuming him, all of them congruent with the concepts of the learned fields. But more, if one chooses to see Abraham as an anomaly, then one can be quite content to let him be still unexplained, if knowledge does not quite cover his case. One can trust to future scholarship when more evidence will be on hand; and this does not make for a paradox, only the acknowledgement and minor discomfort that some things are not yet quite done. But, the point then emanating from this consideration is that becoming responsible intellectually is an achievement that Kierkegaard does not disparage. There is an *ad quem* and it is feasible.

The difficulty that makes for a deep paradox lies not in the knowledge, but in another form in the consciousness of the human. For there is a diseased and sickened consciousness that begins to grow in all of us, even alongside the growth of knowledge. Unless this "growth" is confronted and directly attacked, Kierkegaard finds that all can well be lost. For there is an almost naïve and simple passional notion that gets added to the normal intellective abilities. It is that the human personality itself, the spirit of man, will take care of itself in the growth of knowledge and correlative skills. Because knowledge is accumulated gradually and incrementally, almost as the expansion and fulfillment of native immediacy, so it is assumed that the personality and spirit of a person is achieved by the same lineal and intellective development. The person being normally educated does not typically confront a paradox; and his understanding may be balked but usually by a difficulty for which he is presently unprepared or an ignorance not yet requited. If Abraham had had only more to learn, his frustration could have been temporary; and all of us can understand that kind of dismay. Again, though, the point is that the growth of knowledge-ability is defined to be enough for the development of the personality, for then there would be no paradox and no persistent crises in understanding. At least, this is how it appears to most of us. Everything spiritual gets subsumed under a general single-level learning theory.

However, we often find our wants and wishes to be at odds, and the pursuit of knowledge often augments that kind of self-cognizance. But if this quixotic character of oneself is made manifest as we learn this or that, then the paradoxicality (if that is what we wish to call it) is only in the subject, not in anything objective. It is made out to be a temporary emotional aberration—something that one will get over in time. And that, again, is not quite what makes Abraham difficult to understand. For we all can empathize with psychological conflicts and we all can say things that are consoling, if not profound, about this kind of difficulty.

III

Now to return to the consideration of consciousness again. It is Kierke-gaard's contention that consciousness is not fully developed when an individual learns to intend in cognitive ways the world around him. Or, the development of the capacities to see, to hear, and to know the world around one, even if one should become a virtuoso of science and scholar-ship, is not to become all that a human being should be and can be. Here another kind and quality of consciousness is supposed. Kierkegaard at this juncture surely is not advancing a theory or proposing a novelty. Instead he is putting what is probably a very common, almost commonsensible, awareness into more conceptual and formal terms.[6]

Consciousness becomes something quite different when a person learns to make himself an object of attention, concern, and even knowledge. This is to intend and to purpose oneself: and this kind of transitivity is for Kierkegaard the hallmark of spirituality. This is why he says in *The Sickness unto Death* that Christian heroism consists principally in venturing to be oneself, not being "humbugged the pure idea of humanity or to play the game of marvelling at world-history."[7] The diametric opposite is to be spiritless and that is like never being conscious of and, hence, never learning to be responsible for, what one has made of oneself. Perhaps this is like the state of those the Apostle Paul describes (Ephesians 4) whose minds are futile, whose understandings are darkened, who are alienated from God, who are callous and cannot grieve anymore. Here one has hardness of heart. But to be a self, granted what human beings are, requires that interest and enthusiasm, concern and passions, be developed for the quality of one's own life. Here one cares and manifests a kind of pathos. Thus a self relates and constitutes itself. This has to be an intentional activity and supposes that one takes into consideration what one already is. Here the *a quo* and *ad quem* are different. Hence, too, being a self requires understanding, not of just anything and everything, but of oneself.

This is where Kierkegaard again thought that science and scholarship, and philosophy too, could easily mislead one. Unfortunately, some kinds of knowledge and philosophical reconstructions of that knowledge lead one to the notion that one must surely have to understand the totality first, and that only then will the parts, including the self, be seen in the right perspective. If the whole of history can be made at all sensible, it could seem plausible to think that such an understanding would give one access both to the past and to oneself, as a matter of course. But so, too, with "being," with "reality," with "Nature": for a man seems to be but a part of all these. In this fashion, then, understanding oneself becomes an episode within a broader compass. And this kind of learned and sophisticated mistake is a deeply ingrained one, and it is not quite corrigible by a casual reminder.

In fact, Kierkegaard seems to think this mistake is both logical in form and ethical (or moral) in motivation. For we want to avoid self-concern and all the attendant components of self-consciousness. This is the moral side, for none of us finds that getting clear about ourselves is very pleasant. We begin to feel guilt, we grieve a bit, and we suffer all the wounds—remorse, remembrance of broken promises, slights, jealousies, contriteness—that have given self-consciousness its bad name for so many centuries. The trouble with you, we say to others and perhaps to ourselves, is that you are too self-conscious. "Forget yourself" seems like the open sesame, a command that opened the robbers' den in the *Arabian Nights* and will unfailingly open the self to better health, too.

The logical side is that we subsume the self as a part is to a whole, as a component is to a totality, as an atom is to the molecule, or even as Hegel, as an episode in the temporal unfolding of the System. But the self is not an object like that mode of thought suggests. Nonetheless, the mode of reflection is still suggestive and easy, besides being eminently plausible; and it allows us to think that selves are nothing unless they are like compost, which gradually becomes solid ground—but only after it first ferments, then becomes peat, and then a usable soil. The community or society looks like the reality toward which selves are contributory.

Kierkegaard says, in contrast, that a self is not a substratum, not a hidden essence at all; instead, it is a kind of relating activity, a relation, which by developing a consciousness of itself actually constitutes itself.[8] For this reason being a person involves activities, a willing of a goal for oneself, an emotionally rich concern over what one can be, a thoughtful assessment of what one already is. All of this is a matter of making emotions, pathos, wish, want, hope, understanding, thoughts, not bare essences, hanging in a kind of limbo, but instruments that are directed "to" and are "about" the self. This is the energy of life of which Kierkegaard spoke so often. He could not understand a man of learning developing such a consuming passion for his learning that he would ever give up the endlessly taxing and consuming thought about himself that would make him a responsible human spirit. "Not understanding oneself," then, would be the penalty for being totally objective. Kierkegaard thinks it would be the most frightful way to live: "to fascinate and surprise the world by one's discoveries and one's brilliance, and yet not to understand oneself."[9] This would not be another way to be a self, a genuine alternative; rather it would be a default so serious that there would be no self at all.

For being a self is a matter of wanting, wishing, not just anything, but a certain quality of life and subjectivity. However, only by being a subject can one be a subject, and that is not a transition; it is an energent, a "leap" as Kierkegaard calls it. One must become a subject by making oneself, not others or the external world, one's object. But not disinterestly, for that could only be in virtue of not seeing what is there. For Kierkegaard thought that there was a logical, not a fortuitous and accidental, connection between seeing what one was and a kind of concern. To know oneself was, immediately, and without qualification, to become concerned. It would be impossible in the strongest logical sense of *impossible* to know clearly and acutely what one was and not, therewith, to be passionately involved. That is why self-consciousness is a different kind of transitivity. It is not simply knowledge turned inward. We can be students of other people and neither love them or hate them, without, in fact, caring about them in any way. Here the "about" character of our thought, the reference and predication, is logically independent of any kind of "ought." But with oneself it cannot be so, for to know oneself is like knowing, not a substratum stuff, not an object at all. It is a little like knowing God, who is never an object, but is always a pure subject. So, too, other people may be objects initially to one's glance, but the more pure they are as subjects, the less can they be viewed as objects. But with oneself, there is only the activity or the lack thereof, the relation or the lack thereof, and there is nothing to see but only something to be. There is nothing much else there.[10]

The self is that transitivity that gets its substance by being a "how," by not being a what, a thing, but by making itself a subject. To be a subject at all is to be conscious, to be intending the world in a rich variety of ways. But this one does by no single means, neither by thought, emotion, or will, but by all these and more—by emotions, wish, desire, and love. But to making oneself one's own enterprise and field, this marks out the beginning of a spiritual life. Then guilt, fear of failure, and anxiety get their root in the person.

We are speaking, however, about Abraham, whom Johannes de Silentio cannot understand. Think, therefore, about a kind of self-consciousness that is natural and easy enough. For early in a lifetime, we discover that some things distress us and others please. It is not long before we begin to tune ourselves almost like an instrument in order to gain gratification, enjoyment, and the agreeable in contrast to their opposites. Soon we become conscious of capabilities and powers that we have or do not have by which to find greater pleasure and reduce the pain. All this Kierkegaard has described already in his writings on the aesthetic stage. In a variety of ways, a move can be made to another qualitatively distinct style and manner of intending the self. This is the ethical; and here Kierkegaard is indeed fulsome and detailed. Once more, his point is that an ethical quality can be realized in independence of one's cognitive grasp of the rest of the world. For there are two dialectical streams that meet in the individual, and they never become one. On the one side, there is the skein of concepts within which and by which we construe the world and others as objects. Herewith we know the world and acquire a kind of consciousness that is "about," "to," and "of" that world and all that it contains. This is one conceptual scheme, as moderns would say, or a set of them; but Kierkegaard speaks mostly about a kind of dialectic, a skein of concepts. Nonetheless, the ethical stage also brings into birth another stream of concepts; but they are first (in a logical sense) and foremost developed in virtue of a person's apprehension and consciousness of himself or herself. These are the concepts in which we articulate our understanding of ourselves. They get their content not so much from learned schemes about ourselves as from the informal but necessary kinds of self-judgments by which we must live.

These two kinds of dialectic, one existential, the other cognitive, are not internally related; persons can be religious, aesthetic or ethical and still have the same science or scholarship. But an individual must often entertain two conceptual schemes, one of the former group, while also being informed by general cognition. The individual is the point of synthesis or is the synthesis itself. Kierkegaard would have us remember that all human beings are in this strait, if they develop any consciousness of themselves at all. To have the latter supposes the development of subjectivity and passion, concern and interest, but these in turn are also qualified and determinate in at least one of three ways, aesthetic, moral, and religious.

Something could be said about the generic features of this synthesis, but I refrain because it does not bear directly upon the question of understanding Abraham. Something else and another kind of crisis of consciousness is shown us there. And that is to approach the telling point. Abraham's life shows us something in and of itself; and that feature cannot be adumbrated or lifted up into a higher synthesis. There is no higher conceptual unity or synthesis. A life itself is the synthesis or the crisis, as the case may be, and this is the price to be paid for a highly developed human spirit.

How then was it developed? Kierkegaard supposes Abraham to have been living under ethical categories and, hence, to have evinced an ethical kind of subjectivity, understanding, and consciousness. This means that he cared, and that he strove to construe his life and behavior in accord with laws and precepts. These were not, nor could they be, merely inclinations and hunches, wish-fulfillments or chancy proposals. Rather the ethical must be defensible and public, and in terms that are congruent with something available to all. Laws, rules, and obligations are like that. Here is the arena in which "rightness," "good," and "ought" get their standardization and force. And the point is that a consciousness, a proneness to intend oneself, is thereby given form and morphology. Kierkegaard thought there was something incumbent in human nature itself that would typically lead mankind from the aesthetic to the ethical and not the other way around. But with the ethical comes also a host of new concepts and these, in turn, become a good part of ethical behavior itself, and not just its cause or its symptom. The thought pattern that is produced is both a pattern for the deeds as well as a part of ethical behavior.

Abraham was like good men everywhere, a man subject to ethical judgments and also a subject who could make his judgments and live thereby. But this community of moral understanding can only obtain when and if the proper conditions are met. The rules and laws are not subjective, private, whimsical, or arbitrary. They are public, universal, stateable, and binding on all. But so is an ethical life. The only exceptions that can be envisioned are among those who have chosen not to play the game, who are drop-outs. There are, clearly, nonteleological suspensions, when a will falters, a thought does not obtain, there is a failure of consciousness itself. In effect, there is a suspension of the rule when we circumvent it and no longer admit it to be binding. But then there is usually a lapse in consciousness itself.

Abraham, again, was not guilty of a moral lapse. If so, we could understand him in the loose sense that we all know about moral lapses and suffer them often enough. Abraham was not victimized by a preference, by a wayward disposition, in contraposition to his settled moral conviction. If so, again we all know about such instances and hence he would not be baffling. Kierkegaard's point is that Abraham still has a determinate and ethical quality of consciousness even while he sets out on his trip to Mount

Moriah. He suffers no lapse of that consciousness, but he does suffer a breach of that consciousness in this peculiar way. While willing the law and maintaining a continuity with his fellows and his son in a consciousness that is shared, in concepts that are in common, he now finds a duty from God that he cannot speak about, that is not for everybody, that proposes a way of intending the world and Isaac that seems idiosyncratic, odd, and indefensible. How can we understand that? It is as if the tools of understanding were inadequate.

IV

Here, then, we have a very deep paradox that will not be remedied by information, not by more discursive knowledge, not by enlarging the cognitive conceptual scheme. Nor is it a matter quite of changing God into one more ethical agent, as if he too is and must be part of that game. Must the moral laws obtain for God as philosophers have said about the laws of logic? If so, why? Is it really the case that the paradox is due—as Wittgenstein suggested—to a defective surrounding? If so, it might help to get the surrounding enlarged and bring God in. Let us suppose, for example, that God, indeed, must share the moral consciousness, or more plainly, let us suppose that God is good in the manner that people are. Then the context would not allow for a paradox. God would know everything and his ethicality would be more subtle. The environment would not now be defective—God's command would be thought of as being something like the tragic hero's behavior, which looks paradoxical but is not if you know what the hero knows. This kind of hero is tragic, for he cannot get rid of the tragedy; but the terrible oddness of the paradox and the divided consciousness that ensues is overcome. So, too, if one believed that moral concepts and precepts held for both God and men. Then one could in principle understand God by understanding the moral laws. God would be plausible in the longest possible run.

This, too, is the secret of the great philosophical "isms." For they propose bringing everything under a single conceptual scheme, by reference to which the defective surroundings are rectified. Most such large-scale views tend to place all dichotomies within an underlying synthesis and all disunities within a deep and invisible unity. So, too, with Hegel's philosophy, which envisioned all the conflicts of human consciousness as resolvable once one saw each component as if it were but a phase in the unfolding of an all-inclusive cosmic consciousness. In that view, there are no fundamental paradoxes and no crises of understanding that have an irremediable finality about them. They need not be suffered. For again, Hegel is quick to invoke a picture of rationality, a kind of equivalent of the mind of God, in which diametric opposites, even contradictories, are never quite that; they are always in the process of being resolved. To recall

Wittgenstein's remark again, Hegel is prone to think that paradoxicality lies in the environment's being defective, but only by its never being the totality. When the totality is considered, all paradoxes and contrarieties vanish.

Søren Kierkegaard thought, on the contrary, that Abraham's confrontation with God led to a paradox that was *not* going to disappear even as one began to understand the metaphysics of God and/or reality. For to know God better was precisely to suffer a divided and wounded consciousness. God was not like a totality; instead he was and is a subject, like the individual. The individual becomes a subject by ethical cultivation, and the law itself feeds a consciousness in which obligation rules. Kierkegaard was convinced, as serious students have been for centuries, that obligation roots easily and appropriately in people. One can take obligation out of theories and the social scene, but one can scarcely remove it from people. So deep is the need for an obliged outlook and a life justified by fulfilling an obligation that this way of construing the world and oneself invariably seems like personal maturation and the pinnacle of self-development. So with Kant and Kierkegaard; and so, too, does Kierkegaard think it must have been with Abraham. A consciousness that feels a debt and owes a life of service is not imposed merely from the outside. Instead it is incumbent, and it is a realization of a capacity and not a triviality created by externalities.

So Abraham has a consciousness that is formed and ruled in the direction of being universalized. It is articulated by a rule and by a duty that brings passions and impulses, deeds and proposals, under its sovereignty. This is how it must be with mature and responsible persons. Furthermore, the very logic and morphology of such a consciousness is that it is understandable to the subject, for everything transitive and outward-directed within its competency is ostensibly covered by the rule. What is not so covered is, again, construable by the rule by virtue of its being an exception to the rule, a lapse. Besides, the rule is not a rule if it obtains only for oneself. The logic of a rule is that it must obtain between other ethical agents. It is a guarantor of understanding, but not only for successive moments of time and hence for promoting a kind of self-identity; it proposes a community of persons within whom moral sense can be promoted. It rules between and among all other subjects.

However, the point that gives the poignancy to Abraham is the fact that his consciousness of himself is identified by an ethicality that envelops God, Isaac, the future, Abraham's people, and the promise by which Abraham lives. God also has been seemingly a party to this truly solemn and glorious conception of Abraham's life and destiny. But that would be a small thing if it stayed only a story. Rather, the story proposed a kind of publicly defensible mode of life for Abraham, within which moral factors were operative. Abraham's consciousness of himself, his subtle ways of evaluating his tasks, his self-justification, were all herein bracketed. He was not the tragic hero who had a small but important fund of secret knowledge by which anything odd could be further explained. Everything was explicable by recourse to a plan, his life, the promise, and the future.

Therefore, God's new command meant a terrible breach in Abraham's consciousness. For it was not as if Abraham had failed God. Being a part of a fellowship of the lapsed, most of us are prepared for defection. But here was a more fundamental and terrifying kind of bifurcation. Abraham suffers a call that is urgent and authoritative, a call from God himself, which is unsupported by the context of the promise and not vindicated by the picture of the future. It has no tissue of reliability, no supporting texture, no arena of reasons backing its force. Worse still, Abraham has to reconstitute and realign the most precious achievement of a lifetime, his own consciousness and evaluation of himself and his tasks. He had had years in which to achieve a self-composure and to make himself recognizable to himself. He had gained self-understanding in the only way that any of us can, by becoming a self.

And that is, finally, where the issue lies. To be a self is to have made the self. Most of us do not understand ourselves because there is nothing much to understand. We get a self and something to understand only by constituting ourselves. We have to wish, to hope, to want, to love, to promise—and more. By doing all this we acquire a self. For the self is not a thing but a relation that relates itself to itself. By wanting steadily and long, a kind of definition of the person ensues. We are knowable by the fact that we have always wanted this or that. We become clear even to ourselves, as to who and what we are, by the intensity and constancy of our wants, wishes, and loves. And if we have never wanted or desired with steadiness and intensity, it is also the case that our lives have scarcely any definition at all. We never arrive at the goal of being a true self. This is Kierkegaard's point through his entire authorship and surely also has to be said on behalf of Abraham.[11]

The issue is not abstract. Every person achieves all this only when the wants and hopes, etc., are themselves transitive. That is why consciousness itself comes to define being a self. After a while, Abraham was conscious of himself, but only because by living a promise and by being obligated by a commanded destiny he had acquired thereby his selfhood. Consciousness involves transitivity in two senses. One becomes an identity, first, by wanting, by being obligated, and by wishing with all one's heart. This makes possible the second kind of transitivity, that of being allowed a thought of who and what one is. Abraham had both. There is more, though, for this is the way in which Abraham became a subject rather than an object. To be a subject requires that the transitivity of which one is capable be turned to the task of making something of oneself. This is a capacity; its realization means that one becomes a true self and a human subject.

However, Abraham had a history with a God who was also a person and a subject. God was not a "force" or a blind power or an "id." God was a pure subject. Abraham's life had been put together by a trust in that God whose will and promise encompassed all things. That God had dominion. Because God was a subject, he could not be conceived apart from loving Isaac, fulfilling a promise, realizing the teleology that had been painfully apprehended by Abraham. The seal on all this was an abiding and deep confidence that Abraham had gained concerning God and the people. Abraham's certainty was too deep for a hypothesis and more encompassing than any theory. Abraham's whole life, as well as God and the fate of a people, all hinged on the reliability, predictability, and communicability of that certainty. From that certainty, everything else flowed. And it was Abraham's consciousness that had been the instrumentality for God's promise and for the establishment of the people of God. Had Abraham failed here, then all could have been lost. But he had not failed. He had kept the faith, nurtured the promise, admonished the people, and pro- jected the future with unswerving loyalty.

And then came God's new command! How could this be understood? I think it right to say that Abraham's capacity could not be stretched that far. For a moral kind of understanding is a kind of capacity. It comes like other capacities only when certain conditions are met. When one's reasoning abilities have been nurtured in a moral manner, then they are also limited in that same manner. It is as if a way of forming one's life, by formalized and rule-ordered wants and duties, also provides and forms one's reasons. For the business of reasoning also belongs to people and it, too, reflects what people make of themselves. More than this, it is that the rules of reasoning are the criteria; but the rules of reasoning are finally a part of the very grammar of how we are living, behaving, wanting, and judging. The criteria become manifest in the way we live. And Abraham had so conformed his subjective life that it had become moral; but moral means that it was in accord with a grammar and a kind of rule-consciousness that a way of living, itself, made manifest. To violate the moral consciousness was to trespass upon the very logic within which lives made moral sense. But "sense" and "meaning," "order" and "rational," are all parasitic upon a grammar that our lives lay down.

Abraham had laid down a very rich and sonorous career. Its morphology allowed his consciousness to judge what was sensible, right, and in accord with God's will. He could not doubt that, for doubt would make no sense unless it were within that orbit. Then he meets God again. And what makes God so unfeasible and so difficult now is not that the moral concepts are being stretched a bit to cover new circumstances; instead, these concepts are being abrogated altogether. "Sense" itself is at stake. It makes rubbish of a promise to make it and then destroy the means of effecting it. So, the crisis for Abraham is not something one can get over by a little patience or by rehearsing the fundamentals all over again. Matters are more serious. Another kind of faith, another quality of consciousness in Abraham, is being asked for.

And that is the very point of the paradox. Faith of the Abrahamic sort is a new move for the consciousness itself. It asks that a subject project himself, make sense of his life, not only by congruences that are established in a calculus of right and wrong, but also to be prepared, on occasion, to establish a kind of criterion, to make a certainty, by a community with God himself. Then, between oneself and God a new grammar will develop, a new rule-consciousness will emerge, and a new confidence will be manifested. This kind of living will have to be intentional and willed; it will be teleological, not a lapse. For a moral lapse is like a failure to intend the rule, and it goes on in the absence of a telos. For Abraham, the business of following God looked nonteleological, but, oddly enough, it was not. Only Abraham and God could know that. Toward the rest there had to be silence.

V

Kant says:" 'A conflict of duties (*collisio officiorum s. obligationum*)' would be a relation of duties in which one of them would annul the other. . . . But a 'conflict of duties' and obligation is inconceivable ('*obligationes non colliduntur*'). . . . two conflicting rules cannot both be necessary at the same time."[12] If Kierkegaard is right, Abraham's life and faith have led him to entertain two diametrically different kinds of duty. Thus his consciousness of himself is at stake. How can he go on? Unlike Kant, however, Kierkegaard does not think that there is a single logic or a single set of criteria to which one can have recourse, according to which one duty will appear derivative or lesser. For the criteria, along with the logic and/or the grammar (which provide the criteria), are precisely what either morals or religion themselves establish. They are the source of the criteria. Therefore, the crisis cannot be resolved by recourse to a standard outside the morals, nor do the standards of morals become standard outside the limited moral context. For Kierkegaard would have it that a remark that says ethics is universal does not (because it cannot) make sense unless one thinks of its rules applying only in a context or in a stage of life.

Abraham is also unprepared for a God who is not measurable by the criteria that seem most fundamental and even necessary. For Abraham, like the rest of us, must have thought that the ruled use of "good," "right," "in accord with the promise," and other such working-concepts simply had to obtain for all others and for God. But suddenly he is up against a God who calls for a breach with all that. The break hurts so much because the pathos of Abraham's life and the very quality of his subjectivity are at stake. This is not a matter of rules being abrogated—it is more like a violation of his integrity and a sufferance of an incapacity. His way of coping, his capacity to think the future, all that is in abeyance. And for Kierkegaard, unlike Kant, there is no more fundamental arena of rationality in which such issues can be entertained and perhaps resolved. Making moral sense is part of the enterprise of making sense of our lives. Logic and rationality are not fundamental to all that except in the jejune sense that logic might articulate the common conceptual necessities of our language uses, be they cognitive, moral, aesthetic, or religious. These formal criteria show us that, indeed, we live and think our way into conflicts, but the criteria surely do not get us out of them.

Kierkegaard shows us Abraham, whose life has been defined by a practiced pattern of expectation, promises, and behavior. Surely what it means to say that this is to bring one's particular life under a universal is to note that Abraham's conduct was subject to criteria that were recognizable by both God and other persons—the people living under the covenant. The important point is that what is a universal and recognizable duty is so only because there is a context that has made it possible. That context is neither mankind nor all the world nor everybody; there we would have an instance of an "illegitimate totality." Any totality of which we speak in a responsible way has to be "all of a limited class" or we soon lose our moorings and sense itself. There is nothing being said if we make the totality all of mankind.[13]

Abraham's duties to Isaac and others were duties to particular people, family, friends, and Jews bound by a tradition. There was nothing more fundamental or more dutiful lying behind Abraham's covenanted life. He, too, had had to decide and the duty was the consequence, not the cause. Here, indeed, then, was Abraham's connection with an ordered ethicality. But Kant and most of us would have it that there must be a "categorical imperative" or a necessary duty that embraces and orders all other duties. Or others would conclude that there is some kind of "rational unity of mankind," within which our ad hoc reasons get vindicated, or by reference to which every decision can be explained and made manifest.[14] However, the story of Abraham shows us something else. We do *not* owe our daily reasons or the thrust of our daily speech to intercourse with "all" men. Furthermore, there is no general morality, no standards for all, and there surely is nothing called a duty for all. After receiving God's new command, Abraham suddenly could not speak to Sarah and Isaac, with whom and for whom his life had heretofore been lived. And understanding him, accordingly, became impossible.

But this is to say that the "rational unity" is not all inclusive. On the contrary, Abraham shows us that there are real conflicts. But these conflicts are not just on paper or of a sort that a general logician might celebrate in a pair of contradictory propositions. Here the conflict is suffered. Abraham has no resolution at hand and no higher wisdom to consult. There is no impartial court and no set of hidden reasons to be precipitated out of the confrontation.

This brings us again, therefore, to the issue of what it means to be a self. The self is not an object. (That remark is, of course, a grammatical remark, as Wittgenstein would have said.) There is no truth waiting to be discovered that tells us what we ought to do; neither is there a duty beckoning our resolution and the surcease of the difficulty. Instead, to be a self is to have a capacity for self-clarification only via the "bloody" and long way. There are rival ways of carrying on our lives. If there were not, our selfhood would be a joke and living a lifetime would be like a waste of time. But existing is momentous partly because so much depends upon "how" we do it, not simply "that" we do it.

Kierkegaard uses the story of Abraham to show us that being ethical and being religious are not the same. The temptation is to elide them, and that is what Kant did in his *Religion Within the Limits of Reason Alone.* But there is no vantage point, no logical point of view, outside morality or outside religion that tells us which one we should be. Abraham shows us in peculiarly sharp relief that the point of intersection between the two is very deep. But depth means here not an intellectual complexity. Instead, Abraham's self-consciousness, how he thinks of himself and gives his life a justification, the very criteria that his life have laid down, these are confronted by another set of criteria, another way to be; and there is no friendly assimilation of the one by the other. Instead, there is conflict and momentous consequences.

Abraham can only clear up the conflict in his consciousness by changing that consciousness. This, however, is a resolution. This means that he has to decide; but by so doing he also clarifies his own life. He had no outside recourse, no data to consult, no evidence to assess. This is how deep the difficulties then become. For reasoning and thinking and speaking and understanding all have limits; we can do them only where there are connections, continuities, and a certain kind of rule of good sense. Our reasoning and understanding get noted in the language we speak and in the ways of life we live. So, too, with Abraham. But the link with all this is our decision to share the way of life and to be, hence, a part of the rationality and a subject in the reign of moral order.

The oddness of faith does not lie only in what is believed. Abraham is said to be the father of faith. Now we might be able to see why. For here we can begin to see what is required. A life like Abraham's shows us something that words cannot say. But now it is not merely biographical information that does that job, but the very manner of life and the way Abraham went on. He decided something momentous, and he did it alone and without the guarantee of companionable talk and the support of the environment. His life and his way give us a clue to what faith is. These block out, in a kind of schematic way, the room that faith requires in a life. We begin to see how fear and trembling are a component and appropriate accompaniment. The anxiety is not a symptom of ill-health and temperamental lapses. The fear belongs to Abraham because the question, "What ought I to do?," gets no answer. There can be no answer. There is no way to decide that faith is right or that ethics is better. Here no scale is available to be consulted. Abraham answers with his life—and even then the question is not answered: it simply falls away. Everything "finite," as Kierkegaard says, is suddenly restored. But think how momentous the decision was!

It is almost as if what Abraham's religion requires of all of us is the admission that nothing matters so much as how we live and decide. The force of any society is obviously felt by almost every individual in it. Most of us probably say something about that. We are indebted to our language, for we do not make it as we speak. We are indebted to our common life in a myriad of ways. But being a self is not only to be a by-product. And all that socialization might have lured us from the romance and terror and sheer fun of being a person. For there is a voluntary thrust we all must make if we are going to be faithful to God that is not just the same as trustfulness and loyalty and fidelity within the institutionalized contexts. For Abraham's faith shows us that there are limits on all that rationality and on the moralizing effect of our common life. As selves, we stand outside that tissue. There is no embracing morality and no single standard. God is outside all that, too. But being outside does not mean one must stay outside. To be a moral self is also to join up. But one can fall out, too.

There is, clearly, the nonteleological move, when one does not will at all. Kierkegaard thought this meant an aesthetic mode of life, which, while it was a style of life was not ethical just because of that fact. Then there was a teleological suspension, too. Abraham could not show us the reason for it, but his life shows us—again, it does not say—what is involved.

Is there such a thing as understanding Abraham? Perhaps two reminders are now in order. Kierkegaard's *Fear and Trembling* gives us a kind of understanding that is general and schematic. It shows us via the category of the stages that there is a kind of morphology to one's life and that it is not utterly random and fortuitous. Here Wittgenstein's notion of a "grammar" is useful and begins to move us a little more surely into the details. We begin to get the hang of some human endeavors, not least Abraham's, by knowing where the differences between morals and belief in God, even faith itself, begin to swing off. So much for one kind of understanding: it is slight and perhaps a surface recognition, it is not without its illumination. For we begin to see this via the grammatical remark and see it for ourselves.

The other reminder is of a deeper kind of understanding that is projected for us by this same book. But it is projected and cannot be delivered to us. For it requires a deep kind of activity. If one becomes faithful, then one's consciousness of oneself is moved by the wanting, wishing, and caring that made Abraham faithful and the father of faith. By so doing, one surely would also know God. Within that decisiveness, a new rule, a new life, and a new understanding would ensue. Maybe, then, everything finite would come back again. All of life, the past and the future, would make sense. So it was for Abraham.

Kierkegaard thought that what happened to Abraham on Mount Moriah could also happen on a heath in Denmark. Perhaps it could happen anywhere. The logic that makes it even conceivable is the rational accompaniment to the emotions that were Abraham's—the peculiar fear and trembling that were a sign that his life was being judged and formed.

6. Understanding Abraham: Care, Faith, and the Absurd[1]

EDWARD F. MOONEY

> Once I am dead, *Fear and Trembling* alone will be enough to immortalize my name. It will be read and translated into foreign languages. People will shudder at the terrible pathos which the book contains.[2]

FEAR AND TREMBLING IS BY COMMON CONSENT ONE OF KIERKEGAARD'S MOST important and most trying works. It is perhaps the best known of his texts, and among Kierkegaardian catch-phrases, "the teleological suspension of the ethical" is second in currency only to the infamous "truth is subjectivity."[3] No doubt it has caused many to shudder. The book's "terrible pathos" comes from the wild and disturbing interpretation it gives to the biblical story of Abraham and Issac. How could God have uttered that terrible command, that Abraham's only son be sacrificed? And how could Abraham have assented? Through his mouthpiece, Johannes de Silentio, Kierkegaard seems to argue that, from a rational, ethical perspective, Abraham, the father of faith, must be judged a murderer—and so much the worse for ethics! Faith overrules the ethical prohibition against killing one's son. Obedience to God requires that all other considerations be fanatically suppressed—or so it seems. Faith is utterly absurd. It collides head-on with ethics and reason.

If this initial reading stood, one might shudder not just for Abraham but for reason, faith, and much else, as well. Happily, this first reading, though it has become a standard interpretation of Kierkegaard's position in *Fear and Trembling,* does not stand up. It focuses too fixedly and without sensitivity to context on the startling suggestions of irrationality. And it misses altogether a central story that Kierkegaard is at pains to tell.

I am persuaded that an absolute antithesis between faith and reason, or between ethics and faith, is not Kierkegaard's final word in *Fear and Trembling.* The possibility that Abraham is holy in God's eyes, though condemned by all ethics, is just that—not a final position, but a *possibility,* a teasing, ironic suggestion meant to "awaken us from our dogmatic slumbers." The Kierkegaardian notions of "the absurd" and the suspension of the ethical do not proclaim new dogmas but work as relativizing notions, dialectical weapons meant to break up old dogmas, to rattle the easy assumption that God's ways are those of any reasonable, commonsensical, respectable middle-class inhabitant of Danish Christendom. Surely a major burden of *Fear and Trembling* is to carry out a skeptical, ironical, relativizing attack on current assumptions. But this is not all the narrative contains. The bold, perverse Kierkegaardian penchant for paradox creates the unmistakable *impression* of a thorough-going irrationalism. But beneath this impression lies a positive and constructive—dare one say *reason-*

able?—exploration of human relationship: of separation and attachment, of love and resignation, of care and its display in grief, joy, and welcome. It is this central, neglected story, that I will follow here, letting the more notorious and debated issues unravel as we go. My strategy will be to let the abstractions, paradoxical or otherwise, fall into the framework provided by the underlying story of care and relationship. In a sense, this is Kierkegaard's—or Silentio's—own strategy. The abstract, philosophical question "Can there be a teleological suspension of the ethical?" is raised only *after* the largely neglected, dramatic section entitled "Preliminary Expectoration."[4] I will focus almost entirely on this early section, leaving the question of the "teleological suspension of ethics" for treatment elsewhere.

I

The Knight and his Princess.

In the overall scheme of *Fear and Trembling,* resignation is a transitional stage between lack of faith and faith, between shallow unbelievers and heroic men of faith. Characteristically, Kierkegaard mixes abstraction with dramatic portrayal. Occupying this transitional stage or sphere of existence is "the knight of infinite resignation." Although Silentio gives us several portraits of this knight, one of them is central and developed at length.

> A young swain falls in love with a princess, and the whole content of his life consists in this love, and yet the situation is such that it is impossible for it to be realized, impossible for it to be translated from ideality into reality. The slaves of paltriness, the frogs in life's swamp, will naturally cry out, "Such love is foolishness. The rich brewer's widow is a match fully as good and respectable." Let them croak in the swamp undisturbed. It is not so with the knight of infinite resignation, he does not give up his love, not for the glory of the world.[5]

Though caught up in an unhappy love, the young swain is not shaken by circumstance or opinion. Someone less noble, less knightly, would be swayed by the mediocre "slaves of paltriness"—mediocre and paltry because utterly blind to any real sense of commitment, integrity, or courage. If love for the princess is unrealistic, it should be given up and forgotten. There will be someone else to love soon enough. But the knight disregards such "reasonable" advice. Even though it cannot be "translated into reality," he nurtures his love. It is "the whole content of his life" (even if only an "ideal content").

The knight of resignation

> will have the power to concentrate the whole content of life and the whole significance of reality in one single wish. If a man lacks this concentration,

this intensity, if his soul is from the beginning dispersed in the multifarious,
he will never come to the point of making the movement (of resignation).[6]

The swain's life is concentrated in the "single wish" (or commitment) to
love his princess, come what may. To give up that love outright would be to
lose the defining, stabilizing center of self and world. All would be
shattered.

In Silentio's view, if one invests concern over a number of interests
without a unifying focus, one's integrity is dispersed and diluted. To be
unable to concentrate concern in a single wish (or commitment) implies,
for Silentio, that "emotional investments" will be cautious, tentative,
matters of prudential calculation. What fails here will be made up for
there. This "capitalist's approach" lets gain and loss, lets worth in relationship, be set by "market conditions," by judgments of the public at large.[7]
How escape this sad parody of personal rapport?

Silentio believes that interests must be *focused,* and around an appropriate object. The capitalist perhaps does concentrate his life around a single
commitment: the desire that his lifetime "personal assets" outweigh his
losses. Here one can only make a fundamental judgment of value. Can one
really base one's integrity on taking relationships as items of quantitative
value, their fluctuation in worth attentively observed and manipulated, like
shares on the stock exchange? Silentio mocks such would-be "errand
runners" of the spiritual.[8] The knight of resignation is no opportunist, no
speculator in paying relationships. He takes his love as ultimate.[9]

Another distinguishing feature of the knight of resignation is his courage. This appears strikingly in the "self-sufficiency" of his love (free from
dependent need), and in his independence of mind (unswayed by "what
others would think" about the "foolishness" of his love).[10] But courage
also appears in his refusal to be self-deceived about the absence of any
realistic possibility for his love. He is completely candid with himself. He
does not run from the pain of losing the princess, or pretend that after all
perhaps he didn't love her, or that the impossible can somehow be gotten
around.

Thus far I have tried to distinguish the knight of resignation from the
common crowd, from the "slaves of paltriness." Unlike the crowd, the
knight has commitment, integrity, and courage. He is further than others
along the path from superficiality toward faith. But what accounts for the
title he earns? Why is he a knight of *resignation?*

Silentio speaks of the "movement of resignation" abstractly as "renouncing the finite," "gaining an eternal consciousness," and "transform-
ing temporal love into an eternal one."[11] For those unfamiliar with
Kierkegaard's style (or just suspicious of jargon), it will seem forbidding to
talk of "the finite," "eternal love," or "eternal consciousness." To get by

the opacity of such terminology, we might remind ourselves of Kierkegaard's—and Silentio's—broadest objectives, for there is more here than a tangle of empty rhetoric.

Finite/Infinite, Temporal/Eternal.

Kierkegaard's interest is not in physicalistic descriptions of Nature, but in personal, existential perspectives—perspectives that articulate moral, aesthetic, and spiritual meanings that can animate or inform a human life. Terms such as "the eternal" or "the infinite" shape and energize such interpretative outlooks, evaluative positions, centers from which we meet the world in action and understanding.

To get at the makeup of the physical universe, a scientist (and often a philosopher) discounts personal standpoints, so far as possible, but to understand an existential stance, the opposite is required. However widely it may be shared, such a perspective reflects a particular way things seem to an individual at a particular time in that individual's development; and that personally "owned" position will itself be located within the larger historical time of community and culture. The personal, existential specificity of such a perspective is not a defect but of its essence. Thus, insofar as it figures in an existential perspective, a concept like "the eternal" cannot be defined free from a context of practical, personal concern. It will be part of a complex web of imagery and interpretation. And in working to "get inside" that perspective, we should not expect an inappropriate precision. Rather than a knack for inventing definitions and testing their fit, we need sympathetic, imaginative responsiveness to the way meanings open up and resonate within experience.

"Eternal consciousness" suggests an experiential standpoint that lies in polar contrast to the standpoint of "temporal consciousness." What would it be like to be caught up entirely in the hourly whirl of things, imprisoned by the press of time, never gaining a vantage point outside of, and looking over, the frantic temporal flux? For the knight of resignation, to gain an "eternal consciousness" would be to gain access to such a vantage point, to gain some freedom from the constricting push and pull of the many petty things that shape the ordinary flow of time. "Finite" and "infinite" are a similar pair of polar contrasts. To be enmeshed in the finite would be to have attachments only to particular, finite things, never responding to ideals that overarch particulars, or to totalities (such as the world itself) from which particulars separate out or emerge, or to "things" like the soul or God, which Hegel had identified as "infinite objects." For the knight of resignation, then, to make "the movement of infinity" would be to gain some freedom from the push and pull of petty, senseless things, gain some access to totalities, ideals, or "things" like God.

Renouncing the Finite.

Because the knight's tie to the princess is the unifying focus of his identity, her loss reverberates throughout his experience. It seems that "all is lost," and that he "has no self" (even though from an "objective" position much might seem to remain). Self, relationship, and world are torn asunder, stripped of meaning and reality. However, the swain is no ordinary man. He is a person of exceptional strength and courage, in fact a *knight.* Because of his exceptional resources, the loss of the finite turns out not to be shattering through and through. Something is rescued—though not real rapport with the princess.

The knight renounces the self, relationship, and world constituted by his tie to the princess, and in that movement gains an infinite or eternal self, relationship, and world. In renouncing the princess, or by virtue of that act, the knight discovers (or generates) a new perspective—one that is *not* focused by concern for a single, finite individual. This new perspective places the knight outside the push and pull of petty things; and the "objects" this perspective takes are beyond the finite and temporal, too. This new outlook represents the possibility of surviving the crushing loss of the princess, the possibility of a point of leverage from which the old way of experiencing can be abandoned, and its loss felt as only partial—not the utter loss of point of view itself. This new-found perspective Silentio calls an "eternal consciousness." In it, the knight of infinite resignation finds "peace, rest, and comfort in sorrow."[12]

Hardening oneself to sorrow by renouncing particular intense relationships seems to resemble the stoic reaction to a world of pain and trouble. One seeks immunity from the disturbance of disappointment, anger, and guilt. By withdrawing care, the self shields itself from injury or affliction. By renouncing the finite, its power to provoke passional reaction is defeated. But unlike the stoic who extirpates his love, the knight of resignation transforms it. Its new object is "the eternal being," and a shadow of concern remains as a sorrowful glance at the finite.[13] God, for the knight, is not just an ideal of freedom from attachment and reactive emotion. God is love, a love "totally incommensurate with the finite."[14]

Through resignation, a threefold transfiguration of existence is won. Transfigured first is the tie between the knight and his princess: an earthly, finite love becomes an idealized, eternal love. Then, the object of love is transfigured: a love of the princess becomes a love of God. And finally, the lover himself becomes transfigured: his integrity now is based not on a finite tie to another, but on his "eternal consciousness," on his grasp of a point of leverage on the finite.

Resignation vs. Faith.

The knight of resignation's achievement should not be underrated. He has made an advance on the "slaves of paltriness," the burghers, bishops, or thinkers who take faith to be easily won, something naturally acquired by dint of one's parentage, say, or place of birth. He knows real commitment and real loss. He has moved from the crowd of onlookers and donned the garb of spiritual battle. He knows independence, and does not "find the law for his action in others."[15] Even greater, however, is the knight of faith's achievement.

Resignation, we recall, is but a halfway house, not a destination. The next stage of development is faith. Silentio only partially endorses the moves of resignation, for something is surely wrong with wholesale renunciation of the finite. The knight of faith corrects this defect. The knight of faith renounces the finite, as his predecessor did. But in addition, strange to say, he wins it *back* again.[16] He gains an eternal love, but *temporal* loves are his as well. He is at home in the eternal, but happy also in the midst of the world.

In the last part of this essay, I will consider Abraham, who will be Silentio's central case of the knight of faith. For the moment, we will attend to another knight. In the "Expectoration," Silentio imagines a comic encounter with a knight of faith hardly resembling Abraham at all—or so it seems, for this unassuming gentleman looks for all the world like a tax collector.

> Here he is. Acquaintance made, I am introduced to him. The moment I set eyes on him, I instantly push him from me, I leap backward, I clasp my hands and say half-aloud, "Good Lord, is this the man? Is it really he? Why, he looks like a tax-collector!" However it is the man after all. I draw closer to him, watching his least movements to see whether there might not be visible a little heterogeneous fractional telegraphic message from the infinite, a glance, a smile, a gesture, a note of sadness which betrayed the infinite in its hetergeneity with the finite. No! I examine his figure from tip to toe to see if there might not be a cranny through which the infinite was peeping. No! He is solid through and through.[17]

Being at home in the finite, the knight of faith looks ordinary. There is no betrayal of "the infinite," of a soul withdrawn or distanced. Appearances notwithstanding, Silentio is sure it is a knight of faith he encounters.[18]

> [He] belongs entirely to the world, no Philistine more so. One can discover nothing of that aloof and superior nature whereby one recognizes the knight of the infinite. He takes delight in everything, and whenever one sees him taking part in a particular pleasure, he does it with the persistence which is the mark of the earthly man whose soul is absorbed in such things. . . . *if one did not know him,* it would be impossible to distinguish him from the rest of the congregation.[19]

His delight in earthly things, his joy, is the token of his having welcomed the finite. But how is this man distinguished from a similarly ordinary man who has never undertaken the difficult movement of resignation?

In a passage that, when set against the pathos of Abraham's trial, can be taken only as comic relief, Silentio provides this knight of faith a delightfully banal test.

> Toward evening he walks home, his gait is as indefatigable as that of the postman. On his way he reflects that his wife has surely a special little warm dish prepared for him, e.g., a calf's head roasted, garnished with vegetables. . . . As it happens, he hasn't four pence to his name, and yet he firmly believes that his wife has that dainty dish for him . . . . His wife hasn't it—strangely enough, it is quite the same to him.[20]

His delightful anticipation of his meal is the sign of his harmony with the finite. The fact that he cannot be unsettled or disappointed should his dish "be impossible" (as the swain's love was impossible) is the sign that he has renounced his claim to the finite. He cannot be embarrassed or thrown off stride by the world's unfolding this way rather than that. He welcomes, and is ready to welcome, all. He is unperturbed by change, yet he has in no way diminished his care for even the least particularity of his existence. Abstractly, Silentio characterizes his condition in this way:

> this man has made, and every instant is making, movements of infinity. With infinite resignation he has drained the cup of life's profound sadness, he knows the bliss of the infinite, he senses the pain of renouncing everything, the dearest things he possesses in the world, and yet finiteness tastes to him just as good as to one who never knew anything higher. . . . he has this sense of security in enjoying it, as though the finite life were the surest thing of all. And yet, the whole earthly form he exhibits is a new creation by virtue of the absurd.[21]

Both the knight of resignation and the knight of faith make "movements of infinity," gain an "eternal consciousness" that inures them to change. It would not hurt the young swain, Silentio reflects, to learn that his beloved has married another.[22] But by the same token, Silentio admits, he would be embarrassed were love to become possible—he has written her off, temporally speaking.[23] However it is precisely in this respect that the swain lacks faith. For in addition to the "movement of infinity," the knight of faith can make the move back into the world, finding the taste of the finite good. Unlike the man of resignation, he would be ready to accept the beloved's return. He has not sealed himself off from the possibility of joy. He knows more than resignation, withdrawal, and grief. In *this* respect, he has advanced.

II

Silentio is frankly baffled by the knight of faith. The knight of resignation he can understand, but not the man of faith.[24] How can one renounce finite life, yet embrace it in joy? With his flair for the dramatic, he speaks of faith as a capacity for the impossible, as achieving its goal "by virtue of the absurd." The knight of faith gets back the finite because he believes that "with God, all things are possible by virtue of the absurd."[25]

Silentio has no interest in clearing up this tangle of paradox. He relishes it. What a delicious affront to those "reasonable men" who think the path to faith is wide, well-marked, and smoothly paved—no doubt traversable in a day! But although we may now understand at least one reason why Silentio speaks in this way, we do not need to settle for such a thin rationale. I will try now to spell out some specific complexities of faith that lead to Silentio's paradoxical expressions. In so doing, I in no way wish to dilute Silentio's claim that faith is stunningly difficult to achieve. I begin with a contrast between types of concern.

Proprietary Claim and Selfless Concern.

If we have cared for a fine old watch and suddenly it is stolen, we feel not only sorrow but anger. Our care for the watch will be linked, in a typical case, with proprietary rights. With a deepening of care goes a deepening of possessiveness—and a deepened capacity for hurt, should our possession-related rights be violated. One way to cancel this capacity for hurt is to renounce our proprietary claims. If we disown our possessions, we may be saddened if they are lost or taken but we will at least be spared the added pain of knowing that our rights have been violated.

Much of the stoic hardening of the self to disappointment and change can be interpreted as a narrowing of the area of proprietary claim. Thoreau remarks that a man is rich in proportion to that which he is willing to give up. Giving something up, we cannot be hurt by its being taken away. Silentio speaks of the knight of resignation "waiving claim" to the finite, "renouncing the claim to everything," and "infinitely renouncing claim to the love which is the content of his life."[26] Renouncing all claim to the princess, he saves himself from hurt should she marry another, and from hurt coming from the finite generally. But the fact that the swain would find the return of the princess an embarrassment indicates that the price he has paid for diminished hurt is a narrowing of care.[27] He would be embarrassed by her return because in some sense he has ceased to care: "he no longer takes a finite interest in what the princess is doing."[28]

But not all cases of care are tied up with proprietary claims. I may enjoy and warmly anticipate the appearance of a sparrow at my feeder. Yet I would claim no rights over this object of my care. The matter of its life and death is something over which I waive all claims. Of course, I would feel indignant were someone maliciously to injure it. But in the course of things, the sparrow will go its way and I will adjust myself to its goings and comings. A concern that forgoes proprietary claim one could call selfless.[29]

It would be a concern entirely distinct from the assertion of rights—unless one wanted to speak of the right of the object cared for to its own independence. My joy at the return of the sparrow need be no less for my lacking proprietary claim over it; and my care need be no less for my lacking bitterness or indignation, should it be lost forever.

This distinction between kinds of concern partially clears up the confusing claim that the knight of faith renounces the finite and yet is simultaneously at home in the finite. The knight of faith can both renounce and enjoy the finite because he sees, or knows in his bones, that renouncing all *claim* to the finite is not renouncing all *care* for it. He is at home and takes delight in the finite (witness the tax-collector) because he cares; yet this is a selfless care, for he has given up all proprietary claim. The knight of resignation, on the other hand, cannot distinguish, or blurs together, these two sorts of concern. The swain's care for the princess is diminished as he renounces claim. Hence it seems impossible to him that one might renounce all claim and yet care.

I would like to use this distinction between renouncing claim and renouncing all care to clarify the respect in which, through faith, one could hope to get the princess back. Then I will try to provide a rationale for Silentio's invocation of "the absurd."

Receptivity and Return.

The knight of faith retains an openness to joy and the possibility of love that the knight of resignation sorely lacks. In a way that combines admiration and self-pity, the knight of resignation reflects on the man of faith:

> By my own strength I am able to give up the princess, and I shall not become a grumbler, but shall find joy and repose in my pain; but by my own strength I am not able to get her again, for I am employing all my strength to be resigned. But by faith, says that marvelous knight, by faith, I shall get her by virtue of the absurd.[30]

Having renounced all claim to the princess (but not all care for her), the man of faith is ready to welcome her back. He has the strength, courage, or faith to say, "I shall get her by virtue of the absurd," but he cannot force or coerce her return. By an open readiness to receive her, buttressed by the faith that he will get her back, he can welcome her, if she is given. The knight of resignation, using all his strength for renunciation, lacks faith that love is still possible. He blurs his renunciation. Care as well as claim is renounced, leaving him in no position to receive the princess, were she to be given.

The knight of faith gets the princess back, then, only in the sense that he guarantees that the ultimate obstacle to her return—lack of receptivity—will be absent. He does not by his own strength effect her return, but he provides the condition for her return. The rest is up to God. She will not be returned to his keeping unless he is ready in welcome. He does not believe that the impossible can be gotten around by his efforts, but neither does he believe that what is impossible for him is impossible for God. If he gets the princess (which he has faith that he will), it will be through God—and through his own receptivity to the possibility of her return. In Silentio's view each man gets, spiritually speaking, exactly what he deserves.[31] Therefore he has confidence that once the man of faith has put himself in complete readiness for the princess, she cannot but be given; the knight, having placed himself in the position of selfless love, will reap his reward.

The Absurd.

Silentio says that the knight of faith believes he will get the beloved "by virtue of the absurd." One reason for this phrase is polemical. It works to counterbalance an easy rationalistic optimism, the idea that by calculation of benefits and burdens one can arrive at the decision to opt for faith; the idea that reality can be captured without remainder by some essentially simple conceptual scheme, with no dark spots before which reason must confess its ignorance; the idea that faith is an early, childish stage in the grand, inevitable development of human rationality, which is now, from our present exalted position, easily understood. But there are at least two other considerations, apart from this polemical purpose, which underlie Silentio's talk of the absurd.

As someone placed this side of faith and at most a man of resignation, Silentio is unable to make the discriminations open to the man of faith.[32] The knight of faith could *reject* the idea that "by virtue of the absurd" he will get the princess. To the narrator, the knight *appears* to believe this because, as we have seen above, he cannot discriminate giving up claim to the princess from giving up care for her. He thus believes (falsely) that the knight of faith has given up all care (in his renunciation) and yet *has* care (in his faith). An absurdity indeed!

Secondly, there is Silentio's sense that the knight of faith is involved in some sort of logical contradiction. This knight believes that "with God all things are possible"—that is, he has hope that the princess might be returned. Yet, having passed through the stage of resignation, he also has a clear-headed recognition that the princess is lost. Faith does the impossible, says Silentio. It believes both that the princess is lost (a belief that separates the knight of resignation from those not yet resigned) and that she will be returned (a belief that separates the knight of faith from the knight of resignation). One interpretative option is to accept Silentio's characterization, to assume that faith just *can* embrace such absurdity. However, a more helpful reconstruction is possible. What appears to be a contradiction in beliefs can be understood as part of a complex test of care.

Within the context in which Silentio is working—the context of faith—
these opposing beliefs do not simply cancel each other out. A surface
absurdity remains: love is and is not possible; the princess will and will not
be returned. But a kind of deep structure can be opened up that eases the
offense, for these beliefs function crucially as separate measures of care:
care is taken as a person's capacity first, for dread and grief, and then, for
delight and joy. Faith must be tested and authenticated in two apparently
opposed directions at once. "Absurdly," the knight of faith confronts both
tests at once, for grief and joy, dread and delight, are coequal measures of
care and faith.

The belief that love is impossible (or that the princess is lost) measures a
capacity to acknowledge real loss, without which one's care would be
exposed as shallow and weak. The capacity to feel deep loss—to care—is
authenticated when the swain *does* face the loss of his princess, rather than
flee or evade the fact.

The belief that love is possible (or that the princess will be returned)
measures a contrasting dimension of care. Here, care is sounded out in
terms of a capacity for joyful welcome of what may be given: a capacity to
acknowledge the blessings of existence, appearing wonderously, without
warning or rationale. An inability to rejoice spontaneously at what gifts
time may bring marks a cramped and guarded care. Denying the possibility
of joy (through bitterness, resignation, or "common sense") can deplete
and poison care. The capacity to remain open to joy—to care—would be
authenticated insofar as the swain, moving beyond resignation, could
believe he might get the princess back. This is not a matter of rejoicing
when grief is called for, but of remaining open to the possibility that
occasions for joy have not been utterly erased, even in the moment of
grief.

The "slaves of paltriness" fail the test of care-as-capacity-for-grief by
refusing to acknowledge that a person could feel the sort of deep loss felt
by the swain. But these shallow unbelievers also fail the test of care-as-
capacity-for-joy. Silentio showers contempt on such bland optimism and
fear of sorrow, contrasting it to the real hope and joy, resignation and
grief, of the knight of faith. His is not

> the lukewarm indolence which thinks, "there is surely no instant need, it is
> not worth sorrowing before the time," [or] the pitiful hope which says, "One
> cannot know what is going to happen . . . it might possibly be after all"—
> these caricatures of faith are part and parcel of life's wretchedness, and the
> infinite resignation has already consigned them to infinite contempt.[33]

The knight of faith's beliefs, as tokens of his condition, are distinguished by
their intensity and depth. Having passed the test of care as grief, he moves
beyond resignation toward faith by facing the test of care as joy.

Silentio recognizes that the requirement that one's capacity for joy and grief be authenticated simultaneously may result in the *appearance* of a person capable of neither—the capacity for one, as it were, undermining at that moment the capacity for the other. As he puts it,

> Those . . . who carry the jewel of faith are likely to be delusive, because their outward appearance bears a striking resemblance to that which both the infinite resignation and faith profoundly despise . . . to Philistinism.[34]

But faith accepts this risk—that it be mistaken for Philistinism.

The "absurdity" that entangles the knight of faith—the notion that his capacity for grief and his capacity for joy can be simultaneously tested—exemplifies a more general point concerning "logic" and "emotion." Authenticity may not just permit but may *require* that we acknowledge the simultaneous presence of "contradictory" emotions. Thus one can feel both love and hate toward a demanding master, both disappointment and delight at the failure of a colleague, both anger and happy relief at a snub. Whatever the outcome of a purely logical analysis of these cases (perhaps the air of contradiction is without substance), no one would deny that seemingly incompatible feelings are all too often "illogically" intertwined, and that personal integrity can be quickly undercut by a refusal to acknowledge the full complexity and ambivalence of one's emotions.

It is characteristic not only of specifically religious faith but also of the faith that attends any radical growth or change of self that care be plumbed in both directions. It will be tested both as grief and joy, both as dread of what is about to be painfully lost and as full welcome of the new and uncertain, about to be received. It is characteristic of faith and care that these emotions be mixed and acknowledged as mixed; and that the temptation, in the interest of simplicity or logic, to deny one or another emotion in this tensed ambivalence, be resisted.

III

I have tried to suggest a rationale for the often wildly obscure characterizations Silentio gives of faith. There is the obvious factor of polemical exaggeration and dramatics. Also, there is the fact that from the standpoint of resignation, the contrast between renunciation of claim and renunciation of care will collapse, resulting in the appearance of absurdity: it will appear that the knight of faith cares, and yet has given up all his care. And without care, how can the knight hope to have the princess returned? Finally, there is the fact that from a logical standpoint, the knight of faith appears to hold contradictory beliefs: for example, that he both will and will not have the princess returned. Silentio says the knight of faith believes that "with God, all things are possible." And one might suppose that this meant that God could both return and not return the princess. But our reconstruction took a different tack. The capacity of faith is not the capacity to believe God capable of two mutually exclusive actions, nor the capacity of a person to believe two incompatible propositions, where "believe" means something like "believe that under objective conditions both might be tested and found true." Rather, faith concerns a capacity for care, and the apparently contradictory beliefs were seen to function as measures of grief and dread, of joy and delight, thus authenticating two crucial and apparently opposed dimensions of care.

Our analytical work now accomplished, we can return to the central drama of *Fear and Trembling,* Abraham's trial. At the risk of repetition, it will be worth gathering our insights. We should now be ready to hear that story in a new and compelling way.

Abraham: Dread and Joy.

Abraham's world has revolved not around a princess but around Isaac and God. Now he learns that his relationship with Isaac (and God) will be tried. He must visibly and dramatically reenact, as it were, the "movements" of resignation and faith. His willingness to sacrifice Isaac betokens his renunciation of all claim to Isaac. Yet that sacrifice is predicated on his unceasing love, which is a sign that he has not lost care for the finite.[35] And by faith, he believes that he will get Isaac back "by virtue of the absurd."

The task set for the Knight of Faith is this:

> to live happily and joyfully, every instant to see the sword hanging over the head of the beloved, yet not to find repose in the pain of resignation, but joy.[36]

However, Abraham does not just *see* the sword hanging over the beloved. He is asked to wield it. Hence his sense of doom is intense, and his capacity for joy, made obscure. From the standpoint of faith, the pain of renunciation concerns the loss of the proprietary claim. Giving up the claim means giving up the sense that one has rights over the matter of Isaac's life and death. That will be a difficult renunciation. To Silentio, and perhaps even to Abraham, it will seem dangerously close to losing Isaac outright. Yet Abraham has faith that Isaac will not be lost. His willingness to sacrifice Isaac shows in the most dramatic way imaginable his severing of the possessive tie. Yet in that severing, a selfless care is renewed and released. His greatness is "a two-edged sword which slays and saves."[37]

The complexity of Silentio's position on the relationship between ethics and faith demands a fuller treatment than I can offer here. But I should note that although Silentio tries us with the dizzying, dissociative view that Abraham is murderous, he also gives us ample evidence that what we confront is not murder but sacrifice. Even in the "Expectoration," which does not really explore the issue, Silentio says that if someone did not love

Isaac as Abraham did, then "every thought of offering Isaac would not be a trial, but a temptation," and that such love is "the presumption apart from which the whole thing becomes a crime."[38] In addition, the purpose of murder, ordinarily, is to get rid of someone. Yet Abraham is ready to welcome Isaac back joyously at every moment of his trial.[39] Never does he relax his love or care.

A ritual such as sacrifice is an outward expression for an inward *act:* in this case, undoing possessiveness. Renunciation of possessiveness is more than the self-pitying sense that one is a passive *observer* or *victim* of pain. Abraham cannot chalk up his loss—if it occurs—to some cosmic necessity or tragic fate. He does not just live through that suffering, as he would had God just snatched his son away.

Silentio believes that this aspect of the story is overlooked by his contemporaries. By remembering only that Isaac was returned, the difficulty of sacrifice is brushed aside. Therefore Silentio resolves to force it into view.

> If I were to talk about him, I would first depict the pain of his trial. To that end, I would suck all the dread and distress and torture out of a father's sufferings, so that I might describe what Abraham suffered, while nevertheless he believed.[40]

As we read on, Abraham's joy goes unmentioned. But this emphasis exclusively on pain must be viewed as a polemical corrective, for faith involves not "repose in the pain of resignation" but "living happily and joyfully." Abraham cannot be *that* different from the tax collector. He must take delight in the finite.

What could be meant by Abraham's joy? His unceasing love of Isaac betokens a joy in Isaac's existence, and derivatively, in existence generally. In addition, he does not succumb to hatred or resentment of God or life. The paths of suicide or despair are not his.[41] We must suppose that joy is present inwardly, interwoven with fear and trembling, as a correlate of his capacity to affirm existence through and through, while willingly and without reservation acknowledging the inexpungable facts of parting and loss. But the capacity for joy—however tacit—is buttressed by his belief that Isaac will be returned—not in another life but in this one.[42] This belief is both an expression of his joy and its presupposition. The copresence of dread and joy, grief and delight, is the other side of the paradoxical belief that Isaac both will and will not be lost.

Once, in the prelude to *Fear and Trembling,* Silentio imagined Abraham getting Isaac back, but being so embittered by God's request that he was thereafter unable to care—so in a sense (at least in *that* version of the story) *not* getting back his son.[43] But in the central version, Abraham's unceasing love of both God and Isaac makes Isaac's return both full and fulfilling.

Abraham does not effect his son's return, but he ensures that there is no inner obstacle to his son's full welcome—should he be given. He ensures that his care is unbroken.

Silentio has failed to sort renunciation of claim from renunciation of care, and so cannot understand the sense in which Abraham might believe that "with God, all things are possible." For him, the phrase either signals the shabby optimism of a confused and pitiful hope, or shows that "by virtue of the absurd," God can return Isaac to Abraham's care, even though Abraham has severed all care. But stepping back, we see that Abraham merits Isaac's return by maintaining a selfless love, by sustaining his care even through the dreadful threat of its loss in the act of renouncing the proprietary claim, and in the crisis of ambivalence, of joy and grief, that attends all fundamental change. His openness, his receptivity to the possibility of return even as he gives up all rights in the matter, substantiates his faith and makes fitting his reward.[44]

> Here an eternal divine order prevails, here it does not rain both upon the just and upon the unjust, here the sun does not shine both upon the good and upon the evil, here it holds good that only he who works gets the bread, only he who was in anguish finds repose, only he who descends into the underworld rescues the beloved, only he who draws the knife gets Isaac.[45]

I have tried to give a reading of the first parts of *Fear and Trembling* faithful to the spirit and detail of the text. If I have succeeded, the widespread view of Kierkegaard as an arch irrationalist will seem shallow and naïve beside Kierkegaard's own self-characterization as a needed corrective for the age. Also, I trust we will have gained renewed respect for Kierkegaard's grasp of the subtle fine-structure of care and attachment, of grief, love, and selflessness, of courage, risk, and change of self—venerable philosophical concerns as old as the pursuit of wisdom itself, however frequently we find them cast aside.

7. Kierkegaard's Problem I and Problem II: An Analytic Perspective

JOHN DONNELLY

But . . .when I have to think of Abraham, I am as though annihilated. I catch sight every moment of that enormous paradox which is the substance of Abraham's life, every moment I am repelled, and my thought in spite of all its passion cannot set a hairs-breadth further. I strain every muscle to get a view of it—that very instant I am paralyzed.[1]

I

BY KIERKEGAARD'S OWN ADMISSION FEAR AND TREMBLING WAS ONE OF HIS "most perfect books," sufficient in itself "for an imperishable name as an author," and yet the prevalent view among Kierkegaardian commentators would suggest that such a boast was misplaced when interpreted as claiming *Fear and Trembling* to be a high-grade example of philosophical writing, although perhaps true if interpreted to mean that it is an excellent (notorious) example of the existential style of "doing" philosophy.

The received opinion further contends that the discussion of the "teleological suspension of the ethical" in *Fear and Trembling* is more suitably consigned to crisis theology at best or irrationalism at worst than to serious philosophical investigation. George Schrader writes:

> In *Fear and Trembling*, Kierkegaard makes the trenchant point that . . . insofar as a person is ever called upon to act as an individual, he stands outside the ethical sphere, and thus can find no justification for his action. If ethical justification is equated with rational justification, then the action of the individual *qua* individual must presumably go without any justification whatever.[2]

Brand Blanshard also has adopted a decidedly negative attitude toward Kierkegaard as a potential moralist.[3] In summary, he finds the events described in *Fear and Trembling* "pointless absolutely." Blanshard argues that any nonpurposeful act is irrational and that a nonpurposeful act is just a nonteleological one, so that all nonteleological acts are irrational. Inasmuch as Abraham's intended act of slaying Isaac is described by Blanshard (but not by Kierkegaard) as nonteleological, the verdict of Blanshard is a ready one of moral nihilism.

> In the end Kierkegaard stands, in his thoughts as in his life, a defeated figure. He was like a business man who builds up a commercial empire by condemning and buying up the businesses of all his competitors on the strength of promissory notes which he cannot redeem. He indicts reason; he indicts rational ethics. . . . He invites them all to accept subordination to one

directing hand in return for grandiose, even infinite promises. But, when they present their claims, they find the bank empty. . . . Just how reason is to be rectified or ethics reformed . . . these all important directions never transpire. Faith has leaped so high that it has shot up . . . to where thought and conscience can no longer breathe. These may be poor things, but we know them, and know that they have served us not badly. We shall do well to keep them, even when notes are flourished before us that are stamped in infinite denominations, unless we can be sure that the issuing bank is solvent. That assurance Kierkegaard never supplies.[4]

No doubt if Blanshard's accusation of "moral nihilism" is supportable, then the problematic of the knight of faith in *Fear and Trembling* is more aptly described as the "dysteleological suspension of the ethical." However, this is clearly the point at issue, and Blanshard's failure to establish that point ought not deter philosophers from a literal interpretation of Kierkegaard's expression "teleological suspension of the ethical."[5] Ironically enough, Blanshard approves ("the reconciliation with our moral sense") of Jephthah's vow to offer as a sacrifice the first person he met upon successful return from battle, namely, his daughter! Approval is also afforded Agamemnon's slaying of Iphigenia to appease the wrath of Artemis (could not Abraham be appeasing the wrath of Jehovah?) as well as Brutus' handling of his conciliar duties. Moreover, something is surely remiss about Blanshard's initial assumption (that any nonpurposeful act is irrational) because a person can perform quite un-Cartesianly many acts unaware, that are not thereby irrational. Lastly, the *paradox* of it all is that those who most lambast Kierkegaard's alleged irrationalism oftentimes prove more passionately illogical than the adjudged Kierkegaard (on the received view). Blanshard writes:

> *Ad Hominem* reasoning, besides being distasteful, is never conclusive and is often self-defeating. . . . His [Kierkegaard's] alternations of exaltation and depression, his temptations to suicide, the feverish activity of an over-pressed brain in darkened rooms, the hysterical-sounding claims to being "a genius in a market-town," and his comparison of himself to Christ, the frantic excoriations of church and clergy in his later years, his own report that he had stood on the verge of insanity—it would be a mistake to pass over these things as if they were wholly irrelevant. They suggest . . . that Kierkegaard's singularities of thought were less the product of judicial reflection than the by-product of a sick spirit![6]

II

However, after a number of readings of *Fear and Trembling,* it still occurs to me that a more positive philosophical case can be established against such dismissals, which both the critics and perhaps even Kierkegaard himself might have refused to consider or just failed to realize. That is, I believe that "the teleological suspension of the ethical" raised issues that are of interest to the philosopher, issues that merit something better than simply being assigned to "crisis theology." My motivation is then to provide, not an intrinsically interesting, exegetical exercise in the history of ideas, but rather an attempt to restore some semblance of consistency and coherence to a work of literature generally considered philosphically unrespectable. Accordingly, I would suggest that the analytic philosopher take seriously Kierkegaard's invitation to investigate

> . . . whether in this story there is to be found any higher expression for the ethical such as would ethically explain his conduct, ethically justify him in suspending the ethical obligation toward his son, without in this search going beyond the teleology of the ethical.[7]

> For I should very much like to know how one would bring Abraham's act into relation with the universal, and whether it is possible to discover any connection whatever between what Abraham did and the universal.[8]

It is important to keep in mind that the description of the knight of faith in *Fear and Trembling* transcends the Abraham problematic. Any professed Christian is called upon to be a knight of faith. Kierkegaard is clear on this matter in his *Journals and Papers* #6791, when he writes:

> There was once a man who as a child had learned the story of Abraham, and as usual, knew his lesson brilliantly, inside and out.

> The years went by, and as happens to much of what is learned in childhood, so also here, he found no use for it—and it faded into oblivion.

> In the meantime his life underwent a change; he had severe trials and was involved in a singular conflict that all at once or with one blow placed his life in abeyance, and just that alone gave him plenty to think about.

> This preoccupied him from morning until night, awake and in his dreams, and he became old before his time.

> Fifteen years went by. Then one morning as he woke up the thought suddenly struck him: What you are experiencing is similar to the story of Abraham.

In *Fear and Trembling* Kierkegaard relates the biblical story of Abraham and poses the question whether there can be any ethical justification for Abraham's conduct and, in particular, whether there can be any moral explanation for the intended action of killing his own son, Isaac, out of obedience to a divine command. Such a probing involves the famous "teleological suspension of the ethical," a phrase that seemingly indicates, if affirmed, that any justification of Abraham's conduct, if not blatantly immoral, is clearly amoral, and a defense of a distinctly religious sort:

> Faith is precisely this paradox, that the individual as the particular is higher
> than the universal, is justified over against it, is not subordinate but supe-
> rior—yet in such a way be it observed, that it is the particular individual who,
> after he has been subordinated as the particular to the universal, now
> through the universal becomes the individual who as the particular is superior
> to the universal, for the fact that the individual as the particular stands in an
> absolute relation to the absolute. This position cannot be mediated, for all
> mediation comes about precisely by virtue of the universal; it is and remains
> to all eternity a paradox, inaccessible to thought.[9]

Critics, potential sympathizers, and apparently Kierkegaard himself agree on at least one thing, that at best one may provide a religious justification for Abraham's conduct, whereas any ethical, rational, or philosophical explanation or justification of that conduct is out of the question. (Blanshard even speaks of the "dysteleological" suspension of the ethical!) Much as the mother qua Christian Scientist who allows her only child to die of first-degree burns for lack of readily available proper medical treatment can be said to have a religious explanation for her action, albeit not a moral one, so too it is argued that this is the best that can be said for Abraham's plight qua knight of faith. Indeed, it might be said that Abraham's justification is the less satisfactory of the two, for the mother can justify her conduct by recourse to the religious institution of Christian Science, whereas Abraham qua knight of faith plays a noninstitu-tional role in life and thus forfeits such a defense.

I wish to suggest, however, that these critics, potential sympathizers, and possibly Kierkegaard himself have failed to realize that a plausible defense can be mounted for Abraham qua knight of faith, a defense that is not just of a religious sort but is, rather, distinctly moral, rational, and philosophi-cal in character. In the light of the quotation from *Fear and Trembling* cited above, I suggest that

(1) one can affirm with Kierkegaard that "the individual as the particular is higher than the universal," where *universal* here connotes our
conventional socioethical standards; yet,

(2) also claim with Kierkegaard that "through the universal becomes the
individual who as the particular is superior to the universal," where
the former use of the term "universal" connotes that which is
distinctly moral, and the latter use connotes our conventional socioethical standards, as in (1); so that

(3) one can affirm with Kierkegaard that "the individual . . . stands in
an absolute relation to the absolute," wherein a unique relationship
is established between the knight of faith and his God, a relationship
that is either within the moral sphere or at least consistent with it;
but

(4) one can deny Kierkegaard's assertion that "this position [i.e.,
knighthood of faith] cannot be mediated," in that I can mount a

moral, rational, and philosophical defense for the knight of faith; so
that

(5) I can also deny that the conduct of Abraham is "a paradox inacces-
sible to thought."

To begin our investigation into the complexities of Abraham's plight in
Fear and Trembling, I suggest that we consider the "classic" article by an
analytic philosopher on the subject of the "teleological suspension of the
ethical." James Bogen takes seriously the possibility of finding a philosophical analysis of Abraham's conduct that will allow us to grant him a
moral justification, so that there never would be a "teleological suspension
of the ethical." That is, Bogen seeks to determine whether the philosopher
cannot assign a negative answer to Kierkegaard's "Problem I: Is there such
a thing as a teleological suspension of the ethical?" while granting an
affirmative answer to Kierkegaard's "Problem II: Is there such a thing as
an absolute duty to God?" Bogen's investigation yields the conclusion that
there can be no moral defense of Abraham's conduct, and that there was,
therefore, a "teleological suspension of the ethical" involved in *Fear and
Trembling.* Bogen answers Problem I in the affirmative and Problem II in
the negative. I wish to compliment Bogen on his initial resolve but to
disagree with his conclusions. That is, I wish to claim that we can answer
Problem I in the negative, and Problem II in the affirmative.

I have not overlooked "Problem III" in *Fear and Trembling:* "Was
Abraham ethically defensible in keeping silent about his purpose before
Sarah, before Eleazar, before Isaac?" However, if I can sustain my
position on Problems I and II, then Problem III seems not to be a serious
one, admitting as it would of a yes answer.

III

James Bogen proposes the thesis that Kierkegaard regarded morality as
a system of duties ("Throughout his discussion of Abraham, Kierkegaard
speaks as though morality were a system of duties"),[10] such that one's
moral duties are tied to the position, office, role, or station (i.e., these
terms are used as intensional equivalents herein) one plays in life (". . .
statements of the form 'Y has a duty to do X' can be verified by appeal to
nothing else but the position of the agent").[11] In his article, Bogen presents
us with no formal argument per se; however, to show that this is what duty
consists of in *Fear and Trembling,* we might faithfully argue his case as
follows:

(1) If X is a duty of moral agent A, then X is derivable from position(s)
P_1 v P_2 v P_n that A occupies in life.

(2) It is not the case that X is derivable from either P_1 v P_2 v P_n which A
occupies in life.

(3) Therefore, it is not the case that X is a duty of A.

Applying this line of ratiocination to Abraham's situation in *Fear and Trembling,* we get the following argument:

(1.1) If the act of sacrificing one's son is a duty of Abraham, then the act of sacrificing one's son is derivable from position(s) P_1 v P_2 v P_n that Abraham occupies in life.

(2.1) It is not the case that the act of sacrificing one's son is derivable from the respective positions (i.e., husband, father, head of household, etc.) that Abraham occupies in life.

(3.1) Therefore, it is not the case that sacrificing one's son is a duty of Abraham's.

Bogen proceeds to make two further claims, namely, (i) a denial of any legitimacy to a sense of duty qua man, allowing him (ii) the option to argue for the logical connection between duties and positional contexts:

(i) . . . We do not speak of the duties of human beings *qua* human beings. The everyday concept of duty is such that we are said to acquire duties not . . . simply by being born into the species *homo sapiens*—but by occupying definite positions in society.[12]

(ii) . . . arguments over whether a person acting in a particular capacity has a particular duty must . . . be arguments over the nature of the position he occupies.[13]

Given the above claims, we might present Bogen's next argument to read:

(4) If there are only duties of a positional nature, then any ethical justification of Abraham's conduct must lie in the establishment of a case for citing positional contexts such that Abraham's conduct can be morally explained therein.

(5) There are only duties of a positional nature.

(6) Therefore, any ethical justification of Abraham's conduct must lie in the establishment of a case citing positional contexts such that Abraham's conduct can be morally explained therein.

(7) But there is no possible establishment of a case for citing positional contexts such that Abraham's conduct can be therein explained.

(8) Therefore, there is no ethical justification of Abraham's conduct.

(9) Therefore, the action of Abraham would involve a "teleological suspension of the ethical."

(10) Therefore there is no (morally) absolute duty to God.

Bogen writes:

. . . it would make no sense to say either that Abraham acted out of duty, or that his action was morally right. Because of Abraham's position, none of the moral considerations made relevant to the evaluation of his conduct by the circumstances of his case, justify his conduct. . . . One cannot speak in his case of a duty toward God which conflicts with his duty toward his son in the way in which we can speak of Agamemnon's having a duty (as king) which conflicted with his duties as a father.[14]

It seems to me that there is a twofold way to counter Bogen's basic theme, first, by presenting an argument either to establish a position for Abraham, such that this position calls for Abraham's sacrificing his son, and second, by establishing a case for speaking of duties qua man and showing how the recognition of such a type of duty will allow us to speak favorably of Abraham's conduct. As ways of defending Abraham, both approaches, if successful, would prevent "the teleological suspension of the ethical" from occurring.

I shall opt for the former line of defense of Kierkegaard's account in *Fear and Trembling,* so that I will deny Bogen's premise (2) and (2.1), thereby making the respective conclusions (3) and (3.1) false. I will express some misgivings with premise (4) because of its limited conception of duty, and yet, I will recognize it for the purposes of more fully extending its logic to allow for a novel defense of Abraham. Quite obviously, I will deny the truth of (7) and (8) and, paradoxically enough, of (9) and (10) as well.

It is not at all clear to me, after a great deal of textual exegesis, exactly what Kierkegaard's own views on morality were. Even so, it seems that Kierkegaard did not limit the ethical to a system of duties, as that expression is understood by Bogen. Accordingly, Bogen's account is too narrow in scope both textually and, as we shall see, philosophically. Indeed, one wonders how a Kantian passage like the following can be so structured that it incorporates a specific duty only for a specific position.

> The ethical as such is the universal, and as the universal it applies to everyone, which may be expressed from another point of view by saying that it applies every instant.[15]

Although Bogen's claim then is textually underextended in scope, as well as philosophically limited, it by no means follows that Kierkegaard did not also employ a type of duty much akin to Bogen's analysis. The following passages give substance to Bogen's thesis although, as we shall see, the concept of duty and that of position need to be further delineated. The passages refer respectively to the situations of Agamemnon, Jephthah, and Brutus, and cite the need for the recognition of certain sorts of tasks and responsibilities as required by the respective positions of king, military leader, and Roman consul.

> When an undertaking in which a whole nation is concerned is hindered, when such an enterprise is brought to a stand-still by the disfavor of heaven, when the angry deity sends a calm which mocks all efforts, when the seer performs his heavy tasks and proclaims that the deity demands a young maiden as a sacrifice—then will the father heroically make the sacrifice . . . the whole nation . . . will be also cognizant of his exploit, that for the welfare of the whole he was willing to sacrifice her.[16]

> When the intrepid judge who saved Israel in the hour of need in one breath binds himself and God by the same vow . . . all Israel will lament her maiden

youth, but every free-born man will understand, and every stout-hearted woman will admire Jephtha, and every maiden in Israel will wish to act as did his daughter.[17]

When a son is forgetful of his duty, when the state entrusts the father with the sword of justice . . . then will the father heroically forget that the guilty one is his son, but there will not be a single one among the people, not even the son, who will not admire the father, and when the law of Rome is interpreted, it will be remembered that many interpreted it more learnedly, but none so gloriously as Brutus.[18]

IV

I have already alluded to the philosophical limitations of Bogen's concept of *duty*. Bogen's proposal that Kierkegaard regarded morality as a system of duties implies that the rightness or wrongness of acts depends upon whether the moral agent has a duty to perform X-action or to refrain from X-action. Moreover, the interesting aspect of Bogen's thesis is that a particular moral agent acquires certain duties only by occupying a particular definite position in society. I take it that such an intimate association between the concept of "duty" and the particular status or role maintained by the moral agent commits Bogen to contending that if A claims to be morally justified in doing X because it is A's duty to do X, then this entails that A is acting in K-capacity such that K calls for A's doing X. Agamemnon held the position of "King of the Achaeans," and since his country's welfare depended upon his sacrificing his daughter Iphigenia, it was his duty to sacrifice her.

To question whether A in fact has a duty to do X is to be reduced to asking on Bogen's account whether the legitimacy of the inference from A occupies K-position, and, if A so acts in accordance with K, then is not A obliged to do X? Surely we need not deny that it is the moral duty of rulers to act in their country's best interests, but such an assertion does not have to be analytic, as Bogen insinuates. Indeed, it is often appropriate to ask the open question: "But should kings really always act in their country's best interests?" This appears to be a fair and appropriate question, though Bogen considers it to be closed: "It would then be unreasonable to ask whether Agamemnon was morally bound to sacrifice his daughter *just because* he was military leader, and the invasion depended upon his sacrificing her."[19]

Now Bogen considers the above to be a nonsensical question because of: (a) the soundness of the deductive inference from (i) A occupies K; (ii) K calls for action X; (iii) therefore, A ought to do X; and (b) the definitional equivalence of "A has a duty to do X" with "A occupies K and K requires X." However, while it may be the case that the assertions (i)–(iii) are true, so that one condition of soundness is satisfied, it surely is not obviously the case that the inference is valid, for (iii) contains an "ought" and the premises (i) and (ii) contain only descriptive terms. Also, quite clearly the definiens in (b) can be satisfied, without the definiendum's being satisfied, so that this connotational linkage is rendered somewhat dubious. That is, A may occupy a role or office, in a specific organization or in a particular social system, that requires A to do X, but it need not be the case that A also has a moral duty to do X (i.e., Adolf Eichmann in the Nazi organization could not be said to have had a *moral* duty to kill millions of Jews). Bogen presumably overlooked Kierkegaard's admonition that "It is only the lower natures which find in other people the law for their actions, which find the premises for their actions outside themselves."[20] There appear, then, to be good grounds for disavowing any claim, such as Bogen's, that to say "X is right" or "X is my duty" is logically equivalent to saying "X is required by position K," for clearly the evaluation of moral conduct depends not only on the agent's position but also on the circumstances and motives under which the action in question was or is to be performed.

Bogen further contends that Kierkegaard's conception of morality, viewed as a system of duties, need make no allowances for moral rules or principles (e.g., temptations can be more adequately described as tending to keep one from doing one's duty, rather than as tending to make one break a moral rule). I find such a conception of duties to be too limited. That is, the requirement of a duty for Bogen has simply the stringency of a claim of law, custom, acculturation, etc. I suggest that to say B occupies position F, and B freely accepts the requirements of F, entails that B thereby subscribes (at least implicitly) to the following moral principles (P_1, P_2 . . . P_n) defining that position. Jephthah is King of the Jews and freely accepts the requirements of that office, so that he accordingly submits to uphold such a moral principle as "kings ought always to act in their country's best interests."

Now there is strong textual evidence to support a thesis that Kierkegaard did recognize a hierarchy of duties. Agamemnon is a father and as such has the duty of caring for his daughter's welfare; but he is also a king and as such he has the duty in a higher sense to sacrifice his daughter for the sake of his country's successful invasion against Troy. Bogen wishes to maintain that, in such cases of conflict between fatherly duties and kingly duties, Kierkegaard is forced to resort to the quite arbitrary claim that kingly duties override fatherly duties, a resolution procedure that Bogen finds acceptable. However, if there is a sense of "good reasons" in ethics, then clearly the decision of what action is to be performed must be justified by invoking either prudential or utilitarian considerations, or at least by appealing to an overriding supreme principle. But this is precisely what Bogen's analysis of Kierkegaard has ruled out in claiming that statements such as (1) "It is A's duty to do X" are entirely distinct from and logicall prior to statements such as (2) "It is A's duty to do X in accordance with the dictates of moral principle P to which A freely subscribes." That is, Bogen has erroneously maintained that the connection between one's position and the rules he must obey is different from that between one's position and one's duties, and that indeed the former is decidedly un-Kierkegaardian. Bogen's reading would claim that (3) "A may know what A is to do and do X because A knows X is his duty to do." I would contend that this needs to be reformulated to read (4) "A may know what A is to do and do X because A holds X to be his duty in light of moral principle P." Bogen leaves us with the thesis that the concept of duty is bound to positional usage; but I wish to maintain that such a thesis is philosophically inadequate because the concept of duty is more properly related to the subscription to certain moral principles and their accompanying secondary rules, which principles and rules serve in turn to define the very role or position that an agent is to play in life. Whereas Bogen's account recognizes only a *descriptive* sense of duty, tying it down to certain roles or positions that one plays *in society,* my account recognizes a more properly normative sense of duty, tying it down to certain roles or positions that one plays *in life.* Accordingly, Bogen's analysis of morality in *Fear and Trembling* as a system of duties is fraught with excessive naturalistic shortcomings, limitations that prevent any appreciable understanding of the conduct of the knight of faith.

V

We have seen where, on Bogen's analysis, Agamemnon, the prototype of the tragic hero, is morally justified in causing the death of his daughter because his duties as king take precedence over all other relevant moral considerations. My interpretation would claim that Agamemnon is morally justified in his action because the moral principles governing the position of a king—more properly, defining that position—and its correlative duties override those governing the position of a father. But how are we to handle the case of Abraham, which by Kierkegaard's own admission involves the subordination of the very moral principles upon which a moral evaluation of his conduct could be based? Bogen at this point maintains—quite erroneously, I believe—that Abraham's act would not be performed under circumstances in which the various positions he occupied (i.e., father, husband, tribal leader, etc.) involved duties calling for the killing of Isaac. In one respect, Bogen is quite correct in this matter, for, given even an amended rendition of Bogen's concept of "duty" to avoid his excessively naturalistic assumptions, it still does not follow that such a concept of "duty," what I will call "duty-proper," will allow us to explain morally the conduct of Abraham. By "duties–proper" I refer to the assigned tasks that attach to stations, offices, and roles in society, and that are generally of an institutional sort; thus, one can be in Sartre's "bad faith" or be living an "inauthentic existence" and yet still fulfill the requirements of one's duties-proper. To be living an authentic mode of life, as I understand and employ the expression, is to be the individual in full possession of oneself, Heidegger's "*eigentlich*," which Richard Schmitt translates as "genuinely self-possessed."[21] On the other hand, to be inauthentic, to be living an inauthentic mode of existence, is to be fallen away from oneself (Heidegger's "*uneigentlich*," alienated from self). Likewise, I understand Sartre's "bad faith" to be the practice of self-deception, so that in being "*uneigentlich*" one is also acting in bad faith. More specifically, "Y is a duty-proper act of moral agent A" if and only if: (a) Y is an action required by moral principles P_1, P_2 . . . P_u, and moral rules R_1, R_2 . . . R_n, (b) these principles and rules in turn characterize A's position in the life of the society; (c) A may or may not have voluntarily chosen to subscribe to such principles and rules; and (d) these principles and rules require a specific performance if A is to satisfy the obligatory functions enjoined by such moral principles and rules. This is the realm of *Sittlichkeit*.

Some rules are extremely precise in specification. This is the case in certain institutional associations that speak of the "duties of members," which in my terminology are duties-proper. The tragic hero and the ecclesiastical hero fall into this type of role in that, being functionaries, their respective duties are determined in each case by a set of rules that establishes the character and structure of the institution as a whole. Within such an institutional framework there is no allowance for a *moral* usurper, and the knight of faith is such a person. His is not the domain of "the crowd" or "the numerical."

Can we then establish a special capacity or position for Abraham, such that his action was called for by duty? It seems to me that we can. Whereas Bogen's account allows only for a limited notion of the term *position*, tying it down to fathers, kings, etc.—the sort of institutional offices sanctioned by society—I see no logical objection to our giving the term a more extended meaning, i.e., to our employing it to designate certain mental attitudes, in which a position is a way of looking at something, a way of taking a certain perspective on life. Such an extended sense of *position* allows the term to designate a point of view adopted with reference to a particular subject, such as a certain benevolent attitude toward God. In such an extended sense of the term, *position* clearly transcends man's objective vocational situation as a policeman, attorney at law, priest, etc.—the sorts of offices listed in the *Dictionary of Occupational Titles*. The position "knight of faith" is not to be found in such a directory, but neither would one find Albert Schweitzer's "spiritual adventurer"—a self-description that he preferred to his institutional roles: physician, missionary, musician, etc. Moral agent A fulfills my extended notion of position whenever A has a certain mental attitude or outlook on life such that: (1) A voluntarily subscribes to a certain overriding supreme principle and the more subordinate rules and maxims emanating from it, (2) the conjunction of which serves to characterize A as a moral agent of a special sort. That is to say: for every moral agent A, there is a description F and certain definite moral principles and rules P^R, such that under F, A may be said to subscribe to P^R, which in turn demarcate A as occupying a certain position in life. José Ortega y Gasset declared, "man is impossible without imagination, without the capacity to invent for himself a conception of life to 'ideate' the character he is going to be. Whether he be original or a plagiarist, man is the novelist of himself."[22] I agree. More importantly, Kierkegaard agreed as well.

My extended notion of position accordingly serves to designate a sense in which the term connotes man's more personal role or station in life. Now, if we accept Bogen's use of the term *duty* wherein there are certain positive performances recognized as pertaining to a role or situation in life, which performances are deemed necessary for a satisfactory fulfillment of one's position, then it is likewise incumbent on us to recognize a certain set of activities to which a knight of faith commits himself in accepting a certain station in life. That is to say, in the limited sense (Bogen's use) and the extended sense of the term *position* there is a list of tasks and responsibilities associated with such positions. Such an extended rendition of *position* does justice to Kierkegaard's attack against the sort of moral and religious institutionalism in which moral standards are not necessarily a matter of personal decision by the individual agent in deciding his own destiny, but are to be found instead in the church or moral code into which the individual is inducted as a participant position-bearer.

Some philosophers (e.g., Schrader)[23] would claim that to be an individual in my sense of occupying an extended notion of position in life would be "inauthentic." Although he does not clarify what he means by "inauthentic," I suspect that Schrader has in mind the Heideggerian sense of "*uneigentlich,*" a state of fallen-awayness from self, alienation from self. Schrader might then appeal to the only apparent authenticity of Abraham qua knight of faith, arguing that he is but an individual who is only apparently genuinely self-possessed. That is, Schrader might say that to occupy a limited concept of "position" and "be what we are occupied with" may be more authentic than to "rummage around extravagantly in one's psyche" by occupying an extended notion of "position" in life. If so, then Schrader could be construed as raising two distinct claims against my analysis: (a) the *conceptual* point of questioning what it means to occupy a role or position in life; and/or (b) the *normative* point of asking what it means to be authentic.

However, given the preceding analysis, Schrader would appear ill-advised to be questioning (a), so this leaves us with the point of (b). His argument might now read: I agree with your conceptual point's coherency, but it seems to me that to instantiate it would be to invite moral or institutional havoc (i.e., for Schrader, as for Bogen, both qualifications of "havoc" are synonymous). Suffice it to say that such institutional or moral havoc does not occur as a result of my recognition of an extended notion of position. Even Kierkegaard was clear on this point:

> People . . . are afraid that the worst will happen as soon as the individual takes it into his head to comport himself as the individual. Moreover they think that to exist as the individual is the easiest thing of all, and that therefore people have to be compelled to become the universal. I cannot share either this fear or this opinion. . . . He who has learned that to exist as the individual is the most terrible thing of all will not be fearful of saying that it is great, but then too he will say this in such a way that his words will scarcely be a snare for the bewildered man, but rather will help him into the universal.[24]

Accordingly, I cannot share Schrader's insinuation that Abraham acting in the capacity of a knight of faith is a Quixotic figure. Rather, it seems to me that the knight of faith neither "rummages around in his psyche" nor causes any moral havoc to occur in performing the tasks associated with his noninstitutional role in life. A knight of faith would not have been found in the ranks of the Symbionese Liberation Army, the Manson "family," or Jim Jones' People's Temple. My introduction of an extended notion of position, and its incumbent recognition of "duty-plus" acts, to be shortly elucidated, will show Abraham as an individual to be playing a role that anticipates his very possibilities; yet such a projection need never outrun the categories of the ethical, for it may be a projection in, of, and with the world.

> He constantly makes the movements of infinity, but he does this with such correctness and assurance that he constantly gets the finite out of it.[25]

Another objection that arises has to do with whether talk of "knighthood of faith" is not simply a "category mistake." That is, Abraham is just a father, husband, tribal leader, etc. He occupies only these limited notions of position, and he can be spoken of as a knight of faith only in terms of the manner in which he views these respective institutional roles. By way of analogy: when you have toured the constituent colleges of Oxford, you have toured the university; so too, when you are aware of the institutional roles a man plays in life, you are aware of his knighthood of faith. This objection arises from consideration of the following passage from *Fear and Trembling:*

> [the knight of faith] knows the bliss of the infinite . . . and yet finiteness tastes to him just as good . . . as though the finite life were the surest thing of all.[26]

This objection is perhaps partly correct and partly incorrect. That is, there is a sense in which it may well be a category mistake to speak of knighthood of faith, but there is also a sense in which it is not. Let me explain this seemingly Kierkegaardian reply!

First of all, it might be argued that to ascribe knighthood of faith to Abraham *is* a "category mistake," although I do have some hesitation here in allowing the objection to be judged even partly correct. For it seems a bit queer to have such a supreme moral principle as "One ought to obey the commands of God" determining the institutional roles of husband, father, etc., although Kierkegaard himself in *Fear and Trembling* did speak of a bookkeeper as a knight of faith: "One might suppose that he was a clerk who had lost his soul in an intricate system of bookkeeping, so precise is he."[27] Kierkegaard also spoke of a tax collector, a professor of philosophy, and a servant girl as knights of faith—the last at least showing that the role is not limited to the male of the species. Furthermore, if one is to allow such considerations to deem it a "category mistake" to speak of a precise role of knighthood of faith, then one must qualify this ascription by granting that the awareness of the institutional roles that led to the identification of a knight of faith is to be viewed from the perspective of duty-plus.

Secondly, it seems that there is a stronger sense in which it is not a "category mistake" to speak of the distinct role of a knight of faith, consonant with my extended notion of position. For consider the case of a "hermit" who can be said to occupy no institutional roles whatever (i.e., he has "no ties with the world") and yet fulfills the conditions of being a knight of faith. Here, I believe, we cannot speak simply of knighthood of faith as being just a way of viewing one's institutional roles or of putting such roles in a certain perspective; for, *ex hypothesi*, knighthood of faith is the only role the hermit plays. It is important also to note that in this case, at least, our hermit plays a distinctly moral role, for he is not a derelict or a misanthrope or an urban guerrilla, to name a few noninstitutional roles that are nonmoral.

VI

The introduction of an extended meaning of *position* will, then, allow us to recognize a role such as "knight of faith." And, if there is some legitimate sense in which one can refer to the position, then certain duties are surely part of it. And if this further implies the subscription to certain moral or religious principles, then it is proper to speak of the knight of faith as recognizing such supreme principles as "One ought to offer all things to God" or "One ought always to obey the wishes of God"; for, as Kierkegaard said, such is the principal duty (the "absolute duty") of the knight of faith.[28]

Now, it might be granted that there is a sense in which such a religious man has certain duties to God, for he may occupy a certain office in some religious organization that deems it mandatory for such a person to be duty-bound to obey God. But—and I think that Kierkegaard is correct to insist that such an "ecclesiastical hero" is not a knight of faith—he has not gone far enough to recognize an absolute duty to God alone, a duty that is not mediated by the ethical or religious institution in which he finds himself. However, if we can appreciate the distinction between those tasks that are by social consensus thought essential to a certain duty, and those tasks that go beyond the ordinary implications of duty (although not beyond duty itself), then we can begin to understand Kierkegaard's knight of faith more fully. To the extent that the individual allows himself to be directed by the standards of what existentialists call the "One" (i.e., impersonal collectivity), he never becomes a true self. Indeed, to become an individual is precisely to begin to formulate one's own principles of conduct and to act resolutely in accordance with them. But this is precisely the sort of "personal universalizability" (i.e., moral principles formed out of regard to Kant's first formulation of the categorical imperative) that Kierkegaard is driving at, although it need not be gained at the expense of the "absurd" (e.g., "Either the individual becomes a knight of faith by assuming the burden of the paradox, or he never becomes one. In these regions partnership is unthinkable").[29]

> [the knight of faith] becomes God's intimate acquaintance, the Lord's friend, and (to speak quite humanly) that he says "Thou" to God in heaven, whereas even the tragic hero only addresses Him in the third person.[30]

Certain contemporary philosophers (e.g., Feinberg, Urmson) have lingered for too long in the error of supposing that the moral or religious code must not be in part too far beyond the capacity of the ordinary man in normal circumstances, lest a general noncompliance ensue. Urmson comments: "The basic moral code must not be in part too far beyond the capacity of the ordinary man on ordinary occasions or a general breakdown of compliance with the moral code would be an inevitable consequence; duty would seem to be something high and unattainable, and not for 'the likes of us.' "[31] This has engendered the result that strictly dutiful acts (e.g., Kant's "hard duties"), which require a great deal of self-restraint and suppression of basic desires, have been classified as nondutiful but meritorious supererogatory acts. Feinberg says: "The sacrificial element in supererogatory actions does not necessarily exceed that in the performance of a duty; what it exceeds is the sacrifice normally involved in the doing of a duty."[32] By his "infinite resignation of faith" and his "leap" to the religious stage of life, so these potential sympathizers might argue, Abraham has so obligated himself to sacrifice Isaac; but surely he has no duty to do so, for this is plainly "beyond the call of duty." At most, it is contended, he has a putative duty, but not an actual duty. But it is clearly false that some difficult heroic and saintly acts cannot be classified as morally required acts within the sphere of duty (to be further specified in the realm of "duty-plus"). It is also equally erroneous to infer that supererogatory acts must be better in the moral scale than certain obligatory acts, for surely it is often the case that acts of dutiful heroism are better than heroic acts of supererogation. I am not suggesting that one could formulate complicated rules to determine in just what situation an act is obligatory or not, but I am suggesting that there are some basic requirements in the form of rules or principles that are necessary features of a position and that, should one consider oneself to be in such a position, one is bound thereby, prima facie, to subscribe to in due fashion.

If we are to preserve the conduct of Abraham consistent with the moral sphere, then it is incumbent upon us to delineate further what Kierkegaard means by "absolute duty." If not, then surely Urmson is correct in saying that by any ordinary appeal to our conventional moral standards, it is absurd to claim that Abraham has a duty to sacrifice his son; and Feinberg is also correct in questioning the excessive sacrificial element involved in the performance of such a presumed duty.

I suggest that we speak of a "duty-plus" act (i.e., what Kierkegaard refers to as an "absolute duty") whenever the following situation obtains: X is a duty-plus act of moral agent A if and only if: (a) X is an action required by moral principles $P_1, P_2 \ldots P_n$ and moral rules $R_1, R_2 \ldots R_n$; (b) A has voluntarily chosen to subscribe to such moral principles and rules; (c) these principles and rules in turn characterize A's position in life; and (d) they require a specific performance if A is to satisfy the obligatory functions enjoined by such moral principles and rules.[33] These duties-plus characterize the realm of *Moralität*. For instance, by our ordinary ethical standards it is not normally considered a duty of a particular person to refrain from eating meat, to pray some eight hours a day, or to refrain from speaking to other human beings. Indeed, if there were a Christian who considered it his duty to do all these things, then our normal ethical standards would tell us that it is only a "false modesty" that prompted such a man to say, "I only did my duty," for philosophers tell us that such a person has done more than duty requires. J. O. Urmson makes such a claim (and in so doing an error, in my view) when he remarks: " . . . though he [the hero] might say to himself that so to act was a duty, he could not say so even beforehand to anyone else, and no one else could ever say it. Subjectively at the time of action, the deed presented itself as a duty, but it was not a duty."[34] However, this seems to me to be a clearly inadequate account of the moral religious life, and hence the need to speak of "duty-plus acts" that form a bridge, as it were, between our ordinary moral duties and those supererogatory acts that go beyond the "call of duty." Moreover, there is (or was) a moral agent, namely, Thomas Merton (the author of *The Seven Storey Mountain*) who occupies the position of a Trappist monk, who plays the solitary role of "hermit," so that, should he willingly perform the above-listed acts, it would be only a "misguided modesty" that would have us say, "Thomas Merton is living beyond the call of duty." Bogen, Urmson, and other philosophers holding similar ethical theories have then fallen into the mistake of failing to recognize the equivocation of the term *duty* in the locution "X is a duty of A." That is, they have failed to realize that X may refer to duties-plus (absolute duties) as much as it is normally construed as referring to duties-proper. However, in failing to draw the proper distinction between types of duties, Bogen, Urmson, etc., have mistakenly been led to infer that if X is not a duty-proper it is not a duty *simpliciter*. But this conclusion belies the complexity of the moral life. By our conventional moral standards, we do not ordinarily expect the average moral agent to act like Thomas Merton, or Mother Theresa of Calcutta, or in an even more extreme case, like Abraham, but the resultant psychological disequilibrium should not cause us to list their actions as being necessarily "beyond the call of duty."

> The fortunate chance in life is that the two correspond, that my wish is my duty and vice-versa, and the task of most men in life is precisely to remain within their duty, and by their enthusiasm to transform it into their wish. . . . [But if the knight of faith] would remain within his duty and his wish, he is not a knight of faith, for the absolute duty requires precisely that he should give them up.[35]

VII

There then seems to be a sense in which we can keep Kierkegaard's knight of faith within the ethical sphere, although in the class of duty-plus acts. Much as the premises of an argument are not established by that argument but must be justified elsewhere (or accepted as self-evident), so too the use of "good reasons" to justify a particular moral decision are not established by that decision but are justified in terms of previous decisions. However, in moving to what Kierkegaard characterized (somewhat mis-leadingly) as the "religious stage of life," the fundamental decision to subscribe to the rules governing faithful knighthood cannot be established by recourse to previous decision but must be "created" in the very making of such a decision. Accordingly, a particular moral judgment, such as "Abraham ought to sacrifice Isaac," would be then derivable from the supreme moral religious principle to which Abraham has subscribed, namely, "One ought to obey the mandates of God in all situations, however demanding," or some such variant locution. I suggest that the knight of faith's conduct need not be reduced to irrationality, but may instead be explained by the following moral syllogism:[36] (1) In all situa-tions, a knight of faith ought to obey God's mandates, however onerous;

(2) Abraham chooses to be a knight of faith; (3) Therefore, in all situations, Abraham ought to obey God's mandates, however onerous; (4) God commands that Abraham sacrifice Isaac; (5) Therefore, Abraham ought to sacrifice Isaac. And if by "infinite resignation" is meant the renunciation of the temporal for the eternal, then, given the preceding analysis, a knight of faith is also a knight of infinite resignation.

One's moral duty and obligation can then be either what one must do in order to act consistently with the general institutional principles governing the particular role and contractual situation in which one finds oneself placed in society, or else it can be what one must do if one is to fulfill the requirements of what one feels one ought to do, consistent with the general moral principles governing the particular role and contractual situation in which one chooses to place oneself, as distinct from (and perhaps opposed to) what the conventional moral code dictates that one ought to do. Unfortunately, Kierkegaard seemed to think that this either/or was an exclusive one. (Indeed, his penetrating psychological forays elsewhere into the logic of "the crowd is the untruth" would lend great credibility to such a suggested interpretation.) However, it need not be, and in at least one passage in *Fear and Trembling* Kierkegaard recognized as much: "But for the man also who does not so much as reach faith life has tasks enough, and if one loves them sincerely, life will by no means be wasted, even though it never is comparable to the life of those who sensed and grasped the highest."[37] In any case, Agamemnon and the ecclesiastical hero chose the first horn of this either/or situation, whereas Abraham chose the latter and, with "passionate inwardness," resolved to carry out his self-given prescription. This is why I can find no paradox in the conduct of Abraham, for it is surely no logical contradiction for an individual to remain consistently self-reliant within his chosen set of *moral* religious ideals. Kierkegaard himself was somewhat aware of this, but he did not bring it to its logical culmination, so that the seeming paradox of Abraham's life would be eliminated.

> . . . the significance of the lofty dignity which is assigned to every man, that of being his own censor, is a far prouder title than that of Censor General to the whole Roman Republic.[38]

Moreover, it does not strike me as a strong objection to remark that Abraham's proposed act is simply absurd because there might not be a God. This objection seems to me to be weak, for often we have self-imposed duties and obligations, as when I declare myself a trustee of property for a yet unborn child and then assume certain duties and obligations consonant with such a declaration. It might be objected here, and rightly so, that my example as stated admits of sufficient disanalogous features to make it unable to offset the objection. To be sure, it is arguable that the unborn child is not already an existing person, but even if we grant it the status of a mere biological entity qua fetus, the example is still deficient, for as soon as the "child" comes-into-being there exists a person to whom I have certain obligations and duties. With this criticism I agree. But the initial objection still does not hold; for my example, now slightly amended, might still hold and, indeed, be legally precedential in cases in which a father declares himself a trustee of property for a yet unborn child of his daughter, and the daughter never becomes pregnant before her father's death. Here, *ex hypothesi,* the father had duties and obligations qua trustee to a person who did not exist. So, too, it might also be argued in my defense, that a wife can be said to have duties to her missing husband, although it is questionable whether her husband is still living. If we are to judge Abraham's conduct as absurd, we must *mutatis mutandis* judge the conduct of our hypothetical father and wife to be equally absurd.

> From this, however, it does not follow that the ethical is to be abolished, but that it acquires an entirely different expression, the paradoxical expression— that love to God may cause the knight of faith to give his love to his neighbor the opposite expression to that which, ethically speaking, is required by duty.[39]

VIII

We have now seen how a plausible philosophical defense can be established for the conduct of Abraham qua knight of faith. This defense allows us to give a negative answer to Kierkegaard's Problem I, "Is there such a thing as a teleological suspension of the ethical?" while allowing an affirmative answer to his Problem II, "Is there such a thing as an absolute duty to God?" I now wish to make an exegetical point, the philosophical ramifications of which allow diverse interpretations to our reexamination of the "teleological suspension of the ethical."

Throughout *Fear and Trembling* Kierkegaard uses the terms *temptation* and *trial* in describing the complexities of Abraham's life. Although any distinction between these terms is generally overlooked by philosophical critics of Kierkegaard, so that the two terms are rendered intensional equivalents, it seems to me that such an analysis is most unsatisfactory; a discovery of this unsatisfactoriness will uncover, I believe, poignant exegetical evidence to support (apparently) my analysis of the logic of "position" and "duty," and the preceding defense of Abraham.

> If these three men [Agamemnon, Brutus, Jephthah] had replied to the query why they did it by saying "It is a *trial* in which we are tested," would people have understood them better?[40]

It seems that we may speak of ø as a "temptation" provided that: (a) ø is an action of enticing a person to evil by presenting inducements to his passion or human frailties; or, (b) ø is a severe challenge against a person in the attempt to confute him intellectually in regard to some moral issue; or, (c) $\emptyset$ is an attempt to offset one from his chosen moral plan of life.

Now, we may speak of ψ as a "trial" provided that: (d) ψ is a test of one's beliefs in a certain set of moral principles and rules; or, (e) ψ is an action of testing, "putting to the proof," the moral fitness of some proposed line of conduct; or, (f) ψ is an inquiry to ascertain a certain practical decision; the search for evidence by the examiner to prove a certain set of qualifications in the examinee, such as the endeavor to establish a person's moral commitment to a certain role in life.

The critic might argue here: (1) that if temptations can be described as those actions that attempt to entice a person (either by appeal to his passions or intellectually) from performing his moral duty, and (2) if *temptation* means the same as *trial,* then (3) trials can also be described as those actions that attempt to entice a person from performing his moral duty, so that (4) to describe the testing of Abraham by use of the term *trial* is to cast doubt on any considerations offered to show that he may have a moral duty to sacrifice his son. The critic might proceed by citing Kierkegaard to show that the most one can claim for Abraham's proposed line of conduct, given the univocal sense of *trial* and *temptation,* is some sort of religious justification; but on no account can there be any moral justification of his action. The theist should find no ready solace in the former defense, for it suggests that the knight of faith's tempting God is malevolent. That is, if *trial* is defined as *temptation,* then to characterize the testing of Abraham as a trial is to imply that God's command seeks to direct Abraham away from his moral and rational responsibilities (qua father, husband, etc.), in favor of a religious decision (qua knight of faith). But, if it is the case, as I wish to suggest, that *trial* is not defined as *temptation,* then to characterize the testing of Abraham as a trial is to imply that God's command seeks to direct Abraham to act morally [in the sense of (f)] out of respect for the responsibilities of his role qua knight of faith.

I certainly do not propose to refute the critic's charge that the issue is not always so well-defined; and I will not deny that Kierkegaard gets himself into certain muddles with his "passionate use of language."

> Why then did Abraham do it? For God's sake and for his own sake. . . . The unity of these two points of view is perfectly expressed by the word which has always been used to characterize this situation: it is a trial, a temptation [*fristelse*]. A temptation—but what does that mean? What ordinarily tempts a man is that which would keep him from doing his duty, but in this case the temptation is itself the ethical . . . which would keep him from doing God's will.[41]

> . . . to the question, "Why," Abraham has no answer except that it is a trial, a temptation [*fristelse*].[42]

Accordingly, the two above-mentioned textual references, cited as evidence against my claim for the distinction between *trial* and *temptation*, I shall not deny. However, I will not accept the critic's conclusion that the terms *trial* and *temptation* have the same connotation. Furthermore, I would reply to the critic that he had simply failed properly to consider the possible uses of Kierkegaard's "dialectical method," that is, the way in which he goes about presenting issues in "desultory fashion."[43]

I am not recommending this form of writing, only recognizing it. Since Kierkegaard was fond of indirect communication (Johannes de Silentio wrote *Fear and Trembling*), metaphor, highly imaginative but ambiguous figures of speech, one would do poorly by him to attempt to neatly pigeon-hole Kierkegaard, as the received opinion does, existential dialectic notwithstanding. Josiah Thompson writes: "Instead of thinking of his authorship as having a *single* core of meaning, we might think of it as having (like a multifaceted jewel) many *different* meanings depending on the angle from which it is illuminated."[44]

First of all, Kierkegaard borrowed from an antagonist, Hegel, the belief that from the thesis and antithesis of conflicting claims may well come the synthesis of understanding. This is what he means in saying that like the lyricist he goes about things "dialectically."[45] This procedure is closely associated with his "desultory manner," an expression used by Kierkegaard to indicate the presentation of an issue from all points of view, so that the reader, having seen (as it were) the issue illuminated from all opposing viewpoints, may draw his own conclusions. As the philosopher, Kierkegaard is simply raising the issues; he is the Socratic gadfly. But the reader must make his own personal decision. I would suggest, then, that an appreciation for this maieutic manner of doing philosophy will yield the result that the texts cited by our critic may be construed as simply illustrating a particular point of view, and were not intended to be taken as a definitive solution to the problem.

Secondly, for such a fusion of the two terms as synonymous, there are passages that clearly repudiate such a connotational linkage and, moreover, support my analysis in favor of the distinction.

. . . the whole of life is a trial.[46]

Would not his contemporary age . . . have said of him, "Abraham is eternally procrastinating. Finally he gets a son . . . now he wants to sacrifice him. So is he not mad?—but he always says that it is a trial.[47]

The relief of speech is that it translates me into the universal. Now Abraham is able to say the most beautiful things any language can express about how he loves Isaac. But it is not this he has at heart to say, it is the profounder thought that he would sacrifice him because it is a trial. This latter thought no

one can understand, and hence everyone can only misunderstand the former.[48]

Every instant Abraham is able to break off, he can repent the whole thing as
a temptation [*anfechtung*], then he can speak, then all could understand
him—but then he is no longer Abraham.[49]

Lastly, in reference to the critic's argument, I would simply deny
premise (2), citing the linguistic evidence presented in (a)–(f), so that the
definitional equivalence of (3) fails to be satisfied, thereby rendering (4) a
poorly drawn philosophical conclusion.

IX

Having drawn the above distinctions among types of duties, I now wish
to clarify for the reader some doubtless, lingering difficulties concerning
my analysis of the logic of duty. I wish to claim (1) that duties are tied down
to positional contexts, in the sense of duties-proper, duties-plus, and
oftentimes ultraduties (i.e., supererogatory acts). But, (2) unlike duties-
proper, duties-plus (i.e., what Kierkegaard calls "absolute duties") and
ultraduties are tied down to positional contexts of both a limited and an
extended sort, the latter not recognized as applicable to ascriptions of
duties-proper. So that, (3) to affirm a duty of Abraham in order to meet
Bogen's challenge successfully, it is necessary by (1) to argue for a
positional context for Abraham's proposed action, or else to establish a
case by recourse to basic duties. However, (4) to argue for a defense of
Abraham grounded on basic duties is unlikely to succeed. In addition, (5)
to argue for a defense of Abraham based on duties-proper is also bound to
fail, inasmuch as duties-proper pertain only to institutional roles, and the
knight of faith occupies a noninstitutional role in life.

Moreover, (6) to argue for a defense of Abraham grounded on ultraduties (supererogatory acts) is also unsatisfactory. Such an argument might
proceed by defining "X is a supererogatory act for A" provided that: (i) X
ought to exist; (ii) A is permitted to do X; and (iii) A is permitted not to do
X.[50] It would accordingly claim that the proposed line of conduct of
Abraham fulfills these conditions, and so may be spoken of as a supererero-
gatory act. However, I wish to dispute such an argument; moreover, when
we apply these three necessary and jointly sufficient conditions to the case
of the knight of faith, we see that such an analysis breaks down. That is, the
argument fails because: (i.1) the state of affairs of Isaac's being killed
ought not to exist; (ii.1) Abraham is required to do X, not just permitted to
do X; and lastly (iii.1) since it is forbidden for Abraham not to do X, it
follows that Abraham is not permitted not to do X. Accordingly, we can at
best say, on my analysis so far, that the action of slaying Isaac ought to be

performed, but that it is dubious whether the object of the action ought to exist.

Our antagonists might yet claim hope for their view that Abraham's proposed action is at best supererogatory, and so beg only half-defeat, for it might be conversely argued that Abraham's action is simply "offensive," that is, bad but not forbidden, for consider: "X is an offensive act for A" provided that: (iv) X ought not to exist; (v) A is permitted to do X; and (vi) A is permitted not to do X. They would now claim that the proposed line of conduct of Abraham fulfills these conditions, and so may be spoken of as offensive. But again their analysis is seen to break down. For, while we might agree with condition (iv), surely conditions (v) and (vi) are not satisfied, for reasons already cited in regard to (ii.1) and (iii.1), so that those would-be sympathizers of Kierkegaard who would allow Abraham to have intended to have committed an act of permissive ill-doing, although not a morally wrong act, have failed to provide such a line of defense.

Equally, (7) it is mistaken to assume that I introduced an extended notion of position to justify duties-plus, for they apply as well to institutional roles of a limited sort. It seems that a person may assume a role that is well-delineated by conventional social standards, such as that of a teacher, yet conceive of this descriptive office in such a way that it takes on a prescriptive quality and with it the incumbent duties that go beyond the requirements of our ordinary moral standards. For instance, the following assertion seems blatantly contradictory: (a) "Professor Smith ought to teach his students to the best of his abilities and it is not the case that Professor Smith ought to teach his students to the best of his abilities."

Moral philosophers, like Bogen and Urmson, would no doubt argue here that there is no moral conflict involved in (a), for either Smith ought to teach his students to the best of his abilities or it is not the case that Smith ought to teach his students to the best of his abilities. But such a conclusion bespeaks ignorance of the moral nature of the case. It seems that the first conjunct in (a) could be uttered by an educational progressivist (e.g., Dewey), while the latter conjunct could be what society expects of him qua teacher, viewing his role as that of an educational traditionalist (e.g., Locke). Here we have an institutional role (teacher) that presents Smith with conflicting claims, and with the practical problem of deciding wherein his actual duty lies. With the view to reaching a "way out" of our newly discovered conflict, I suggest that the seeming contradiction of (a) begins to dissolve when it is reformulated to read: (a.1) "Professor Smith [conceives his role in life to be such that he] ought to teach his students to the best of his abilities; but [viewed *publici juris*] it is not the case that Professor Smith ought to teach his students [i.e., he need not be acquainted with their psychological and social problems of adjustment to the curriculum structure] to the best of his abilities."

That is, viewed *publici juris,* viewed from the perspective of duty-proper, to say "It is not the case that Professor Smith ought to teach his students to the best of his abilities" implies that teaching is a self-justifying activity, so that it need not attain the achievement status of education (i.e., learning); that is, "teaching" may be, as Ryle points out, simply a "task verb." However, viewed from the perspective of duty-plus, to say "Professor Smith ought to teach his students to the best of his abilities" implies that Smith's teaching is not intrinsically worthwhile in itself unless it attains the appropriate state of learning in the pupils under Smith's tutelage. Accordingly, two people may fit the same institutional role in society, yet conceive of their role in such a manner that the position itself demands dissimilar performance, often even conflicting duties for them. My normative solution to the above conflict is that Smith's duty-plus requirement takes precedence over his duty-proper. Unfortunately, what is a duty-plus act for Smith, viewed from the perspective of duty-proper, becomes a supererogatory act *publici juris.*

However, (8) I do need an extended notion of position to allow us to speak of Abraham's noninstitutional role in life, qua knight of faith; and (9) because noninstitutional roles are not recognized by conventional moral standards, and since society applies duties-proper only to its institutionally recognized roles, it follows that only duties-plus can be ascribed to certain noninstitutional roles in life.

X

I wish to claim that, although there is a supreme moral religious principle in Abraham's ethical categories—namely, "One ought to obey the commands of God above all else"—we might nonetheless also agree with 1 John 4:20 that such a principle "contextually implies" that "One ought not to perform gratuitous injuries to one's neighbors" or some such variant locution (cf. 1 John 4:20: "If a man says, I love God, and hates his brother, he is a liar").[51]

What do I mean by "contextual implication"?[52] Suppose that we speak of statement S as contextually implying S^1 if and only if: for any person P, if P knew the normal conventions of language L, P would be able to infer S^1 from S in the context in which S and S^1 occur. That is, all I wish to maintain is that if a moral agent subscribes to the moral religious principle "One ought to obey the commands of God" (as the knight of faith does), then in all probability (i.e., there is strong inductive evidence to suggest) he also subscribes to the moral principle "One ought not to perform gratuitous injuries to one's neighbors" or "one ought not intentionally kill another innocent person against that person's wishes"—albeit, conversely, this is not the case.[53]

In his essay "That Individual" Kierkegaard supports nicely this matter of contextual implication.

> And to honour every man, absolutely every man, is the truth, and this is what it is to fear God and love one's "neighbour." . . . But never have I read in Holy Scripture the commandment, Thou shalt love the crowd—and still less, Thou shalt recognize, ethico-religiously, in the crowd the supreme authority in matters of "truth."[54]

XI

The reader might here ask: Okay, perhaps you have made the Abraham problematic rather intelligible and certainly not absurd, but is there no way in which Abraham (consistent with his newly recognized knighthood of faith) can avoid sacrificing Isaac? Happily, I believe there is a way. The contextual implication just mentioned in Abraham's conceptual moral framework would suggest that:

(1) Abraham qua knight of faith ought to sacrifice Isaac, and yet

(2) Abraham qua knight of faith ought not to sacrifice Isaac.

But (1) and (2) are moral contraries that can both be false. Hence, Abraham could *abstain,* where this reads:

(3) It is not the case that Abraham qua knight of faith ought to obey the command of God to sacrifice Isaac *and* it is not the case that Abraham qua knight of faith ought not to obey the command of God to sacrifice Isaac.

The action in (3) results from taking seriously the question: assuming that the divine command is legitimate, why did God command Abraham to sacrifice Isaac, if there is present this contextual implication between the moral religious principle "One ought to obey the commands of God" and "One ought not to perform gratuitous injuries toward one's neighbors"?[55] For us to answer this question, we must recall that I previously argued (in Part VIII) for the need to draw a distinction between *temptation* and *trial,* and argued that the latter term most aptly characterized the state of affairs surrounding the situation of Abraham. I still wish to maintain such an argument; but I now want to add that the use of *trial* to describe the relationship between Abraham and the divine mandate applies to the testing of Abraham to see whether Abraham understood the ramifications of his supreme moral religious principle "One ought to obey the commands of God" and in particular how it contextually implies "One ought not to perform gratuitous injuries to one's neighbors" or "one ought not to intentionally kill another innocent person against that person's wishes." That is, the divine command is not to be acted upon with the result that Isaac is sacrificed. It is "idle" in this sense. Accordingly, although the argument presented in Parts I–VII is interesting and I believe valid, it is much too vulnerable to the sophisticated critique of philosophers like Kai Nielsen who would suggest that ethicoreligious claims are *often* clearly immoral, as (1) might well have been. However, the putative demands of (1) and (2) are to be acted upon to the extent that they force Abraham to understand the principles defining his role qua knight of faith, and reach a decision about what line of conduct to adopt. Such a decision is found in (3). Accordingly, if by "infinite resignation" is meant the renunciation of the temporal for the eternal, then the knight of faith in opting for (3) is no knight of infinite resignation. In Ortega y Gasset's words, we might describe a knight of faith as a "kind of ontological centaur, half immersed in nature, half transcending it." However, the knight of faith's form of life is not that of what Kierkegaard termed "life's neuter gender." He is not a "pure hermaphrodite."

It might be suggested that my solution (3) of Abraham's plight is too cautious; why not just affirm (2) instead? To such a question I would invoke the traditional reply "that the ways of God are often mysterious," so that it may be the case that God's command is not "idle," but was intended to be acted upon, so that the basic arguments of Parts I–VII could now be used to justify Abraham's conduct, and (1) be satisfied. Nonetheless, on my interpretation of *Fear and Trembling,* I have described Abraham as betting on (3), so that even a knight of faith can be allowed to abstain—in fear and trembling!

It now becomes clear, I hope, that Kierkegaard's Problem I allows of a negative answer, and his Problem II, of an affirmative one.[56]

8. Is the Concept of an Absolute Duty toward God Morally Unintelligible?

C. STEPHEN EVANS

IN THE COURSE OF HIS TREATMENT OF THE BIBLICAL STORY OF ABRAHAM'S willingness to sacrifice Isaac at God's behest, Johannes de Silentio, the pseudonymous author of *Fear and Trembling,* raises a profound and troubling question for the theistic philosopher: "Is there such a thing as an absolute duty toward God?"[1] By an absolute duty toward God, Johannes means a specific, absolutely overriding duty to obey God's commands. This duty is so absolute that it takes precedence over every other concern, even the loftiest moral obligation. Such an absolute duty is carefully distinguished from moral duties per se, though the author acknowledges that in some sense moral duties themselves are duties toward God:

> One has therefore a right to say that fundamentally every duty is a duty towards God; but if one cannot say more, then one affirms at the same time that properly I have no duty towards God. Duty becomes duty by being referred to God, but in duty itself I do not come into relation with God. Thus it is a duty to love one's neighbour, but in performing this duty I do not come into relation with God but with the neighbour whom I love. If I say then in this connection that it is my duty to love God, I am really uttering only a tautology, inasmuch as "God" is in this instance used in an entirely abstract sense as the divine, i.e., the universal, i.e., duty.[2]

Johannes continues that from this perspective the ethical becomes the whole content and limit of man's ethicoreligious life, and God "becomes an invisible vanishing point" (*FT,* p. 78). He seems by this to mean that a religious life that equates God's commands and one's moral duties contains no distinctively "religious" elements. In such a religion, the term *God* does not refer to a person who makes known his desires and commands, but is simply an abstract, personified way of talking about one's moral duties.

The conception of the ethicoreligious life that Johannes refers to here is actually worked out in detail in Kant's *Religion Within the Limits of Reason Alone.* Kant there says that "religion is (subjectively regarded) the recognition of all duties as divine commands."[3] Kant declares that the moral life and the true religious life are indistinguishable. Belief in creeds, performance of religious activities and rituals, membership in ecclesiastical bodies are all religiously worthless, and represent religious fantasies and superstition except insofar as they represent means toward the furtherance of the natural religion, which consists of pure moral faith. Kant asserts that the following principle requires no proof: "*Whatever, over and above good life-conduct, man fancies that he can do to become well-pleasing to God is mere religious illusion and pseudo-service of God.*"[4] Interestingly enough, Kant considers the same issue as Johannes, whether or not a father could be commanded by God to kill his son, and concludes that since such a command contradicts morality it "cannot, despite all appearances, be of God."[5]

Johannes agrees that this is true *if* there is no such thing as an absolute duty toward God:

> If in any way it might occur to any man to want to love God in any other sense than that here indicated (moral service), he is romantic, he loves a phantom which, if it had merely the power of being able to speak, would say to him, "I do not require your love. Stay where you belong." If in any way it might occur to a man to want to love God otherwise, this love would be open to suspicion, like that of which Rousseau speaks, referring to people who love the Kaffirs instead of their neighbours. (*FT*, p. 78)

Kant's pure moral faith would be characterized by Johannes as preeminently a religion of "immanence," which presupposes that there is nothing in human existence that is "incommensurable" with the ethical life.

If there is then to be an *absolute* duty to God, Johannes believes that the duty must be essentially nonmoral in character; the knight of faith acts in a sphere "beyond good and evil." To this end Johannes develops the notion of an absolute duty to God by claiming that Abraham's act in being willing to sacrifice Isaac constitutes a "teleological suspension of the ethical." Abraham must be distinguished from the tragic hero who sacrifices his child for the sake of some higher duty; Abraham "overstepped the ethical entirely" for the sake of some higher nonethical telos (*FT*, p. 69).

Interestingly enough, in delineating this religious duty from ethical duties Johannes employs precisely the criteria that Kant employs to distinguish his "pure moral faith" from superstition and fanaticism: universality and rational intelligibility.[6] Johannes agrees that the ethical is the universal, but says that faith is the paradox that the individual as the particular is higher than the universal (*FT*, p. 65). The ethical is the rationally intelligible; faith is the absurd (*FT*, pp. 66–67). The ethical is the publicly communicable; faith is concealed even when it expresses itself in speech (*FT*, pp. 91, 122–29). Thus the sphere of faith and the sphere of ethical duty are incommensurable. The moral sphere presupposes only immanent, rational principles; the sphere of faith presupposes some actual, direct relationship between the individual and God, who is conceived of not as the abstract voice of duty but as a distinct person, with wishes and desires, capable of giving commands and then rescinding those commands. An absolute duty to God could only come from some specific communication or special revelation from God, directed to individuals. This is precisely the sort of claim that, on Kant's view, entails that a religion lacks the most important criterion of truth—universality.[7] For it is obvious that such a revelation, dependent upon contingent historical facts for its transmission, could never be the ground of a moral duty in Kant's sense.

Johannes de Silentio accepts these conclusions—yea, glories in them. He does not try to evade the conclusion that the knight of faith, conceived as the man who has received a special command from God and fulfills his absolute duty, acts in ways that are, judged by universal rational principles, absurd. For the point of his book is not to *defend* faith. Those who wish to defend faith are portrayed as whores who pretty the cheeks of theology to sell her charms to philosophy (*FT,* p. 43). The book is a polemical slam against those who twaddle about "going beyond" faith. Johannes de Silentio wishes to make clear the *difficulties* connected with faith. When one is aware of these difficulties, one is not tempted to provide a spiritual analogue to the Dutch merchants, who dumped several cargoes of spices into the sea to raise the price (*FT,* p. 129). No need to prop up the price of faith artificially, for the sake of giving a spiritually advanced generation enough to do! The generation has enough to do in realizing that the notion of a spiritually advanced generation is a fraud, and that the difficulties of faith remain the same in every age (*FT,* pp. 130–31). Faith is incommensurable with the rationally intelligible principles immanent in human reason—not exactly the sort of thing to be concerned about "going beyond."

One can sympathize with the aim of this polemic without agreeing completely with its content. One can agree with Johannes that Kant's argument that the life of faith and the life of moral effort are indistinguishable is mistaken, and yet feel uneasy about the precise manner in which Johannes contrasts them. One can agree that faith is not reducible to morality, that it has an autonomous content, but yet quarrel with the way in which Johannes conceives of that content.[8] One can chuckle at the barbs directed against the Danish Hegelians who sputtered about "going beyond" faith, but nonetheless be genuinely disturbed at the effect the book might have on the sincere religious believer, who is troubled by the implied picture of God as a nonmoral, capricious despot who commands his followers to perform morally vicious acts for no intelligible reason except as a test or trial of the followers's devotion. These qualms lead one to ask: Can the irreducibility of faith to moral duty be defended without implying a conflict between the two? Put in terms of the central focus of this paper, the question becomes: Is the notion of an absolute duty to God absolutely heterogeneous with moral duty? Or, at least, have we accurately characterized the distinction between such a special, religious duty and a moral duty by regarding the latter as essentially rational, intelligible, and communicable, and the former as absurd, unintelligible, and incommunicable?

Ultimately, then, I wish to quarrel with the characterization of faith as contramoral and contrarational. But it seems crucial to me to see that it is the way Johannes characterizes rational moral duties that underlies his description of faith. It is against the backdrop of a specific conception of the moral and rational that Abraham's act is judged to be absolutely heterogenous with human moral and rational standards. What I wish to suggest is that if these conceptions of morality and rationality are modified, it is possible to characterize faith in less paradoxical terms, yet still preserve Johannes' central contention: that the life of faith possesses an integrity of its own that is not reducible to the categories of the moral life as ordinarily understood.

What does Johannes have in mind when he talks about the ethical?[9] The notion is actually not terribly clear. Johannes says many times that the ethical is "the universal" and feels no need to characterize it in detail. As a part of "the universal human" presumably he was dealing with something that each individual was already familiar with. But he does tell us that the ethical as the universal applies to everyone and applies every instant (*FT*, p. 64). Also, as the universal the ethical is the manifest, the revealed (*FT*, p. 91), by which he seems to mean the ethical is essentially communicable—in principle understandable by all. Perhaps the clearest picture of Johannes' conception of the ethical emerges when we look at the tragic heroes, the beloved sons of ethics, whom he contrasts with Abraham. Agamemnon's sacrifice of Iphigenia to appease an angry deity and save the mission that concerned the whole nation, Jephthah's sacrifice of his daughter to keep his vow and preserve the victory of Israel, and Brutus' impartial justice in executing his treasonous son all seem to Johannes to fall under the blanket of ethics. To sacrifice a child to save a nation or to maintain the state is ethically intelligible to Johannes. This suggests that despite the Kantian sound of "the universal," Johannes' conception of the ethical is essentially Hegelian. The highest ethical duties are concretely embodied in societal institutions. In Abraham's case the family represents his highest ethical duty (*FT*, p. 70). The tragic hero who is connected with the state "lets one expression of the ethical find its *telos* in a higher expression of the ethical" (*FT*, p. 69). The ethical relation between parent and child is reduced by the tragic hero to a "sentiment which has its dialectic in its relation to the idea of morality" (*FT*, p. 69).

The actions of these ethical heroes are said to be universally intelligible; everyone in Greece, Israel, and Rome would understand and approve the acts of Agamemnon, Jephthah, and Brutus. Abraham's act, on the other hand, stems from a purely private relationship that he enjoyed with the deity. At a specific moment in time the deity approached Abraham as an individual and gave him a specific, private message. This message, according to Johannes, is private not merely in the sense that only Abraham happened to receive it but in the further sense that only Abraham could understand it. Abraham cannot speak; he cannot "utter the word that explains all" (*FT*, p. 124). Even the superficially similar case of the Greek bridegroom who must break off his engagement because the augur has foretold that a misfortune would follow the marriage is different. "Everything depends upon how this man stands related to the utterance of the augurs. Is this utterance *publici juris* or is it a *privatissimum*" (*FT*, p. 102)? Johannes asserts that the notion of an augur announcing to an individual the will of heaven is essentially intelligible to all. Abraham's situation is not.

It is not certain that this notion of a communication that is intelligible only to the recipient is coherent. If the message is understandable only to Abraham, not merely in the sense that only Abraham happened to hear it or in the sense that it is in a code that only Abraham happens to be able to decipher, but in the radical sense that it is logically impossible for anyone other than Abraham to understand it, then it is not at all clear what "understanding" such a message means. *What* does Abraham understand? The notion of a communication to Abraham that is essentially private seems to presuppose the soundness of the (perhaps questionable) notion of a radically private language.

Perhaps Johannes' real point can be salvaged if we abandon the thesis that Abraham's message was logically unintelligible to anyone else, and replace it with a different account of Abraham's inability to communicate his duty to anyone else. On this revised account it is not just the fact that Abraham was Abraham that enabled him to understand the message, but the fact that Abraham enjoyed a direct, special relationship with God. Abraham knows God as an individual; he knows God is good, and he loves and trusts God. Although he does not understand God's command in the sense that he understands why God has asked him to do this or what purpose it will serve, he does understand that it is indeed God who has asked him to do this. As a result of his special relationship, Abraham's trust in God is supreme. This trust expresses itself cognitively in an interpretive framework by which he concludes, all appearances to the contrary, that this act really is the right thing to do in this particular case. God would not in fact require Isaac of him (*FT*, p. 46); or even if God did do this thing, he would nonetheless receive Isaac back and "grow old in the land, honored by the people, blessed in his generation, remembered forever in Isaac" (*FT*, p. 35).

Abraham's willingness to sacrifice Isaac might be compared with the confidence of a knife-thrower's assistant in the accuracy of the knife-thrower's aim. Both Abraham and the knife-thrower's assistant perform acts that seem so risky to an outsider as to appear almost mad. The two men of faith, however, because of their trust in another person, regard their acts rather differently. The analogy ends here, of course. The knife-thrower's assistant's motivation is probably economic gain, while on most accounts, Abraham's act was motivated by a desire to please God and obtain an eternal happiness. The source of their trust is different as well. The knife-thrower's assistant's faith is grounded in the inductive evidence that he has concerning the performer's accuracy. According to Johannes, no empirical considerations of probability supported Abraham's conviction that God was trustworthy. Abraham's trust was faith in the truest sense of the word. Though perhaps grounded in his experience of God it was by no means a belief to be treated as an experimental hypothesis, but a conviction to be clung to through thick and thin. There is also the important difference that the knife-thrower's assistant has no moral obligation to the knife-thrower and certainly no religious obligation, while Abraham regards himself as obligated to obey God's command. Abraham's trust was the ground of his *act* in the sense that it made it possible for him to believe that this was his duty, but the trust should not be understood as the ground of the *duty*. Abraham viewed the act as his duty because he believed it was God who had asked him to do it. But without his supreme trust in God, such a command would surely have led Abraham to repudiate the Lord as a moral monster.

That some would regard such a trusting belief as itself "the absurd" and such an "interpretive framework" as itself madness is undeniable. Perhaps this is Johannes' point in saying that Abraham believed "by virtue of the absurd." But let us be clear that if this is indeed Johannes' view, it represents an abandonment of the claim that God's command to Abraham and Abraham's act of obedience are *essentially* unintelligible and incommunicable to anyone else. For his position is now only that God's command to Abraham is intelligible only in light of an interpretive framework of Abraham's, a framework he adopted because of his supreme trust in God, with whom he had a special direct relationship. There is no reason in principle why Abraham's act would not be intelligible to someone else who enjoyed the same sort of relationship to God and considered God's command to Abraham from the same interpretive framework. And even someone who did not share that relationship and framework could at least understand that, from the perspective of someone else who did, such a command *might* be understandable, though if he had no comprehension of or empathy for such a viewpoint, he might well simply judge it as madness or gross immorality.

"Very well," Johannes might reply. "You say in effect that to another man of faith, Abraham's act might be intelligible; not being a man of faith, I cannot say. In any case Abraham's act and God's command are still not intelligible as *moral* duties, they are not universally understandable, but are comprehensible instead only from the perspective of those who, as individuals, enjoy a special, direct relationship to God. Abraham's case is still morally and rationally unintelligible."

It is at this point that we must call Johannes' understanding of morality and rationality into question. Johannes seems to assume that my ethical relations with my fellow men are governed solely by abstract, universal considerations that are intelligible to all men regardless of the concrete historical relationships in which they participate. If an act is moral, Johannes seems to say, then anyone ought to be able to perceive it as moral, regardless of what experience he may or may not have had, regardless of whether the individual has been in a similar situation, regardless of the interpretive framework in terms of which one act is classified as "murder," another as "legal execution." This account of moral judgment is surely oversimplified.

To help us see this point more clearly, let us look at the criticisms addressed by Sir David Ross to another ethical perspective, ideal utilitarianism, the view that moral duties are essentially a function of our obligation to maximize good.

> The essential defect of the "ideal utilitarian" theory is that it ignores, or at least does not do full justice to the highly personal character of duty.[10]

> It says, in effect, that the only morally significant relation in which my neighbors stand to me is that of being possible beneficiaries by my action. They do stand in this relation to me, and this relation is morally significant. But they may also stand to me in the relation of promisee to promiser, of creditor to debtor, of wife to husband, of child to parent, of friend to friend, of fellow countryman to fellow countryman, and the like; and each of these relations is the foundation of a prima facie duty, which is more or less incumbent on me according to the circumstances of the case.[11]

Ross asserts that the particular, concrete, historical relationships that we enter into are the ground of our moral duties. This implies at least two things. If duty is highly personal, then my specific moral duties must always be seen in the light of the specific relationships that I have to my fellows. It makes a difference whether the person I confront is a parent, friend, creditor, or stranger. Although I must treat all men morally, the specific character of a moral act cannot be determined in abstraction from the particulars of the situation.

Moreover, and this is of special importance, we might infer from this that these concrete relations not only help to shape my duty; they may also influence my ability to understand and know my duty. It is surely the case that a lack of familiarity with these relationships, whether grounded in the individual's failure to meaningfully participate in these relations, or simply in their nonexistence in a particular culture, would make it difficult or impossible to understand the duties in question. Thus an individual who did not live in a state could not be expected to understand an obligation to be loyal and patriotic to one's state, though he might of course understand loyalty to his family or tribal unit. The responsibility to repay a debt would be unintelligible in a culture where the institution of borrowing did not exist. (Whether there is such a culture I do not know.) Thus on Ross's view both my actual duties and my ability to understand those duties may be somewhat dependent on the nature of the actual relationships in which I participate as an individual.

Johannes de Silentio is obviously not an ideal utilitarian, and Ross's criticisms obviously do not apply directly to his ethical view. But there is a parallel in that Johannes, too, seems to see all moral obligations as stemming from one, abstract principle, universally intelligible regardless of the specific historical relations in which individuals find themselves. For Johannes the only ultimately significant moral relationship in which I stand to my neighbors is that embodied in "the idea of the universal." But it is highly questionable whether such a universal morality, grounded in principles that are intelligible to human reason as such, may not be a "fantastic" notion. Johannes himself sees these universal obligations as embodied in human institutions like the family and the state, but he seems to assume that these institutions are themselves universally intelligible spheres of human activity. Even if this were the case it would still be questionable to claim that one's knowledge of one's duties towards the family, the state, etc. is independent of one's historical, cultural understanding of these entities. I am not here challenging the objectivity of morality, but the notion that concrete moral principles can be understood in the abstract apart from a concrete, historical context. Still less could the morality of a particular act be understood in abstraction.

If Ross's view of moral duty is correct, what sort of moral duties might be grounded in a creature-Creator relationship? The relation of a created individual to God the Creator, assuming God is a personal entity rather than a suprapersonal "ground of being," is clearly a unique one, quite different from the relationship of debtor to creditor, child to parent, etc., and the idea that such a relationship to God would give rise to moral obligations is not necessarily incoherent. Such a duty would certainly be *different* from other concrete moral duties, but the difference would not be correctly characterized by asserting that ordinary moral duties are intelligible and communicable, while a duty toward God is absurd and incommunicable. The intelligibility of both sorts of duties would be rooted in one's understanding of the respective sorts of relationships, and the interpretive framework derived from that understanding which is employed in characterizing moral choices.

One disanalogy between an absolute duty to God and other moral duties would be that, if the religious perspective is correct, the creature-Creator relation that gives rise to the duties in question is in one sense independent of the activity of the creature. This is not usually the case with other

Rossian moral relations. Normally it would be impossible for me to have a friend and be obligated to a friend whom I do not know about. However, from a religious perspective one's duties as a creature to one's Creator may be very real even if I do not know my Creator. The relationship of trust to which we have attached so much importance is not the ground of my religious duty, but the essential condition for understanding these sorts of duties and discovering what my actual duties are. But this disanalogy is probably not complete. It is plausible to assert that there may well be other moral relationships that exist independently of my awareness of those relationships and that give rise to duties of which I am ignorant.

Another difference between a duty to God and other sorts of duties is that it is plausible to maintain, as Johannes does, that an obligation toward God would be absolute in the sense of taking priority over all other obligations. But such a situation would not differ *in principle* from other situations where our prima facie duty is overridden by more pressing obligations. That a duty to God would be different from other sorts of duties is undeniable, but the difference would not be that the one is rational and intelligible and the other is absurd, as judged by some "absolute standard." If one wished to emphasize the differences between other moral duties and one's special duties to God one might adopt the convention of restricting the term "moral duty" to those other duties. Someone who wished to emphasize the analogy between one's special religious duties and ordinary moral duty might wish to use the term "moral duty" in a more inclusive sense. Neither convention should blind its user to the actual similarities and dissimilarities that hold. It is probable that the more restricted sense of "moral duty" more accurately reflects ordinary usage, especially insofar as that usage is shaped by individuals who do not possess the active trust in God that is a prerequisite for understanding one's special religious duties. Kierkegaard himself seems to feel that lives characterized by such faith are rather rare, even (or perhaps especially) amidst established Christendom.

This account does not, then, imply that the life of faith is reducible to a life of moral effort, as that phrase is generally understood. The autonomous content of the life of faith would center in the specific, historical relationship to God that makes intelligible the notion of an absolute duty to God. Belief that special historical communications that one has received are communications from God would be impossible without the sort of personal trust that we have characterized Abraham as possessing. The exercise of this personal trust is a distinctive element in the life of faith that is irreducible to the moral life as it is ordinarily conceived, and certainly irreducible to the moral life as described by Johannes. To that extent, Johannes' contention is justified. But the autonomous character of faith is not accurately characterized by asserting that one's religious duties are absurd and incommunicable while moral duties are rational and universally intelligible. In fact, the two types of duties are similar in important ways, and the intelligibility of each is a function of one's personal relationships.

But what is the significance of this discussion? Does anyone enjoy such a special relationship to God? *Fear and Trembling* only hints at the answer to these questions.

> For when the individual by his guilt has gone outside the universal he can return to it only by virtue of having come as the individual into an absolute relation with the absolute. (*FT*, p. 108)

> As soon as sin makes its appearance ethics comes to grief precisely upon repentance; for repentance is the highest ethical expression, but precisely as such it is the deepest ethical self-contradiction. (*FT*, p. 108 n.)

> An ethics which disregards sin is a perfectly idle science; but if it asserts sin it is *eo ipso* well beyond itself. (*FT*, p. 108)

The significance of Johannes' contention that faith is not reducible to the life of moral striving cannot be seen until the individual comes to see that the life of moral striving is bankrupt. To the man who sees himself as outside the ethical, alienated from the ideal not merely in the sense that he fulfills it imperfectly, but in the radical sense that he cannot even begin to approximate that ideal—to that man Abraham appears as "the guiding star which saves the anguished" (*FT*, p. 35). For Abraham's story is an anticipation of the case of the Christian believer, who by an historical relationship with the God in time, accomplishes a repetition—a rebirth in which the condition for the fulfillment of the ethical requirement is provided and "the whole of life and of existence begins afresh."[12]

This new state, Kierkegaard believes, is made possible only by a life of commitment to Jesus Christ. This life of commitment includes an acceptance of Jesus' life as "the Pattern" for the believer's life, and an obligation to obey Jesus' commands. On Kierkegaard's view, those commands do not consist of "simple ethical teachings" but may require of the believer acts that go far beyond the boundaries of ethics. The believer may be called to become a eunuch for the kingdom of God (Matthew 19:12), and his absolute commitment to Jesus even reduces his familial obligations to a relative status. Thus the believer may appear to the one who lacks this commitment to be a person who "hates" his father and his mother (Luke 14:26). The believer might even be asked to sell all his material possessions and give them to the poor (Mark 10:21).

The person who lacks this trust in Christ will find these commands unintelligible, just as he will find Christ's claims about himself unbelievable. But the trusting believer will see things otherwise. Because he believes Christ to be God, he regards these commands as *duties*. What I have tried to argue is that his action in accepting such obligations, while certainly distinct from the moral life as ordinarily conceived, may be analogous in important ways to the way other "ordinary," nonreligious duties are understood and accepted.

9. Abraham's Silence and the Logic of Faith

DAVID J. WREN

TO BE OBSERVED DOING SOMETHING ODD CAN BE AN UNNERVING EXPERIENCE. For most of us, the first hint of an eye looking quizzically in our direction will not only bring a warm glow of embarrassment to our face, but also a flurry of explanations to our lips. Sometimes these will be no more than silly excuses, notable perhaps for their ingenuity but not for one moment intended as serious justification for our actions. When we have been caught slipping food to the dog underneath the dinner table despite all our promises to the contrary, there is little that can be said. We may make a half-hearted attempt to excuse our actions, but we will not attempt to justify them. But this feeling that we need to give an account of our actions can represent more than an embarrassed reaction to being caught. It may also be the sign of a deep appreciation of the nature of the ethical life.

One of the characteristics that we demand of those who claim to be ethical is that their actions be done for good reasons rather than haphazardly or as a matter of personal whim. If someone borrows our car and returns it damaged, explaining its somewhat modified shape by saying that he had a sudden urge to argue with a tree, we would be entitled to consider his reasons suspect and his action irresponsible. Such a man would not even seem an appropriate candidate for the designation "ethical." On the other hand, if we are told that the car was damaged because running it into a tree was the only alternative to killing a pedestrian, we would have to acknowledge that the action was justified. The saving of a life is a powerful reason for acting that cannot easily be set aside.

But there are many circumstances in which there is no ready agreement about the adequacy of the reasons that may be given to justify particular choices. The table of contents of any book on contemporary moral problems will remind us of some of the more controversial areas. Such topics as abortion and capital punishment provide an opportunity for reflection and discussion precisely because the difficulty of these issues is recognized. In each case, we are willing to allow that there are good reasons to be found on both sides of the controversy, and this, of course, is what makes such issues all but impossible to settle to everyone's satisfaction. Yet here, too, we still demand that whether or not a particular person does what we would have done (or what we think we would have done), he still must act for good reasons if his action is to be accounted ethical. Any such judgment about the reasons for an action will, of course, depend on our ability to discern them, either by observation or by their being explained to us. It is surely this recognition that lies behind the conviction of the ethical man that he has not only an obligation to act in certain ways but also an obligation to account for his acts.

In *Fear and Trembling,* Kierkegaard acknowledges this aspect of the ethical life when he points to its characteristic as the revealed.[1] Where the reason for an action or the principles that govern a man's life remain hidden, then quite clearly we can reach no judgment about their propriety. This is usually no accident. When an apparent act of kindness is motivated by the hope of reward, it is hardly politic to reveal that motive. But where there is ethical conviction, there is not only no need to hide one's motives; there is every reason to make sure that they are clearly understood. The desire to explain at this point marks an appreciation of what it is to be ethical.

This desire to open one's actions for public understanding is an important feature of the ethical life. It is obviously not enough, however, that our actions simply stand revealed. When Kierkegaard talks of the ethical man as aspiring to the glory of having his actions understood by every noble mind,[2] there is clearly implicit a requirement that the actions be approved. Oftentimes our actions may be understood only too well—and every noble mind would join in condemning them. It may be cynical to suggest that whenever we cannot understand someone's actions we should assume that they are motivated by selfishness, but far too often for comfort, however, the actions of others do become comprehensible (and we can assume that they can and do say the same of us). Where we would distinguish a person as ethical, we must not only understand his actions but recognize his reasons for them as worthy of approval.

Since we have noted the possibility of honest disagreement among ethical men, any test we apply to such reasons will have to be to some degree formal in nature. We have already recognized the inadequacy of reasons that trade on personal whim and idiosyncrasy, yet we must still allow for cases in which some noble minds would approve our reasons as good even though they themselves would not have acted as we have. It is here that we come to the feature of the ethical life that Kierkegaard calls the relationship to the universal.

There are some counter-Hegelian overtones that influence the way this relationship is discussed in *Fear and Trembling,* but Kierkegaard's point is basically a simple one. If an action is to be judged ethical, the actor must believe that the reasons that governed his action would compel anyone else in his situation to act in the same way. This is not to say that others actually will agree that his choice was right; it is to say that he genuinely *believes* that the others should act as he has. This is the essence of what we mean by duty. If we are to act ethically, then we must act not for some personal reason but out of a sense that there is an obligation that lies on any man in our circumstances. It is this sense of acting out of a duty that lies not only on him but on others, too, that moves the ethical man to reveal his actions and to seek the understanding of the noble. And from the other side, we can look on it as a mark of ethical development in a man when more and more of his life becomes comprehensible to those who can wield the concept of duty.

Kierkegaard looks to the tragic hero as the supreme example of the ethical life. Here we have the man whose respect for duty comes not with the bonus of a pleasant respectability but at the cost of all his natural desires and inclinations. The illustration that Kierkegaard borrows from Euripides is particularly telling. When Agamemnon is told that the sacrifice of his daughter, Iphigenia, is demanded by the goddess Artemis, his natural reaction is to want to save his daughter. And his desires here are supported by his duty as a father. But he has another and greater duty as a king. He must consider the general welfare of all his people, and it is this welfare that is being threatened by the anger of the goddess. His decision to renounce his own desires and his duty to his daughter in favor of his wider, public duty is a terrible and agonizing one that takes full measure of the hero. Yet it is a decision that can be understood and commended by those who share his devotion to duty. Indeed, it is this common understanding of the overwhelming claims of duty that bears the tragedy to us and gives us some understanding of the torment of his soul. Few of us can claim the depth of devotion to duty that was Agamemnon's, for the material of heroism is not commonplace; but it is our sense of duty that provides the link which makes him comprehensible. To a person without such a sense, Agamemnon is indecipherable; at best he seems stupid, at worst, criminal.

The enduring recognition of *Iphigenia in Aulis* as one of the great dramatic tragedies says much for the persistence of the sense of duty and for the fact that men can be awakened to an understanding of moral matters. There is no lengthy explanation on the part of Agamemnon designed to initiate us into his dilemma; it is simply assumed that he has a direct claim on our understanding, and many have found that he does. But there are occasions when we find someone's actions puzzling and need an explanation before we can make sense of what he has done. Often it is simply that we do not know enough about the situation that faces him, or sometimes it is that we need to know why he acted as he did. But regardless of whether the understanding of the action is immediate or the product of a lengthy explanation, it is the hallmark of the ethical man that his actions can be understood and his reasons approved by those who share his commitment to the ethical.

Kierkegaard's fascination with the example of Agamemnon and Iphigenia is clear. Throughout *Fear and Trembling,* he keeps returning to the theme, which provides him with a perfect counterpoint to his consideration of the story of Abraham's willingness to sacrifice Isaac. The similarities are clear. Both stories tell of a sacrifice demanded as an obligation to a deity and a sacrifice that is all but impossible to make. But Kierkegaard is more concerned with the differences, which make of Abraham a figure more puzzling and unsettling than Agamemnon could ever be. His purpose in discussing the Abraham story is to throw some light on the concept of religious faith and he does this by focusing in turn on three problems raised by the story. In this essay, we are concerned with the third of these, the problem of Abraham's silence.

Over and over, Kierkegaard remarks on the difficulty of understanding Abraham's actions. But if this is a problem for readers of the story, how much more of a problem it must have been for Abraham's immediate family. Most of us have at some time or other puzzled those who are close to us by the way we have acted, but most of us would also acknowledge that they have a right to expect an explanation. But from Abraham no explanation is ever forthcoming; he remains silent.

There are many possible explanations for someone's keeping silent about the reasons for his actions. One of the simplest and most obvious is that he has no reasons. If we ask a child, "Why did you do that?" we should not be surprised by the response, "I don't know." This does not always mean that the action was involuntary. The question "Why did you slam the door?" may get this reply because the child is simply not aware that it was the wind that made the door close so fast. But when the child claims not to know why he set fire to the cat, it is likely that his action had no reasons. It takes a certain maturity to have reasons for one's actions, and we recognize this when we do not hold very young children morally responsible for what they do. Part of the problem with children is that they do not have sufficient experience to foresee the consequences of what they do, but once they get beyond that stage, we can only attribute this lack of reasons to a lack of personal maturity and to an unformed character. In this latter case, it is not a question of a lack of understanding of the world but a lack of self-understanding.

But silence does not necessarily indicate a lack of self-understanding. On the contrary, it is sometimes an accurate self-understanding that makes it clear to us that there is nothing to be said. Let us imagine a person who has a fanatical devotion to playing backgammon. If we met him, we might politely try to understand the roots of his fascination and ask him to explain what is so gripping about the game. Undoubtedly we would then be subjected to a voluble and enthusiastic account of the peculiar pleasure that it provides, and we might be persuaded to give the game a try. Should we still fail to understand his enthusiasm, there would be little point in his offering further explanation. He would recognize, one hopes, that liking backgammon is a matter of personal taste and that any further explanation would be useless and inappropriate. Thus explanation and understanding would founder on the level of personal differences. In large areas of human life this is what must be expected. In such circumstances, silence is the necessary corollary of individuality.

Where silence stems from either of these reasons, it is something that is founded in the particular personal make-up of the individual and would seem to fall neatly within Kierkegaard's category of aesthetic silence. Kierkegaard's aesthetes do not spring to mind as notable examples of silence; indeed, it would be hard to imagine a more talkative bunch of people. The one compulsion that they all seem to share is the desire to put every aspect of their innermost lives into words, be it in the after-dinner speech or the diary. Such behavior is of course a literary necessity, for the reader would gain little insight into the lives of those who remained stubbornly silent. Despite this lack of quiet aesthetes, however, Kierkegaard rightly saw that there would be times when silence would be characteristic of the aesthetic life. We have seen two contexts in which there is silence because there is nothing that can be said, either because of a lack of any developed character or because of highly personal idiosyncrasies. But Abraham seems to fit neither of these.

If the story in question were the only mention of Abraham in the Bible, then it might be possible to believe that he did not explain his action because he did not understand it himself. But we do know more of him. He is no pawn moved about through life in a state of helpless confusion; he is a man capable of strong and decisive leadership. Indeed, to ascribe his readiness to sacrifice Isaac to lack of personal maturity on Abraham's part and to account for his silence by saying that he did not understand why he was prepared to perform the sacrificial act comes close to portraying him as criminally insane.

If this view of Abraham does not fit the facts, are we any closer to an explanation if we attribute his inability to explain his deeds to their foundation in personal idiosyncrasies? It is sad but true that now and again through history we come on an individual who can take a strange kind of perverted pleasure in the murder of a son, and it is surely to the credit of the rest of us that there is nothing that could be said that would enable us to understand this source of pleasure or in any way to approve it. The story of such a man might well be used as a warning to us of the dangers of failing to keep the darker side of our personal inclinations within proper bounds. But Abraham comes to us not as a warning but as an example to be followed. We cannot then ascribe his silence to the limitations of personal idiosyncrasy, nor can we blame any difficulty that we have in understanding him on personal differences. But there is another possibility.

We have been concerned with situations in which someone was unable to explain his actions. There are also cases, however, of those who could explain their actions but choose not to do so. Again, Kierkegaard directs us to the story of Agamemnon. In order not to cause Iphigenia needless suffering, Agamemnon tries to hide what he must do from her for as long as possible. This is the way of the aesthetic hero who keeps his silence in order to spare another the agony that torments him. We can admire Agamemnon's behavior all the more because we can imagine how much the sympathy and understanding of those he loved would have meant to him as he struggled with his terrible problem. As it happened, events conspired against Agamemnon: his purposes were revealed and he was challenged with the role of the ethical hero. But at this early point in the drama, he can be understood in aesthetic terms because his actions are determined by what is accidental to him, *his* knowledge of what the future demands.

While the desire to spare others unnecessary suffering can provide a genuine opportunity for heroism, Kierkegaard is aware of the dangers of this kind of silence. It is very hard to be sure that our keeping silent is simply aimed at sparing another. Sometimes by not explaining our actions, we are trying to avoid hearing all the arguments against our proposed line of conduct. In contrast, the ethical hero is one who reveals his purpose and has the courage to live with all the reasons against what he proposes to do.[3] This provides us with another illustration of the importance for the ethical life of openness about one's actions. The ethical man can take some comfort in the knowledge that everything that could be said against his action has been said and that he has therefore been forced to examine his action carefully, overlooking no possible aspect of it.[4]

If it is necessary to examine with extreme care anyone who claims that his silence is for the benefit of another, before accounting him an aesthetic hero, it is even more necessary to examine the case of Abraham. He simply does not fit into the category of the aesthetic at all! Agamemnon's silence was intended to spare Iphigenia the knowledge of what had to be done, and his final decision is based on his consideration of the welfare of his people. At no point do considerations of his own desires or personal benefit enter in. But Abraham's silence is not designed to spare Isaac suffering and cannot be justified in aesthetic terms. Indeed, as Kierkegaard points out, "in general, Abraham's whole task of sacrificing Isaac for his [Abraham's] own sake and for God's sake is an offense to aesthetics, for aesthetics can well understand that I sacrifice myself, but not that I sacrifice another for my own sake."[5]

Abraham's silence cuts him off from any consideration within ethical categories, but equally we cannot account for his silence in terms of those other circumstances that might lead a man to offer no explanation. Yet his silence is offered to us as an example to be followed.

We have seen that Abraham's silence was not of his own choosing and that it was not the case that he did not know what he was about. And if his silence stems from personal idiosyncrasy, then he makes no sense as an example unless we mean to equate that with faith. However, he does seem to share something with the man who acts for peculiarly personal reasons: the inability to explain himself. Even if he were to speak day and night, he could not make himself understood.[6]

The problem is not the act itself. That we can understand the sacrifice of an offspring is made clear by the story of Agamemnon. But Abraham cannot tell us that he is acting for the general welfare. He might be able to make his action comprehensible for a moment if he were to explain that he was being tempted,[7] but he would as quickly become incomprehensible again if he went on to reveal that the temptation was to do his fatherly duty by Isaac. How can we understand a man who is a failure if he fulfills his ethical obligations, a man who must not do what all men must do? Indeed, the more deeply a man is concerned for the ethical, the more Abraham will seem a figure of offense. One might imagine no higher feeling for the ethical than that which sees one's ethical duties as duties owed to God, one might even imagine Abraham agreeing. But there is more to his silence than this.

For a man of a religious disposition who has come to look on his duties as being owed to God, it would not seem an unnatural step to believe that God, on occasion, may require some specific task of him. To admit the possibility that life can be understood in a religious way is also in part to acknowledge that there can be a direct relationship to God that goes beyond anything that is mediated through our sense of universal obligation. While the specific task that is set for Abraham may be hard to understand, it would be possible for those with some awareness of the religious attitude to understand his plight if he were to explain that he was fulfilling the command of God. While we might dispute whether God could ever truly issue such a command, it would certainly be possible to appreciate the nature of the obligation felt by Abraham.

We can imagine the agony of any religious man who feels called on by God to sacrifice his son and can admire the man who would refuse even at the cost of his soul. Such a conflict between temporal and eternal happiness, between duty to others and duty to God, presents a cruel but comprehensible choice, and would be a fit subject for high drama. Of this, Abraham could have spoken and wrought the tears of his hearers. But Abraham could not explain.

What made the problem so intense and so personal for Abraham was that he had already received God's promise that through Isaac his descendents would be a blessing to the whole world. Thus he was faced with a situation in which God's promise and God's command seemed to be in direct conflict. Yet he determined to obey the command. To the outsider such a course must seem the highest folly. Surely, Abraham must have been mistaken about what God demands and Isaac has become the hostage to his unwillingness to recognize his error. Or perhaps Abraham is not mistaken and it is God who now abrogates his covenant, but can such a God *merit* a sacrifice of this kind? In either case, Abraham's action seems to be without reason.

To read the story at a later date is to have all the advantages of hindsight and to be able to see as obvious what Abraham must have struggled to believe, that it was only a test of his faith. But this temptation to collapse the ending into the story only serves to cloak its real significance. We must not make Abraham's task an easy one. As he took the long journey to Mount Moriah, he knew how his actions would appear to others, and he must have been tormented by the apparent absurdity of his accepting both God's promise and God's command. Abraham knew that the seeming absurdity of his situation formed a total barrier between himself and all others such that he could never explain his decision to anyone. And yet he persevered, and accepting by faith what seemed absurd, he reached the triumphant climax of his ordeal. For such, we hail him as one of the highest examples of religious faith.

Abraham's silence was the silence of the man of faith. Where he differed from those who watched his actions was in his willingness to accept and guide his life by what appeared to them to be absurd. To those who did not share his personal relationship to God, there was nothing that could be said that would make any sense. In Abraham's silence we see an important aspect of the nature of faith, the barrier that it erects between the believer and the unbeliever. It is this that Kierkegaard discussed under the rubric of the Absurd.

In his *Journals,* Kierkegaard characterizes the absurd as "the negative criterion . . . of the relationship to the divine" and goes on to remark that "to a third person, the believer relates himself by virtue of the absurd."[8] In other words, to the onlooker who stands outside the relationship to God of the man of faith, both that relationship and the man of faith himself are incomprehensible. Yet we must remember that this is the appearance that is given *to the outsider.* Abraham's faith did not involve him in believing what was actually absurd; by faith, what appeared absurd was transformed. Yet his task was a test of faith, for he did not by some magic of faith avoid being aware of how his actions appeared to others and, at times, even to himself; "in every weak moment," Kierkegaard observes, "it is more or less absurd to him."[9] It is the absurd that calls forth faith and provides the test of strength.

Abraham was totally cut off from all other men because his relationship to the divine was peculiarly personal. The promise and the command were to him alone. If, therefore, we look to this story for an example of the faith that is distinctively Christian, we may be misled. Kierkegaard acknowl-

edges in his *Journals* that he uses the story of Abraham to illustrate the
formal definition of faith. "That there is a difference between the absurd in
Fear and Trembling and the paradox in the *Concluding Unscientific Postscript* is quite correct. The first is the purely personal definition of existential faith—the other is faith in relationship to a doctrine."[10] Thus, while we
may look to Abraham for a general illustration of the kind of passion that
we call faith and the way in which it can govern a man's life, we should not
go beyond this.

Later in the same entry, Kierkegaard elaborates on the distinction in a
way that has sparked a great deal of controversy. He describes Abraham as
believing by virtue of the absurd, while the Christian believes the absurd.[11]
This suggests that the Christian faces a difficulty that Abraham did not.
While the absurd, the apparent conflict of God's promise and God's
command, provided the opportunity for Abraham's faith, there is nothing
inherently absurd in what he believed, namely, that he was being tested. It
simply does not seem that he could have had any good reasons for
believing it. Only in that sense can we say that his belief was unreasonable.
In the case of Christianity, however, it is the very content of the belief itself
that is seen as absurd, and hence Christian faith would seem to be
unreasonable in a much stronger sense. Thus while Abraham was silent
because he could not explain his reasons, the Christian seems to be
condemned to silence not simply by the reasons for his believing but by the
very content of his beliefs.

The question of whether Kierkegaard is arguing that Christianity is
irrational in content has been much argued. On the side of those who claim
that he is can be placed several passages in the *Postscript*. We find
reference to the Christian's having to endure the crucifixion of the understanding[12] and his having to believe against the understanding.[13] Yet there
is much to be cited in favor of the opposing view. Shortly after the remarks
that we have just quoted, Kierkegaard writes, "Christianity as a thought
project is not difficult to understand, the difficulty, the paradox is that it is
real."[14] At several earlier points in the *Postscript*, he has written along
similar lines. He claims that it is an easy matter to know what Christianity
is and that we do not need a vast array of scholars to help us understand
it.[15] It would seem difficult then to believe that he holds that the content of
the Christian faith is irrational, for that would hardly give us something
easy to understand, it would simply give us nonsense. But what then is
meant by the crucifixion of the understanding and believing the absurd?

We need to remember that both remarks must strictly be attributed to
Climacus who, although he makes a number of philosophical remarks with
which Kierkegaard would agree, is not Kierkegaard. Climacus is not a
believer but someone who observes Christianity from the outside. Thus
what he says is based on a descriptive knowledge of Christianity and not on
how it appears to the man of faith. This he acknowledges when he admits

that while he knows what Christianity is, he does not know what it is to be a Christian.[16]

The notion of the absurd, or the paradox, is once again one that refers to the front that is presented to the outsider, only here it is the content that represents the difficulty. And what causes this difficulty with the content is the idea that it is real. Such a radical affront is given to all normal expectations by the claim that "God has come into being, has been born, has grown up and so forth, precisely like any other individual human being, quite indistinguishable from other human individuals,"[17] that the more we try to understand it in terms of our normal categories, the more absurd it seems. This is no paradox that results from the incompleteness of human knowledge, for there is no further information that would make the Incarnation an ordinary occurrence.

On the contrary, the more we reflect on them, the more striking the Christian teachings seem to be, for they put our knowledge of God at the mercy of objective uncertainty. Thus when the outsider is forced to the conclusion that the Christian faith is absurd, there are two main elements that prompt this judgment. First, he is faced with the fact that it claims that our eternal happiness is to be based on a relationship to something historical, which by that fact can only be objectively uncertain. Secondly, he is confronted with the difficulty that this historical fact is of its own nature contradictory to all thinking.[18] It is not only one of a kind, but one of such a kind as defies all explanation. In the light of this, the judgment that such a teaching is absurd seems almost modest.

The absurd thus represents the barrier that comes between the unbeliever and the believer, a barrier that marks the limits of reason and prevents the believer from making himself understood. The silence of faith is the reflection of its presence. The only way in which the absurd is at all open to the understanding of the outsider is when he can recognize that it is not something that can be understood by reason. To be sure, this is an advance of a limiting, negative kind, but once reason is prepared to admit the limits set by the presence of the absurd, then the way is open to appropriate the paradox by the only possible means, the passionate inwardness of faith. "If the Paradox and Reason come together in a mutual understanding of their unlikeness, their encounter will be happy, like love's understanding. . . . "[19]

We have seen Kierkegaard's contention that the silence of the man of faith results from the presence of the absurd as an absolute barrier between believer and unbeliever, but we might well wonder if this is not some crafty apologetic move adopted as a desperate ploy by someone who has discovered an inability to explain his faith rationally. Before we make any attempt to assess Kierkegaard's position, we will need to clear away some possible confusion.

In this day and age, we are inclined to think that the belief that the earth is flat is an absurd one. We do not do this because of any difficulty in understanding the meaning of the belief. On the contrary, it is because we do understand it that we describe it as absurd; there is no way that such a belief can be harmonized with any reasonable interpretation of the evidence we have.

If this is the kind of situation in which Christianity makes its demand for faith, then it would be guilty of a flight into irrationalism. To make faith the guarantee of truth where the evidence is lacking seems to have considerable analogies to the behavior of a small boy who is convinced that no one can see him when he closes his eyes, or to the ostrich that buries its head in the sand in order to be invisible to its enemies. Clearly in neither of these cases does the belief that something is true make it so. The boy will come to see that the evidence does not support his belief and he will abandon it. The ostrich is a more difficult case. It never seems to learn that its belief is false. Indeed, it might argue, if it had any philosophical inclinations, that its continued survival provides an excellent pragmatic justification of its belief. But this is because it is not aware of all the evidence; we, of course, know that its continued survival is due not to its odd behavior but to the fact that, contrary to its belief, it has no natural enemies. And so generations of ostriches will go on burying their heads. But all their believing does not make what they believe true.

However, this is not Kierkegaard's position. The difference between the Christian believer and the unbeliever is not simply their failure to agree on the truth of certain claims. Rather, the unbeliever does not understand what it is to be a Christian. Faith, then, is not a means by which statements open to public understanding are accepted as true even though evidence for them is inadequate or nonexistent. Faith is the key to understanding. It is the position that has traditionally been expressed by the phrase *Credo ut intelligam,* "I believe in order to understand." Here we are faced with beliefs that are described as absurd because they are not understood.

When Wittgenstein was asked whether he could imagine himself as a disembodied spirit, existing after death, he did not reject the belief because of the lack of evidence, but said that he was unable to answer because of his lack of understanding. "I'd say: 'I'm sorry. I (so far) connect nothing with these words.' "[20] This provides us with an important illustration of the problems surrounding the question of understanding, and the need to be very clear about where the lack of understanding lies. There is obviously a sense in which Wittgenstein did understand the question; all the words were perfectly familiar to him. Yet he was unable to see what they meant when they were used in the context of religious belief. In this case, a description of how the words are used in the religious context might have helped him understand and give an answer to the question. But there is the possibility of a different situation. Wittgenstein also considered the instance of belief in the Last Judgment. Here he claimed that he would understand such a belief in an *important* sense. He had read certain books and was able to see how this concept functioned in the religious context. Yet again he questioned whether he really did understand,[21] for he acknowledged that he was unable to put the words to any use in his own life. This led him to distinguish between the ways in which a belief may be absurd in the manner to which we have already drawn attention. There would be the case in which we would say, "This is believed on insufficient evidence," which would be appropriate in those instances in which a belief struck us as "a bit absurd." However, there would also be those cases in which the belief seemed to be altogether absurd and was not understood at all. In these cases, it would not be a matter of evidence.[22]

We have made use of the example from Wittgenstein in part because he points to the same relationship between the absurd and the inability of the outsider to understand that was made by Kierkegaard, and in Wittgenstein's case there can be no question of any kind of religious apologetic. But there is a further point to be made. While Kierkegaard comes to his position from his reflection on the nature of religious faith, Wittgenstein arrives at a compatible position as a result of his analysis of the nature of the concept "understanding."

He argues that the ability to put a concept to use in ways that are in harmony with the previous usage is the sign of understanding. We know, for example, that a child has understood the word *cat* when it can make acceptable use of the word. The child no longer, for instance, points at dogs or makes oinking sounds along with saying *cat*. But it would not be enough to be able to say *cat* only in those instances where it has heard the word used; this might simply be parroting. We require the use of the word on some new occasion before we can be certain that it has been understood, and not just any new occasions, but appropriate ones.

If this is what counts as understanding, then it follows that if we are going to credit someone with the ability to understand Christian concepts, they must show that they have the ability to use them in an appropriate way. But, for Christianity, this appropriate way includes the requirement that the various concepts not be used in a mere verbal way, but only in the context of certain behavior, attitudes, commitments, and beliefs. In the New Testament, we are reminded constantly of the emptiness and hypocrisy of mere outward profession. Surely this is the thrust of the remark that faith without works is dead. Only where there is the presence of certain subjective qualifications are Christian concepts put to proper use. It follows that the man who stands outside the context of faith can *never* meet the criteria for understanding.

Thus philosophical analysis of the notion of "understanding" points us in the same direction as does Abraham. Between the believer and the unbeliever there is a barrier that would seem to compel silence. Yet unlike

Abraham, Christians are not silent; indeed, they are commanded to proclaim their faith. Here we can begin to see why it has traditionally been claimed that faith is a gift of God. Where Christianity is the absurd, incomprehensible to the outsider, nothing that the believer can do will change that; in and of itself, his preaching is worthless. Understanding requires a changed life on the part of the *hearer,* and when someone does come to see that the gospel makes sense and that it can govern his life, we can only ascribe the change to the work of the Holy Spirit. The Christian preaches out of obedience, not because he claims that preaching has any effects. It is the grace of God that enables the hearer to understand. It is this grace of God that puts an end to the Christian's silence.

10. Sounds of Silence

MARK C. TAYLOR

Silence is the snare of the demon, and the more one keeps silent, the more terrifying the demon becomes; but silence is also the mutual understanding between the Deity and the individual.[1]

PARADOXES

FEAR AND TREMBLING IS A BOOK RICH IN PARADOX—PARADOXES TOO TANGLED to be unraveled by speculative reflection, paradoxes that strike the reader dumb. One of the most perplexing paradoxes is the mere fact that the book was written. Consider the author: Johannes de Silentio. Consider the central character: Abraham, who not only does not speak, but who cannot speak. Consider the book's preoccupation: silence. A book by Johannes de Silentio, about a person named Abraham who cannot speak, devoted to an exploration of the significance of silence. There would not seem to be much to say. Indeed to try to say anything would seem to land one in self-contradiction. But perhaps that's the point, or one of the points. Let's see about that.

Johannes seems obsessed with the theme of silence. Throughout much of the book, he approaches silence indirectly, discussing it in the context of other issues, touching it briefly when he peeks through cracks in the System. As his reflections draw to a close, however, silence assumes center stage. The entire third "Problem" addresses the question: "Was it ethically justifiable for Abraham to keep silent about his project before Sarah, before Eleazar, before Isaac?" (*FT*, p. 91). Too often this section of *Fear and Trembling* is read either as a repetition of points stated more precisely in Problems I and II, or as musings on Kierkegaard's personal experience that stray from the primary concerns of the work. But such judgments are usually rash, insensitive to the care with which Kierkegaard composes his works. Johannes' probing of the question posed in Problem III discloses that his discussion has been moving consistently toward silence. Dialectician that he is, Johannes' ending clarifies his beginning and the path he has been following. Silence has much to say (if speak it can) about the complex ethical and religious issues with which Johannes grapples throughout the book: the nature of language, the relationship between faith and reason, between faith and the demonic, between faith and ethics, between aesthetics and ethics, between inwardness and outwardness, between individuality and universality, between isolation and community. We could go on.

To the reader familiar with the Kierkegaardian corpus, Johannes' comments on silence focus a theme that runs throughout the pseudonymous authorship. In fact, it is difficult to appreciate the significance of Abraham's silence without coming to terms with what other pseudonyms have to say about the matter. In the pages that follow, we approach the role of silence in the life of the believer by setting Johannes' reflections within the context of Kierkegaard's dialectic of the stages of existence as developed in the pseudonymous authorship. Silence means different things at different stages of existence. Silence is not always faithful.

But before we "leap" into the stages, a further word about our author and his principal character. Both are silent, though in different ways. And that difference is important. The suggestion that Johannes remains silent might strike one as odd. After all, he writes a book, quite a complex book. Isn't Kierkegaard's use of the pseudonym Johannes de Silentio for such a loquacious author another of his notoriously ironic twists?[2] Perhaps. But the matter is somewhat more complex. As we have suggested, one always must attend to the point of view expressed by Kierkegaard's writings. Johannes is a poet, albeit a poet with considerable dialectical acumen. He is neither a philosopher who spins speculative webs nor a man of faith who silently suffers fear and trembling. His lyrical dialectic or dialectical lyric is an attempt to fathom the movements of faith by reflecting upon faith's father—Abraham. Johannes admits: "The poet cannot do what the other [i.e., the believer] does, he can only admire, love and rejoice in the hero" (p. 30). His book does not so much reveal a faithful perspective, as it describes the way faith appears to nonfaith. Abraham constantly eludes Johannes' grasp. With Sarah, Johannes is left to watch Abraham from afar. Johannes cannot ascend Moriah.

To the extent that he seeks to comprehend and to render comprehensible the knight of faith, Johannes fails—and must fail. He confesses, "when I have to think of Abraham, I am as though annihilated. I catch sight every moment of that enormous paradox which is the substance of Abraham's life, every moment I am repelled, and my thought in spite of all its passion cannot get a hairs-breadth further. I strain every muscle to get a view of it—that very instant I am paralyzed" (*FT*, p. 44). Johannes ends as he began, dumbfounded before the paradox of faith. The lesson of his journey: a deeper comprehension of Abraham's incomprehensibility. Though Johannes tries to speak, in the face of Abraham he remains mute.

Abraham does not try to speak, he endures silence. A man of faith *cannot* speak; he *must* be silent. The believer's silence is, however, qualitatively different from the silence of the poet. Faithful silence is unique. To hear it, we must listen to other sounds of silence.

STAGES AND SILENCE

When analyzing any theme central to Kierkegaard's thought, it is necessary to keep in mind his notion of the stages of existence. Each of Kierkegaard's pseudonyms presents a distinctive perspective on life, articulates a different world view, depicts an alternative *Lebenswelt*.[3] Throughout the pseudonymous authorship, three primary stages of existence are defined: the aesthetic, the ethical, and the religious. In some contexts, Kierkegaard suggests that further refinements of this basic threefold schema are necessary. For instance, he differentiates the immediate and the reflective aesthetic and identifies two forms of religiosity. Kierkegaard insists that while the three stages are closely related, they retain a certain autonomy. Every perspective carries with it criteria and norms by which individuals might guide their lives. A person can move from one stage to another only through resolute decision. When such a choice is made, a person's world quite literally changes. Worn forms give way to novel patterns for ordering experience. The unimportant suddenly becomes important, while what had been important fades into unimportance.

In the context of our present discussion, we must recognize that Kierkegaard's view of the stages of existence conditions his interpretation of silence. Paradoxical though it may appear, silence assumes various forms. It has a different role to play at each stage on life's way. The meaning and significance of silence are not fixed, but change from stage to stage. By exploring what pseudonymous representatives of the stages have to say about silence, we begin to see the ambiguity and the density of the notion, and to glimpse its importance for faithful existence.

AESTHETIC CONCEALMENT

The aesthetic stage is, perhaps, the most misunderstood of the three Kierkegaardian stages of existence. Many commentators characterize aesthetic existence as the life of pleasure seeking. The aesthete, it is argued, is one who lives primarily for the purpose of gratifying his desires.[4] In the egoistic quest for pleasure, the aesthete is oblivious to moral obligation and to religious concerns. Another way of characterizing the aesthetic stage that finds support in secondary literature identifies it with the stance of theoretical speculation. A person is regarded primarily as an observer to whom objects become manifest. The aim of such a perspective is objective comprehension, rather than moral action or religious devotion.[5] These two views of the aesthetic stage seem to stand in tension. On the one hand, the aesthetic stage is seen as a form of life in which one is governed by sensuous inclination, and on the other hand, as a mode of existence preoccupied with objective thought. It must be acknowledged that there is an element of truth in each of these points of view. The problem with secondary interpretations has been that they have tended to stress either the dominance of sensuous inclination or the priority of theoretical speculation to the exclusion of the other. As a matter of fact, the aesthetic stage is composed of two poles: immediacy and reflection. The failure of analysts to recognize this bipolarity and the propensity to analyze only one of the two poles has necessarily resulted in the failure to arrive at a satisfactory view of this stage. These insights only compound the problem of grasping the nature and significance of silence. We must consider how both aesthetic immediacy and reflection bear on Kierkegaard's view of silence. We will discover that in neither instance is silence broken and disclosure effected. The sources of immediate and reflective silence are, however, quite different.

IMMEDIATE MUSICALITY

Don Juan, as characterized in Mozart's opera of the same name, is for Kierkegaard an ideal example of a person whose life is governed by the attempt to gratify desire. He is what Kierkegaard calls the "sensuous-erotic genius,"[6] who engages in endless erotic adventures in an effort to satisfy his seemingly insatiable lust. Don Juan is so driven by the power of passion that he cannot properly be called an individual person. Rather his life is a reflex of desire, a concrete expression of the natural force of sensuousness: "Here we do not hear Don Juan as a particular individual, or his speech, but we hear a voice, the voice of sensuousness, and we hear it through the longing of womanhood."[7] Kierkegaard makes this point more graphically when he describes Don Juan as "flesh incarnate, or the inspiration of the flesh by the spirit of the flesh."[8] He elaborates: "If I imagine a particular individual, if I see him [Don Juan] or hear him speak, then it becomes comic to imagine that he has seduced 1,003; for as soon as he is regarded as a particular individual, the accent falls in quite another place. When, on the contrary, he is interpreted in music, then I do not have a particular individual, but I have the power of nature, the demonic, which as little tires of seducing or is done with seducing as the wind is tired of blowing, the sea tired of billowing, or a waterfall of tumbling downward from the heights."[9]

For a person who remains bound to such natural sensuality, self-conscious reflection has not yet emerged. The entire immediate aesthetic form of life is prereflective; Don Juan neither thinks nor speaks. His relations with women are not marked by carefully planned plots of seduction such as those formulated by his reflective counterpart, Johannes the seducer. He simply overpowers women through the natural force whose embodiment he is. Even those with whom Don Juan comes into contact are not self-conscious persons so far as Don Juan's awareness goes, but are extensions of the natural power so fully present in him. The prereflective character of Don Juan's existence makes it impossible to express his essential character in words. As the foregoing quotation suggests, only music can communicate pure sensuality. Kierkegaard contends that since music is the medium from which reflection is furthest removed, it is ideally suited to convey the potency of the sensuous erotic genius. Music can express motion, and hence can capture the breathless pace of Don Juan's abrupt movement from one sensual encounter to another. "The most abstract idea conceivable is sensuous genius. But in what medium is the idea expressible? Solely in music. It cannot be expressed in sculpture, for it is a sort of inner qualification of inwardness; nor in painting, for it cannot be apprehended in precise outlines; it is an energy, a storm, impatience, passion, and so on, in all their lyrical quality, yet so that it does not exist in one moment but in a succession of moments, for if it existed in a single moment, it could be modeled or painted. . . . it has not yet advanced to words, but moves always in an immediacy. Hence it cannot be represented in poetry. The only medium which can express it is music."[10]

Words, language, thought are unable to capture immediacy. "Language involves reflection, and cannot, therefore, express the immediate. Reflection destroys the immediate and hence it is impossible to express the musical in language."[11] As the most complete expression of the sensuous-erotic genius, Don Juan "has not yet advanced to words." Music is his element, thought, reflection, language his destruction. Of the immediate aesthetic, Kierkegaard writes: "There the sensuous has its home, there it has its own wild pleasures, for it is a kingdom, a state. In this wild kingdom, language has no place, nor sober minded reflection. There sound only the voice of elemental passion, the play of appetites, the wild shouts of intoxication; it exists solely for pleasure in eternal tumult. The first born of this kingdom is Don Juan."[12] Either Don Juan remains mute, or he ceases to be a sensuous-erotic genius. "The crucial point in this interpretation of Don Juan has already been indicated above: as soon as he acquires speech, everything is altered."[13]

We conclude that the first pole of the aesthetic stage is best described as immediacy *prior* to reflection. One cannot think or speak without negating immediacy. Don Juan's sensual gratification *must* be enjoyed in silence. It should be apparent that by *silence* in this context, we do not mean the absence of sound. Sensual passion has many sounds. But such noise rarely breaks silence and, indeed, often thickens its veil. *Silence* might better be understood as the absence of communication or self-expression. So long as Don Juan continues to be fully immersed in prereflective sensual immediacy, he knows nothing—nothing about himself, his world, or other persons. It is impossible for him to communicate with others or to express himself in an intelligible manner. Silence hovers over the immediate aesthetic stage of existence, even amid its sometimes noisy clamor. Curious sounds of silence.

REFLECTIVE SECRETS

Our exploration of immediacy has already pushed us beyond its bounds and pointed us in the direction of reflection, the other pole of the aesthetic stage. In the second volume of *Either/Or,* Kierkegaard, under the guise of

Judge William, writes: "There comes a moment in a man's life when his immediacy is, as it were, ripened and the spirit demands a higher form in which it will apprehend itself as spirit."[14] This higher form of spirit is reflection. In order to understand Kierkegaard's argument at this point, it is important to recognize that he makes no sharp distinction between thought and language. Relying on Hegel, he argues: "Whereas the philosophy of the recent past had almost exemplified the idea that language exists to conceal thought (since thought simply cannot express *das Ding an sich* at all), Hegel in any case deserves credit for showing that language has thought immanent in itself and that *thought is developed language*. The other thinking was a constant fumbling with the matter."[15] In other words, thought and language are two sides of the same coin—thought internalized language, and language externalized thought. Taken together, they constitute the human capacity for reflection. We can now understand Kierkegaard's contention that "reflection is the negation of immediacy"[16] to mean that immediacy is abrogated with the development of the ability to think reflectively and to use language correctly. In one of his earliest writings, Kierkegaard expresses the point in these terms. "Cannot consciousness then remain in immediacy? This is a foolish question, for if it could, no consciousness would exist. If this immediacy be identical with that of an animal, then the problem of consciousness is done away with. But what would be the result of this? Man would be an animal or in other words, he would be *dumb*. That which annuls immediacy, therefore, is language [*Sproget*]. If man could not speak then he would remain in immediacy."[17] But exactly how do reflective thought and language "annul" immediacy?

In immediate aesthetic existence, both the world and the self are fully indefinite, so indefinite that at the initial stage of immediacy they remain undifferentiated. The world is a confusing array of sense impressions, and the self a mass of conflicting, contradictory emotions and desires. Immersed in this ceaseless stream of sensual flux, the self is aware neither of itself nor of particular objects within its ambience. Such indefiniteness escapes language. "The immediate is really the indeterminate, and therefore language cannot properly apprehend it; but the fact that it is indeterminate is not its perfection but an imperfection."[18] Language, however, does not remain silent before immediacy. Language and reflective thought seek to inform immediate sense experience, thereby bringing form to formlessness. The most important distinction that cognition and the ability to use language make possible is, of course, the conscious differentiation between self and world: "Here there is in fact a certain degree of self-reflection, and so a certain degree of observation of oneself. With this certain degree of self-reflection begins the act of discrimination [*Udsondringsakt*] by which the self becomes aware of itself as something essentially different from the environment, from externalities and their effect upon it."[19] In short, language and thought render possible consciousness of one's world and self-consciousness. The fundamental distinction between self and world (or subject and object) having been established, further refinements develop until each side of the polarity is clearly resolved. A person gradually becomes aware of himself as a center of conscious reflection distinct from objects around him and from other cognitive subjects. Such "acts of discrimination" order chaotic, indefinite, indeterminate immediacy and open new forms of experience.

These insights are important for our study of silence. The ability to reflect and to use language properly allows a person to know himself and the objects and selves that make up his world. It should be stressed that thought and language are not to be understood as idiosyncratic or private. Kierkegaard is persuaded by Enlightenment efforts to interpret reason and language in terms of universality. Persons share common cognitive and linguistic structures. The consequence of this position is that the attempt to bring rational order to disordered sense experience actually is an effort to express experience in universal terms which are, in principle, comprehensible to all rational beings. Another way of making this point is to say that the development of cognitive and linguistic facility establishes the possibility of communicating with other persons. Through reflection we are able to represent to ourselves what we experience, and by language we can address ourselves to other persons. Surely this does not imply that we always understand completely what we are thinking or what another person is saying. Kierkegaard's point is that without the presupposition of common cognitive and linguistic structures there is not even the possibility of communication among selves.

But, of course, this is only half the story. The opportunity for communication carries with it the possibility of the refusal to communicate. Put in other terms, the acquisition of the capacity to use language opens the possibility of intentional silence or deliberate concealment. Only linguistic beings can keep secrets. The reflective-aesthetic stage of existence is characterized by various modes of purposeful silence. There are secrets and there are secrets.

Before describing these forms of silence in detail, it might be helpful to distinguish reflective secrets from the noisy silence of immediacy. We have seen that Don Juan is the paradigm of the sensuous-erotic genius, whose entire life is devoted to pleasure seeking. As a creature of desire, he remains prereflective; Don Juan "has not yet advanced to words." Indeed were he able to think and to speak, he would negate his immediacy and move to the reflective pole of the aesthetic stage. Since he can neither think nor speak, it is not possible for him to express himself or to communicate with others in an intelligible manner. Consequently for all his passionate noise, a certain silence continues to surround Don Juan. If he is to remain a sensuous-erotic genius, breaking this silence is simply impossible. Clearly the case of the reflective aesthete is quite different. No longer completely controlled by desire, he is able to reflect in a rational way and to communicate intelligently. If he chooses, he can overcome silence by speaking. The necessity attached to the silence of immediacy is gone from reflective silence. Nevertheless, it seems to the reflective aesthete that there are good reasons to guard silence.

Kierkegaard's most extensive consideration of reflective silence is presented in Problem III of *Fear and Trembling.* Although not always carefully distinguished, we can identify four primary forms of silence that are typical of the reflective pole of the aesthetic stage: *playful, deceitful, heroic,* and *demonic* silence. In each instance, silence is freely chosen, though the reasons for the choice vary greatly.

The simplest form of reflective silence is playful silence, and Kierkegaard does not discuss it in much detail, for he takes it to be a common and obvious occurrence. He sees playful silence most adequately represented in the drama of his day. Kierkegaard is thinking primarily of the kind of intentional secrecy that lies at the heart of comedy.[20] Mistaken identity, careful disguise, white lies, puns, and irony all generate comic situations. Of course, such playful silence is not restricted to the stage; it is an important part of the drama of everyday life. Lovers, friends, parents, children all playfully conceal. Such secrecy is fun—it enhances the enjoyment of life. What would Christmas be to a child if his parents kept no secrets? Is courtship possible without coy silence? As the comic ending reveals, when the playful secret is told, all live happily ever after.

Not so with deceitful silence. In the course of his pseudonymous authorship, Kierkegaard devotes considerable attention to the problem of deceitful secrecy. In *Fear and Trembling,* this issue is raised in the context of his consideration of Agnes and the Merman.[21] At the beginning of his relation with Agnes, the Merman's silence is deceitful. He intends to seduce her, but recognizes that he will never accomplish this end without practicing some deceit. Therefore he develops a careful strategy to veil his real purpose. In his cunning he intends to take advantage of Agnes' innocence.[22] Johannes de Silentio explains, "The merman was a seducer. He had called to Agnes, had by his smooth speech enticed from her the hidden sentiments, she has found in the merman what she sought, what she was gazing down after at the bottom of the sea. Agnes would like to follow him" (*FT,* pp. 102–03). The implications of the Merman's deceitful silence become more evident when we recognize his close affinity to the other great seducer of the pseudonymous authorship—Johannes, whose diary constitutes a major part of *Either/Or.* A brief consideration of Johannes the seducer will help us to understand the Merman more fully and to clarify further the relationship between immediacy and reflection.

It is significant that Kierkegaard selects a seducer and the intrigue of a seduction to present his analysis of the reflective aesthetic in *Either/Or.* By doing so, he establishes a conscious parallel with the "first born" of the kingdom of immediacy, Don Juan. The two seducers represent the tension between the immediate and the reflective poles of the aesthetic stage. Though Don Juan and Johannes are both seducers, the similarity in their erotic adventures ends here. Don Juan, as we have seen, is the embodiment of the power of sensuality. He conquers women by the sheer strength of his eroticism, rather than by a carefully developed and skillfully executed plan of seduction. Only music is able to express the power of his immediacy. Johannes, on the other hand, seduces only one woman. He brings about this seduction by an intricate plan that is described in tortuous detail in his diary. The prosaic form of the diary is most appropriate for recording Johannes' endless reflection and plotting. The basic difference between Don Juan and Johannes creates a different interest for the reader. "The immediate Don Juan must seduce 1,003; the reflective need only seduce one, and what interests us is how he did it. The reflective Don Juan's seduction is a sleight-of-hand performance, wherein every single little trick has its special importance; the musical Don Juan's seduction is a handspring, a matter of an instant, swifter done than said."[23] In the case of Don Juan, the immediate fact of his sexual conquests arrests our attention, while in that of Johannes, the long and involved reflection in which he engages is of interest to us.

Johannes selects as the victim of his plan a young girl by the name of Cordelia. The reader, however, learns very little about Cordelia herself, for she is seen through the plotting eyes of Johannes. Johannes views Cordelia, as he does other characters in the intrigue, as an object to be manipulated for his own purposes. His aim is to fashion her into the sort of person who can fulfill his lustful desires. Any form of deception is permissible so long as it advances his sinister end. In carrying out his scheme, Johannes shows total disregard for Cordelia's feelings. His comments about the culmination of the affair reveal the mood in which he approaches the entire undertaking:

> Still, it is over now, and I hope never to see her again. When a girl has given away everything, then she is weak, then she has lost everything. . . . I do not wish to be reminded of my relation to her; she has lost the fragrance, and the time is past when a girl suffering the pain of a faithless love can be changed into a sunflower. I will have no farewell scene with her; nothing is more disgusting to me than a woman's tears and a woman's prayers, which alter everything, and yet really mean nothing. I have loved her, but from now on she can no longer engross my soul.[24]

Johannes' strategy is successful, for Cordelia remains ignorant of his real intention up to the moment of seduction. This means, however, that Johannes' triumph brings defeat and disillusion to Cordelia. When the deceitful secret is told, Cordelia is crushed. Deceitful silence, like playful silence, is undertaken for the purpose of maximizing pleasure. But unlike playful silence, deceitful silence involves the enjoyment of only one of those concerned, and this at the expense of the other. It takes little imagination to recognize the significance of this form of silence in relations among many persons. Not only amorous adventures are fueled by such secrecy. Deceit wears many faces. Despite its various forms, deceitful silence usually springs from selfish sources and issues in the violation of other persons. Betrayal exacts a price. But reflective silence can fall to still greater depths. Deceitful silence can become demonic.

In order to understand Kierkegaard's complex analysis of silence, it is essential to recognize his distinction between deceitful and demonic silence.[25] Let us return to the Merman and Agnes. Unlike Johannes, the Merman does not carry through his plan of seduction. At the climactic moment, he "collapses, he is not able to resist the power of innocence, his native element is unfaithful to him, he cannot seduce Agnes. He leads her back again, he explains to her that he only wanted to show her how beautiful the sea is when it is calm, and Agnes believes him" (*FT*, p. 104). Having turned away from his deceitful end, the Merman faces two options: "repentance; and Agnes and repentance. If repentance alone takes possession of him, then he is hidden; if Agnes and repentance take possession of him, then he is revealed" (*FT*, p. 105). The Merman could, of course, repent, disclose his corrupt intention to Agnes, and ask her forgiveness. Though no doubt the naïve young girl would be distraught by the revelation, it is possible that Agnes would forgive the Merman and that they could establish a solid relationship on a firm foundation of mutual trust and understanding. But the Merman might also repent of his intention without revealing himself to Agnes. Johannes de Silentio explains:

> Now in case repentance grips the Merman and he remains concealed, he has clearly made Agnes unhappy, for Agnes loved him in all her innocence, she believed that at the instant when even to her he seemed changed, however well he hid it, he was telling the truth in saying that he only wanted to show her the beautiful calmness of the sea. However with respect to passion the Merman himself becomes still more unhappy, for he loved Agnes with a multiplicity of passions and had besides a new guilt to bear. The demonic element in repentance will now explain to him that this is precisely his punishment, and that the more it tortures him the better. (*FT*, pp. 105–06)

The psychological dynamics of the demonic, as Kierkegaard defines it, are extraordinarily complex. Presumably the Merman's repentance is genuine. The loving trust of Agnes dissipates his deceitful lust and awakens a new form of love. In the face of this novel affection, his earlier desire seems cruel and evil. Thus he regards the pain and unhappiness wrought by repentance as just punishment for a heinous scheme. But precisely this understanding of the inward suffering occasioned by deceitful deeds can lead to demonic silence. Paradoxical though it may seem, misery can become attractive, and suffering one's raison d'être. Johannes insists that "there is no doubt that he [the Merman] can talk" (*FT*, p. 106). Moreover, we have seen that speaking opens the possibility of overcoming pain through Agnes' forgiveness. But the Merman chooses to remain silent. His relation to his suffering is ambivalent. On the one hand he is repelled by it and wants nothing more than to be free of it, while on the other hand, he is attracted to it and refuses to part with it. The attachment to one's own corruption and suffering that leads a person to guard silence and to turn his back on the possibility of forgiveness is what Kierkegaard means by the demonic.

In *The Concept of Dread,* Vigilius Haufniensis explains more fully the nature of demonic silence. "The demonic," he suggests, "is dread of the good."[26] This point is clarified when the good is defined as "the reintegration of freedom, redemption, salvation, or whatever name one would give it."[27] When one becomes attached to his corruption and the unhappiness it brings, he tends to avoid the good that might allow forgiveness and the alleviation of inward misery. A person closes in on himself, refusing the communication with others that could rob him of his beloved suffering. Kierkegaard explains the demonic in terms of such self-closure. "The demonic is closed-upness [*det Indesluttede*] and the unfreely revealed [*det ufrivilligt Aabenbare*]. These two traits denote, as they should, the same thing; for the closed-up is precisely the dumb [*Stumme*], and if it has to express itself, this must come about against its will when freedom lying prone in unfreedom revolts upon coming into communication with freedom outside and now betrays unfreedom in such a way that it is the individual who betrays himself against his will in dread."[28] Demonic silence can be broken only by freely speaking to another. "The closed-up is precisely the dumb; language, the word is precisely the saving thing, that which delivers from the empty abstraction from the closed-up."[29] Though this disclosure always is possible for this form of reflective aesthetic existence, suffering itself provides too much pleasure, perverse though it may seem, to permit self-revelation.

For Kierkegaard, demonic silence is the most dangerous, though not the most terrifying, sound of silence. It represents a complete reversal of the proper state of affairs. Evil, corruption, unhappiness are loved, and good, wholeness, happiness are hated. Instead of seeking release from corruption through communication with and forgiveness of other persons, one closes in on himself and suffers silently.[30] Reflective silence need not, however, always be demonic; at times it even can be heroic.

The final expression of silence characteristic of the reflective aesthetic stage is heroic silence. As the name implies, this form of silence seems to be more nobly motivated than the other forms. Kierkegaard develops his understanding of heroic silence by examining the aesthetic hero. His discussion at this point lays the groundwork for his consideration of the role of silence at the ethical and the religious stages of existence. In the concluding pages of the book, Kierkegaard contrasts the aesthetic hero, the tragic hero, and the knight of faith. The form of silence peculiar to each character provides the key that unlocks the significance of this comparison.

The distinguishing mark of heroic silence is the willingness to keep what at times can be a painful secret in order to save another person from misfortune. Johannes de Silentio makes this point concisely when he writes: "Aesthetics permitted, yea, required of the individual silence, when he knew that by keeping silent he could save another" (*FT*, p. 121). Heroic silence is, therefore, the precise reverse of deceitful silence. While deceitful silence promotes secrecy in order to maximize one's own pleasure in a way that usually brings pain to another, heroic silence willingly incurs suffering in order to save another from unhappiness. Throughout *Fear and Trembling* several illustrations of heroic silence are offered. Johannes' simplest example of heroic silence concerns two persons secretly in love, "although they have not definitely avowed their love to one another" (*FT*, p. 94). Before this love can find expression, the girl's parents compel her to marry another person. Filial piety leads her to comply with the wishes of her parents, though the marriage cannot quell her first love. "She conceals her love, so as not to make the other unhappy" (*FT*, p. 94). Out of deference to the well-being of his beloved's family, the young man "resolves magnanimously to remain in his concealment, 'the young girl shall never get to know it, so that she may perhaps become happy by giving her hand to another' " (*FT*, p. 95). In both cases, "concealment is a free act, for which they are held responsible by aesthetics" (*FT*, p. 95). The action of each person is intended to be a noble expression of love, but only misunderstanding and unhappiness follow.

Johannes presents a more complex instance of the same basic situation by elaborating a story suggested in Aristotle's *Poetics*. When a young bridegroom consults the Delphic oracle on his wedding day, "the augurs foretell him that a misfortune will follow his marriage" (*FT*, p. 98). Johannes notes the peculiarity of this situation: "Usually it is all the afflictions and difficulties of the finite which like evil spirits separate the lovers, but love has heaven on its side, and therefore this holy alliance overcomes all enemies. In this case it is heaven itself which separates what heaven itself has joined together" (*FT*, pp. 98–99). This unexpected development poses a dilemma for the bridegroom. "What then is he to do? (1) Shall he preserve silence and celebrate the wedding?—with the thought that 'perhaps the misfortune will not come at once, at any rate I have upheld love and have not feared to make myself unhappy. . . .' (2) shall he keep silent and give up celebrating the wedding? In this case he must embroil himself in a mystification by which he reduces himself to naught in relation to her. . . . Or (3) shall he speak?" (*FT*, p. 100). From the aesthetic point of view, the choice is clear: the bridegroom must remain silent and refuse to marry in order to protect his beloved from misfortune.

Johannes cites Faust as another case of heroic silence. "Faust," he notes, "is a doubter" (*FT*, p. 116). Faust carries through his resolution to doubt so thoroughly that the certainties upon which most people build their lives vanish before him. Were he to reveal his doubt to others, misery would befall them, for they would be plunged into the anxiety that uncertainty brings. But "Faust is a sympathetic nature" (*FT*, p. 118), and for the sake of the race as a whole, "he keeps silent, he hides the doubt in his soul more carefully than the girl who hides under her heart the fruit of a sinful love, he endeavors as well as he can to walk in step with other men, but what goes on within him he consumes with himself " (*FT*, p. 118).

The final representative of heroic doubt is Agamemnon in Euripides' *Iphigenia in Aulis*. Johannes' study of Agamemnon is particularly important, for it at once discloses some of the ambiguities of heroic silence and points to the ethical interpretation of Agamemnon as a tragic hero. The problem facing Agamemnon is whether he should reveal to others the necessity to sacrifice Iphigenia for the welfare of the state as a whole. Johannes explains the situation: "When the hero ensnared in the aesthetic illusion thinks by his silence to save another man, then it requires silence and rewards it. . . . Agamemnon must sacrifice Iphigenia. Now aesthetics requires silence of Agamemnon inasmuch as it would be unworthy of the hero to seek comfort from any other man, and out of solicitude for the women too he ought to conceal this from them as long as possible" (*FT*, p. 96). Again there is no doubt that Agamemnon *can* reveal to others his intention to kill Iphigenia, and that they will understand his plight, admire his courage, and share his misery. "The aesthetic hero *can* speak, but will not" (*FT*, p. 122). He keeps silent for two reasons. The first has become apparent in what has gone before. By remaining silent, Agamemnon attempts to protect those around him from unnecessary sorrow. Eventually, of course, the secret must be told and the dreaded suffering will ensue. Nevertheless, the aesthetic hero is persuaded that he should forestall such misery for as long as possible.

Johannes' remarks reveal another deeply hidden motive for Agamemnon's silence. Though ostensibly undertaken for the advantage of another person, heroic silence also benefits the aesthetic hero. Indeed from an aesthetic point of view, heroic identity is contingent upon remaining silent. Silent suffering is a trial the hero must pass. When this is recognized, it becomes apparent that heroic silence can easily slip into demonic silence. The misery one silently endures can become a source of pleasure and the basis of one's self-understanding and self-esteem. The very act by which one seeks to spare another person unhappiness brings a form of suffering that is not unsatisfying to the silent individual. The psychodynamics of silence again prove to be quite involved. Kierkegaard relentlessly probes the ambivalence and ambiguity of silence's sources.

Our long and involved analysis reveals that silence reigns throughout the aesthetic stage of existence. Aesthetic silence assumes many forms, ranging from the seeming necessary silence of the sensuous-erotic genius to reflective secrets willingly kept for playful, deceitful, demonic, and heroic purposes. Though aesthetic noise may often sound, at no point is there communication between persons or genuine self-expression. To realize such possibilities, we must advance from the aesthetic to the ethical stage of existence.

ETHICAL COMMUNICABILITY

Occupying a middle position between the aesthetic and the religious stages, the ethicist breaks the silence that surrounds him on both sides. Johannes de Silentio identifies the peculiar character of ethical communicability by comparing it to the willing silence of the reflective aesthete, on the one hand,[31] and to the necessary silence of the knight of faith, on the other. In the next section of our discussion, we will attempt to distinguish the ethical and the religious responses to silence. For the moment, we must try to understand the ethicist's view of silence by contrasting it with insights garnered from our exploration of aesthetic silence. This issue takes us to the heart of the difference between the aesthetic and the ethical stages of existence.

Johannes begins his analysis of Problem III by observing,

> The ethical as such is the universal, again, as the universal it is the revealed [det Aabenbare]. The individual regarded as he is immediately, that is as sensually and psychically determined, is the concealed [det Skjulte]. So his ethical task is to develop out of his concealment and to become revealed in the universal. Every time he wills to remain in concealment, he sins and lies in temptation [Anfægtelse], out of which he can come only by revealing himself. [FT, p. 91)

In Concluding Unscientific Postscript, Johannes Climacus makes this point more concisely when he notes the difference between the aesthetic and the ethical stages in Either/Or: " 'the expression which sharply differentiates between the ethical and the aesthetic stage is this: it is every man's duty to reveal himself'—the first part [i.e., the aesthetic stage] was concealment."[32] These texts suggest the most important features of the different views to silence held by the ethicist and by the aesthete.

We have already seen that the entire aesthetic stage remains wrapped in silence. Though necessity attaches to the silence of immediacy, reflective silence is voluntary. Reflective secrets always can be told. The reasons for keeping silent are many and complex—ranging from the demonic to the heroic. From the ethical viewpoint, silence is regarded quite differently. The ethicist directly opposes all forms of silence, regardless of motivation.

Within the ethical framework, as Kierkegaard defines it in his pseudony-mous authorship, secrecy, silence, and concealment are never justifiable. An individual has a moral obligation to reveal himself through free communication with other persons. As Johannes de Silentio maintains, "For the ethical view of life, it is . . . the task of the individual to divest himself of inward determinants and to express himself in an outward way" (*FT*, p. 119). Judge William, Kierkegaard's ethical paradigm, echoes this sentiment when he declares to the secretive seducer, Johannes, "I say that it is every man's duty to become revealed."[33] In sum, although "aesthetics required concealment and rewarded it, ethics required revelation and punished concealment" (*FT*, p. 96). But what is the basis upon which the ethicist so violently opposes silence and concealment, and so strongly urges self-expression and revelation? To answer this question, we must probe more deeply the major coordinates of ethical existence.[34]

From the ethical point of view, life is understood primarily in terms of free decision. While the aesthete avoids decision through either immersion in sensuous inclination or endless reflection, the ethicist constantly admon-ishes the individual to realize his potential through the free resolution of his will. From the ethical perspective, the self is not actualized until the will is engaged. Apart from resolute decision, a person remains an indetermi-nate bundle of conflicting desires and contradictory possibilities. As the name of this stage of existence implies, the ethicist is not indifferent to the nature of the decisions that are made, but insists that an individual's will always be guided by moral law. When we seek to uncover the meaning of duty, we discover that moral obligation is consistently interpreted in terms of universality. Each of the three "Problems" in the latter part of *Fear and Trembling* begins with the assertion, "The ethical as such is the universal" (*FT*, pp. 64, 78, and 91). The notion of duty characteristic of Kierkegaard's ethical stage is, therefore, reminiscent of Kant's categorical imperative, according to which the morality of a proposed action is determined by its ability to be universalized, i.e., to be applied under any circumstance.[35] Johannes de Silentio lends credence to this line of argument by maintain-ing, "The ethical as such is the universal, and as the universal it applies to everyone, which may be expressed from another point of view by saying that it applies at every instant" (*FT*, p. 64).

In light of this interpretation of duty, the fundamental struggle of morality involves the conflict between universality and particularity. Each individual is called upon to forego idiosyncratic inclination in order to further the good of a larger community. Immorality, by contrast, is the subordination of common moral precepts to personal desire. In Johannes' own words,

> The individual determined sensually and psychically is the individual who has his *telos* in the universal, and his ethical task is to express himself constantly

in it, to annul [*ophaeve*] his individuality in order to become the universal. As soon as the individual would assert himself in his particularity over against the universal he sins, and only by recognizing this can he again reconcile himself with the universal. Whenever the individual after he has entered the universal feels an impulse to assert himself as the particular, he is in temptation, and he can labor himself out of this only by penitently abandoning himself as the particular in the universal. (*FT,* pp. 64–65)

For the purpose of our analysis, it is important to recognize that the universality of moral laws, in principle, renders them comprehensible to all rational beings. Man's ethical dilemma is not knowing the good, but willing it. This same universality allows an individual to explain any moral decision to another person with the confidence that he will understand and appreciate the basis of the choice. Morality presupposes such communication and consent among rational agents. We can summarize the ethical point of view by saying that while the possibility of moral action depends upon free communication among rational persons in which universal precepts of conduct are identified, the actuality of moral community rests upon the willingness of particular agents to subject personal interests to the universal moral laws that reason defines. Let us consider each of these points in turn.

The basis of the ethical insistence that moral relationships involve common allegiance to universally binding rules of action should be apparent from what has gone before. Without shared moral principles, every individual would be left to follow his selfish desires. The ethicist holds that a Hobbesian war of all against all would result. The reason for the necessity of free communication among moral agents is not quite as evident. Exploration of this issue, however, takes us to the heart of the ethical aversion to silence. From an ethical perspective, to remain silent and to refuse to express oneself in an honest and forthright way is to negate the very possibility of moral relationships. The ethical substance of a community depends upon honest self-expression among its members. In short, moral community is impossible without communication. Through language, one expresses the universal principles informing moral action. This is what Johannes means when he claims that language "translates me into the universal" (*FT,* p. 122). The ethicist believes all forms of silence to be deceptive and deceitful. Secrecy and concealment unravel the very moral fabric of a society. Although a silent agent might act *in accordance* with duty, it is not evident to the community at large whether he acts *from* duty. Consequently the ethicist argues that a person is duty bound to speak, to come out of concealment and to reveal publicly the ground of his deeds. Silence is a moral transgression in which one refuses to express himself in terms of universality and clings to particularity. We can now discern the reasoning behind Johannes' contention that the "ethical task is to develop out of this concealment and to become revealed in the universal" (*FT,* p. 91).

We might best summarize the difference between aesthetic and ethical responses to silence by comparing their diverse interpretations of Agamemnon.[36] Recall the situation: It has been disclosed to Agamemnon that he must sacrifice his daughter, Iphigenia, for the welfare of the state as a whole. This is not a question of negating his fatherly duty, but of having this obligation subsumed by a wider responsibility to the entire state. The dilemma Agamemnon faces is whether he should keep his duty secret or should reveal it to those around him. "Aesthetics," we have seen, "permitted, yea, required of the individual silence, when he knew that by keeping silent he could save another" (*FT,* p. 121). In other words, the aesthete holds that Agamemnon should remain silent about his intention to kill Iphigenia in order to spare others the unhappiness that necessarily would follow the revelation of his intention. Indeed, such silence is seen as heroic, for one voluntarily incurs suffering for the sake of the well-being of others. Ethics disagrees. For the ethicist, Agamemnon is obliged to break his silence and to speak. He must explain to his daughter, his wife, and the whole state the demand that duty is making upon him. The assumption of the universality of moral obligation assures Agamemnon that others will understand his intention, respect his courage, and share his sorrow. To the extent that Iphigenia can appreciate the ethical perspective on life, she has to admit the propriety of her father's intention and admire his resolve to carry out his duty, regardless of cost. To do otherwise would be to give personal desire or pleasure priority over moral responsibility. Of Agamemnon, ethics says, "The genuine tragic hero sacrifices himself and all that is his for the universal, his deed and every emotion with him belong to the universal, he is revealed, and in this self-revelation he is the beloved son of ethics" (*FT,* p. 122). When Agamemnon discloses the ground of his deed, the sacrifice of Iphigenia strengthens the moral fabric of the society by manifesting the absolutely binding character of duty. If the most powerful citizen must willingly subject his strongest desire to the dictates of morality, should not every person conscientiously carry out his duty? Had Agamemnon followed the aesthete's counsel and remained silent, the consequence of his act might have been quite different. With no explanation from Agamemnon, people would be left to speculate about his motives. No doubt many would see the deed as ruthless murder, the cruelest violation of duty. The moral character of his intention would likely go unfathomed. Agamemnon's apparent immorality would fracture the moral structure of his world. If Agamemnon himself can act in such a manner, what harm can follow from the moral laxity of ordinary citizens? The recognition of the possibility of such dire consequences leads the ethicist to oppose all forms of silence and to demand truthful self-revelation.[37]

At the ethical stage of existence, silence is never heroic. To the contrary, "Silence is the snare of the demon" (*FT,* p. 97). But this is not the end of Johannes' tale, for he suggests that from another point of view, silence is "the mutual understanding between the Deity and the individual" (*FT,* p. 97).

DUMB BELIEVERS

"It was early in the morning, Abraham arose betimes, he embraced Sarah, the bride of his old age, and Sarah kissed Isaac, who had taken away her reproach, who was her pride, her hope for all time. So they rode in silence along the way, and Abraham's glance was fixed upon the ground until the fourth day when he lifted up his eyes and saw afar off Mount Moriah, but his glance turned again to the ground. Silently he laid the wood in order, he bound Isaac, in silence he drew the knife—then he saw the ram which God had prepared. Then he offered that and returned home" (*FT,* p. 28). "Abraham keeps silent—but he *cannot* speak" (*FT,* p. 122).

We would seem to have come full circle: from silence and concealment, through communication and revelation, back to silence and concealment. Abraham, the paradigmatic knight of faith, not only does not speak, but cannot speak. Like the silence of aesthetic immediacy, faithful silence seems necessary. This apparent circularity is not accidental. Kierkegaard understands the stages of existence to be dialectically interrelated. Each succeeding stage displaces its predecessor from a position of centrality while at the same time taking it up within itself, giving the former stage a relativized status.[38] Thus ethical existence preserves aesthetic determinants, and the religious stage conserves important features of aesthetic and ethical forms of life. When we arrive at Kierkegaard's final stage of existence, we again find many of the themes and problems characteristic of his first stage. Most notably, after moving beyond the ethicist's talkativeness, we once more are able to hear sounds of silence. Our journey, however, has not been for naught. Aesthetic and religious silence are "worlds" apart. We could not grasp the uniqueness of Abraham's silence without having considered the significance of silence for aesthetic and ethical existence. As Johannes de Silentio observes, "It is incumbent upon me to examine dialectically the part played by concealment in aesthetics and ethics, for the point is to show the absolute difference between aesthetic concealment and the paradox [i.e., faith, or religious silence]" (*FT,* p. 94).

Abraham believes that God has issued a demand for him to sacrifice his son, Isaac. Unlike Agamemnon, Abraham's intended deed serves no higher ethical purpose. The sacrifice is not directed to the welfare of a larger social group, but is undertaken solely for the sake of Abraham

himself. It is a trial by which Abraham attempts to establish his identity as
a believer. Johannes states the difference between Agamemnon and
Abraham concisely when he writes, "The tragic hero renounces himself in
order to express the universal, the knight of faith renounces the universal
in order to become himself" (*FT*, p. 86). This does not mean that Abraham
is ignorant of or insensitive to his ethical responsibility to Isaac. Since each
stage preserves (though it also relativizes) its predecessors, the knight of
faith remains bound by moral obligation. "Abraham's relation to Isaac,
ethically speaking, is quite simply expressed by saying that a father shall
love his son more dearly than himself" (*FT*, p. 67). As opposed to the
ethicist, however, the believer does not absolutize duty but stands ready to
suspend it in light of a higher obligation to the transcendent God. It is
essential to stress that *suspend* does not mean "negate." Precisely the
coincidence of ethical obligation and the divine dictate to transgress
morality creates fear and trembling for the knight of faith.

These remarks enable us to see that Abraham can never relinquish his
ethical responsibility to Isaac. Were he to do so, his apparent trial of faith
would become the most outrageous temptation. To the extent that Abraham maintains his ethical relation to Isaac, he is obliged not to conceal
himself, but to communicate freely and honestly with his son. As we have
seen, the ethical point of view insists that silence poisons human relations
and destroys moral community. For Abraham the dreaded conflict between ethical and religious commitments becomes real. His relation to
God makes it *impossible* for him to speak to Isaac, to Sarah, or to anyone
else. He *cannot* fulfill the ethical mandate to reveal himself, though this
might be his strongest desire. Unlike the reflective aesthete, Abraham's
silence is not volitional. In a manner reminiscent of the immediate aesthete, though for very different reasons, Abraham is unable to speak. But
why? Why can't Abraham speak? Why must he remain silent?

The necessity of Abraham's silence is a function of the nature of his
relationship to God. Johannes argues,[39]

> Faith is precisely this paradox, that the individual as the individual is higher
> than the universal, is justified over against it, is not subordinate but supe-
> rior—yet in such a way, be it observed, that it is the individual who, after he
> has been subordinated as the individual to the universal, now through the
> universal becomes the individual who as the individual is superior to the
> universal, for the fact that the individual as the individual stands in an
> absolute relation to the Absolute. This position cannot be mediated, for all
> mediation comes about precisely by virtue of the universal; it is and remains
> to all eternity a paradox, inaccessible to thought. (*FT*, p. 66)

In this extraordinarily complex but important passage, Johannes points out
that the faithful person stands in a direct, an immediate, a private relation
to God. Only a solitary self can meet God. As Johannes puts it, in faith

"the individual is only the individual" (*FT*, p. 80). The relationship to God cannot be mediated through other persons, but must be direct, ummediated. If an individual abrogates his isolation, even out of ethical obligation to another person, he negates the possibility of an absolute (i.e., faithful) relation to the Absolute. We must meet God alone, "for only the individual becomes a knight of faith as the individual, and this is the greatness of this knighthood . . . but this is also its terror" (*FT*, p. 82).

The radical individuality of the believer's relation to God is the basis of faithful silence. Such individuality cannot be articulated in or mediated by language. In our examination of ethical communicability, we have seen that language always translates into universality (*FT*, p. 122). But such a transformation of individuality into universality would be the annulment of the most essential feature of the God relation. "Abraham cannot be mediated, and the same thing can be expressed also by saying that he cannot talk. As soon as I talk I express the universal, and if I do not do so, no one can understand me" (*FT*, p. 70). The very nature of language, i.e., its universality, renders it impotent to capture the moment of faith.[40] If Abraham tries to explain his trial to others, he necessarily misrepresents it. "Therefore if Abraham would express himself in terms of the universal, he must say that his situation is a temptation, for he has no higher expression for that universal which stands above the universal which he transgresses" (*FT*, p. 71). And yet we have seen that "Faith is precisely this paradox that the individual, as the individual is higher than the universal" (*FT*, p. 66). When faith is defined in this way, concealment becomes necessary. "If there is not a concealment which has its ground in the fact that the individual is higher than the universal, then Abraham's conduct is indefensible, for he paid no heed to the intermediate ethical determinants" (*FT*, p. 91).

Johannes' analysis of religious silence might become clearer by noting another way in which he poses his argument. He insists that the faithful relation to God is thoroughly private. In faith, three's a crowd! To make his point, Johannes returns to the case of the young bridegroom who consulted the oracle on his wedding day and learned that misfortune would follow his marriage. In an effort to illuminate the crisis of faith, the plot is changed. No longer is misfortune predicted by an oracle that can be understood by all. Rather the revelation of impending unhappiness is made to the bridegroom alone; it is fully private. Johannes maintains that in this situation, free disclosure no longer is possible. "In case the will of heaven had not been announced to him by an augur, in case it had come to his knowledge in an entirely private way, in case it had put itself into an entirely private relationship with him, then we encounter the paradox . . . then he could not speak, however much he might wish to" (*FT*, p. 102). To speak is to disrupt the privacy that is essential for the proper relationship between an individual and God.[41]

The believer's thoroughly individual and absolutely private relationship to God forces his faith into the hidden recesses of inwardness. At one point, Johannes characterizes faith as the "paradox that inwardness is higher than outwardness" (*FT*, p. 79). The ethicist, we recall, contends that inwardness must always manifest itself outwardly—"it is every man's duty to become revealed." Though the knight of faith recognizes this ethical obligation, he is unable to fulfill it. Johannes goes so far as to suggest that faith remains so hidden that the believer's "outward appearance bears a striking resemblance to that which both the infinite resignation and faith profoundly despise . . . to Philistinism" (*FT*, p. 49).

"Abraham keeps silent—but he *cannot* speak." The character of the faithful relation to God makes speaking impossible and necessitates silence. "So the reason for his silence is not that he as the individual would place himself in an absolute relation to the *universal*, but that he as the individual was placed in an absolute relation to the *absolute*" (*FT*, p. 103). Believers are by nature dumb! And to nonbelievers this dumbness is more than muteness. Johannes says of the knight of faith, "Humanly speaking he is crazy and cannot make himself intelligible to anyone" (*FT*, p. 86). *Cannot* make himself intelligible . . . : that is an essential point about faithful silence. Since language renders the individual universal and the private public, "faith is the paradox that the individual absolutely cannot make himself intelligible to anybody" (*FT*, p. 81). Intelligible to anybody . . . : that, too, is essential. Not only is the believer unable to express himself to others; he cannot even make his trial comprehensible to himself. Faith involves an absolute paradox that shatters human reflection—shipwrecks understanding. After all, Abraham's conviction that he should kill Isaac might be a horrible temptation rather than a trial of faith. Wrapped in silence, unable to communicate with others or to become intelligible to himself, the knight is gripped by fear and trembling. "Therein lies the distress and anguish. For if when I speak I am unable to make myself intelligible, then I am not speaking—even though I were to talk uninterruptedly day and night. Such is the case with Abraham. He is able to utter everything, but one thing he cannot say, i.e., say it in such a way that another understands it, and so he is not speaking. The relief of speech is that it translates me into the universal" (*FT*, p. 122). Abraham's single effort to speak confirms the necessity of his silence. His words conceal rather than reveal. "Hence he is speaking no untruth, but neither is he saying anything, for he speaks a foreign language" (*FT*, p. 128).

Johannes concludes that the believer simply is unable to become articulate about his faith. Faith cannot be mediated through language or rational thought. It is unmediated, immediate. Our circle seems complete, for we have returned to immediacy. But immediacy with a difference, "For faith is not the first immediacy but a subsequent immediacy" (*FT*, p. 92). As Kierkegaard puts it in his Journals, "faith is immediacy after reflection."[42]

We have seen that aesthetic immediacy is immediacy prior to reflection. For the sensual aesthete, reflection has not developed and individual selfhood has yet to emerge. At the first pole of the aesthetic stage, one remains a prereflective bundle of desires and sensations. The acquisition of the ability to think rationally and to use language properly negates immediacy. But the immediate aesthete has not yet advanced to this stage. The absence of individual selfhood and the inability to use language necessitate the silence of aesthetic immediacy. For the knight of faith, immediacy negates, and is not negated by, reflection. He is able to speak, but cannot. The direct, unmediated, radically privatized and individualized relation of the believer to God cannot be conveyed in the universal categories of thought and language. Not the absence of individual selfhood, but its most extraordinary expression strikes the believer dumb. The silence of immediacy, be it before or after reflection, is always necessary. While bearing a certain formal similarity to each other, the necessary silence of the sensuous erotic genius and of the believer are quite different. These two sounds of silence represent opposite stages on life's way. Though we begin and end with silence, our beginning and ending are not identical. The journey from and to silence is only apparently a circle.

Abraham, the knight of faith, "is unable to speak, he speaks no human language. Though he himself understood all the tongues of the world, though his loved ones also understood them, he nevertheless cannot speak—he speaks a divine language . . . he 'speaks with tongues' " (*FT*, p. 123). A frightful sound of silence.

COMMUNITY AND COMMUNICATION

Rarely has an author so carefully probed the nature and significance of silence. By placing his consideration of silence within the context of his notion of the stages of existence, Kierkegaard illuminates the different forms silence can assume and the contrasting roles it can play in a person's life. In *Fear and Trembling*, however, Kierkegaard's primary concern is faith. Through the pseudonym of Johannes de Silentio he explores the nature of faithful existence. In the course of his inquiry, Johannes discovers that silence is an intrinsic dimension of the life of faith. The analysis of aesthetic and ethical responses to silence in *Fear and Trembling* has as its end a clarification of the importance of silence at the religious stage of existence. In concluding our study, we shall attempt to suggest some of the problems inherent in Kierkegaard's view of faithful silence.

As the history of scholarship amply demonstrates, commentators have little trouble identifying points of disagreement with Kierkegaard's view of faith. Quite often, however, critiques are directed at Kierkegaard from a perspective outside his authorship, and thus seem to be beside the point. Writers are seldom patient enough to try to elaborate their misgivings by developing the internal weaknesses of Kierkegaard's position. Instead of leveling a broadside attack on Kierkegaard's admittedly problematic representation of religious belief, we shall attempt to criticize faithful silence within the terms Kierkegaard himself defines.

If our interpretation is correct, the necessity of the believer's silence is a function of the nature of his relationship to God. In order to meet the wholly other God, a person must distance himself from others and journey alone. The highly individualized and completely private relation between the believer and God make self-revelation impossible and concealment unavoidable. As Johannes puts it, faith is a paradox that "does not permit of mediation, for it is founded precisely upon the fact that the individual is only the individual" (*FT*, p. 80). Our question for Kierkegaard is a simple one: Is the individual ever only the individual? Does not the individual require the other in order to be himself? Are not individual and community bound in an unbreakable dialectic of mutual constitution and definition?

We can make our point in philosophical terms by arguing that solely independent individuality is an impossibility. Being-for-self necessarily entails being-for-an-other. That which "is equal to itself and is for-itself is such only in its absolute difference from every other. And this difference implies a relation with other things, a relation which is the cessation of its being-for-itself."[43] The insight, of course, is Hegel's. In the second chapter of the *Phenomenology*, he argues: "The thing is set up as having a being of its own, as existing for itself, or as an absolute negation of all otherness; hence it is absolute negation merely relating itself to itself. But this kind of negation is the cancelling and superseding of *itself,* or means that it has its essential reality in another."[44] In other words, individuality cannot define itself apart from otherness. By this very fact, otherness ceases to be merely other and becomes constitutive of the individual's identity. "It is precisely through the absolute character and its opposition that the thing relates itself to others, and is essentially this relation, and only this. The relation, however, is the negation of its independence, and the thing collapses through its own essential property."[45] Relations between self and other are internal, mutually defining. Individuality comes to expression only through a relationship with otherness:

> The object [or person] is really in one and the same respect the opposite of itself—for itself 'so far as' it is for another, and for another 'so far as' it is for itself. It is for itself, reflected into self, one; but all this is asserted along with its opposite, with its being for another, and for that reason is asserted merely to be superseded. In other words, this existence for itself is as much unessential as that which alone was meant to be unessential, viz. the relation to another.[46]

If we accept Hegel's contention that individuality cannot be defined simply by opposition to otherness, but arises only by virtue of the internal relation between self and other, the character of a person's relation to God takes a form quite different from that suggested by Kierkegaard. Even if we were to agree with Kierkegaard's insistence that only a concrete individual is able to establish a relation with God, we can now see that such individuality does not necessarily involve complete isolation from other persons. To the contrary, the dialectical connection between relation-to-self and relation-to-an-other means that for an individual to become related to God, he cannot negate but must cultivate and deepen his relations with other persons. From this point of view, faith no longer leads to isolation, but enhances community. Moreover since the basis of Kierkegaard's faithful silence is the isolated individuality requisite for a proper relation between believer and God, the perception of the dialectical interplay between individual and other reopens the possibility of communication for the believer. Perhaps believers need not always be dumb.

Paradoxes. *Fear and Trembling* is a book rich in paradox—paradoxes too tangled to be unraveled by speculative reflection, paradoxes that strike the reader dumb. One of the most perplexing paradoxes is the mere fact that the book was written. But perchance a deeper paradox is that an essay has been written about a book about silence . . .

11. On Faith

NANCY JAY CRUMBINE

FAITH IS THE COMPLETE AND YET INTERNALLY COMPLEX RELATION TO THE PAST that gives meaning to the present and the future. As the still center of all dynamic action, faith is the dimension of life that, literally, makes human life possible. Faith is the trust that allows what is to be for us both intelligible and meaningful at the same time. Every human dwells, however unconsciously, within faith.

Faith is a dimension of the relation between self and world that cannot be comprehended in any linear account because it constitutes a contextual fullness that underlies all possible linear directions. Like silence, faith preceeds speech, but also, like silence, faith is what allows speech to carry meaning.[1] The nothingness of silence would be deafening, and therefore language impossible, without the relation we call faith. The linguistic world within which human acts take place is literally rooted in this trust in and reliance upon what is beyond the world of language, what is present once the familiar is eliminated.

The "act" of faith is less an act than a rhythm of being that has its source in prelingual, prereligious, and prephilosophical encounters with the world, yet finds its sustenance in a developing participation with finitude. Faith's sustained relation with finitude is so familiar that it is often overlooked. Its infinite relation is so elusive, indeed, that it is often either entirely forgotten or it is rigidified into symbols that lose its meaning. The paradoxes of faith's appearances accurately reflect the fact that faith is itself the paradox, that the self becomes itself only by losing itself, that the finite and infinite grant each other meaning in their mutual intimacy within the participating individual.

The relation of the human to what is prior to language, to what allows language to carry meaning, is essentially private. The contextual fullness of faith, as immersed within finitude itself, is structured by the private recollections that make up the individual subject. The difficulty inherent in becoming private, in developing and relying upon this prior background of private context, explains the rarity of individuals who consciously stand in relation to the world through this richness of recollective context.[2] An analysis of the nature of the private, of the prepolitical life of the subject in relation to what is hidden, constitutes the first part of the understanding of faith, for without privacy there is no self within which faith might take its focus.

The alinear fullness of privacy develops within and from the recollective powers of the subject. The greater these powers, the more developed the subjectivity. Faith's paradoxical nature as both prelinguistic and participatory, as a relation to finitude through unlimited dimensions of that finitude, gains in meaning when we begin to understand this paradox within the paradoxical framework of recollection itself. In the fullness of recollective involvement within both the private and public realms faith emerges as that relational prerequisite for all free action. Once the necessity of privacy is established, the path into its fullest utilization, its fullest development, must be understood in recollection.

Recollection is the active, expressive, and private reunion with the past as it informs and grants significance to the present. A reunion of and with the wholeness of things, recollection is the way one sees dimension and therefore is the vision not only of events but of the shadows and darknesses that surround and connect those events. It is the process by which the individual is recalled to the unifying darkness from which the present is brought to light and without which the dimension of the present is lost. With recollection the organic development of an individual's fullest uniqueness seems not only possible but actual.

Memory as a reunion with context is distinct from knowledge, a mode of separation from context. Where knowledge effects a disengagement, dividing and setting into relief the "thing" known, the process of recollection effects the reunion of "thing" presented with its historical and contextual depth. While the reunion with its history necessarily complicates the event or "thing" beyond analysis, it at the same time provides a space for resolving problems that cannot be solved on the two-dimensional plane of knowing. The contradictions (implicit and explicit) in existence itself require an openness to the realm of memory, in which one form of clarity is given up for another, the clarity of division and linear analysis for the clarity of unity and context.

Like the cycles of decay that eventually produce the richest soils, the process of forgetting and recollection qualitatively changes the events of experience, allowing perspective for the individual remembering by providing depth and context for the event itself. This change is constituted by the transformation of consciousness of things from the view of them in the light of reason to the consciousness of them as they have developed and decayed by themselves. Without the continual prodding and often confused assistance of consciousness, forgotten events take on characteristics that are incapable of developing elsewhere. Left to their own processes, put away in the private realm, these for-a-time unremembered particulars not only provide a basis for action when recalled, but continually and silently provide significance and grounding for all interaction within the public realm.

Recollection is the reflective and dimensional depth of privacy itself. As such it is the prelinguistic background of all meaningful silence. In the absence of "presentation," memory transforms the absence into a fullness, transposing the present into the organic development of its past. Just as, without silence, language is hollow and poetry impossible, so it is that private recollections ultimately grant meaning and interpret events in the present, however public these may be. While the public qua public has its own means of recollection in the myths and rituals of tradition, it is the more creative, multidimensional and imaginative recollections of which individuals are capable that ground that tradition and keep it dynamic and alive. In the extent to which private recollective powers are allowed to merge into and with the communal works, and in the extent to which authority is granted to this dimension of experience, the health and survival of communities is determined. Just as speech gains its significance from what transcends it in the supportive silence of its origins, so the public realm (the realm in which speech takes place) gains its strength and vitality from the transcendent recollections of private and preverbal memories of individuals.

The internal rhythm of recollection is sacrifice, the giving up of the present for the sake of, and in reliance upon, the larger context that the past alone can provide. Sacrifice is a mode of consciousness that relates to the world by giving up particulars in order to receive them again in a renewed context. In this rhythm of recollection, the particularized present is given up for its alternative presentness within its historical context. As a continuous mode of relation it is a rhythmic exchange between the individual consciousness and the multiple possibilities of the world's presence. The art of sacrifice is never evidenced in one act but is rather a giving and receiving in which the activity and passivity of the world's interaction become indistinguishable.[3] Sacrifice is a giving up that by its very nature constitutes a receiving. It is a commitment to absenting for the sake of a renewed present, a commitment to forgetting for the sake of a renewed recollection.

Recollection presupposes sacrifice, and it is within sacrifice that faith exposes the depths of its paradoxes. The rhythm of offering up the actual for the sake of the possible, which is so necessary to sustain the recollective relation to one's context, concretizes itself not only in the sacrifice of language and community but in the sacrifice of hope as well. In these sacrifices the fullness of recollection is allowed to give meaning to the present and thus allow for a previously impossible reunion with language and community. In the profundity of this sacrifice is the meaning of faith itself. Neither privacy nor recollection would make sense without it.

Unless faith is born of such sacrifice, unless it thereby constitutes a reunion with self in the completeness of its confessional recollection, granting it authority would be a perversion. Conjoined with the centrality of privacy is the "scandal" of faith itself: that the individual is higher than the universal, that faith, this relational context born of recollective openness, has authority over all human acts and relations. The absoluteness of this stance, the totality of the sacrifice required, is the most difficult aspect of faith to grasp; it is also the most indispensable. Faith without authority, being in relation to this fullness of context without necessarily granting it absolute sovereignty, is not yet to be in true relation. For the relation that is sacrifice is precisely the relation that offers up everything to possibility, and the very nature of faith is that this possibility, in turn, then dictates and determines a meaning based on the recollective depths of what is not yet actualized. This possibility exists completely (or not at all), for it is the possibility of the roots of action, not the possibility of one action over another. Faith, in this sense, is not only the requisite support without which action is absurd; it is the source of human beginnings, a source that is singular and therefore either absolutely determining or not determining at all.

These four aspects of faith—its nature as private, recollective, sacrificial, and absolutely authoritative—all have meaning only when one understands that faith is infinitely a matter of finitude. It is, unlike dread, primarily a relation of the individual to finitude and to the tasks of finitude, and as such it constitutes a reunion with self, not a loss of self within some sort of mystical union with the divine.[4] This reunion with self, as the self immersed in the here-and-now from which recollection originally emerges, is no isolated apolitical being but rather the self as it emerges from and returns to its participative context. In this respect it is important to stress the prepolitical (as opposed to apolitical) nature of faith, and to seek to discover in acts of faith the source of community that is at the heart of even (and especially) the most profound individualism. The involvement in finitude, which is faith's paradoxical strength, turns out to be the very context that makes the public and universal sensible through its grounding in the individual.

The contrast of two characters with radically differing qualities points up the significance of recollective privacy and its relation to authority, sacrifice, and politics. Meursault, the protagonist of Albert Camus' novel *The Stranger,* represents in every respect the complete antithesis to faith. Excluded from the contextual support of faith by virtue of his confused relation to privacy, Meursault is incapable of recollection or sacrifice and is ultimately unable to participate in either private or public life. Kierkegaard's Abraham of *Fear and Trembling,* in contrast, is one who embodies the privacy of faith in its relation to the authority it claims and to the sacrifice through which faith is expressed, who founds a nation with this privacy, and whose faith is the basis of the very conception of law itself.

In contrasting Meursault and Abraham (and thus to some extent Camus and Kierkegaard) I will make clear my own conception of faith, as well as make some interpretative claims regarding Kierkegaard. In particular, I wish to disengage discussion of Kierkegaard's view of faith from the all too common identifications with "existentialisms," on the one hand, and "rationalisms," on the other. Kierkegaard avoids both schools of difficulties by reuniting himself with the silence of Abraham on the one side and with the tradition of recollection on the other.

I wish also to put aside once and for all the charge, perennially leveled against Kierkegaard, that his religiousness disallows politics. If absurdity is a challenge to human interaction, then it must be Camus' understanding of the term, not Kierkegaard's, that constitutes that challenge. For Kierkegaard, the concept of the absurd and its significance for the recollective individual is the very prerequisite and basis for meaningful participation. Without it—and this constitutes the whole thrust of *Fear and Trembling*—Isaac, who is the hope and promise of the nation, is lost.

I

Faith, as the prerequisite for participation, is the context and mode of relation from which an individual participant emerges. Because it is the ontological richness of privacy that makes public action possible, without faith human interaction is mere sequence.

In conjunction with the word *solitude,* privacy is part of a vast continuum of meaning that stretches from the fullness of religiousness (which solitude at its best can imply) to the sense of privacy as privation or undesired alienation of an individual from her/his community.' Even at this far negative end of the spectrum, aloneness implies a strength or positivity born of that "privation."[6] And again, even at this extreme end there is a unifying thread that makes the private and solitary different from the public and communal. This thread goes from the banal to the profound, from the most concrete elements of the finite to the most elusive qualities of the infinite. We call this unity the background, to which silence bears witness and from which faith derives its meaning. It is background to which we move in our longing for privacy, and background we seek when we desire solitude.

Background informs and directs the present. The background of any given moment is what of the past and future can emerge at that moment as present. Only individuals can accomplish this task of presentation, for it is in the originative nature of individuality that memory and foresight emerge as significantly unifying. The present has meaning by virtue of the private recollections and dreams of the individuals who participate in it.

In order to appreciate the significance of background one needs only to regard a life without it: the infamous Meursault. In this contemporary "hero" we see individuation without context, separation without recollection, "integrity" without silence. Meursault dwells on the border of a completely revealed life of publicly confessed behavior and of the false hope that meaninglessness nevertheless has meaning. His pathos is the consequent indifference by which he relates to everything and for which he must ultimately be condemned.

Meursault is a man intent on revealing himself. He wants to present himself without exaggeration or ambiguity, to state his feelings simply, without passion or guilt, and to eliminate all possibility of privacy. He wants to bring himself to light, to make public all that he is. One seeks in vain for anything behind or between the continual series of events and reactions that Meursault relates. What is not told, is not.

Having done away with all sense of privacy and background, Meursault in turn refuses or is unable to recognize the privacy of others. What he sees of others is only what is presented to him most obviously. In the case of Marie and his mother, recognition of them as human is completely lacking. His interaction with Marie is based entirely on his assessment of his own feelings; he never once recognizes that *she* might have feelings, too. In the case of the nameless, faceless Arab, the light of Meursault's revelatory quest does away with the other's identity altogether.[7] Such solipsism is the direct result of failing to recognize in oneself—and to grant authority to—the silent, private dimensions of experience.

Meursault's isolation from the private realm is a consequence of his refusal to enter into the dimensions of temporality. In dwelling within a sort of eternality of the present he refuses to recollect or foresee, and thus refuses to connect, reflect upon or make judgments upon experiences. His memory is used as a tool of repetition, not of review, as a form of reshowing, not of interpretation or inquiry. Tradition is ignored, the lived experience from which memories derive their meaning is forgotten, and only affect remains. Dimensions inherent in the feeling, given meaning by the context in which it arose, are lost with the refusal to remember the source of the feelings, the refusal to recollect. The ironic result of Meursault's drive toward the simple and honest is that by eliminating all but the articulate present, by remembering and presenting only the visible reaction, the intensity of the emotion is greatly reduced. Moreover, the reduction of experience to immediate public articulation is, in Meursault, so immediate that there is never a possibility for development of genuine feeling. His integrity is mere immediacy, a journalist's integrity of events transformed instantaneously into articulations and caught thereafter in the eternal stillness of speech. It is said and it is done. The moment stillborn into what only in the most myopic perspective could be called truth.

While he defies the depth—and, not incidentally, the complexity—that the past contributes, he likewise refuses direction from the future. He frees himself within a limitless present, thereby eliminating the shackles of reminiscence as well as hopes, goals, and fantasies of the future. But the absence of direction in his life, like the absence of tradition, leaves him completely open to environmental occurrences. Without the support of tradition, he is a series of affected moments. Without a sense of direction into the future, his life is not only serial but random as well. Without orientation or relation to either future *or* past, the background that gives privacy fullness and public interaction meaning is eliminated.

What nevertheless appeals to Meursault is that, without past and future, he can achieve a sort of perfect integrity, for the present seems to him to become completely revealable. In fact, however, it becomes completely transparent. In his drive to reveal himself completely, he exhibits nothing very interesting. What makes the present "presentable" is the background that grants it dimension; the background of Meursault's present is eclipsed entirely by his compulsion to put everything in the light. The light of his so-called integrity transforms everything and not only conceals background but disallows its development. Even when the deed is done, even when the cycle of nature itself is broken by the blindness of this light, Meursault (and one must wonder about Camus here) does not understand his crime. He describes the court trial as a sentimental attack by a tradition gone senile. Yet what he is ultimately condemned for is his refusal to be human, his incapacity to recognize others, his refusal to enter into temporality and to be mortal among other mortals. It is this refusal to participate in the confusions and complexities of temporality that condemns him. In this regard, he mirrors the naïveté of modernity itself, and is rightfully called a hero of our age, an age in which the easy escape from mortality seems to be the dominant theme of both individual life and cultural life—a refusal to participate, as though by not participating one is thereby no longer implicated.

An endless string of continuously abortive beginnings, which disallows participation, marks Meursault as the absurd hero. He is master of the ever-dying creation, the artist of artists in a world where vision is limited to the belief that articulation of feelings is the ultimate possibility not only for truth but beauty as well. As artist of the absurd, his creation is a sacrifice of meaning and community for "confession." The sacrifice is made, however, in the hope of regaining meaning and community. But he loses both forever by virtue of the meaninglessness of the "confession" itself. Just as his speech fails to be recollective, so also it fails even to be confessional, for it is an empty reporting, an objective repetition, without judgment, unity, or passion. Lacking the element of growth that these elements would make possible, it is not really a confession at all. Quite the opposite of Kierkegaard's inwardness of passion, Meursault's subjectivity is objectified and becomes the universal in which he dwells and to which he grants all authority. By gaining himself in this fashion, he loses himself in the fashion here described.[8]

Without entrance into temporality and the connectiveness that that would allow, and without otherness of events and people—without, in other words, the self as private recollection and projection and as a separate interactive being-with-others—there is nothing present with which interaction can take place. In the eternal light of immediacy in which Meursault dwells, self is lost, and participation (and therefore politics) is impossible. Life is not only absurd for Camus' Meursault; it is ultimately unlivable.

II

Regardless of what Camus may have suggested in the *Myth of Sisyphus,* for Meursault, at least, the question of suicide was answered affirmatively long before we meet him in the book. His rejection of temporality (and therefore of privacy and political action) marks the absurdity he stands for more as an answer than as a question. Meursault's absurd is not something that cannot be understood; neither does it mean that life is too paradoxical or contradictory or even meaningless; it means that what appears to be life is mere fantasy and illusion, and that human existence really is an already-terminated sickness unto death.

For Kierkegaard, on the other hand, the absurd, presented as it is through the paradoxes and contradictions of existence, is a question and a beginning—an occasion for rebirth and reentry into the very finitude that it confounds. What distinguishes the different reactions to the absurd, as between Camus' Meursault and Kierkegaard's Abraham, is not the choice of rationality or irrationality (or the distinction between existentialists who leap and those who do not leap). Rather the differences between the two individuals are inherent in their total relationship to temporality and in their speech about it. As Meursault loses himself through his determination to articulate and immortalize feelings, so Abraham gains himself through his trustful entrance into mortality and his silent reflection of it.

Abraham, perhaps the most private character in all history and literature, is ever emerging from and receding into the background and mystery that continually surround him. His dimensions are sketched by this darkness and his acts are shrouded in the silence from which his power originates. The sacrifice of Isaac gains its significance as an act of faith by virtue of the richness of this privacy, its groundedness in the recollective context from which both Abraham and Isaac emerge, and the ultimate expression of this contextual depth in Abraham's life of silence. In Abraham's relation to temporality we can begin to discover the groundedness of faith and can begin to make sense of an act that is otherwise contradictory and meaningless. Within the relation to this private temporality three distinguishable elements make up the contextual fullness called faith: (1) recollection, the mode of the relation itself, (2) the rhythm of sacrifice that is inherent in recollection and necessitates and makes meaningful the paradoxes of faith, and (3) the absolute authority with which Abraham endows this sacrificial rhythm and that finally distinguishes the person of faith from a nihilist such as Meursault. From the combination of these three elements an understanding of the definition of faith as the unequivocal and private recollective rhythm of sacrifice will emerge.

The easiest way to concretize the meaning of sacrifice as it relates to recollection and faith is to inquire into Abraham's sacrifice of Isaac. Who is Isaac such that his sacrifice entails his very preservation? Why should his sacrifice be the basis and originative force from which both private and public fullness emerge?

Isaac is not "presented," but is merely present—present as mystery. The story tells us only that Abraham loved him. To discover his significance, the reader must remember not only the facts of Isaac's birth and growing up but the significance of those events and their relation to Abraham and Abraham's past. The fullness of that past, back through Adam, is requisite for the recollective wholeness that makes Isaac the incredible figure that he is. As the hope of Israel, as Israel's very continuance, Isaac is Israel's past as it projects forward. He is, in a sense, recollection itself, the very significance of the past as it holds possibilities, and is a promise, for all future meaning.

Isaac is both past and future, recollection and hope. The story of his sacrifice is the story of the crucial transition between past and future, wherein the sacrifice of Isaac as past is required for the birth of Isaac as future. Hope must be sacrificed so that recollection can emerge. The possibility of the nation, in other words, is sacrificed for the actuality of its becoming within the richness of its recollective consciousness.

The most common obstacle to recollective existence is a falsified and fanciful relation to the future that obscures the pastness of the present. Indeed, once authority is granted to this recollective background, to the private, hope has already been sacrificed. It is no mistake then that the sacrifice portrayed here as an expression of faith is the sacrifice of hope for recollection. For it is in the doing away with the most basic hope, in the acceptance of an utter meaninglessness, that recollection is able to take over sufficiently to provide meaning. This paradox is at the heart of Abraham's situation, for faith is by definition the sacrifice of every hope: "Only he who draws the knife gets Isaac."[9] It is in the trusting in the totality of what lies behind what appears that allows what appears to become as significant. In this trust, even murder is transformed into holiness and sacrificial expression.[10]

In sacrificing Isaac, Abraham is putting in abeyance any claim to understanding, any hope of knowing, what is taking place. The sacrifice of knowledge, like the sacrifice of hope (if they can be distinguished at all), is a sacrifice that institutes and assures the groundedness of knowledge. As we have seen, the claim to infinite knowledge, knowledge without a basis in background, without an ontological footing, becomes the unlivable visibility of Meursault. What was meant to support becomes, in its exaggerated powers, the source of the individual's destruction and the context for Meursault's killing of the Arab. In stark contrast to the heightened visibility of Meursault's present, Abraham relies not on what is seen or known but on the dark background of his selfhood. But for this grounding, Isaac's sacrifice would be transformed into the demonic negativity of murder.

Sacrifice as redemption is possible only in the realm of absolute responsiveness. Short of complete response, short of sacrificing everything—all hope, all claim to understanding all that one has ever loved—everything is lost. As we have defined it, the very meaning of sacrifice is a giving up of one's momentary interpretations in favor of the larger contextual realm assessible only through the most private, silent, recollective mode of being. No compromise can be reached between the recollective and epistemic forms of inquiry: they are direct opposites. Either one bases one's actions on the infinite dimensions of historical context, or one proceeds in a linear and teleological fashion. It is here that the locus of the absolute either/or choice of faith is to be found.

The absoluteness of this either/or takes its roots in the necessity of refusing an either/or interpretation on another level. The recollective realm can be given absolute priority because it contains both the finite and infinite dimensions of experience, because it alone does not require an either/or decision between Isaac, the earthly hope, and God, the divine recollection. By choosing recollection over hope one chooses the possibility of having both. In the absoluteness of Abraham's commitment to the recollective realm of experience is his freedom to sacrifice what he "knows" will also thereby be redeemed.

This can be seen most clearly in the pictures Kierkegaard draws of the Abrahams who fail, who have not remained silent and unhesitating but who speak, question, blame, or despair. In each of the four imaginative portraits prefacing *Fear and Trembling* Abraham is presented in inauthentic relation to his recollective privacy. Failing to hold absolutely to his stance within the recollective realm, he is forced, in each case, into an either/or situation in which he must lose Isaac as surely as if he had literally slain him. What becomes clear in each portrait is that the failure is due to the assumption by each of the four imaginary Abrahams that the only response to the situation is one of resignation; each, that is, perceives the situation as an impossible one requiring compromise. Yet it is the very impossibility of compromise, the requirement that everything be sacrificed in order to gain the totality of divine support, the very paradoxical requirement that Abraham commit himself infinitely to the finite, that the actual Abraham so wisely and so faithfully embraced. A review of the four failures will help illuminate this arational truth, to which the actual Abraham bears witness.

In the first portrait, Abraham tries to tell Isaac what is being required of them. Isaac does not understand, of course, and begs for his life. Abraham then feigns madness, in an attempt to preserve Isaac's faith in the divine (to which Isaac then calls out), but in the process he destroys Isaac's trust in his finite parentage.

> But Abraham said to himself, "I will not conceal from Isaac whither this course leads him." . . . And Abraham's face was fatherliness, his look was mild, his speech encouraging. But Isaac was unable to understand him, his soul could not be exalted; he embraced Abraham's knees, he fell at his feet imploringly, he begged for his young life, for the fair hope of his future. . . . He climbed Mount Moriah, but Isaac understood him not. Then for an instant he turned away from him, and when Isaac again saw Abraham's face it was changed, his glance was wild, his form was horror. He seized Isaac by the throat, threw him to the ground, and said, "Stupid boy, dost thou then suppose that I am thy father? I am an idolater. Dost thou suppose that this is God's bidding? No, it is my desire." Then Isaac trembled and cried out in his terror, "O God in heaven, have compassion upon me. God of Abraham, have compassion upon me. If I have no father upon earth, be Thou my father!" But Abraham in a low voice said to himself, "O Lord in heaven, I thank Thee. After all it is better for him to believe that I am a monster rather than that he should lose faith in Thee."[11]

By speaking, Abraham eliminates the background in which the vertical and horizontal can be retained together and through which losing and gaining become roads to each other. Without this unifying context of background, he is reduced to an either/or situation in which he is forced to disengage himself from (despair of) finitude in order to retain trust in the divine. For Isaac, this has disastrous consequences, for he is thereafter cut off from the horizontal participation that was to lead to nationhood requiring trust for both its inception and development. The pathos of Abraham's well-meaning deception is poignant, for in trying to retain part of Isaac, Abraham loses him entirely.

In the second portrait, Abraham fails in the opposite direction. While he does not speak, he is yet resigned to his fate in the worst possible way:

> Silently he laid the wood in order, he bound Isaac, in silence he drew the knife—then he saw the ram which God had prepared. Then he offered that and returned home. . . . From that time on Abraham became old, he could not forget that God had required this of him. Isaac throve as before, but Abraham's eyes were darkened, and he knew joy no more.[12]

His silence here is an aesthetic concealment born of the despair of the infinite. While such silence allows Isaac the freedom to grow, it only strengthens the nihilism that has overcome Abraham. Abraham clings to the earthly—"and Abraham's glance was fixed upon the ground until the fourth day when he lifted up his eyes and saw afar off Mount Moriah, but his glance turned again to the ground"[13]—and in sequential monotonous rhythm he goes through the motions of the sacrifice. Deaf to the divine dimension of this silence, he is resigned to the meaningless sequence of this disconnected temporality. The bitterness and distrust that result from this resignation are the results of what Kierkegaard later calls the demonic potential of silence wherein truth is concealed rather than disclosed by the absence of speech. The inauthentic silence portrayed in this story is the counterpart to the naïveté of speech in the first story. Both approaches fail to establish trust, the one in the divine, the other in the finite. In the second story Isaac retains his faith and willingness to relate to the finite and infinite, but Abraham has lost faith in the divine, and thus, we can conclude, despairs of the nation as covenant.

The third imaginary Abraham is portrayed as privately ethical and reflective. The unhappiness here resides in the haunting suspicion, with which Abraham lives the rest of his life, that his willingness to sacrifice Isaac was wrong.

> It was a quiet evening when Abraham rode out alone, and he rode to Mount Moriah; he threw himself upon his face, he prayed God to forgive him his sin, that he had been willing to offer Isaac, that the father had forgotten his duty toward the son. Often he rode his lonely way, but he found no rest. He could not comprehend that it was a sin to be willing to offer to God the best thing he possessed, that for which he would many times have given his life; and if it was a sin, if he had not loved Isaac as he did, then he could not understand that it might be forgiven. For what sin could be more dreadful?[14]

While in the second story Abraham blames the divine, in the third rendering the inclination to blame (a kind of cause-effect compulsion) is directed against himself. In both stories there is a resignation that results in the divisive need to attribute blame for a situation that, if understood in its proper context of recollection, would be wholly amoral. In this second search for blame, Abraham is portrayed as failing in the same way as that in which Adam and Eve failed, by seeking knowledge in matters beyond the reaches of knowledge. Just as (according to Kierkegaard) Adam and Eve chose a grasping return to finitude as an escape from the infinite vastness of dread, so Abraham finds it easier to seek a causal explanation within himself than to dwell within the silence and paradoxes of divine motivation and recollective fullness.

The second and third stories show the effect on Abraham of his being able to go only as far as ethics, only as far as the universal and communal realm wherein resignation and/or desire for knowledge is the highest stage of development. While these stories show Abraham as appearing to be politically conscious of universal laws, we see that by his very appeal to them he loses the possibility of community. In both cases Abraham clings to the earthly—in one case because he blames the divine, and in the other because by blaming the earthly he can lock himself in constant struggle within it.

While the second and third stories show how Abraham is lost, the first and last show the two alternative effects on Isaac. In the first Isaac is forced to lose trust in Abraham and finitude; in the last he is forced to lose trust in the divine. As we turn to this last story, we see the intentional deceit on the part of Abraham and the mere sham that silence can become. Here Abraham completely destroys any potential relation to faith that Isaac might have had.

> But Abraham prepared everything for the sacrifice, calmly and quietly; but when he turned and drew the knife, Isaac saw that his left hand was clenched in despair, that a tremor passed through his body—but Abraham drew the knife.
>
> They returned again home, and Sarah hastened to meet them, but Isaac had lost his faith. No word of this had ever been spoken in the world, and Isaac never talked to anyone about what he had seen, and Abraham did not suspect that anyone had seen it.[15]

Whether it is deceit perpetrated by silence or more actively produced through speech—whether there is a loss of trust in the divine dimensions or the finitude into which one is born—the possibility of the recollective participation is destroyed for the individual who is forced to resign himself or herself to pull back from one of the two realms necessary for meaningful action. In all four portraits, Abraham loses Isaac by cutting off the potential for his full development. Under the either/or framework into which Abraham forces him, Isaac is unable to become himself, unable to become that fullness of private and public individual that is the promised hope of Israel. Wherever a strict either/or has developed—whether from resignation or deceitfulness—faith, as the rhythm of sacrifice within the intermeshing of the finite and infinite dimensions, has already become impossible.

This uncompromising absoluteness that alone makes possible the "both/and" fullness of faith becomes more approachable when it is remembered that what Abraham did does not matter so much as how he did it. And the "how" of the real Abraham's life centers in the absoluteness of his life as born entirely from within, a life based absolutely on the private recollective realm of his own inwardness. The commitment of the actual Abraham is a commitment to the earthly, to the finitude of his own facticity as he has evolved through it. His willingness to sacrifice Isaac portrays the grounding of that finitude in the infinite reaches of Abraham's recollective commit-

202 Nancy Jay Crumbine

ment to finitude. The divine dimension *is* "subjective" in the sense that it is through the infinitude and the infinite possibilities of recollection that Abraham is able to ground his particular acts, his particular mortal life, in something larger. It is through an involvement with finitude, not a cloistering or separation from it, that Abraham gains access to the recollective realm in which "divine" requests not only make sense but open up possibilities of meaning and community otherwise unattainable. It is in the lifting of the knife that the miracle of Isaac as the possibility of Israel takes place. With this act, with this absolute willingness to participate in the finite however difficult or impossible to understand, the covenant itself is made possible. In the lifting of the knife, and only at that point, does the possibility of Israel become a reality.[16]

The willingness to participate in finitude, to participate recollectively in the realm of interaction and particularity, is the central factor in understanding the person of faith and distinguishing that person from the nihilism of a Meursault. The person of faith enters the realm of temporality with a particular act that finds its basis in a way of being that is grounded in the infinite depth attainable through recollection. The act of faith is an entrance into the public realm from a basis in the recollective, unifying, and organically developed privacy of the individual's past. It is an entrance into finitude by way of the infinite dimensions that surround and ground that very finitude. The trust that is made possible through the recollective relation to the infinite grounds and makes possible the sort of absolute commitment to finitude witnessed in Abraham.

Meursault, on the other hand, devoid of recollective sensitivity and committed to the "integrity" of the present, attempts to extend the finite realm infinitely, turning temporality into an endless series of disconnected, meaningless objects of observation. The possibility of participation and human interaction is thus eliminated from the start by virtue of the atomistic temporality that, left to its own unlimited possibilities, levels everything into a valueless two-dimensional rigidity. There is no perception of life here because the perceiver is no longer living.[17]

Faith, as the contextual trust expressed in acts of finite commitment, is the ground for meaningful communal interaction. While its development is unequivocal and private, faith's expression results in compromise and openness. While its growth evolves from the past, its recollective strength issues into an unconcealment of the future. While its very essence is its rhythmic sacrifice of the individual's meaning, faith remains the basis of meaning to which the individual in sacrifice necessarily is returned. Faith, as the unequivocal and private recollective rhythm of sacrifice, is thus the ground for the most concrete, public, and forward-looking acts of self-assertion and political power. An openness to it and an understanding of it is thus not a command from on high but a responsibility born of our most earthly facticity. For it is by virtue of our rootedness in the entanglements of finitude that the uprooting of them through the recollective rhythm of faith remains not merely an activity of leisure but an increasingly relevant—and profoundly political—necessity.

12. Faith Is as Faith Does

JERRY H. GILL

Some things cannot be said; they show themselves.
Wittgenstein

MY THESIS IS THAT THE STANDARD INTERPRETATIONS OF KIERKEGAARD'S understanding of Abraham as the paradigm of faith are essentially wrong-headed. In his exploration of the notion of faith Kierkegaard is *not* contrasting belief as mental assent based on reasons against belief as a "cognitive leap" based on no reasons at all. He *is,* rather, challenging the whole notion that belief could ever be simply a matter of mental assent, with or without reasons. His contrast is between this view, which underlies the whole Western philosophical tradition from Plato through Descartes, Hume, Kant, and Hegel, and the Hebrew–Christian perspective, which posits faith as a way of life, as a way of being in the world. Although *faith as a way of life* is not to be equated with mental assent, it can be understood as incorporating it. The basis of a faithful way of life is *trust,* and it is trust embodied in faithfulness that is exhibited by Abraham.

My own interpretation would suggest that *Fear and Trembling* is meant to be understood as *ironic,* in the sense that it provides an analysis of faith as unanalyzable—an understanding of that which it claims is *un*understand-able. The paradox of faith, together with its essential consequences, is quite clearly delineated and argued for. The irony of this situation was either lost on Kierkegaard or it was intentional on his part. In light of the obvious brilliance and self-consciousness of his authorship I find the former possibility untenable. His intended meaning, I submit, was to offer a "dialectical corrective" to the traditional view of faith as mental assent in order, by means of a reductio ad absurdum, to call attention to the true character of faith. Thus he juxtaposes an irrationalist view of faith, through de Silentio, to the rationalist view in order to give rise to a higher view.

There are three standard interpretations of *Fear and Trembling* on the market. The first views the book as a poorly reasoned defense of the traditional view that sees faith as believing "*because* it is absurd."[1] The second interprets it as a brilliant critique of the rationalist tradition that sees faith as mental assent to cogent argument and evidence.[2] The third and more sophisticated view contends that Kierkegaard was not an irra-tionalist at all; rather, he presents a case for a holistic understanding of faith that integrates reason and will.[3]

The former two interpretations are inadequate because they both con-strue the crucial issue as a dichotomy between faith as mental assent *with* reasons and faith as mental assent *without* reasons. To my mind, however, Kierkegaard's main concern is with contrasting faith as mental assent with faith as a way of living, i.e., with truth as a quality of life not as a quality of propositions. Thus he is not to be seen as an irrationalist, as the third interpretation mentioned above correctly perceives. This third interpretation is misleading, however, because it gives the impression that Kierkegaard's holistic understanding of faith is to be found *in* the text, *directly*. My contention is that his holistic, neither-rationalistic-nor-irrationalistic view of faith is only dialectically suggested *by* the text by means of "*indirect communication*." The support for this contention is presented on the following pages.

I

To begin with the internal evidence, consider SK's use of the pseudonym, Johannes de Silentio. Time and time again one encounters interpretations of *Fear and Trembling* that present it as Kierkegaard's own view of faith. This is true, moreover, with regard to nearly all his pseudonymous works. We are frequently told that Kierkegaard says this or that, without the slightest consideration being given to the fact, let alone the intricacies, of his pseudonymous authorships. In this instance, the very use of a pseudonym, to say nothing of the implications of the name "de Silentio" itself, ought to serve as a warning against any direct interpretation. Kierkegaard himself specifically cautioned his readers not to equate his views with those of his pseudonyms.

Moreover, the particular pseudonym of *Fear and Trembling,* Johannes de Silentio, carries with it special significance. I have in mind more than the well-known facts pertaining to Kierkegaard's remaining silent about his hopes of regaining Regina. It will not do to dismiss the pseudonym, let alone the whole of *Fear and Trembling,* as mere narcisicism. For the work stands by itself as a powerful exploration into the meaning of faith in relation to understanding and ethics. No, the name de Silentio symbolizes the main theme of the whole work, namely, that faith cannot be spoken about. The author himself claims to be reduced to silence by the phenomenon of Abraham, and the latter is described as being forced to remain silent about his intentions vis-à-vis Isaac. Furthermore, the motto (about Tarquinius' message) that appears on the title page with de Silentio's name signifies the importance of indirect, parabolic communication to the interpretation of this work.

What is of special significance for the interpretation I am advocating is that in spite of his overt and repeated acknowledgment that faith cannot be conceptualized, de Silentio proceeds to give a rather thorough analysis of both Abraham's faith and its conceptual consequences in relation to ethical categories. De Silentio has not remained silent. Now either he has *done* the very thing he says is impossible, or he has *tried* to do it in order to illustrate how futile it is. This latter possibility suggests an ironic interpretation of his analysis of faith wherein, as with Tarquinius' beheading of the poppies, actions are meant to speak more effectively than words.

De Silentio makes it quite clear, especially in his "Preliminary Expectoration," that he is at least one step removed from having faith himself. He says he can "describe" the movements of faith without being able to make or perform them. He claims to be related to Abraham as the poet is related to the hero. Perhaps de Silentio can be described as having attained unto "religiousness A" (the knight of infinite resignation), but clearly he denies both being "in" faith and being able to understand faith. Yet in spite of these admissions, philosophers and theologians alike have frequently interpreted de Silentio's account of faith as if it were Kierkegaard's view. It would seem, rather, that given these admissions the reader should expect *Fear and Trembling* to be off the mark in one way or another. My suggestion is that it is intentionally off the mark in presenting an irrationalist view of faith that, like its rationalist counterpart, must be discarded if one is to come to understand faith as a way of life rather than as mere cognition or volition.

In light of the foregoing considerations, it is more than possible that de Silentio's accusations against the rationalist thinkers of his day who sought "to go further than faith" are meant to be applied to the irrationalist view as well. Like Heraclitus' disciple, who sought to extend and thereby improve upon his master's teaching,[4] those who interpret *Fear and Trembling* as a brilliant argument for and analysis of the "leap of faith" are really guilty of going beyond Kierkegaard in such a way as to return to the position he had abandoned. For to read de Silentio's work as a direct *argument* for an alternative view of faith, albeit a volitionalist instead of a ratiocinationist view, is to ignore the force of indirect communication embodied in the pseudonym.

Secondly, consider the actual content of *Fear and Trembling*. The first third of the book deals with Abraham as a phenomenon and its dominant theme is de Silentio's inability to understand this phenomenon. The prelude sets the tone for the whole work, and here de Silentio tries four different ways of exegeting the Abraham and Isaac passage, but all to no avail. He concludes by saying, "No one is so great as Abraham! Who is capable of understanding him?" However, the prelude is followed by the "Panergyric upon Abraham" and the "Preliminary Expectoration" in which Abraham is not only praised for his faith, but precisely wherein that faith consisted is spelled out in some detail. We are told, quite straightforwardly, that faith consists in believing the paradox by virtue of the absurd and in making the double movement of infinite resignation and returning to the finite.

What is to be made of the tension between the posture assumed by de Silentio at the close of his prelude ("he sank down with weariness, he folded his hands . . .") and his extended analysis of the faith of Abraham in the two succeeding sections? If the account of Abraham's faith is taken as a straightforward interpretation, then the overall claim that faith is ineffable is obviated and de Silentio—and Kierkegaard as well—is guilty of a glaring self-contradiction. If, however, de Silentio's account of Abraham's faith is viewed as ironic, then the tension between the prelude and the analysis is resolved in a way that points beyond the account per se to faith as a lived reality.

Moving on, it is important to note that the rest of *Fear and Trembling* (Problems I, II, and III) is introduced at the close of the "Preliminary Expectoration" in the following words:

> It is now my intention to draw out from the story of Abraham the dialectical consequences, inherent in it, expressing them in the form of *problemata*, in order to see what a tremendous paradox faith is, a paradox which is capable of transforming a murder into a holy act well-pleasing to God, a paradox which gives Isaac back to Abraham, which no thought can master, because faith begins precisely there where thinking leaves off.[5]

There is something very out of place about this sort of talk from one who has already declared that faith is incomprehensible to reason. The vocabulary employed in this transitional paragraph, as well as that used in the actual "drawing out of the dialectical consequences" that follows, smacks far too much of the likes of Kant and Hegel to go unnoticed. Kierkegaard was far too bright to miss the irony here, and far too self-aware as a literary artist to let it stand for effect only. I think he meant it to trigger the reader's awareness of the futility of a detailed *analysis* of faith as an unanalyzable phenomenon.

Although on one level de Silentio's analysis of faith in Problems I, II, and III can be said to run contrary to the main themes of Kant's and Hegel's ethics, at a deeper level they can be seen to depend upon those very themes. Take, for example, the famous notion of "the teleological suspension of the ethical" (Problem I). In addition to the fact that such a rationalistic mouthful ought instantly to be suspect when it stands at the heart of an existentialist presentation, it should be clear that the concept itself is only understandable given the very categories against which it is used to enveigh. For not only is the notion of transcending the category of duty itself dependent upon what can only be described as a "higher duty," but the term '*teleo*logical' makes it quite obvious that the suspension of the ethical can only be undertaken with a "higher end" or rationale in view.

To put the matter a bit differently, in the case of Abraham—and in all cases of faith—the particular or the individual is said to supercede the universal. Yet, this very possibility is explained—and can only be explained—in abstract or universal categories, such as "the particular" or "the individual." Moreover, we are told that "no man is excluded from faith" (i.e., it applies to all men *universally*) and "all human life is unified" in faith. The same situation obtains with regard to the notion of an absolute duty toward God (Problem II). Here, in fact, the transcending of the ethical is expressed straightforwardly in terms of the crucial ethical category, namely *duty* toward God. And certainly de Silentio is urging that it is *imperative* that all men come to faith! The final section of *Fear and Trembling* (Problem III) argues the case for Abraham's silence about his intentions being seen as another facet of his suspension of the ethical. Here again the form of the discussion would seem to belie its main emphasis. It is both argumentative and wordy, and it seeks to justify Abraham's silence while maintaining that no justification is necessary or possible.

Furthermore, the discussion concludes with de Silentio distinguishing between two senses of *understand* vis-à-vis Abraham. The first allows one to speak of understanding him as one would be said to understand a paradox, i.e., recognize that it is, indeed, a paradox, while the second implies the ability to behave as Abraham did, i.e., appropriate his way of being in the world as one's own.[6] What is of greatest import here is that a clear-cut clue is dropped as to the real issue in *Fear and Trembling,* namely the contrast between theorizing about faith and living it. Despite his protestations to the contrary, de Silentio has managed to provide a great deal of theorizing about a fideistic view of faith. Nevertheless, he tips his hand as to the value of such theorizing when he acknowledges that he cannot put it into practice. Those who focus on Abraham's ability to *believe the absurd*—including de Silentio—have missed the point. The prodigious nature of Abraham's faith had, rather, to do with his ability to *live trustingly and obediently*.

One final piece of internal evidence, namely the dialectical structure of the work as a whole. After considering many seemingly parallel cases in the field of literature, de Silentio turns to Abraham's case and explains that his investigations have been offered "not as though Abraham's case would thereby become more intelligible, but in order that the unintelligibility might become more desultory."[7] By this he would seem to mean that his overall purpose is *not* to give a systematic account of faith, but rather a many-sided, fragmented, dialectical account. Thus, to take his voluntarist interpretation of Abraham as a straightforward presentation of the nature of faith would be as misguided as following the traditional rationalist interpretation of faith as mental assent. Thus, in *Fear and Trembling* two equally absurd views of faith are contrasted, the rationalist being presented negatively and the irrationalist positively. The latter is a *corrective,* not in the sense of a replacement, nor in the sense of striking a "happy medium," a compromise between reason and will. Rather, it is a corrective in the sense that it is hoped that out of the conflict created by the juxtapositioning of these equally one-sided views will dawn an awareness of the true character of faith as something to be *lived,* not defined or argued about.

I think a valuable clue to this dialectical understanding of the views of de Silentio can be found in his remarks about the knight of faith in the "Preliminary Expectoration." If we take the criterion for distinguishing between the knight of infinite resignation and the knight of faith—the former is recognizable by means of the "spiritual" quality of his demeanor while the latter is not—and apply it to de Silentio's own account of Abraham we get surprising—and dialectical—results. For certainly the praise that is heaped upon Abraham as the one and only prodigy, as the father of faith, singles him out as exceedingly spiritual and thus disqualifies him as a knight of faith. Another way to put this is to remind ourselves that the knight of faith so integrates the infinite into the finite that he becomes indistinguishable from other men. If Abraham was as extraordinary as de Silentio makes him out to be, he could hardly be a knight of faith.

Once again I am led to the conclusion that de Silentio's account of faith as belief by virtue of the absurd undercuts itself and must, therefore, either be dismissed as confused or interpreted as a profound display of irony. The latter move seems more promising in light of the considerations on the foregoing pages. There are, moreover, certain pieces of external evidence that strongly support the likelihood of this interpretation. It is time to turn to them.

II

The obvious place to begin when considering external evidence relevant to interpreting *Fear and Trembling* is with Kierkegaard's own remarks about his pseudonymous authorship in *The Point of View for My Work as an Author*. There he introduces his notion of "indirect communication" and suggests its three-fold application. First, the pseudonyms provided Kierkegaard with a kind of "literary distance" that enabled him to function as a creative artist without becoming overly didactic and/or dogmatic as a theological and/or philosophical thinker. At this level the pseudonyms also allowed him some distance between his authorship and his personal life. Second, his pseudonymous authorship served his purpose of attracting the attention and identifying with the mode of existence of the members of "Christendom." This aspect of indirect communication coincides with Kierkegaard's religious motivations, and constitutes the main concern of *The Point of View*.

At a deeper level, however, the pseudonymous authorship and the notion of indirect communication serve Kierkegaard in an existential sense. For by these means he is able to *present*, rather than merely *describe*, various modes of existence, and such presentation is necessary to the task of facilitating existential encounter. Spiritual truth cannot be communicated directly, by description, but can only be suggested or evoked indirectly, by example, analogy, parable, and metaphor. Indirect communication preserves the sanctity and integrity of the individual so necessary to the spiritual dimension of existence. Thus Kierkegaard's pseudonymous authorship is essential to his task of reorienting his readership in general and to the particular concerns of *Fear and Trembling* in particular. For to write a book *explaining and describing what faith is* would be to violate both the character of faith itself and the spiritual integrity of the reader. Instead, Kierkegaard has written a book, by means of Johannes de Silentio, that in purporting to explain what faith is, clearly displays what faith *is not*.

It is important to bear in mind that the sword of *Fear and Trembling* is two-edged. With one edge, its contents, it undercuts the possibility of conceiving of faith in a rationalistic way, as the natural outcome of a well-reasoned consideration of evidence, duty, etc. With the other edge, its form, it undercuts the possibility of conceiving of faith as an arbitrary act of the will in a cognitive and moral vacuum. It is this second edge that has been ignored by interpreters of *Fear and Trembling,* thus producing the impression that Kierkegaard's view of faith is irrationalist in character. To interpret the work in this way is to ignore completely the obvious implications of Kierkegaard's important notion of indirect communication.

In addition, it is important to bear in mind that this double-edged sword is not presented in a straightforward fashion in any of Kierkegaard's works. His holistic and integrated view of faith can only be seen from the vantage point of an overview of his entire authorship. The mistake of most of those who defend Kierkegaard against the charge that he is an irrationalist is to write as if Kierkegaard actually expresses his view directly in works like *Fear and Trembling* and *Concluding Unscientific Postscript,* or as if he merely overstated the case in these works in order to strike a more reasonable balance. This is a mistake because it robs these profoundly creative works of their existential power. They must not be interpreted in such a way as to compromise their force. Rather they must be seen, in light of Kierkegaard's remarks about indirect communication, as *authentic* presentations of various extreme points of view—and not as balanced or knowingly overstated positions. Kierkegaard's own view must be discerned in and through those of his various pseudonyms, indirectly and dialectically.

It is this dialectical character of Kierkegaard's work that is so forcefully and insightfully developed in Louis Mackey's *Kierkegaard: A Kind of Poet.* Mackey argues in this book that "Kierkegaard's work is poetry because it traffics in possibilities. It is the poetry of existence because the possibilities it exhibits for contemplation are also idealities that challenge the will to the ethical activity of realization."[8] This way of putting it dovetails nicely with the above account of indirect communication as a dialectical presentation of possible modes of existence with an eye to evoking an existential commitment without invading the privacy of the individual and without reducing truth about living to dissertations *about* the truth about living.

Two further quotations from Mackey serve to substantiate the interpretation for which I have been contending. First, speaking about the pseudonyms as forms of indirect communication, Mackey says:

> The essence is the same in all its manifestations: to interpose between author and reader an anonymous object so articulated by the author that it deploys upon contact into a phalanx of possibilities for the reader. Such communication is indirect because it turns author and reader away from each other toward "some third thing, something more abstract, which neither of them is." Indirect communication uses the example image "to turn the spectator's eye in upon himself, and thus repel him through placing the possibility between the example and the spectator as something they both have in common. . . ." [footnote 62] Such indirection is a communication of subjective truth because the impersonality of the object returns the reader to the arena where the possibilities it displays must be acted on: his inwardness.[9]

Second, speaking about indirect communication as a form of poetry, he says:

> The heresy of paraphrase and the intentional fallacy tempt the reader of Kierkegaard as they tempt readers of poetry generally. The pitfalls of the latter trap those earnest endeavors to determine what Kierkegaard "really means"—which, if they do not conveniently leave out everything that conflicts with what the scholar thinks Kierkegaard ought to mean, conclude either that Kierkegaard is a fool deaf to the most resounding self-contradictions or that he is saying something so precious and so deep that it can't help sounding silly. Taken as instruments of his intent, his works add up to magnificent nonsense. But the truth is that Kierkegaard the poet of inwardness did not "really mean" anything. His "intent" is to exfoliate existential possibilities, not to offer a systematic appraisal of reality as seen from his point of view; like all poets he is concerned not with mentioning but with making.[10]

Now it is important to bring all this to bear on *Fear and Trembling* specifically, something that Mackey himself does not do. Johannes de Silentio personifies a particular mode of existence, one which is able to see that faith does not fit neatly within the categories of traditional rationalistic and ethical philosophy and theology. But this mode of existence can only express these insights by taking an irrationalist view of faith and explaining it in that fashion. The irony of this posture is that even an irrationalist account of faith must make use of the very rational and ethical categories it is seeking to debunk. Moreover, any direct presentation of faith is going to nullify itself in the process because faith is a way of living and as such can only be communicated indirectly, poetically. Interpreted in this dialectical fashion, *Fear and Trembling* must be seen as a means of calling attention to

the existential character of faith—as a way to *exist* in the world—and not as
a direct account and/or explanation of faith.

A parallel case-in-point is that of the *Concluding Unscientific Postscript.*
A specific application and extension of Mackey's general position to this
particular work is made by Henry E. Allison in his article "Christianity and
Nonsense."[11] He argues that the standard interpretation of the *Postscript*
as a presentation of Kierkegaard's position that "subjectivity is truth" is a
misguided interpretation. To begin with, such an interpretation ignores the
significance of the pseudonymous author, Johannes Climacus, who describes himself as a "humorist" who is climbing, "from below," toward an
understanding of what it means to become a Christian, without himself
having yet achieved that state. It would seem obvious that the account of
Christian belief offered from this mode of existence is not to be taken as
reliable, let alone as Kierkegaard's own view. Climacus' humor clearly
takes the form of irony.

More importantly, Allison points out, to ignore the ironic force of the
Postscript is to be led into a paradox of self-reference. For the main theme
developed by Climacus is that "an existential system is impossible";
nevertheless both the structure and the content of the *Postscript* qualify it
to be classified as an existential system. Its structure is that of a philosophical argument and its content consists of a very thorough analysis of what it
means to think subjectively or existentially. Thus Climacus has produced a
highly powerful argument to show that Christian belief can never be the
result of rational argument, and he has done so in order to promote
Christian belief. It would seem that either Climacus, and ultimately
Kierkegaard as well, will have to be dismissed as self-contradictory, or the
irony of the pseudonym will have to be taken seriously.

> The starting point of his trouble, the decisive passage which gives rise to the
> misologistic consequences is the assertion: "When subjectivity is the truth,
> the *conceptual determination* of the truth must include an expression of the
> antithesis to objectivity." The key words here are "conceptual determina-
> tion" for they make clear that Climacus' misologism is a direct consequence
> of the conceptualization of the "principle of subjectivity"! But to conceptual-
> ize is to objectify, and, as we have seen, to speak objectively about inward-
> ness (and Christianity, it will be remembered, is the highest form of
> inwardness) is stupidity. Thus, unless we are to view Kierkegaard as guilty of
> the author's artistry, the intent of which is not to "prove" the superiority of
> Christianity or even to show us in a theoretical way that the absolute paradox
> makes a kind of sense as *supra rationem* which is lacking in garden variety
> nonsense, but rather to help us realize existentially what it means to become
> a Christian, and to see that the only valid concept which we can form about
> Christianity is that it defies conceptualization. Moreover, it is only in light of
> these considerations that we can appreciate the significance of Kierkegaard's
> reflection: "Dialectically it is easy to see that Johannes Climacus' defense of
> Christianity is the most extreme that can be made and only a hair's breadth

from an attack." [footnote 10] It is the most extreme that can be made because it consists essentially in pointing to its utter incommensurability with all human categories, and the "hair's breadth" which distinguishes this from an attack is nothing more than the double reflection of the subjective thinker. If this be omitted, and the *Postscript* viewed as an essay in existential apologetics, then it is indeed an attack for it leads to the ultimate identification of Christianity and nonsense.[12]

This then is precisely the sort of interpretation I have been urging with respect to *Fear and Trembling*. Both of these works need to be seen within the framework of Kierkegaard's overall authorship and his stress on indirect communication. Then they will be understood as profound displays of dialectical irony that serve (as Allison quotes Wittgenstein)[13] to elucidate the character of Christian faith by embodying postures that themselves have to be transcended once they have been understood. We must throw away the ladder after we have climbed up it. Although this is not the place to go into the matter, it should be pointed out that Kierkegaard's master's thesis, *The Concept of Irony*—which usually goes unmentioned in standard interpretations of his work—contains many prefigurations of the posture he later assumed in his pseudonymous authorship.

III

By way of conclusion I should like to offer an additional piece of external evidence on behalf of the interpretation of *Fear and Trembling* defended here. To a large extent the persistent tendency to interpret this work as proposing an irrationalist view of faith is to be explained, I think, by the fact that faith is commonly thought of, by religious and nonreligious folk alike, as a kind of commodity that one either has or does not have. More often than not this commodity is construed as some sort of emotional state that enables one, to quote the infamous Sunday school lad, "to believe what you know isn't so." I do not think there is a shred of biblical evidence to support such a view, and moreover I think it was part of Kierkegaard's purpose to point this out. Faith is a quality of life—a life based in trust and characterized by faithfulness. It certainly is not mental assent, but neither is it an emotional state or a superhuman act of the will. The following considerations should make this clear.

There are four main senses in which the terms *faith* and *believe* are used in the New Testament. As near as I am able to tell, on the basis of both firsthand and secondhand study, these uses correspond quite well with those of the Old Testament. At any rate, the focus of my concern is on the Christian concept of faith. The four New Testament uses can be subsumed under two main grammatical heads, verbs and nouns. The following analysis follows this format.

The use of the verb πιστεύω (*pisteúo*), "to believe," divides into two main categories depending upon the preposition used directly after it. There is the use wherein the verb 'to believe' is followed by the preposition ὅτι (*hoti*), "that." In such cases these two terms are then followed by a direct object in the form of a preposition. A dummy sentence illustrating this usage would be: "Joe believes *that* Bob is happy." This use of the notion of belief focuses on what might be termed the "cognitive dimension" of faith, since what is believed may be either true or false. Second, there is the use wherein the verb "to believe" is followed by the preposition ἐν or εἰς (*en* or eis), "in" or "on." In such cases these two terms are followed by a direct object which is in the form of a noun. A dummy sentence illustrating this usage would be: "Joe believes *in* Bob." This use of the concept of belief focuses on what might be called the "commitment dimension" of faith, since what is believed in may prove to be either trustworthy or untrustworthy.

Examples of usages that illustrate the "belief *that*" dimension of the concept of faith are plentiful both in the Gospels and in the Epistles. In Matthew 9:28 Jesus asks: "Believe ye *that* I am able to do this?" In Mark 24:11 he says: "Whatever you ask in prayer, believe *that* you receive it, and you will." Jesus prays in John 11:42: "I have said this on account of the people standing by, *that* they may believe that Thou didst send me." Paul writes in Romans 10:9: "Believe in your heart *that* God raised him from the dead . . . ," and again in I Thessalonians 4:14: "Since we believe *that* Jesus died and rose again."

Examples of usages that illustrate the "belief *in*" dimension of the concept of faith are also quite plentiful. In Matthew 18:6 Jesus says: "Whoever causes one of these little ones who believe *in* me." John 3:16 reads: "Whoever believes *in* him should not perish . . . " and 7:31 reads: "Many of the people believed *in* him." In Romans 4:24 Paul refers to those "who believe *in* him that raised from the dead Jesus our Lord." Finally, Titus 3:8 expresses concern "that those who have believed *in* God may be careful to apply themselves to good deeds."

Now a brief word about the relationship between these two dimensions of faith. I do not think there is as much difference between the two as most writers on the contemporary theological scene would have us believe. There is a great deal of commitment involved in cognitivity and a great deal of cognitivity involved in commitment. The traditional interpretation of the relationship between the two would argue that "belief *that*" must precede "belief *in*" in order to assure objectivity. The more contemporary, "existentialist" interpretation argues that "belief *in*" must precede "belief *that*" in order to assure authenticity. I am convinced that it is impossible to separate these two dimensions of human experience, that they function in a reciprocal relationship with each other, and if either one of them is missing something vital is absent from faith. The best model for understanding this relationship is that of interpersonal relations. One's commitment to another person hardly arises in a vacuum. Rather, it arises within a physical and historical context of interaction between two people who are striving to be open and honest with one another. At the same time, it remains true that to a large degree the quality and depth of the relationship is a function of the attitudes that the persons *initially* bring to the encounter. We tend to get what we expect. Belief *in* and belief *that* arise reciprocally and simultaneously.

Next, attention should be given to the noun uses of faith. The use of the noun πίστις, "faith," and the associated noun πιστός (pistis, pistos), divides into two categories depending upon whether it is preceded by the definite article. If there is a definite article ("*the* faith"), the term is being used to denote the Christian world view and life style as a whole. In other words, to speak of *the* faith is to speak of the established beliefs and practices of those who call themselves Christian. There are any number of examples of this usage in the New Testament, especially in the Pastoral and General Epistles. Thus Timothy is referred to as a "son in *the* faith" in Timothy 1:2. Some are said to have "erred from *the* faith" (1 Timothy 6:10), while concern is expressed that still others may "be sound in *the* faith" (Titus 1:13).

We come now to the use of the concept of faith that causes the most confusion. In the vast majority of cases wherein the noun use of the term *faith* occurs without the article, one or more of the following factors is also present. First, faith is often spoken of as something that can be seen, i.e., it is *tangible*. Matthew 9:2 reads: "Jesus, *seeing* their faith, said to them." Luke 5:20 reads: "When he saw their faith, he said to them." Paul often speaks of having "*heard* of" the faith of Christians in various cities, such as Ephesus (1:15), Colossae (1:4), and Rome (1:8). Second, faith is often spoken of as something that is *active*. Witness the frequency of such phrases as "your faith *has made* you whole," "*justified* by faith," and "by faith" various Old Testament heroes accomplished great *deeds* (cf. Hebrews 11:4 ff.). This surely is the point of the Epistle of James when it argues that "faith without *works* is dead." Third, faith is often spoken of in *quantitative* terms, as something one can have more or less of. Sometimes people are said to have "*little* faith," sometimes they are said to have "*great* faith," and sometimes they are encouraged to "*increase*" their faith. Finally, and most importantly, people in the New Testament are frequently upbraided for not having faith, or for not having enough faith. Thus faith is a *responsibility*.

My main contention is that in all these cases the term in question would better be translated as "faithfulness" rather than as "faith." In other words, the primary emphasis is upon the ethical dimension of faith, and not upon some sort of psychic state that is a function of the will. A state of mind is not tangible, active, or quantitative (you are either in it or you are not), and it is not something that a person can be required to have. Faithfulness, on the other hand, as a form of behavior, *is* tangible, active, and quantitative, and it can be required of persons. In the same way as Jesus' commanding his disciples to "love their neighbor" makes it necessary to interpret Christian love (ἀγάπε, agápe) as a way of life rather than as an emotional condition, so his requiring his disciples to "have faith" makes it necessary to interpret the concept of Christian faith as a form of behavior, rather than as a mental condition or volitional act.

In conclusion, I submit that a great deal of the confusion surrounding our talk about Christian faith stems from a failure to interpret properly this fourth use of the concept in the New Testament. If we think of faith as a mental state, we are constantly being put in the position of defining it as "believing what you know isn't true," and of going around trying to "grunt up" our psyche by sheer will power. In short, we run the risk of confusing faith with hope! For a quick confirmation of the foregoing interpretation, I invite the reader to open a concordance to the listings under "Faith" and read through the entries with this translation ("faithfulness") in mind. Of course, a full substantiation of the interpretation would involve careful exegesis of several key passages. I here offer a few translations of texts that have been particularly troublesome, suggesting that the improvement of understanding that accompanies them will serve to establish my overall contention. "Jesus, seeing their *faithfulness,* said to them" (Matthew 9:2); "The just shall live by *faithfulness*" (Romans 1:17); "If you have *faithfulness* as a grain of mustard" (Luke 17:6); "Now *faithfulness* is the assurance of things hoped for, the conviction of things not seen. For by it [*faithfulness*] the men of old received divine approval." (Hebrews 11:1,2).

Thus, in addition to believing *that* certain things about Jesus Christ are true and believing *in* Jesus Christ, Christian faith is nothing more than living a life that is *faithful* to such commitments. Nor is it less! My overall thesis is that this is the insight that constitutes the burden of Kierkegaard's *Fear and Trembling*. Faith *is* as faith *does*.

CONCLUDING UNPOETIC POSTSCRIPT

Toward the end of his life Kierkegaard wrote "A Sad Reflection" in his journal in which he lamented the fact that the riches of his life's work would be inherited, unfortunately, by "the Professor." He followed this with a note:

> And even if the "Professor" should chance to read this, it will not give him pause, will not cause his conscience to smite him; no, this too will be made the subject of a lecture. And again this observation, if the Professor should chance to read it, will not give him pause; no, this too will be made the subject of a lecture. For longer even than the tapeworm which recently was extracted from a woman . . . even longer is the Professor, and the man in

whom the Professor is lodged cannot be rid of this by any human power, only God can do it, if the man himself is willing.[14]

It has been a source of no small amount of frustration and disappointment to me that I was unable to express the burden of this paper in a form more fitting to its character and to Kierkegaard's artistic genius. I honestly tried. As yet, however, my facility for indirect communication is not sufficiently developed even to begin to do justice to such a task. Therefore I have produced a very "professorial" sort of essay, offering as my sole excuse the possibility that the whole issue of interpreting Kierkegaard's works is confusing enough already without the addition of yet another layer of indirect communication.

Besides, even though the professor stands below the poet, the poet in turn stands, as Johannes de Silentio admits, below the hero. Nevertheless, the poet has his task and so does the professor. At the highest level, faith must be lived, it cannot be *stated*. But to *show* that this is so is the task of the poet. And to *state* that *this* is so is the task of the professor.

Notes

1. THE PROBLEM OF THE *AKEDAH* IN JEWISH THOUGHT

1. Louis Jacobs, "Akedah" in *Encyclopedia Judaica,* Vol. 2 (1972), pp. 480–84.

2. In his *Anatomy of Faith* (New York: Harcourt, Brace, 1960), pp. 130–52.

3. Ibid., p. 147.

4. See the discussion in Reuben Margaliout's commentary to tractate Sanhedrin, entitled: *Margaliyot Ha-Yam* (Jerusalem: Mosad Harav Kook, 1958), Part II, No. 10, p. 128.

5. Shalom Spiegel, *The Last Trial* (New York: Schocken, 1969).

6. Relevant to this question is a Responsum of Rabbi Meir ben Baruch of Rothenburg (died 1293). Here (*Teshuvot Pesakim U-Minhagim,* ed. I. Z. Kahana [Jerusalem: Mosad Harav Kook, 1957–62], Part II, No. 59, p. 54) Meir discusses a case arising out of certain tragic events that occurred in the city of Koblenz, where on 2 April 1265 a man killed his wife and four children by his own hand in order to save them from torture and forcible conversion; he had intended also to kill himself, but Gentiles prevented his doing so. Asked whether the unfortunate man must do penance for the murder of his family, Meir replies that he is quite sure that it is permitted—indeed, obligatory—to commit suicide in order to avoid apostasy, but that he is not at all sure that it is permitted to murder others for the sake of the "sanctification of God's name." Nevertheless, Meir concludes that this, too, must be permitted, since we know that many of the saints killed themselves and their families when threatened with forcible conversion. He concludes that the man must not be allowed to undergo any penance, for if he did penance it would imply that the saints of old were wrong.

7. This does seem to be the meaning of the quotation by Satan from Job, see Reuben Margaliout, op. cit., No. 17, p. 129, and the sermon by Hayyim Jeremiah Plensberg (nineteenth century) in his: *Divrey Yirmiyahu,* S. P. Garber, Part I, Vilna, n.d., to the *Akedah* narrative, pp. 157–60.

8. Cf. the comment of the Hasidic master, Rabbi Mordecai Joseph Leiner of Izbica (died 1854) in his *Mey Ha-Shiloah,* Vol. II, ed. M. J. Leiner (New York: Sentry Press, 1973), p. 12, that the command to Abraham was conveyed in an ambiguous manner and that Abraham had doubts whether it was really a divine command, since it involved the prohibited act of murder. Abraham emerged victorious from the test because he refused to allow his love for Isaac to persuade him that God could not really have commanded him to commit murder. This author quotes the Zohar (I, 120a) to the effect that Abraham saw his vision of this command "as in a glass darkly."

9. *The Guide of the Perplexed,* III, 24, trans. S. Pines (Chicago: University of Chicago Press, 1963), pp. 500–02.

10. Bahya Ibn Asher, *Commentary to the Pentateuch,* Vol. I, ed. C. B. Chavel (Jerusalem: Mosad Harav Kook, 1966), pp. 192–94.

11. Plensberg, op. cit., states that, on the face of it, the *Akedah* is extremely strange. The command to commit a murder seems "a very ugly thing" for God to

do and appears to involve, in fact, a profanation of God's name. But Abraham had hitherto only known the love of God. In order to become the perfect man of faith he had to learn to obey God and fear him even when commanded to do something that made it extremely hard to believe in God's goodness!

12. J. B. Soloveitchick, "Ish Ha-Halakhah," *Talpiot* 2 (1944): 651–735.

13. J. B. Agus, *Guideposts in Modern Judaism* (New York: Bloch, 1954), pp. 37–38.

14. W. Gunther Plaut, "Notes on the Akedah," *Central Conference of American Rabbis Journal* 17 (January 1969): 45–47.

15. Franz Rosenzweig, *Star of Redemption,* second ed. (1930), trans. William W. Hallo (London: Routledge & Kegan Paul, 1971), Part III, Introduction, pp. 265–67.

16. Ernst Simon, *"Torat Hayyim,"* *Conservative Judaism* 12 (Spring 1958): 16–19.

17. *Guide of the Perplexed,* III, 32.

18. Cf. Jiri Langer: *Nine Gates,* trans. Stephen Jolly (London: James Clarke, 1961), p. 156. Under the heading *And now something for Kierkegaard,* Langer gives this interpretation of the *Akedah,* which he attributes to the eighteenth-century Hasidic master Rabbi Shmelke of Nikolsburg:

> The significance of Abraham's testing lies not in the fact that his obedience to the Lord's command made him prepared to offer up his only son for love of God, but in the way he behaved when God ordered him to set his son free and let him live. In other words, its significance lies in the fact that God declined the offering the moment after He had demanded it. If Abraham had rejoiced because the life of his beloved son was saved, or if he had grieved because he had not been allowed to show his love for God by actually carrying out his sacrifice—in either of these cases he would have failed the test. But Abraham rejoiced—as can be seen from a careful reading of the Scriptures—that, in carrying out God's new command, to spare his son, he was allowed to bring to God a still greater sacrifice than the actual offering up of Isaac would have been. In being prepared to offer his son to God, he showed that for him the command to sacrifice was something even higher than his love for his child. But when God gave His second command, Abraham gave up the performance of this sacrifice, in other words, he sacrificed even that sacrifice which had previously become so dear to him, for this was the only way he could show his infinite love to the Creator. He rejoiced in the new sacrifice whose significance lay essentially in the fact that he had renounced the offering up of his son. This is the climax of his testing.

2. ABRAHAM AND ISAAC:
A HERMENEUTICAL PROBLEM BEFORE KIERKEGAARD

1. Søren Kierkegaard, *Fear and Trembling,* trans. Walter Lowrie (Princeton: Princeton University Press, 1968), pp. 66–67.

2. Ibid., p. 41.

3. Ibid., p. 48.

4. Augustine, *The City of God,* Bk. 16, c. 32, *On The Trinity,* Bk. 3, c. 11, 25; Abélard, *Ethics* c. 3; Aquinas, *Summa Theologica,* I-II, 94, 5; 100, 8; II-II, 104, 4.

5. Joseph Hall, "Contemplations: The Second Booke" in *Works,* Vol. 1 (London: 1647), p. 796.

6. Voltaire, *A Philosophical Dictionary,* Vol. I (London: 1843), p. 15.

7. Andrew Fuller, "Expository Discourses on the Book of Genesis" in *Complete Works,* Vol. 1 (London: 1856), p. 386.

8. Stephen Charnock, "A Discourse of the Necessity of Christ's Death" in *Works,* Vol. 2 (London: 1699), p. 599. Hereafter: Charnock, 2.

9. Thomas Chubb, *Some Observations . . . Occasioned by the Opposition made to Dr. Rundle's Election* (London: 1735), p. 31, but cp. pp. 36f. Hereafter: Chubb, 2.

10. Thomas Chubb, "The Case of Abraham . . . In Answer to Dr. Stone's Remarks" in *Four Tracts* (London: 1734), p. 87. Hereafter: Chubb, 1.

11. David Collyer, *The Sacred Interpreter* (London: 1815), Vol. I, p. 161. See also, William Chillingworth, *Nine Sermons* in *Works* (London: 1719), p. 86; Chubb, 1, pp. 94, 98, 118; Robert Jenkin, *The Reasonableness and Certainty of the Christian Religion* (London: 1734), Vol. II, p. 332; Gregory Sharpe, "Notes Historical, Chronological, and Critical" added to his translation of Baron Holberg's *Introduction to Universal History* (London: 1758), p. 62n; Thomas Stackhouse, *A Compleat Body of Speculative and Practical Divinity* (London: 1743), p. 336.

12. Fuller, op. cit., p. 385.

13. Stackhouse, op. cit., p. 336.

14. Fuller, op. cit., p. 386.

15. Charnock, 2, p. 599.

16. Isaac Barrow, *The Works (Being All his English Works),* ed. by J. Tillotson, 3 vols. (London: 1716), Vol. II, p. 288, Vol. III, pp. 363f; Charnock, 2, p. 599; Fuller, op. cit., p. 386; Hall, op. cit., p. 796; Charles Leslie, *A Short and Easy Method with the Jews* (London: 1848), p. 12 (hereafter: Leslie, 1); also "The Truth of Christianity Demonstrated" in *A Short and Easy Method with the Deists* (London: 1851), pp. 111f (hereafter: Leslie, 2); Jenkin, op. cit., Vol. I, p. 26, Vol. II, pp. 333f; John Pearson, *An Exposition of the Creed* (London: 1880), pp. 290f; Stackhouse, op. cit., pp. 336, 338; John Tillotson, *Works,* ed. by Ralph Barker, (London: 1712), Vol. I, p. 21; Thomas Wilson, "Notes on the Holy Scriptures," in *Works,* Vol. VI (Oxford: 1859), pp. 35f (hereafter: Wilson, 2).

17. Pearson, op. cit., pp. 290ff, 306, 366.

18. Jenkin, op. cit., Vol. II, pp. 332-34.

19. Daniel Waterland, *Scripture Vindicated in Answer to a Book entitled Christianity as Old as the Creation* in *Works,* Vol. IV (Oxford, 1843), p. 204.

20. Chubb, 1, p. 99; cf. "Bayle," p. 95. "Bayle" refers to the additional note on Abraham in the translation and augmented edition of Bayle's *General Dictionary, Historical and Critical,* edited by John Peter Bernard, Thomas Birch, John Lockman, and others (London: 1734). The note is not signed. At the end of Volume 10 it is stated that unmarked articles such as this were composed by "George Sale, or communicated by other Hands to the editors."

21. Matthew Tindal, *Christianity as Old as the Creation* (London: 1730), p. 97.

22. Voltaire, op. cit., p. 18.

23. John Leland, *An Answer to a Book Intituled Christianity as Old as the Creation,* Part II (London: 1740), p. 387.

24. Hall, op. cit., p. 796.

25. Sharpe, op. cit., p. 62n.

26. Tillotson, op. cit., p. 12; cf. Stephen Charnock, "A Discourse upon God's Knowledge" in *Works,* Vol. 1, (London: 1699), p. 175; "Bayle," p. 95.

27. Tillotson, op. cit., p. 12. It is not clear why Tillotson misquotes. Cf. Fuller, op. cit., p. 386.

28. Charnock, 1, p. 175.

29. Tillotson, op. cit., p. 12.

30. Leland, op. cit., p. 387.

31. Cf. "Bayle," p. 95.

32. Chillingworth, op. cit., p. 86; cf. Charnock, 2, p. 599; Hall, op. cit., p. 796.

33. Hall, op. cit., p. 792.

34. Cf. David Hartley, *Observations on Man, His Frame, His Duty and His Expectations,* Second Part (London: 1749), p. 131, who apparently sees no problem.

35. "Bayle," p. 95.

36. Loc. cit.

37. Wilson, 2, p. 36; cf. p. 35.

38. Chubb, 2, pp. 35ff.

39. John Abernethy, *Sermons on Various Subjects,* Vol. 4 (London: 1751), p. 7.

40. Tillotson, op. cit., p. 12; cf. Chubb, 1, pp. 94–7, 118; Sharpe, op. cit., p. 62n; Stackhouse, op. cit., p. 336; Wilson, 2, p. 35; Beilby Porteus, *Sermons on Several Subjects* (London: 1810), Vol. I, p. 47.

41. Hartley, op. cit., p. 132.

42. Chillingworth, op. cit., p. 33; cf. p. 86.

43. Thomas Chubb, "An Answer to Mr. *Stone*'s second remarks upon the case of *Abraham*" in *Some Observations . . . Occasioned by the Opposition . . .* (London: 1735), pp. 66–68. Hereafter: Chubb, 3.

44. Chubb, 1, p. 94; cf. pp. 97, 118.

45. Cf. Joseph Butler, *Analogy of Religion* (London: 1765), p. 267. Hereafter: Butler, 1.

46. Cp. Sermons 2 and 3 on the supremacy of conscience in Joseph Butler, *Fifteen Sermons Preached at the Rolls Chapel* (London: 1765). Hereafter: Butler, 2.

47. William Law, *The Case of Reason or Natural Religion, Fairly and Fully Stated,* in *Works,* Vol. 2 (London: 1892), pp. 87f.

48. Samuel Clarke, *XVII Sermons on Several Occasions* (London: 1724), pp. 254f, (hereafter: Clarke, 1); cf. Edmund Law, "Preface" to his translation of William King, *The Origin of Evil* (London: 1739), pp. 319f; Tillotson, op. cit., p. 15; Isaac Watts, *Logick, or the Right Use of Reason* (London: 1782), p. 272.

49. William Law, op. cit., p. 88.

50. Waterland, op. cit., p. 201.

51. Chubb, 1, p. 92; cf. pp. 85–94; Chubb, 3, p. 58.

52. Chubb, 3, pp. 63f.

53. Immanuel Kant, *Lectures on Ethics,* tr. L. Infield (London and New York: 1963), p. 22; cf. pp. 51f, (hereafter: Kant, 1); cf. also Chubb, 1, p. 90.

54. Tillotson, op. cit., p. 15.

55. Waterland, op. cit., p. 201.

56. Cf. Samuel Clarke, *Sermons on the Following Subjects* ed. by John Clarke, Vol. VII (London: 1731), p. 209, (hereafter: Clarke, 2); Collyer, op. cit., p. 162; John Conybeare, *Sermons* (London: 1757), Vol. II, pp. 254–56, who tries to make God's authority less disturbing by holding that it is directed by "unerring wisdom"; Fuller, op. cit., p. 386; Edmund Law, op. cit., p. 319; William Law, op. cit., p. 88; Watts, op. cit., p. 272; Wilson, 2, pp. 35f.

57. Chubb, 3, pp. 58, 63.

58. Chubb, 1, p. 94.

59. Chubb, 1, p. 115; cf. pp. 104–18; Chubb, 2, pp. 31–35.

60. Chubb, 1, p. 88; cf. Chubb, 3, p. 59.

61. Chubb, 2, pp. 34f; Chubb, 3, pp. 64f.

62. Chubb, 1, pp. 95ff.; Chubb, 3, p. 59.

63. Cf. Jenkin, op. cit., Vol. II, p. 233; Leland, op. cit., pp. 384ff.

64. Tillotson, op. cit., p. 14; cf. Hall, op. cit., pp. 794f; Stackhouse, op. cit., p. 337.

65. Fuller, op. cit., p. 385.

66. Hall, op. cit., p. 795.

67. Stackhouse, op. cit., p. 336n, who attacks this view in Shaftesbury and Marsham; Tindal, op. cit., p. 97; cp. Waterland, op. cit., p. 201.

68. Hall, op. cit., pp. 794–96; cf. Wilson, 2, p. 35.

69. [Patrick Delaney], "A Professed Friend to an Honest Freedom of Thought in Religious Enquiries," *Revelation Examined with Candour,* Vol. 3, (London: 1763), p. 64; cf. Hall, op. cit., pp. 795f, who has Isaac encouraging Abraham when he "had somewhat digested his thoughts" after being told of his fate.

70. Samuel Ogden, *Sermons,* Vol. II (Cambridge: 1780), p. 198.

71. John Locke, *An Essay Concerning Human Understanding* in *Works,* Vol. I (London: 1768), Bk. IV, Chap. 17, para. 24; Chap. 19, para. 4. Hereafter: Locke, 1.

72. "Bayle," p. 95; Conybeare, op. cit., pp. 250ff.

73. Stackhouse, op. cit., p. 337.

74. Tillotson, op. cit., p. 12; cf. pp. 13f; Stackhouse, op. cit., p. 337.

75. Chubb, 3, pp. 59, 64f.

76. Stackhouse, op. cit., p. 339.

77. Ibid., p. 337; Tillotson, op. cit., p. 13.

78. Conybeare, op. cit., p. 251.

79. Ibid., p. 252; Stackhouse, op. cit., p. 337; Tillotson, op. cit., p. 13.

80. Conybeare, op. cit., p. 251; Stackhouse, op. cit., p. 337.

81. Tillotson, op. cit., p. 14.

82. Conybeare, loc. cit.

83. Stackhouse, loc. cit.

84. Hall, op. cit., p. 794.

85. Tillotson, op. cit., p. 13.

86. Chubb, 1, p. 97.

87. Tillotson, op. cit., p. 15; cf. p. 19.

88. Conybeare, op. cit., p. 253; cf. pp. 258f.

89. Waterland, op. cit., p. 202.

90. Stackhouse, op. cit., p. 337; Tillotson, op. cit., pp. 12–14.

91. Hartley, op. cit., p. 131.
92. Conybeare, op. cit., p. 254; cf. p. 250; Collyer, op. cit., p. 162; Wilson, 2, p. 36.
93. Tillotson, op. cit., p. 17.
94. Ibid., cf. p. 16; "Bayle," p. 95; Clarke, 2, p. 209f; *The New Whole Duty of Man*, (London: n.d.), 20th ed., pp. 253f.
95. Clarke, 2, p. 210; cf. "Bayle," p. 95, for another expression of this Cartesian conviction that God will keep us from error.
96. Immanuel Kant, *Religion within the Limits of Reason Alone*, trans. T. M. Greene and H. H. Hudson (New York: Harper Torchbooks, 1960), p. 175 (hereafter: Kant, 2); Immanuel Kant, *Der Streit der Facultäten* in *Werke*, Band VII (Berlin: 1902–), p. 63 (hereafter: Kant, 3).
97. Clarke, 2, p. 209; cf. Collyer, op. cit., p. 162; Conybeare, op cit., pp. 254ff, Hall, op. cit., p. 795; Hartley, op. cit., pp. 131f; Stackhouse, op. cit., p. 339; Tillotson, op. cit., p. 15; Waterland, op. cit., p. 201; Wilson, 2, pp. 35f.
98. William Law, op. cit., p. 88.
99. Cf. Chubb, 2, pp. 31ff; Chubb, 3, pp. 58, 66.
100. Cf. "Bayle," p. 95; Conybeare, op. cit., pp. 256ff; Hall, op. cit., p. 795; Thomas Wilson, "Sermons" in *Works*, Vol. III (Oxford: 1847), p. 229, (hereafter: Wilson, 1); Wilson, 2, p. 35.
101. Waterland, op. cit., p. 202; cf. Hall, op. cit., p. 795.
102. Tillotson, op. cit., p. 15; Tindal, op. cit., p. 97.
103. William Hurd, *A Complete and Impartial View of All Religions* (Manchester: 1814), p. 8.
104. Cf. Stackhouse, op. cit., p. 336n; Tindal, op. cit., p. 97; cp. Leland, op. cit., p. 387; Waterland, op. cit., p. 201.
105. Cf. Conybeare, op. cit., p. 256.
106. Cf. Hurd, op. cit., p. 8; Stackhouse, op. cit., pp. 337, 339; Tillotson, op. cit. p. 16.
107. Collyer, op. cit., p. 162; Tillotson, op. cit., p. 16.
108. John Toland, *Christianity Not Mysterious* (London: 1696), p. 137.
109. Clarke, 1, p. 250; cf. pp. 248, 250f; Conybeare, pp. 256ff; Fuller, op. cit., p. 386; Hall, op. cit., p. 796; Hurd, op. cit., p. 8; Pearson, op. cit., p. 366; Waterland, op. cit., p. 202; Wilson, 1, p. 229; 2, p. 35.
110. Jenkin, op. cit., Vol. II, pp. 333f; cp. Charnock, 2, p. 599, who is not sure that Abraham's comment in Genesis 22:8 can be used to show that he knew what was going to happen.
111. Delaney, op. cit., p. 65.
112. Chubb, 1, p. 98.
113. "Bayle," p. 93n.
114. Tindal, op. cit., p. 97; cf. Chubb, 2, pp. 36ff.
115. Waterland, op. cit., pp. 201, 201n; cf. p. 204.
116. Ibid., 204; cp. "Bayle," p. 93, where it is suggested he might have lied to his servants.
117. Conybeare, op. cit., p. 246; cf. Barrow, Vol. III, pp. 13f; Clarke, 1, p. 247.
118. Cf. Hartley, op. cit., pp. 131f.
119. Cf. Stackhouse, op. cit., p. 337; Tillotson, op. cit., p. 12.
120. Wilson, 1, p. 229; cf. Wilson, 2, pp. 35f; Hall, op. cit., p. 796.

121. Cf. Clarke, 1, p. 256; Conybeare, op. cit., pp. 265f.

122. Barrow, op. cit., Vol. III, p. 14; cf. Collyer, op. cit., p. 162; Hartley, op. cit., pp. 131f; Stackhouse, op. cit., pp. 338f.

123. Tillotson, op. cit., pp. 14f, 19; cf. pp. 11, 20.

124. Clarke, 1, pp. 249f.

125. Voltaire, op. cit., p. 18.

126. Cf. Barrow, op. cit., Vol. III, p. 14; Fuller, op. cit., p. 385; Hall, op. cit., p. 795; Waterland, op. cit., p. 201.

127. Cf. Hall, op. cit., p. 795; Lancelot Andrewes, *A Pattern of Catechistical Doctrine* (Oxford: 1846), p. 178.

128. Cf. Charnock, 2, p. 599; Leslie, 1, p. 12; 2, pp. 111f; Stackhouse, op. cit., p. 340; Tillotson, op. cit., p. 21; Wilson, 2, p. 35f.

129. Hall, op. cit., p. 796; cf. Chillingworth, op. cit., p. 33; Fuller, op. cit., p. 386; Tillotson, op. cit., p. 20.

130. Wilson, 2, p. 36.

131. Hurd, op. cit., p. 8; cf. Leland, op. cit., p. 387; *The New Whole Duty of Man,* pp. 253f.

132. Stackhouse, op. cit., p. 339.

133. Cf. Collyer, op. cit., p. 162; Hall, op. cit., p. 796; Henry Hammond, *Paraphrase and Annotations Upon the New Testament* (London: 1689), on Hebrews 11:19.

134. Fuller, op. cit., p. 386.

135. Clarke, 1, p. 254.

136. Tillotson, op. cit., p. 17; cf. p. 19; Clarke, 1. pp. 250ff; Toland, op. cit., pp. 136ff.

137. Barrow, op. cit., Vol. III, p. 386.

138. Tillotson, op. cit., pp. 16f; cf. "Bayle," p. 95; Wilson, 2, p. 36.

139. Conybeare, op. cit., p. 254; cf. p. 250.

140. Stackhouse, op. cit., p. 340.

141. Conybeare, op. cit., pp. 258f; cf. Clarke, 1, p. 248; Hall, op. cit., p. 796.

142. Fuller, op. cit., p. 385.

143. Tindal, op. cit., p. 97; cf. Chubb, 2, pp. 31ff, 36.

144. Tindal, op. cit., p. 97; cp. Leland, op. cit., p. 387, for reply.

145. Voltaire, op. cit., p. 18.

146. Hurd, op. cit., p. 8.

147. Cf. Voltaire, op. cit., p. 16.

148. Theophilus Gale, *The Court of the Gentiles,* (Oxford: 1672), Part I, "Advertissements."

149. John Edwards, *A Discourse Concerning the Authority, Stile, and Perfection of the Books of the Old and New-Testament* (London: 1693), pp. 132f; cf. Gale, op. cit., Bk. 2, p. 7f; Edward Stillingfleet, *Origines Sacrae: or a Rational Account of the Grounds of Natural and Revealed Religion* (Cambridge: 1702), pp. 407f.

150. Stackhouse, op. cit., p. 339n.

151. Waterland, op. cit., p. 204; cf. pp. 203f.

152. Kant, 2, p. 175.

153. Immanuel Kant, *Critique of Practical Reason,* trans. T. K. Abbott (London: 1909), p. 121.

154. Cf. Chubb, 3, p. 65.

155. Kant, 3, p. 63 (my translation).

156. Barrow, op. cit., Vol. II, p. 288; Vol. III, p. 14. The formal contradiction of his "to believe things incredible" can be excused as preacher's rhetoric.

157. Stackhouse, op. cit., pp. 336f.

158. Chubb, 2, p. 37; cf. pp. 30f.

159. Barrow, op. cit., Vol. III, p. 14.

160. Locke, 1 Bk. IV, Chap. 17, para. 24.

161. Cf. Chillingworth, op. cit., Chap. ii, pp. 110–16.

162. John Locke, *Essays on the Law of Nature,* ed. by W. Von Leyden (Oxford: 1954), pp. 201f; cf. p. 84.

163. Tillotson, op. cit., p. 15; cf. p. 16.

164. Cf. "Bayle," p. 95.

165. John Locke, *A Second Vindication of the Reasonableness of Christianity* in *Works,* Vol. III, (London: 1768), p. 190.

166. Ibid., p. 191—and the preface to his *Paraphrases.*

167. Locke, 1, Bk. III, Chap. 9, para. 22f.

3. FOR SANITY'S SAKE: KANT, KIERKEGAARD, AND FATHER ABRAHAM

1. Immanuel Kant, *Critique of Pure Reason,* trans. Norman Kemp Smith (London: Macmillan, 1956), p. 650 (A829,B857). Note that the "I" in the quotation is neither an existential nor a romantic ego. The ego thus indicated is the Kantian moral self.

2. Robert L. Perkins, "Kierkegaard's Epistemological Preferences," *International Journal for Philosophy of Religion* 4 (1973): 197–217.

3. Søren Kierkegaard, *Concluding Unscientific Postscript to the Philosophical Fragments,* trans. David F. Swenson and Walter Lowrie (Princeton: Princeton University Press, 1941), p. 182.

4. Immanuel Kant, *Foundations of the Metaphysics of Morals,* trans. Lewis White Beck (New York: Liberal Arts Press, 1959). The regressive nature of Kant's arguments is quite evident in titles of the first two sections: "Transition from the Common Rational Knowledge of Morals to the Philosophical" and "Transition from the Popular Moral Philosophy to the Metaphysics of Morals."

5. Søren Kierkegaard, *Point of View,* trans. Walter Lowrie (London: Oxford University Press, 1939).

6. I realize that this last sentence *and* the last few paragraphs are a considerable assertion about philosophical method. This is not the forum in which to defend the truth of these thoughts—though I do consider them true. Kierkegaard research still lacks a major literary analysis, i.e., an analysis of its literary form according to the canons of literary criticism.

7. Robert L. Perkins, "Hegel and Kierkegaard: Two Critics of Romantic Irony," *Review of National Literatures* 1 (1970): 232–54. See also Bradley R. Dewey's perceptive analysis of "The Erotic Demonic in Kierkegaard's *Diary of the Seducer*" in *Scandinavica* 10 (1971): 1–24.

8. Søren Kierkegaard, *Either/Or, A Fragment of Life,* trans. David F. and Lillian Marvin Swenson, Vol. 2 (Princeton: Princeton University Press, 1949).

Stages on Life's Way, trans. Walter Lowrie (Princeton: Princeton University Press, 1945).

9. Immanuel Kant, *Religion Within the Limits of Reason Alone,* trans. with introduction and notes by Theodore M. Green and Hoyt H. Hudson, with a new essay by John R. Silber (New York: Harper & Brothers, 1960). Special attention should be called to the ad hoc distinction between positive and natural religion. No other distinction worked such a pernicious influence on Kant's philosophy of religion, for it turned him away from the phenomenon of religion and imposed a theory on his thought.

10. There are many discussions of this point. Allen W. Wood, *Kant's Moral Religion* (Ithaca: Cornell University Press, 1970), is one of the best. See also John Silber's essay referred to above, "The Ethical Significance of Kant's Religion." See also Michel Despland, *Kant on History and Religion* (Montreal: McGill-Queen's University Press, 1973).

11. Immanuel Kant, *Foundations of the Metaphysics of Morals,* trans. Lewis White Beck (New York: The Liberal Arts Press, 1959), p. 39.

12. Ibid., p. 9.

13. Ibid., pp. 59–64.

14. Ibid., pp. 85–86.

15. This quotation from the Abbott translation was cited by Emil L. Fackenheim in *Quest for Past and Future* (Bloomington: Indiana University Press, 1968), p. 221. The reference in the above mentioned Beck translation is pp. 49, 51. Fackenheim's essay is most suggestive. See also his *Encounters Between Judaism and Modern Philosophy* (New York: Basic Books, 1973), especially the second chapter, "Abraham and the Kantians." See also George A. Schrader's "Autonomy, Heteronomy and Moral Imperatives," *The Journal of Philosophy* 60 (1963): 65–77.

16. See John R. Silber, "The Importance of the Highest Good in Kant's Ethics," *Ethics* 53 (1963): 179–97. See also the excellent treatment in Wood, op. cit., pp. 69–99. This discussion centers in Book II of *The Critique of Practical Reason,* trans. by Lewis White Beck (New York: The Liberal Arts Press, 1956).

17. G. W. F. Hegel, *The Philosophy of Right,* trans. T. M. Knox (Oxford: Oxford University Press, 1958), pp. 86–103.

18. On the latter point see my "Hegel and the Secularization of Religion," *International Journal for Philosophy of Religion* 1 (1970): 130–46.

19. Søren Kierkegaard, *Fear and Trembling,* trans. Walter Lowrie (Princeton: Princeton University Press, 1968), 64–78.

20. The issue of the inclination in Kant and Kierkegaard was explored first and excellently by George Schrader in "Kant and Kierkegaard on Duty and Inclination," *The Journal of Philosophy* 65 (1968): 688–701.

21. Ibid., p. 30.

22. Immanuel Kant, *Streit der Facultäten* in *Prussische Akademie Ausgabe,* 7:43. Also, *Religion Within the Limits of Reason Alone,* 175.

4. ABRAHAM AND HEGEL

1. See "On the Proof of the Spirit and of Power" in *Lessing's Theological Writings,* trans. Henry Chadwick (Stanford: Stanford University Press, 1957), and

Kierkegaard's discussion in *Concluding Unscientific Postscript,* trans. David F. Swenson and Walter Lowrie (Princeton: Princeton University Press, 1941).

2. There is something ironic about the self-conscious modernity of the Enlightenment. For a thorough account of its equally self-conscious appeal to pagan antiquity see Peter Gay, *The Enlightenment: An Interpretation,* Vol. 1, *The Rise of Modern Paganism* (New York: Knopf, 1968).

3. In the same year that *Fear and Trembling* appeared, Feuerbach raised exactly these same two issues in the preface to the second edition of *The Essence of Christianity.* See *The Fiery Brook: Selected Writings of Ludwig Feuerbach,* trans. Zawar Hanfi (Garden City: Doubleday, 1972), pp. 248–49.

4. Søren Kierkegaard, *Fear and Trembling,* trans. Walter Lowrie (Princeton: Princeton University Press, 1968), p. 43. Cited henceforth as *FT.*

5. In addition to the passage cited above this theme is alluded to in numerous passages outside the Preface and Epilogue as well. See *FT,* pp. 26, 37, 48, 61, 79, 124.

6. Matthew 13:45–46. Kierkegaard complains that the Christianity of Christendom has become "a superficial something which neither wounds nor heals profoundly enough." *Training in Christianity,* trans. Walter Lowrie (Princeton: Princeton University Press, 1941), p. 139.

7. *FT,* p. 23, his ellipsis. On life as a gift and a task, see the critique of romantic irony in *The Concept of Irony,* trans. Lee Capel (New York: Harper & Row, 1965), pp. 293f. For an autobiographical account of what Kierkegaard understood by the concept of a task, see *Either/Or,* trans. Walter Lowrie (New York: Doubleday, 1959), II, pp. 271f.

8. In the year before he wrote *FT* Kierkegaard began but did not finish or publish an essay on doubt and modern philosophy. It is available to us as *Johannes Climacus or De Omnibus Dubitandum Est,* trans. T. H. Croxall (Stanford: Stanford University Press, 1958).

9. *FT,* p. 23.

10. See Hegel's 1802 essay entitled *Verhältniss des Skepticismus zur Philosophie* and the echoes of it in *Encyclopedia* (henceforth: *Ency.*) ¶39 and the *Zusätze* to ¶24 and ¶81. *Zusätze* will henceforth be indicated by a *Z* after the paragraph number, e.g., ¶24Z and ¶81Z.

11. Implicitly challenged here is the transition from the *Phenomenology* to the Hegelian system. We are to be prepared for the ether of the latter by passing over the phenomenological highway of doubt and despair in which our confidence in the ordinary deliverances of consciousness is shaken. The doubt that is prerequisite for faith Kierkegaard calls irony and infinite resignation. It "rescues the soul from the snares of relativity." *Concept of Irony,* p. 113. Phenomenological doubt is similarly a prerequisite for Hegelian speculation. Hegel stresses the difficulty of this path, but it is so far from being the task of a lifetime that the system presupposes its achievement. By contrast, Kierkegaard makes suffering a permanent element of faith in so far as faith involves the perpetual, lifelong task of dying to immediacy. See *Postscript,* pp. 386–448.

12. *FT,* pp. 130–31.

13. *FT,* p. 24. Cf. pp. 38, 53, 77, and the suggestion on p. 26 that if only he were a learned exegete who knew Hebrew he would understand Abraham. In the *Postscript* Kierkegaard develops the formula that existence plus reflection produces

passion, and he stresses passion as an essential element in what he calls "essential knowledge." See pp. 313 and 176–77.

14. *FT.*, pp. 130–31. Quickly returning to the satirical mood, Johannes concludes with a reference to the disciple of Heraclitus who went beyond his master by reverting to the Eleatic thesis that motion was impossible.

15. See note 11.

16. *FT,* p. 24.

17. *FT,* p. 29.

18. Cf. *Postscript,* p. 33, and the whole discussion of truth as subjectivity. In the *Postscript* and *The Concept of Dread,* Kierkegaard constantly worries the question of the appropriate mode for discourse about God. Among the indications that this issue is already at work in *FT* are the fact that the section entitled "Problemata: Preliminary Expectoration" is framed by a satirical but plainly serious discussion of how and how not to preach about Abraham and the fact that Johannes worries about speaking humanly and not inhumanly about his theme (pp. 45, 74). Closely related to Kierkegaard's thought here is Luther's distinction between the true knowledge of God and self, in which one actually experiences his sinfulness, and the "speculative" knowledge in which this does not occur. See the 1535 "Lectures on Galatians," in *Luther's Works,* ed. Jaroslav Pelikan (St. Louis: Concordia, 1963), Vol. 26, pp. 131, 148, 288, and the discussion of Psalm 51 in Vol. 12, pp. 310f., 385, 403. The difference between Kierkegaard and Hegel on this point is partially expressed by the fact that the former sharply distinguishes worship from comprehension (*Training in Christianity,* p. 139), while the latter sees philosophy and worship as the same (*Lectures on the Philosophy of Religion,* trans. E. S. Haldane [London: Routledge & Kegan Paul, 1962], Vol. I, p. 20; German text in *Werke in Zwanzig Bänden,* Theorie-Werkausgabe von Suhrkamp Verlag, Vol. 16, p. 28). Where paragraph numbers are not at hand double references will be given, though with abbreviations after the first reference to a text. Thus *Religion,* I, 20 = *Werke,* 16:28. I have felt free to modify existing translations slightly without mention.

19. *Ency.* ¶12.

20. There are five main points in Hegel's critique: (1) Strictly speaking, there is no such thing as immediate knowledge, for knowledge implies content, while a purely immediate awareness would be entirely indeterminate, void of any content whatever. (2) Since one's principle is devoid of content, it is entirely arbitrary what eventually gets affirmed as immediately given. The certainty and self-evidence claimed for immediacy are no guarantee of truth whatever. (3) Since the truth is to be determined by the unchecked subjectivity of private opinion there is a socially anarchist implication to this philosophy. (4) Paradoxically, there is an uncritical conservatism as the usual result, for what is self-evident is most likely to be what is traditional and familiar. (5) Especially since immediacy has been appealed to on behalf of religious ideas that reason had been unable to support, it must be noted that the Christian religion has always had something quite different in mind when it speaks of faith, for it always affirms a specific content and an authority beyond that of private certainty.

21. "*unmittelbar von der Vorstellung zugegeben,*" *Ency.* ¶1.

22. *Ency.* ¶12 and ¶68, *Religion,* I, 166 = *Werke,* 16:161.

23. *Ency.* ¶67, *Religion,* I, 74, 132–34 = *Werke,* 16:78–79, 130–31, *Lectures on*

the Proofs of the Existence of God (henceforth: *Proofs*), in *Religion*, III, 177 = *Werke*, 17:368–69.

24. *Religion*, I, 43, 116, 119 = *Werke*, 16:49, 115, 118, and *Proofs*, III, 160–61 = *Werke*, 17:353.

25. *Ency.* ¶3, 4, & 6, and *Proofs*, III, 203 = *Werke*, 17:391.

26. *Ency.* ¶2, *Proofs*, III, 203 = *Werke*, 17:392, and *Religion*, I, 116 = *Werke*, 16:115.

27. *Ency.* ¶3. Cf. ¶66 and the Preface to the *Phenomenology*, which also contains a penetrating critique of the allegedly immediate as the merely familiar.

28. *Religion*, I, 65, 117, 145 = *Werke*, 16:70, 116, 141.

29. *FT*, 58, 79, 92. Cf. *Stages on Life's Way*, trans. Walter Lowrie (Princeton: Princeton University Press, 1967), p. 364, and *Søren Kierkegaard's Journals and Papers*, trans. Hong and Hong (Bloomington: Indiana University Press, 1970), II, 12, where Kierkegaard writes (in 1848) that "faith is immediacy or spontaneity after reflection." In any earlier entry (from 1836, on p. 3), he writes: "What Schleiermacher calls 'religion' and the Hegelian dogmaticians 'faith' is, after all, nothing else than the first immediacy, the prerequisite for everything—the vital fluid—in an emotional-intellectual sense the atmosphere we breathe—and which therefore cannot properly be characterized with these words [faith and religion]." We have seen that this would be a mistaken reading of Hegel, and Kierkegaard does not level this charge against either Hegel or his own contemporaries in *FT*. It is *Bildung* and not the first immediacy that he finds them confusing with faith.

30. "There is nothing, neither in heaven nor in nature nor in the realm of spirit nor anywhere else which does not contain immediacy as well as mediation, so that these two determinations show themselves to be unseparated and inseparable." *Hegel's Science of Logic*, trans. W. H. Johnston and L. G. Struthers (New York: Macmillan, 1929), II, 80 = *Wissenschaft der Logik*, ed. Georg Lasson (Hamburg, 1967), I, 52. Cf. *Proofs*, III, 175 = *Werke*, 17:367.

31. *Ency.* ¶1 and ¶5.

32. *Proofs*, III, 201–02 = *Werke*, 17:391.

33. The polemic is, if anything, more vehement in the *Phenomenology of Spirit*. Page references will be given first to the Baillie translation (New York, 1931), and then to the Hoffmeister edition (Hamburg, 1952). We read that *Vorstellung* is an imperfect form in which the mediation process is incomplete and which manifests a defect in the connection between thought and being. Consequently, for the true content to attain the true form it is necessary to attain *die höhere Bildung* of the concept (763–64 = 531–32). At the level of *Vorstellung* the content of faith is degraded (*herabsetzen*) (768 = 535). Its understanding of the Incarnation is "the spiritless recollection of an historical figure taken as an individual and its past" (765 = 533). It is thereby reduced to an "inconceivable happening," an "indifferent objective fact" (775 = 541). Self-knowledge is not really possible at this level, nor can truth be at one with certainty (783, 798 = 547, 556). By contrast with *Wissenschaft*, the perfect form of spirit's self-knowledge, religious consciousness is "crude," "barbarian," and "harsh" (802 = 559).

34. *Religion*, I, 118–38 = *Werke*, 16:117–35.

35. Ibid., I, 138–41 = 16:135–38.

36. Ibid., I, 142–45 = 16:139–42.

37. Ibid., I, 146 = 16:142. Cf. 156 = 152.

38. Ibid., I, 147–48 = 16:143 = 44. Cf. *Ency.* ¶1 and *Proofs,* III, 201–02 = *Werke,* 17:391.

39. *Religion,* I, 155, 165 = *Werke,* 16:151, 160 Cf. *Ency.* ¶4, *Religion,* I, 2–3 = *Werke,* 16:12–13, and *Proofs,* III, 161 = *Werke,* 17:353. From this point of view it is no accident that the idea of the paradox and of the absurd, so central to *Philosophical Fragments* is already introduced in *FT.* As early as *The Concept of Irony* Kierkegaard had expressed his distrust of the recollection model. "As Socrates so beautifully binds mankind firmly to the divine by showing that all knowledge is recollection, so Plato . . ." (pp. 67–68). Beautiful? Yes, but not finally tenable, even for Socrates, who ends up ignorant.

40. *Religion,* I, 4–6 = *Werke,* 16:14–15. Cf. *Ency.* ¶6 on philosophy's attitude toward is and ought, and the Preface to the *Phenomenology,* where Hegel first wrote, "But philosophy must beware of wishing to be edifying." Baillie, p. 74 = Hoffmeister, p. 14.

41. The line from the Jutland pastor is the last line of *Either/Or.* The other quotations are from Kierkegaard's oft-cited Gilleleie journal of August 1835. See *The Journals of Kierkegaard,* trans. Alexander Dru (New York: Peter Smith, 1959), pp. 44–45.

42. "It must be possible for the 'I think' to accompany all my representations; for otherwise something would be represented in me which could not be thought at all, and that is equivalent to saying that the representation would be impossible, or at least would be nothing to me. . . . For the manifold representations, which are given in an intuition, would not be one and all *my* representations, if they did not all belong to one self-consciousness." Kant, *Critique of Pure Reason,* trans. N. K. Smith (London: MacMillan, 1956), B131–32.

43. *FT,* p. 132.

44. Quoted from a Berlin review of a book by C. F. Goeschel in Emil Fackenheim, *The Religious Dimension in Hegel's Thought* (Bloomington: Indiana University Press, 1967), p. 192. My italics.

45. *Ency.* ¶3. Cf. *Religion,* I, 24–25 = 16:32–33.

46. *Proofs,* III, 164 = *Werke,* 17:356 and *Religion,* I, 132 = *Werke,* 16:130.

47. *Proofs,* III, 180–81 = *Werke,* 17:372–73 and *Religion,* I, 4 = *Werke,* 16:13. Cf. p. 7 = p. 16.

48. *Religion,* I, 133f. = *Werke,* 16:131f.

49. *FT,* p. 44.

50. Hegel's "Aristotelian" priority of intellectual over moral virtue receives a variety of expressions. In note 18 his identification of philosophy with worship has already been noted. In *The Philosophy of History* (henceforth *History*), tr. J. Sibree, New York, 1956, he writes, "The *ne plus ultra* [*die letzte Spitze*] of inwardness is thought" (p. 439 = *Werke,* 12:521). In *Proofs* he goes further, first identifying thought and inwardness, then preceding to describe thinking reason, the essence of the human spirit, as itself divine (III, 157–58 = *Werke,* 17:349–50). Cf. *Religion,* I, 33 = *Werke,* 16:40.

51. *The Journals of Kierkegaard,* p. 187, his italics. Cf. *FT,* p. 66, and *The Sickness Unto Death,* p. 214.

52. In the third discussion the description of Abraham's being lost does not come in the opening paragraphs but at pp. 122 and 129. Though Kierkegaard could not have known it, Hegel did write a very bitter polemic against Abraham. It

belongs to the essay we know as "The Spirit of Christianity and its Fate," one of Hegel's early, unpublished theological projects. It is by his *Volksreligion* criterion that Abraham is so severely judged, a fact of considerable interest. For if Stephen Crites is right in suggesting that the mature Hegel sees secular Protestantism as the *Volksreligion* of modern Europe, then Hegel's early essay would confirm Kierkegaard's view that he ought to repudiate Abraham. See *In the Twilight of Christendom* (Chambersburg: American Academy of Religion, 1972), pp. 41f and 55.

53. *FT*, pp. 68, 70, 72, 85, 87. Cf. *The Sickness Unto Death*, p. 179. For typical Hegelian statements of the state as universal see *The Philosophy of Right* (henceforth: *Right*), ¶260 and ¶270 *Anmerkung*. Cf. *Die Vernunft in der Geschichte* (henceforth: *Vernunft*), hrsg. von Johannes Hoffmeister (Hamburg: Felix Meiner, 1955), pp. 114–15, where the same identification occurs along with a further identification as *das Heilige*. See note 70 below. This passage, compared with *Right*, ¶267, ¶273 and ¶276, indicates that Hegel means by the state not the narrowly political entity we call the government, but the whole institutionalized life of a people.

54. Both in *FT*, p. 65, and in *Training in Christianity*, p. 88, where he complains about the deification of the established order, Kierkegaard makes specific reference to a central portion of Hegel's analysis of *Moralität*, the discussion in *Right* entitled "Good and Conscience," ¶129–140. He finds the limitations Hegel there places on personal conscience to be part of his deification of *Sittlichkeit*.

55. *FT*, p. 80, my italics and ellipsis. The second italicized formula is repeated at pp. 66, 72, 91, 120, 122, and 129. The possibility that Abraham might be lost is always associated with the possibility that this principle may be false.

56. *FT*, pp. 70 and 88. Cf. pp. 97, 102, and *The Sickness Unto Death*, p. 179, where the central category "before God" is explicitly contrasted with the universality of state or nation.

57. *Training in Christianity*, p. 89. See note 54.

58. *FT*, pp. 64 and 91.

59. " . . . it is the particular individual who, after he has been subordinated as the particular to the universal, now through the universal becomes the individual who as the particular is superior to the universal . . . " *FT*, p. 66.

60. Though Nietzsche and Heidegger esteem the individual above "the herd" and "the they," Kierkegaard would find their accounts equally flat or two-dimensional.

61. *FT*, p. 65. Cf. the end of the passage cited from page 80 above (note 55).

62. *FT*, pp. 33, 45, 51, 61.

63. *FT*, p. 78.

64. *Right*, ¶270Z and *Vernunft*, p. 114.

65. See especially the closing sentence of *Right*, ¶360. Also *Vernunft*, p. 123, *Religion*, I, 247 = *Werke*, 16:236–37, and *History*, p. 417 = *Werke*, 12:497.

66. *Right*, ¶270Z.

67. For typical examples see the critique of Jacobi in *Glauben und Wissen*, the critique of Fries in the Preface to *Right*, and the critique of romantic irony in *Right*, ¶140Z.

68. *Ency.* ¶552Z.

69. *Religion*, I, 102–03 = *Werke*, 16:103.

70. *Vernunft*, pp. 111, 114–15.

71. *History*, pp. 422, 442, 449 = *Werke*, 12:502–03, 524, 531. Hegel only appears to qualify the last statement, for he writes, "Or, if religion be looked upon as higher and more sacred, it must involve nothing really alien or opposed to the constitution."

72. *Right*, ¶270Z and *Vernunft*, p. 112. On the ethical as the actuality of the truth, see *Ency.* ¶552Z and *History*, p. 446 = *Werke*, 12:527–28. By the Idea Hegel understands the unity of *Begriff* and *Objektivität*, of ideal and real, *Ency.* ¶213, which explains why it is possible for him to speak of the Idea of the state as "this actual God." *Right*, ¶258Z.

73. A more complete account of Hegel's position would require detailed analysis of his interpretation of the Trinity. In the *Phenomenology* and in *Religion* the tendency is to make God the Son, i.e., Jesus primarily of causal importance in relation to God the Spirit, which spirit turns out to be the human spirit of modern Christendom.

74. *Right*, ¶270Z and *Religion*, I, 251 = *Werke*, 16:240. For Hegel's assimilation of the laws with the divine will and divine commands see *Religion*, I, 249 = *Werke*, 16:239 and *History*, p. 423 = *Werke*, 12:503–04.

75. Religion, III, 138 = *Werke*, 17:332.

76. *Right*, ¶272Z. In a footnote to his translation Knox reminds us that Kant referred to states as *Erden-Götter* in his essay, *Über den Gemeinspruch: mag in der Theorie richtig sein, taugt aber nicht für die Praxis*. The contrast is quite pointed, for while Hegel speaks of veneration, Kant sternly admonishes states for making war and reminds them of their duty to enter into an international federation bound by international law.

77. *Ency.*, ¶552Z, my italics.

78. Cf. Kierkegaard's quotation of Luke 14:26 about hating one's family in order to be a disciple of Christ. *FT*, p. 82.

79. For other references see *Religion*, I, 250f. = *Werke*, 16:239f., and III, 138f. = 17:332f. Also *History*, 380f. = *Werke*, 12:457f., and 422f. = 12:502f. Hegel gave special attention to this theme in an address on the three hundredth anniversary of the Augsburg Confession. See *Berliner Schriften*, hrsg. von Johannes Hoffmeister (Hamburg, 1956), pp. 44f.

80. Cf. Franz Rosenzweig, *Hegel und der Staat* (Berlin: Oldenbourg, 1920) II, 79f., and the discussion by Michael Theunissen in *Die Verwirklichung der Vernunft* (Tübingen: de Gruyter, 1970), pp. 25f. For discussion of Hegel's attitude toward the Reformation and the French Revolution see the two essays dealing with these themes in Joachim Ritter's *Metaphysik und Politik* (Frankfurt: Suhrkamp, 1969). Also included is a sympathetic treatment of Hegel's view of the relation of *Moralität* to *Sittlichkeit*, centering in the notion that freedom must be institutionalized.

81. See previous paragraph but one, my italics. Cf. *Religion*, I, 252–55 = *Werke*, 16:242–44, *Right*, Preface and ¶270Z, and *History*, p. 417 = *Werke*, 12:496–97, where we read concerning the Reformation, "Time, since that epoch, has had no other work to do than to shape the world through this principle. . . . Law, property, ethical life, government, constitution, etc. must be conformed to general principles, in order that they may accord with the concept of free will and be rational."

82. *History*, p. 424 = *Werke*, 12:504.

83. *History,* pp. 447f. = *Werke,* 12:529f. and *Religion,* III, 149f. = *Werke,* 17:342f.

84. *History,* p. 457 = *Werke,* 12:540. Cf. *Right,* ¶258Z and ¶270Z on Hegel's treatment of the obvious defects in the actual vis-à-vis the Idea.

85. These phrases are from the New Testament accounts of Jesus Christ as the definitive incarnation of God. See Colossians 1:15 and Hebrews 1:3 in *The New English Bible* (New York: Oxford University Press, 1961, 1970).

5. ABOUT BEING A PERSON:
KIERKEGAARD'S *FEAR AND TREMBLING*

1. Remarks to this effect and the quotation can be read in the "Appendix," p. 225ff., in *The Concluding Unscientific Postscript,* trans. David F. Swenson (Princeton: Princeton University Press, 1941).

2. The quotations are from *Philosophical Remarks,* ed. Rush Rhees, trans. Raymond Hargreaves and Roger White (New York: Barnes & Noble, 1975), "Foreword," p. 7.

3. C. S. Lewis, "On Criticism," in *Of Other Worlds,* ed. Walter Hooper (London: Bles, 1966), pp. 56–57.

4. Søren Kierkegaard, *Fear and Trembling,* trans. Walter Lowrie (Princeton: Princeton University Press, 1945), p. 15. Other references hereafter are to the same translation unless otherwise noted. The occasional Danish references are to the convenient new edition of the *Samlede Vaerker* (Copenhagen: Gyldendal, 1963). *Frygt og Baeven* is in Vol. 5, pp. 7–112.

5. Kierkegaard would have enjoyed Wittgenstein's discussion of paradoxicality in the *Remarks on the Foundation of Mathematics,* in which part of his aim is to show that the paradoxes alluded to by certain theorists of mathematics can be taken care of by harder thought and by confining the discussion to narrower limits. "Something surprising, a paradox, is a paradox only in a particular, as it were defective, surrounding. One needs to complete this surrounding in such a way that what looked like a paradox no longer seems one." Ludwig Wittgenstein, *Remarks on the Foundation of Mathematics,* ed. G. H. von Wright, Rush Rhees, and G. E. M. Anscombe, trans. G. E. M. Anscombe (Oxford: B. Blackwell, 1956), p. 186.

6. "I have no wish to discover novelties, but rather it is my joy and my darling occupation to think about things which seem perfectly simple." Søren Kierkegaard, *The Concept of Dread,* trans. Walter Lowrie (Princeton: Princeton University Press, 1944), p. 76.

7. Søren Kierkegaard, *The Sickness unto Death,* trans. W. Lowrie (Princeton: Princeton University Press, 1941), p. 4.

8. *Sickness unto Death,* p. 17.

9. *Papirer,* Vol. VII, part i, p. 135 (entry no. 200). The page citation is to the new printing, with reediting by Niels Thulstrup (Copenhagen: Gyldendal, 1968). The translation here is my own.

10. Here the argument of the *Postscript* is presupposed. But Kierkegaard also said these things in numerous places in his *Journal.*

11. This is the thrust of *Either/Or,* especially volume II. But, again, it is the theme of the entire "stages" notion. For the "stages" are like the "grammar" for

the task of becoming a self. Søren Kierkegaard, *Either/Or*, 2 vols., trans. David F. and Lillian Marvin Swenson and Walter Lowrie (Princeton: Princeton University Press, 1971), pp. 465 and 370.

12. "Introduction to the Metaphysics of Morals." This is printed in Immanuel Kant, *The Doctrine of Virtue*, trans. Mary J. Gregan (Philadelphia: University of Pennsylvania Press, 1964), p. 23.

13. My debt to the theory of logical types is plain. And convenient references here could include several of Bertrand Russell's logical writings. Note Alfred North Whitehead and Bertrand Russell, *Principia Mathematica* (Cambridge: Cambridge University Press, 1925), Vol. 1 (especially the "Introduction" and first chapter). Also Willard Van Orman Quine, *From a Logical Point of View* (Cambridge: Harvard University Press, 1961), p. 90f., where Russell's idea of types is stressed as a solution to paradoxes arising in logical theory. My use of the idea is only suggested by the components of the argument. Russell does something quite different.

14. This kind of point is made by Karl Popper in *The Open Society and Its Enemies* (London: G. Routledge & Sons, 1945), Vol. II, p. 213.

6. UNDERSTANDING ABRAHAM: CARE, FAITH, AND THE ABSURD

1. In preparing this essay, I have benefited from discussion with Bruce Russell and Kurt Roggli, and from correspondence with Professor Robert L. Perkins. In the background throughout was Henry G. Bugbee, Jr.'s essay, "Loneliness, Solitude, and the Twofold Way in which Concern Seems to be Claimed," *Humanitas* 10 (November 1974): 313–27.

2. *The Journals of Søren Kierkegaard*, trans. A. Dru (Oxford: Oxford University Press, 1938), entry 965.

3. Two recent sympathetic reconstructions of the argument are found in Louis Mackey, *Kierkegaard: A Kind of Poet* (Philadelphia: University of Pennsylvania, 1971), pp. 206–27, and in Gene Outka, "Religious and Moral Duty: Notes on Fear and Trembling," in G. Outka and J. Reader, eds., *Religion and Morality* (New York: Anchor, 1973), pp. 204–54. For a hostile reading, see Brand Blanshard, "Kierkegaard on Faith," *The Personalist* 49 (1968): 5–23.

4. Literally, a preliminary "spewing out" of a number of themes and problems. In the last two-thirds of the book, Silentio proceeds with more show of rationality and organization.

5. *Fear and Trembling*, trans. Walter Lowrie (Princeton: Princeton University Press, 1968), p. 52. Cited hereafter as *FT*. At this point in the argument, "he does not give up his love" means he will not love another person. Later when Silentio wants to highlight the transformation of the young swain's love, he can be described as giving up his love—not in the sense of loving another person, but in the sense of withdrawing love from finite beings.

6. *FT*, p. 53.

7. Ibid.

8. *FT*, p. 54.

9. It might be argued that personality is not based on "one big concern" any more than knowledge is based on a single foundation. But some commitments are

more important than others, and in some cases "all of existence" can seem to stand or fall with a single "ultimate concern."

10. *FT*, p. 55.

11. *FT*, p. 59.

12. *FT*, p. 56.

13. *FT*, p. 54.

14. *FT*, p. 45.

15. *FT*, p. 55.

16. *FT*, pp. 48, 58, 59.

17. *FT*, p. 49.

18. Sometimes Kierkegaard is saddled with the view that because the knight of faith cannot be distinguished from the tax-collector or Philistine, therefore only the person himself can know if he is of faith. But both this passage and the one next quoted show that Kierkegaard did not believe that it was impossible to distinguish the knight of faith or the tax collector from the Philistine. The difference can be perceived, although no explicit criteria is formulated to help an uninitiated observer to perceive the difference.

19. *FT*, p. 50. Emphasis added.

20. Ibid.

21. *FT*, p. 51.

22. *FT*, p. 55.

23. *FT*, p. 55. "He no longer takes a finite interest in what the princess is doing."

24. *FT*, pp. 57, 48.

25. *FT*, p. 57.

26. *FT*, pp. 54, 59, 57.

27. Silentio uses the idea of embarrassment with regard to his own response, had Isaac been returned to him as a man of resignation, rather than a man of faith. *FT*, p. 46. But the case is clearly parallel to that of the princess.

28. *FT*, p. 55.

29. On selflessness, see Iris Murdoch, *The Sovereignty of Good* (New York: Schocken, 1971). The applicability of the contrast between claim and care to the case at hand was inspired by Henry Bugbee's discussion in the essay cited above, footnote 1.

30. *FT*, p. 60.

31. *FT*, p. 38.

32. *FT*, pp. 44, 48.

33. *FT*, p. 48.

34. *FT*, p. 49.

35. *FT*, p. 42.

36. *FT*, p. 61.

37. *FT*, p. 42. It can hardly go unnoticed that this is a story of fathers and sons, and that it provides the reverse side of the story so often told in terms of the agony, trial, and rebellion of the son. As I have unfolded the drama, it concerns the trial of sustaining care without possessiveness. In some sense, we cannot lay claim to control or possess "our" children. Yet as Ernest Becker argues in *The Denial of Death* (New York: The Free Press, 1973), there is a powerful human urge to attain a kind of immortality through claiming our children as our self-perpetuation. In this

perspective, God's demand (and later retraction) is best understood not as raising the issue of infanticidal aggression toward sons by fathers; see David Bakan's *The Duality of Human Existence* (Boston: Beacon Press, 1966), Chap. 4. Instead, it raises the issue of granting sons (and fathers) the separateness-in-love each must ultimately need and deserve. God will demand the son's sacrifice to halt the father's immortality project, his urge toward an ultimate will-to-power that, because of its limitless, death-denying scope, is not properly human, but the prerogative of the gods.

38. *FT,* pp. 42, 46.

39. *FT,* p. 46.

40. *FT,* pp. 63, 64.

41. Cf. *FT,* p. 35.

42. *FT,* p. 34f.

43. *FT,* pp. 28, 46.

44. Is faith based on the promise of a reward? Abraham is assured that Isaac will be returned, just as the swain, were he of faith, would be assured of the return of the princess. But faith is not based on this assurance—as if one were to take faith as a reasonable gamble, given one's calculation of the probability of reward. Nor is the hope of reward in any way objectively guaranteed—quite the contrary; if it were, there would be no "fear and trembling." Assurance is an articulation of faith, a measure of one's capacity for care and celebration, the existential counterweight to resignation's dread and grief. Assurance of reward is not a basis for faith, but its expression and display.

45. *FT,* p. 38.

7. KIERKEGAARD'S "PROBLEM I" AND "PROBLEM II": AN ANALYTIC PERSPECTIVE

1. Søren Kierkegaard, *Fear and Trembling,* trans. Walter Lowrie (Princeton: Princeton University Press, 1968), p. 44. Cited hereafter as *FT.*

2. "Kant and Kierkegaard on Duty and Inclination," *Journal of Philosophy* 65 (1968): 688. Cf. "The story of Abraham contains therefore a teleological suspension of the ethical. As the individual he became higher than the universal. This is the paradox which does not permit of mediation. It is just as inexplicable how he got into it as it is inexplicable how he remained in it." *FT,* p. 77.

3. "Kierkegaard on Faith," *The Personalist* 49 (1968): 5–23. Walter Kaufmann writes: "Kierkegaard rashly renounced clear and distinct thinking altogether." *Existentialism from Dostoevsky to Sartre* (New York: The New American Library, 1975), p. 18.

4. Ibid., p. 22. Cf. H. J. Paton, *The Modern Predicament* (London: Allen & Unwin, 1955), p. 120 on *FT:* "What makes it nauseating as a professedly religious work . . . we may pity his unhappy and diseased temperament, but neurosis is a poor qualification for setting up as a religious guide."

5. The label "moral nihilism" is a fuzzy one. However, there are two popular (although incompatible) senses of the expression under which moral nihilism involves either: (a) the denial of any good or evil in the world, or (b) the denial that there can be a justification for ultimate moral principles. I believe Kierkegaard's *FT*

would not fall under the classification of moral nihilism with regard to (a), although such an epithet is applicable to Kierkegaard under sense (b). However, under (b), Kierkegaard would find good *rationalistic* company with the likes of Mill, Ayer, Hare, etc.!

6. Blanshard, op. cit., p. 16.

7. *FT*, p. 67.

8. *FT*, pp. 69–70.

9. *FT*, p. 66. I realize that *FT* is written under a pseudonym, Johannes de Silentio, but I shall take the liberty (since my analysis is intended to be philosophical and not literary) of referring to Kierkegaard as the author of *FT*.

10. James Bogen, "Kierkegaard and the Teleological Suspension of the Ethical," *Inquiry* 5 (1962): 306.

11. Ibid., p. 312.

12. Ibid., p. 308.

13. Ibid., p. 311.

14. Ibid., p. 314.

15. *FT*, p. 64.

16. *FT*, p. 68.

17. *FT*, p. 68.

18. *FT*, pp. 68–69.

19. Bogen, p. 312.

20. *FT*, p. 55.

21. Richard Schmitt, *Martin Heidegger on Being Human: An Introduction to Sein und Zeit* (New York: Random House, 1969), p. 265, n. 11.

22. "Man Has No Nature," in *Existentialism from Dostoevsky to Sartre* (New York: New American Library, 1975), ed. Walter Kaufmann, pp. 155–56.

23. *Existential Philosophers: Kierkegaard to Merleau-Ponty*, ed. George Schrader (New York: McGraw-Hill, 1967), p. 24.

24. *FT*, p. 85.

25. *FT*, p. 51.

26. *FT*, p. 51.

27. *FT*, p. 50.

28. Cf. John Donnelly, "Moral and Religious Assertions," *International Journal for Philosophy of Religion* 2 (1971), pp. 53–55.

29. *FT*, p. 82.

30. *FT*, p. 88.

31. J. O. Urmson, "Saints and Heroes," in *Essays in Moral Philosophy*, ed. A. I. Melden (Seattle: University of Washington Press, 1958), p. 212. Cf. *Søren Kierkegaard's Journals and Papers*, ed. and trans. Howard V. Hong and Edna H. Hong (Bloomington: Indiana University Press, 1967), Vol. 1, #989, 990, 1007.

32. Joel Feinberg, "Supererogation and Rules," *Ethics* 71 (1961): 280.

33. The following passages point to the recognition of duties-plus by Kierkegaard in *Fear and Trembling*: "The absolute duty may cause one to do what ethics would forbid . . ." (*FT*, p. 84). " . . . Yea, he would be offended if anyone were to say of him . . . 'I do not remain standing by any means, my whole life is in this' " (*FT*, p. 131).

34. Urmson, p. 203.

35. *FT*, p. 88, fn. 1.

36. A particular line of defense in morals often argues that a specific moral judgment is right in that it is implied by some moral rule or set of rules, which in turn are derived from some more general ethical principle. The argument cannot continue ad infinitum, so that ultimately to question the basic principle involved (e.g., benevolence, utility, or Abraham's "One ought to obey the commands of God," etc.) is senseless, for such principles define the very game or position one plays in life.

37. *FT*, p. 131.

38. *FT*, p. 59.

39. *FT*, p. 80. Cf. "The divine can very well move in an earthly context, and it does not require the annihilation of the earthly as a condition for its own appearance, just as the spirit of God revealed itself to Moses in the burning bush, which burned *without being consumed." Journals and Papers*, Vol. 1, #833.

40. *FT*, p. 69.

41. *FT*, p. 70.

42. *FT*, p. 81.

43. " . . . I entered into the . . . discussion . . . not as though Abraham would thereby become more intelligible, but in order that the unintelligibility might become more desultory" (*FT*, p. 121).

44. *Kierkegaard* (New York: Doubleday, 1972), p. vii.

45. Cf. *FT*, p. 99.

46. *FT*, p. 63.

47. *FT*, p. 87. Cf. *Journals and Papers*, Vol. 3, #3020.

48. *FT*, pp. 122–23.

49. *FT*, p. 124.

50. It needs to be pointed out that (i) and (iii) are not inconsistent, and this is so because (i) refers to the "ought to be," that is, to the state of affairs that it would be desirable to bring about as the result of A's practical action in the best of all possible worlds, but because of certain contingent factors involved in the situation (e.g., time, physical incapacity, etc.), A is permitted not to do X, so that (iii) is satisfied. For example, policemen ought to protect the lives of their precinct citizens, but suppose it's the case that Policeman Kopp alone is working the night shift, and is patrolling streets K, L, M, N, which conjunctively comprise his precinct, and Kopp is currently situated on street M at t_1, and a rape is taking place at t_1 on N street, and a robbery on K at t_1. Here, Kopp will probably decide that his duty lies in disrupting the rape, so that, because of the given contingencies of the situation, he is permitted not to disrupt the robbery, although ideally as in (i) it ought to be disrupted as well.

51. Cf. *FT*, p. 82, pp. 84–85, for a somewhat different version of the Golden Rule.

52. Cf. P. H. Nowell-Smith, *Ethics* (Baltimore: Penguin, 1954), p. 80.

53. The statement "Jones is a teacher" both logically entails and contextually implies "Jones instructs at least one pupil," but it only contextually implies "Jones instructs two pupils."

54. In Walter Kaufmann, ed., *Existentialism from Dostoevsky to Sartre*, p. 99.

55. It has not been my intention to discuss the question of the veridicality of the divine command to Abraham, or indeed the difficult epistemological issue of

ascertaining the authenticity of any such putative revelations. I have assumed throughout my essay that the command is veridical (Kierkegaard said on p. 36 of *FT:* "he knew that it was God the Almighty who was trying him") and as a consequence pondered how it could jell with a knight of faith's autonomous practical reasoning.

56. Parts of this paper are taken from my article, "Re-examining Kierkegaard's 'Teleological Suspension of the Ethical' " in *Logical Analysis and Contemporary Theism,* ed. John Donnelly (New York: Fordham University Press, 1972), pp. 294–331. It might be suggested that my analysis of the knight of faith's plight keeps Abraham within the moral sphere quite arbitrarily. One might contend that such a method of justifying the knight of faith's conduct would place no moral constraints upon a knight of faith's possible behavior. I confess that I find such a concern somewhat puzzling since the critic often insists upon the teleological suspension of the ethical (as a protest against rationalistic tendencies in philosophical theology, be they Hegelian or analytic) as much as I try to avoid it. In short, this criticism would read my accounting of the events in *Fear and Trembling* as too *prescriptive,* as that term is used in linguistic metaethics. Why, it might be wondered, could one not, *mutatis mutandis,* develop a formal theory of prescriptive universalizability that had such a supreme principle as, "one ought to obey Charles Manson at all costs" or "one ought to obey the commands of Jim Jones above all else"? I would quickly emphasize that the solution in part XI of my paper had hardly any immoral consequences. And the tentative solution offered in part VII at least had the effect of showing that the Blanshard, Bogen analyses could be extended to allow an understanding of Abraham qua knight of faith akin to that of Agamemnon, Jephthah, and Brutus.

In reply to such a possible critique, I would point out that I am not sympathetic to prescriptivism, although there are many passages in the Kierkegaard corpus that suggest his own possible sympathy to such a metaethical framework, chronological considerations notwithstanding. Rather, like the so-called descriptivists, I believe there is a *content* to moral discourse, having to do with the somewhat open-textured notion of that which contributes to human flourishing. I agree with Geoffrey Warnock, Peter Geach, et al., that when we are confronted with moral decisions we do not choose what are to be reasons for choosing, as there are already antecedently existing facts being circumscribed by considerations of human welfare. Rather than expatiate upon such a descriptivistic moral psychology, I would simply point out that the knight of faith's supreme principle does not lead to morally monstrous behavior. I am not suggesting that (Christian) religious belief and moral belief are identical, only that they are compatible to the extent that no orthodox (Christian) religious principle can lead to a *clear* violation of a moral principle—that is, a moral principle that is agreed upon by both secular deontologists and teleologists. I think it manifestly clear that allegiances to Charles Manson, Jim Jones, and even the more institutional religious demagogues do not satisfy this requirement.

I hold that the recognition of absolute duties (or what I termed "duties-plus") de facto fosters human welfare, so that I am not confusing a coherent moral life with a rationally justified moral life. The third stage on life's way positively enriches the second stage and contributes to a person's innate teleology. Unlike a purely second-stage descriptive account of morality that allows us to answer the question of meaning *in* life, the third stage provides the rational apotheosis to the question of the meaning *of* life.

8. IS THE CONCEPT OF AN ABSOLUTE DUTY TOWARD GOD MORALLY UNINTELLIGIBLE?

1. This discussion of Johannes de Silentio's view of the Abraham story should *not* be taken as a discussion of Kierkegaard, or as implying anything about Kierkegaard's own view of morality and religious faith. The question of Kierkegaard's relation to the pseudonymous books is a complex one that will not be considered at all in this essay.
2. Søren Kierkegaard, *Fear and Trembling,* trans. Walter Lowrie (Princeton: Princeton University Press, 1968), p. 78. Parenthetical page references in the text are to this edition of *Fear and Trembling,* abbreviated *FT.*
3. Immanuel Kant, *Religion Within the Limits of Reason Alone,* trans. Theodore Greene and Hoyt Hudson (New York: Harper & Row, 1960), p. 142.
4. Ibid., p. 158.
5. Ibid., p. 82. Kant specifically mentions the Abraham story on p. 175.
6. Ibid. See pp. 94, 100, 158–63, and numerous other passages.
7. Ibid., p. 100.
8. In fact, I believe it is a mistake to regard Johannes as representing Kierkegaard's own view of the positive content of faith. Johannes is a man who does not possess faith and who does not claim to understand it.
9. Here I use the terms *ethical* and *moral* as synonyms. The Hegelian distinction is irrelevant to this essay.
10. Sir William David Ross, *The Right and the Good* (Oxford: Clarendon Press, 1930), p. 19.
11. Ibid., p. 22.
12. Søren Kierkegaard, *The Concept of Dread,* trans. Walter Lowrie, 2nd ed. (Princeton: Princeton University Press, 1957), p. 16 n.

9. ABRAHAM'S SILENCE AND THE LOGIC OF FAITH

1. Søren Kierkegaard, *Fear and Trembling,* trans. Walter Lowrie (Princeton: Princeton University Press, 1968), p. 91. Cited hereafter as *FT.*
2. *FT,* p. 86.
3. *FT,* p. 97.
4. *FT,* p. 123.
5. *FT,* p. 122.
6. *FT,* p. 122.
7. *FT,* p. 71.
8. Søren Kierkegaard, *Journals and Papers,* trans. Howard and Edna Hong (Bloomington: Indiana University Press, 1967). Vol. 1, p. 7.
9. Ibid., p. 7.
10. Ibid., p. 8.
11. Ibid., p. 8.

12. Søren Kierkegaard, *Concluding Unscientific Postscript,* trans. David F. Swenson (Princeton: Princeton University Press, 1944), p. 500. (Cited hereafter as *CUP*).

13. *CUP,* p. 504, 513.

14. *CUP,* p. 514.

15. *CUP,* pp. 330–31.

16. *CUP,* p. 330.

17. *CUP,* p. 188.

18. *CUP,* p. 513.

19. Søren Kierkegaard, *Philosophical Fragments,* trans. David F. Swenson, 2nd. ed. (Princeton: Princeton University Press, 1962), p. 61.

20. Ludwig Wittgenstein, *Lectures and Conversations on Aesthetics, Psychology, and Religious Belief,* ed. Cyril Barrett (Oxford: Oxford University Press, 1966), p. 65.

21. Ibid., p. 58.

22. Ibid., p. 60.

10. SOUNDS OF SILENCE

1. Søren Kierkegaard, *Fear and Trembling,* trans. Walter Lowrie (Princeton: Princeton University Press, 1968), p. 97. Cited hereafter as *FT.* In some instances, I have altered the translation of Kierkegaard's texts. The Danish edition upon which my retranslations are based is: *Søren Kierkegaards Samlede Værker,* eds. A. B. Drachmann, J. L. Heiberg, and H. O. Lange (København: Gyldendalske Boghandel, 1901 ff.). Hereafter quotations from *Fear and Trembling* are cited by page number in the text of the essay.

2. For a detailed consideration of Kierkegaard's use of indirect communication, see the second chapter of my book, *Kierkegaard's Pseudonymous Authorship: A Study of Time and the Self* (Princeton: Princeton University Press, 1975).

3. I do not mean to suggest that this is the only way in which the stages of existence can be interpreted. Actually they can be understood in a variety of ways. For an analysis of this matter, see my *Kierkegaard's Pseudonymous Authorship,* op. cit., pp. 62ff.

4. For example, F. C. Fischer, *Existenz und Innerlichkeit: eine Einfuhrung in die Gedankenwelt Søren Kierkegaards* (München: Beck, 1969), p. 17; and Martin Heinecken, *The Moment Before God* (Philadelphia: Muhlenberg Press, 1956), p. 247f.

5. For example, Stephen Crites, "Introduction," *Crisis in the Life of an Actress* (New York: Harper Torchbooks, 1967), pp. 19–28.

6. Søren Kierkegaard, *Either/Or,* Vol. 1 trans. David and Lillian Swenson (Princeton: Princeton University Press, 1971), Vol. 1, p. 86.

7. Ibid., p. 95.

8. Ibid., p. 87.

9. Ibid., p. 91.

10. Ibid., p. 55.

11. Søren Kierkegaard, *Johannes Climacus, or De Omnibus Dubitandum Est,* trans. T. H. Croxall (Stanford: Stanford University Press, 1967), p. 147.

12. *Either/Or,* I, p. 55.

13. Ibid., p. 104.

14. Søren Kierkegaard, *Either/Or,* Vol. 2 trans. Walter Lowrie (Princeton: Princeton University Press, 1971), Vol. 2, p. 193.

15. Søren Kierkegaard, *Journals and Papers,* ed. and trans. Howard V. Hong and Edna H. Hong (Bloomington: Indiana University Press, 1970), no. 1590.

16. Søren Kierkegaard, *The Point of View of My Work as An Author: A Report to History,* trans. Walter Lowrie (New York: Harper Torchbooks, 1962), p. 73.

17. *Johannes Climacus or, De Omnibus Dubitandum Est,* op. cit., pp. 148–49.

18. *Either/Or,* 1, p. 69.

19. Søren Kierkegaard, *The Sickness Unto Death,* trans. Walter Lowrie, (Princeton: Princeton University Press, 1970), p. 188.

20. *FT,* pp. 93ff.

21. *FT,* pp. 103ff.

22. In light of issues to be discussed in what follows, it is important to recognize that the Merman is unable to carry out his planned seduction. Agnes' innocent trust frustrates his deceitful intentions, and the Merman silently repents. At this point, however, deceitful silence is transformed into demonic silence.

23. *Either/Or,* 1, p. 98.

24. Ibid., pp. 439–40.

25. At this point, I must differ with Louis Mackey's otherwise fine study of Kierkegaard. Mackey comments: "And there is demonic silence: The enforced secrecy of a man committed to evil. John the Seducer is bound to silence by his nefarious purpose; his way of life includes a commitment to that silence without which he cannot carry through his program of betrayal." *Kierkegaard: A Kind of Poet* (Philadelphia: University of Pennsylvania Press, 1972), p. 220. See also "The View from Pisgah: A Reading of *Fear and Trembling,*" in *Kierkegaard, A Collection of Critical Essays,* ed. Josiah Thompson (New York: Doubleday Anchor, 1972), pp. 394–428. It would seem that Mackey identifies deceitful and demonic silence. At any rate, he refers to Johannes as demonic. In view of Kierkegaard's careful description of the demonic, however, it is inaccurate to regard Johannes as demonic. Why this is so will become apparent in what follows.

26. Søren Kierkegaard, *The Concept of Dread,* trans. Walter Lowrie (Princeton: Princeton University Press, 1957), p. 109.

27. Ibid., p. 106.

28. Ibid., p. 110. By this time the reasons for my uneasiness with Mackey's interpretation of Johannes the seducer as demonic should be apparent. At no point does Johannes indicate any remorse for his deed. In our last picture of him, his carriage is hastily leaving the scene of the seduction and taking him toward another erotic adventure. Without repentance, a sense of corruption, and inward suffering and unhappiness, the demonic cannot be present for Kierkegaard. Johannes might be deceitful and even despicable, but he is not demonic.

29. Ibid., p. 111.

30. In order to complete our remarks on Kierkegaard's presentation of demonic silence in *Fear and Trembling,* it is necessary to note that he also cites the case of Sarah and Tobias (pp. 111ff.). This example differs slightly from the primary part of his analysis of Agnes and the Merman. In this instance, the source of demonic silence has not arisen through one's own agency, but has happened to

one, something that fate or the gods preordained. Despite this significant difference, the dynamics of demonic silence remain the same. Revelation would bring relief from suffering, and can be freely chosen. To remain closed-up is to forego the possibility of reconciliation and to remain attached to one's misery.

31. At the outset of our discussion of the ethical stage of existence, it will be helpful to note that in *Fear and Trembling* Kierkegaard devotes little attention to the relationship between the ethical existence and the immediate pole of the aesthetic stage. In connection with the issue of silence, he is more concerned with the interplay between the ethicist and the reflective aesthete. This does not imply, of course, that Kierkegaard is insensitive to the complex problems involved in the relationship between the ethical stage and immediacy. Indeed precisely this issue is the primary concern of Judge William's essay entitled "The Aesthetic Validity of Marriage" in the second volume of *Either/Or*. What concerns Kierkegaard in *Fear and Trembling* is the tension between the willing silence of the reflective aesthete and the ethical imperative to disclose oneself.

32. Søren Kierkegaard, *Concluding Unscientific Postscript*, trans. David Swenson and Walter Lowrie (Princeton: Princeton University Press, 1971), p. 227.

33. *Either/Or*, 2, p. 327.

34. Like each of the Kierkegaardian stages, the ethical life-view is rather complex. In the context of the present discussion, we can only suggest its most outstanding features. I have considered the ethical stage in some detail in the fifth chapter of my book, *Kierkegaard's Pseudonymous Authorship: A Study of Time and the Self*, op. cit., pp. 185ff.

35. In other works, most notably *Either/Or* and *Stages on Life's Way*, Kierkegaard attempts to develop the concrete meaning of universal principles of morality. It would seem, however, that the Judge conceives of ethical obligation as little else than the conscientious fulfillment of civic obligation—securing a good position in society, marrying, and raising a family. He writes: "I will here pronounce at once my view of what an extraordinary [*ualimindelige*] man is. The truly extraordinary man is the truly ordinary [*almindelige*] man. The more of the universal-human an individual is able to realize in his life, the more extraordinary he is. The less of the universal he is able to take up into his life, the more imperfect he is. He is then an extraordinary man to be sure, but not in a good sense" (*Either/Or*, 2, p. 333).

36. Johannes de Silentio also suggests the ethical critique of other instances of heroic silence that we explored in the previous sections of our study. See pages 95ff., 101ff., and 120ff.

37. As heirs of Freud, we are struck by the apparent naïveté of many of the ethicist's suggestions. Can an individual ever plumb the depths of his motives? Is it possible for a person to be truthful about himself, not to mention honestly revealing himself to another person? Is not self-disclosure often simply a different form of self-concealment?

38. It should be evident that there is a remarkable parallel between Kierkegaard's dialectic of the stages and the structure of Hegel's dialectic.

39. Lowrie's translation of this passage is rather problematic. He uses both *particular* and *individual* for Kierkegaard's *Enkelte*. This confuses the text. *Individual* more accurately represents Kierkegaard's meaning and should be used throughout.

40. We might point out that Kierkegaard's contention that language is able to

represent only universality raises interesting epistemological issues. It would seem to follow that the concrete particularities of sense experience can never be known accurately or expressed cogently.

41. The problem of silence and concealment haunted Kierkegaard's personal life. He understood his relation to Regina after the model of Abraham's relation to Isaac. He was plagued by the question of whether he could or should reveal his religious vocation to Regina.

42. *The Journals of Søren Kierkegaard,* ed. and trans. Alexander Dru (New York: Oxford University Press, 1938), no. 754.

43. Jean Hyppolite, *Genesis and Structure of Hegel's Phenomenology of Spirit,* trans. S. Cherniak and J. Heckman (Evanston: Northwestern University Press, 1974), p. 116.

44. G. W. F. Hegel, *The Phenomenology of Mind,* trans. J. Baillie (New York: Harper Torchbooks, 1967), p. 174. In this context, Hegel is addressing the problem of objects. His analysis, however, can be applied to persons.

45. Ibid., p. 174.

46. Ibid., p. 175.

11. ON FAITH

1. For an analysis of the Abraham/Isaac story in terms of silence, see Nancy Jay Crumbine, "On Silence," *Humanitas* 11:2 (1975): 147–65.

2. The word *recollective,* including its derivatives, is to be understood throughout the paper in the sense of re-collective, a unifying and re-organizing mode of response, a re-thinking, a re-union with one's past.

3. This act of sacrifice is what Kierkegaard means by subjectivity. The fact that it is the recollective and not the rational ability of Abraham wherein the paradox of his belief is made sensible has its basis in the unity of subjectivity and is the point that Kierkegaard makes when he talks of truth as neither rational nor irrational but as something subjective. Anything true is, for Kierkegaard, recollective and contains necessarily the contextual fullness that memory alone can provide. As the depth of inwardness that allows the decay and transformation of things to take place, subjectivity *is* the individual's recollective consciousness. The task of becoming subjective is essentially the task of becoming recollective, where this means a striving toward a grounding of all one's actions in the private realm of one's memories as these are interconnected in the context of historical experience.

4. While the contextual fullness of faith is immersed within finitude itself, the way to this still center of finitude is through the giving oneself over to the infinite vastness of nothing. The statement, "Only by losing oneself does one gain oneself," means in this context that it is through the loss of the familiar self that the relation of self and world emerge in a renewed and meaningful way. In this meeting of the individual and nothing, this confrontation of the self not only with its demise but with the dissolution of its world as well, faith emerges as a possibility for the first time.

While no analysis of faith can be complete without an analysis of dread, it is beyond the scope of this paper to deal with it, as it is a topic in itself. It is important to point out, however, that for Kierkegaard dread is the prerequisite for authentic religiousness and explains the otherwise apparently simpleminded notion of the either/or. Within the context of dread the either/or is the exact opposite of simplicity and holds within it the truth not only of Kierkegaard's insights but of the Augustinian tradition itself. To some extent I hope the analysis of faith here presented will contribute to an understanding of this, perhaps Kierkegaard's greatest contribution to philosophic thought.

5. It is indicative of the modern confusions to which Kierkegaard spoke that the word "privacy" connotes a defensiveness or an intentional hiddenness as if in reaction to the encroachment of the public vision. To the most contemporary minds the word even suggests a paranoia where the need for privacy becomes desperate and unfillable. Often when we think of the private we think of keeping others out as with property, or in the secrecy and exclusiveness of clubs that cater to this paranoia. The irony of the confusion of privacy and paranoia is of course that the more paranoid we become the more we disallow the privacy that is a reunion with self.

6. In the grandeur of Sherwood Anderson's *Winesburg, Ohio,* for instance, we understand something about the majesty inherent in the most simple tragedies of privacy.

7. Light spacializes and demarcates linearly thereby. Camus' visual intensity precludes the behind-the-scenes give-and-take that makes interaction possible. Everything is rigidified in the light. Contrast Camus' primary sense with Nietzsche's claim that genuine reflection and insight is born of a person with a highly developed sense of smell, where he means to suggest by this the ambiguity, subtlety, and organic wholeness of things that smell alone can perceive. The sense of smell (metaphorically, of course) picks up the more ethereal unquantifiable aspects of things, aspects of things that are perceivable in the dark. The least-developed of the human senses, it holds possibilities for us of perceiving the least-known aspects of the world, and of discovering these in a radically new way.

8. Augustine's *Confessions* is an excellent example of a confession born of the most intense recollective maturity, which thus carries the significance that confession is meant to carry. Through it Augustine regains himself subjectively, passionately, and entirely. It is a profoundly private reunion which, at the same time, reestablishes Augustine with a community and tradition that then sustains his recollective rhythm.

9. Søren Kierkegaard, *Fear and Trembling,* trans. Walter Lowrie (Princeton: Princeton University Press, 1968), p. 38.

10. Gertrude Stein claimed that with her line "A rose is a rose is a rose" the rose was experienced again for the first time in two hundred years. Similarly, Kierkegaard revitalized the cliché-ridden notion of faith by doing nothing less radical than pointing out that faith is not unconnected with contradiction, hopelessness, and murder.

11. *Fear and Trembling,* p. 27.
12. Ibid., p. 28.
13. Ibid., p. 28.
14. Ibid., pp. 28, 29.
15. Ibid., p. 29.
16.   Time past and time future
Allow but a little consciousness.
To be conscious is not to be in time

But only in time can the moment in the rose-garden,
The moment in the arbour where the rain beat,
The moment in the draughty church at smokefall
Be remembered; involved with past and future.
Only through time time is conquered.

From T. S. Eliot's *Four Quartets,* in *The Complete Poems and Plays 1909–1950* (New York: Harcourt, Brace, & World, Inc., 1962). Used by permission of Harcourt Brace Jovanovich (New York) and Faber & Faber (London).

17. In contrast, the madman is so thoroughly alive that life's very possibilities are smothered by the exuberance. Unlike Meursault, the person of madness enters the realm of temporality frantic to participate in the public and to share her/his highly developed world of privacy. Unlike the person of faith, however, this private dimension is wholly unrecollective, ununified, and undeveloped, being more of a dispersion of the past rather than a reunion with it. Madness is made up of a completely unrecollective privacy built upon some finite interest from which action emerges not as a particular act in relation to an infinite concern and sensitivity but as a particular act passionately carried out on the basis of some finite concern. The act of madness is an entrance into the public realm, then, from a basis of the private chaos of disjointed finite events. It is an entrance into finitude by way of finitude, bringing nothing with it to ground the participation of the individual or the public itself. The act is merely another act. It brings no depth with itself and it is not able to give dimension to other acts. Madness is meaningless. Moreover, as meaningless, as coming from the infinite finitude of an unrecollective consciousness and entering into the realm of finitude that relies on the individual to establish its grounding, it is itself a sort of infinity and constitutes in fact the individual's desire to connect with an infinite dimension. Meaningless, it is not an act of participation, although the individual wishes it were; its source, however, in the chaos of her/his private world makes the act impossibly alien to the public. In so far as it is not a participatory act, it is an act that pushes beyond the limits of the public, destroying the finitude that is so essential to public life. It is, of course, for this reason—this misplacement of the realms of the finite and infinite, this attempted transposition of temporality into limitless possibilities—that the mad person is a social and political threat. And it is because the distinction between the person of faith and the person of madness is too often misunderstood that the person of faith is perceived so incorrectly as a threat to the public realm. The case of Socrates is the classic example of this confusion. A creative force who tried to push the public realm back to an ontological grounding, he was perceived as being just the opposite—as a threat to the state. What the Athenians who condemned Socrates could not distinguish was the difference between the recollectively private as originative ground of the public and the unrecollectively private as the actively dissipating force against the public.

12. FAITH IS AS FAITH DOES

1. Arthur Murphy's "On Kierkegaard's Claim that Truth is Subjectivity" in *Essays on Kierkegaard,* ed. Jerry H. Gill (Minneapolis: Burgess, 1969).
2. William Barrett's *Irrational Man* (New York: Doubleday, 1958).

3. David Swenson's review of *Fear and Trembling* in *The Philosophical Review* and Alastair McKinnon's "Kierkegaard: 'Paradox' and Irrationalism" in *Essays on Kierkegaard,* op. cit.

4. *Fear and Trembling,* trans. Walter Lowrie (Princeton: Princeton University Press, 1968), p. 132.

5. Ibid., p. 64.

6. Ibid., p. 129.

7. Ibid., p. 121.

8. *Kierkegaard: A Kind of Poet* (Philadelphia: University of Pennsylvania Press, 1971), p. 288.

9. Ibid., p. 284.

10. Ibid., p. 290.

11. In *Essays on Kierkegaard,* op. cit. (First printed in *The Review of Metaphysics* 20 [1967]: 432–60.)

12. Ibid., p. 148.

13. Ibid., p. 127.

14. Robert Bretall, ed., *A Kierkegaard Anthology* (New York: Modern Library, 1946), p. 432.

Index